THE JALAYIRIDS

The Royal Asiatic Society was founded in 1823 'for the investigation of subjects connected with, and for the encouragement of science, literature and the arts in relation to Asia'. Informed by these goals, the policy of the Society's Editorial Board is to make available in appropriate formats the results of original research in the humanities and social sciences having to do with Asia, defined in the broadest geographical and cultural sense and up to the present day.

The Monograph Board
Professor Francis Robinson CBE, Royal Holloway, University of London (Chair)
Professor Tim Barrett, SOAS, University of London
Dr Evrim Binbaş, Royal Holloway, University of London
Dr Barbara M. C. Brend
Professor Anna Contadini, SOAS, University of London
Professor Michael Feener, National University of Singapore
Dr Gordon Johnson, University of Cambridge
Dr Rosie Llewellyn Jones MBE
Professor David Morgan, University of Wisconsin-Madison
Professor Rosalind O'Hanlon, University of Oxford
Dr Alison Ohta, Director, Royal Asiatic Society

For a full list of publications by the Royal Asiatic Society see www.royalasiaticsociety.org

THE JALAYIRIDS

DYNASTIC STATE FORMATION IN THE MONGOL MIDDLE EAST

Patrick Wing

EDINBURGH
University Press

For E. L., E. L. and E. G.

Edinburgh University Press Ltd
The Tun – Holyrood Road
12 (2f) Jackson's Entry
Edinburgh EH8 8PJ
www.euppublishing.com

Typeset in 11/13 JaghbUni Regular by
Servis Filmsetting Ltd, Stockport, Cheshire

A CIP record for this book is available from the British Library

ISBN 978 1 4744 0225 5 (hardback)
ISBN 978 1 4744 0226 2 (webready PDF)
ISBN 978 1 4744 1093 9 (epub)

Contents

List of Illustrations vi
Acknowledgements vii
Abbreviations for Primary and Secondary Source Texts ix

1 Introduction and Sources for the History of the Jalayirids 1
2 Tribes and the Chinggisid Empire 29
3 The Jalayirs and the Early Ilkhanate 48
4 From Tribal Amirs to Royal In-laws 63
5 Crisis and Transition (1335–56) 74
6 Shaykh Uvays and the Jalayirid Dynasty 101
7 Dynastic Ideology during the Reign of Shaykh Uvays 129
8 Challenges to the Jalayirid Order 147
9 Conclusions and the Legacy of the Jalayirids 185

Maps and Genealogical Chart 202
Bibliography 209
Index 224

Illustrations

Figure 2.1 The *altān urūgh*: Chinggis Qan and his descendants 37
Figure 2.2 Ilkhan rulers 38
Figure 4.1 The Jalayir *güregen* relationship 66
Figure 4.2 Amīr Chūpān at the centre of the Ilkhanid ruling elite 68
Figure 4.3 Shaykh Ḥasan Jalayir and the Ilkhanid royal house 68
Figure 4.4 The Chubanids 69
Figure 5.1 Factions following Abū Sa'īd's death 76
Figure 6.1 The ancestry of Shaykh Uvays 102
Figure 9.1 *Mi'rāj-nāma* attributed to Aḥmad Mūsá 188
Figure 9.2 Abduction of Zal by the Simurgh, from a *Shāh-nāma* manuscript 189
Figure 9.3 *Dīvān* of Sulṭān Aḥmad, Baghdad, 1403 190
Figure 9.4 Wedding day of Humāy and Humāyūn 192

Map 1 Jalayirid dynasty 202
Map 2 Jalayirid dynasty, c. 1353 204
Map 3 Jalayirid dynasty, c. 1400 206

Genealogy of the Jalayirid dynasty 208

Acknowledgements

It is a pleasure to acknowledge the many colleagues, friends and family members who have supported this project over the years. While I have benefited from the generosity of so many individuals, I of course am solely responsible for all errors and shortcomings in the present work. I first met the Jalayirids at the University of Chicago, where I wrote a dissertation in the Department of Near Eastern Languages and Civilizations. I must above all thank my advisor, teacher and mentor John Woods, who continues to guide and inspire me. I am grateful also to Cornell Fleischer for his wisdom and ceaseless encouragement. Additional thanks are owed to my teachers at Chicago, Fred Donner, John Perry and Holly Shissler, and to Bruce Craig and Marlis Saleh at the University of Chicago's Regenstein Library, where much of the research for this project was conducted. Furthermore, I would never have started down the road of Mongol and Middle East history without the support and example of Jo-Ann Gross at the College of New Jersey.

I am indebted as well to a number of scholars and friends who have supported me in Chicago, Redlands, Ghent and beyond. Thanks to Judith Pfeiffer for her constant support and motivation, and to Evrim Binbaş for his encouragement and for helping to bring this work to publication. Thanks also to Denise Aigle, Thomas Allsen, Kristof D'hulster, Peter Golden, Beatrice Manz, John Meloy, David Morgan, Carl Petry, Warren Schultz, Jo Van Steenbergen, İsenbike Togan and Bethany Walker.

I am fortunate to enjoy the support of my colleagues in history at the University of Redlands, Bob Eng, Kathy Feeley, John Glover, Kathy Ogren, Matthew Raffety and Jim Sandos, and to have been assisted by two Faculty Research Grants from the University of Redlands, in 2009–10 and 2013–14. I would like to thank the librarians at the University of Redlands's Armacost Library, with particular appreciation to Sandy Richie, without whom my research could not have continued at Redlands.

I must express my gratitude to the Royal Asiatic Society for supporting the project, particularly to Alison Ohta, and the two anonymous readers.

I owe a great deal of thanks to Edinburgh University Press, in particular to the editorial talents of Nicola Ramsey and Ellie Bush. I would like to gratefully acknowledge the following institutions for granting permission to reproduce images: The British Library Board: Add. 18113, fol. 45v; Freer Gallery of Art, Smithsonian Institution, Washington, DC: Purchase, F1932.37; Roland and Sabrina Michaud/akg-images.

Finally, thank you to my family for their unwavering support and love.

Abbreviations for Primary and Secondary Source Texts

Ahrī/*TSU*	Abū Bakr al-Quṭbī al-Ahrī, *Ta'rīkh-i Shaikh Uwais (A History of Shaikh Uwais): An Important Source for the History of Ādharbaijān in the Fourteenth Century*, trans. J. B. Van Loon (The Hague: Mouton & Co., 1954).
Astarābādī/*Bazm*	'Azīz b. Ārdashīr Astarābādī, *Bazm u Razm*, intro. Köprülüzāde Meḥmed Fu'ād Bey [Mehmed Fuad Köprülü] (Istanbul: Evḳāf Maṭba'ası, 1928).
Babinger/*GdO*	Franz Babinger, *Die Geschichtesschreiber der Osmanen und ihre Werke* (Leipzig: O. Harrassowitz, 1927).
Brockelmann/*GAL*	Carl Brockelmann, *Geschichte der Arabischen Literatur* (Leiden: Brill, 1949).
BSOAS	*Bulletin of the School of Oriental and African Studies*
CAJ	*Central Asiatic Journal*
Dawlatshāh/*Taz̲kira*	Dawlatshāh Samarqandī, *Taz̲kirat al-Shu'arā'-yi Dawlatshāh Samarqandī*, ed. Muḥammad 'Abbāsī (Tehran: Kitāb-furūshī-yi Bārānī, 1337 [1958]).
Faṣīḥ Khvāfī/*Mujmal*	Faṣīḥ al-Dīn Aḥmad Faṣīḥ Khvāfī, *Mujmal-i Faṣīḥī*, ed. Maḥmūd Farrukh (Mashhad: Kitābfurūshī-yi Bāstān, 1339 [1961]).
Ghiyāth/*Ta'rīkh*	'Abd Allāh b. Fatḥ Allāh Ghiyāth, *al-Ta'rīkh al-Ghiyāthī*, ed. Ṭāriq Nāfi' al-Ḥamdānī (Baghdad: Maṭba'at As'ad, 1975).
Ḥāfiẓ Abrū/*ZJT*	Ḥāfiẓ Abrū, *Z̲ayl-i Jāmi' al-Tavārīkh*, ed. Khānbābā Bayānī (Tehran: 'Ilmī, 1317 [1939]).
Ḥāfiẓ Abrū/*Zubda*	Ḥāfiẓ Abrū, *Zubdat al-Tavārīkh*, ed. Sayyid

	Kamāl Ḥājj-i Sayyid Javādī (Tehran: Vizārat-i Farhang va Irshād-i Islāmī, 1380 [2001]).
HJAS	*Harvard Journal of Asiatic Studies*
Ibn 'Arabshāh/*'Ajā'ib*	Muḥammad ibn Aḥmad b. 'Arabshāh, *'Ajā'ib al-Maqdūr fī Nawā'ib Tīmūr*, ed. 'Alī Muḥammad 'Umar (Cairo: Maktabat al-Anjilū al-Miṣriyya, 1399 [1979]).
Ibn Bībī/Erzi	Ibn Bībī, *El-Evāmirü'l-'Alā'iyye fī'l-Umūri'l-'Alā'iyye*, ed. Adnan Sadık Erzi (Ankara: Türk Tarih Kurumu Basımevi, 1956).
Ibn Bībī/Houtsma	Ibn Bībī, *Histoire des Seldjoucides d'Asie Mineure d'après l'Abrégé du Seldjouknāmeh d'Ibn-Bībī*, ed. M. Th. Houtsma (Leiden: Brill, 1902).
Ibn Ḥajar/*Durar*	Aḥmad ibn 'Alī b. Ḥajar al-'Asqalānī, *Durar al-Kāmina fī A'yān al-Mi'a al-Thāmina*, ed. 'Abd al-Wārith Muḥammad 'Alī (Beirut: Dār al-Kutub al-'Ilmiyya, 1977).
Ibn Ḥajar/*Inbā'*	Aḥmad ibn 'Alī b. Ḥajar al-'Asqalānī, *Inbā' al-Ghumr bi-Abnā' al-'Umr* (Hyderabad: Maṭba'at Majlis Dā'irat al-Ma'ārif al-'Uthmāniyya, 1967).
Ibn Taghrī Birdī/*Manhal*	Abū al-Maḥāsin Yūsuf b. Taghrī Birdī, *al-Manhal al-Ṣāfī wa al-Mustawfī ba'd al-Wāfī*, ed. Muḥammad Amīn (Cairo: al-Hay'a al-Miṣriyya al-'Āmma lil-Kitāb, 1984–).
Ibn Taghrī Birdī/*Nujūm*	Abū al-Maḥāsin Yūsuf b. Taghrī Birdī, *al-Nujūm al-Zāhira fī Mulūk Miṣr wa-al-Qāhira*, ed. William Popper (Berkeley: University of California Press, 1960).
JESHO	*Journal of the Economic and Social History of the Orient*
JNES	*Journal of Near Eastern Studies*
JRAS	*Journal of the Royal Asiatic Society*
Khvāndamīr/Humā'ī	Ghiyāṣ al-Dīn b. Humām al-Dīn Khvāndamīr, *Tārīkh-i Habīb al-Siyar fī Akhbār-i Afrād-i Bashar*, ed. Jalāl al-Dīn Humā'ī (Tehran: Kitāb-khāna-yi Khayyam, 1954).
Khvāndamīr/Thackston	Ghiyāṣ al-Dīn b. Humām al-Dīn Khvāndamīr, *Habibu's-siyar, Tome Three, The Reign of the Mongol and the Turk*, ed. and trans. Wheeler

	Thackston (Cambridge, MA: Department of Near Eastern Languages and Civilizations, Harvard University, 1994).
Kutubī/*TAM*	Maḥmūd Kutubī, *Tārīkh-i Āl-i Muẓaffar*, ed. ʻAbd al-Ḥusayn Navāʼī (Tehran: Kitābfurūshī-yi Ibn Sīnā, 1956).
Maqrīzī/ʻAshūr	Taqī al-Dīn Aḥmad b. ʻAlī al-Maqrīzī, *Kitāb al-Sulūk li-Maʻrifat Duwal al-Mulūk*, ed. ʻAbd al-Fattāḥ ʻAshūr (Cairo, 1972).
Maqrīzī/Ziyāda	Taqī al-Dīn Aḥmad b. ʻAlī al-Maqrīzī, *Kitāb al-Sulūk li-Maʻrifat Duwal al-Mulūk*, ed. Muḥammad Muṣṭafá Ziyāda (Cairo: Lajnat al-Taʼlif wa-al-Tarjama wa-al-Nashr, 1934).
Mīrkhvānd/*Rawża*	Muḥammad b. Khvāndshāh Mīrkhvānd, *Tārīkh-i Rawżat al-Ṣafāʼ* (Tehran: Markazī-yi Khayyam Pīrūz, 1959–60).
Nakhjivānī/*Dastūr*	Muḥammad bin Hindūshāh Nakhjivānī, *Dastūr al-Kātib fī Taʻyīn al-Marātib*, ed. ʻAbd al-Karīm ʻAlīūghlī ʻAlīzāda (Moscow: Izd-vo ʻNaukaʼ, Glav. red. vostochnoĭ lit-ry, 1964–76).
Naṭanzī/Aubin	Muʻīn al-Dīn Naṭanzī, *Extraits du Muntakhab al-tavārīkh-i Muʻīnī (Anonyme d'Iskandar)*, ed. Jean Aubin (Tehran: Librairie Khayyam, 1957).
Qazvīnī/*Nuzhat*	Ḥamd Allāh Mustawfī Qazvīnī, *The Geographical Part of the Nuzhat-al-Qulūb*, ed. Guy Le Strange (Leiden: Brill; London: Luzac & Co., 1915–19).
Qazvīnī/*TG*	Ḥamd Allāh Mustawfī Qazvīnī, *Tārīkh-i Guzīda*, ed. ʻAbd al-Ḥusayn Navāʼī (Tehran: Amīr Kabīr, 1362 [1983]).
Qazvīnī/*ZTG*	Zayn al-Dīn b. Ḥamd Allāh Mustawfī Qazvīnī, *Ẕayl-i Tārīkh-i Guzīda*, ed. Īraj Afshār (Tehran: Naqsh-i Jahān, 1372 [1993].
Rashīd al-Dīn/*Jāmiʻ*	Rashīd al-Dīn Fażl Allāh Hamadānī, *Jāmiʻ al-Tavārīkh*, ed. Muḥammad Rawshan and Muṣṭafá Mūsavī (Tehran: Nashr-i Alburz, 1373 [1994]).
Rashīd al-Dīn/*Shuʻab*	Rashīd al-Dīn Fażl Allāh Hamadānī, *Shuʻab-i Panjgāna* (Istanbul: Topkapı Sarayı Müzesi Kütüphanesi, Ahmet III ms. 2937).

Ṣafadī/*A'yān*	Khalīl ibn Aybak al-Ṣafadī, *A'yān al-'Aṣr wa-A'wān al-Naṣr* (Beirut: Dār al-Fikr al-Mu'āṣir and Damascus: Dār al-Fikr, 1998).
Samarqandī/*Maṭla'*	Kamāl al-Dīn 'Abd al-Razzāq Samarqandī, *Maṭla'-i Sa'dayn va Majma'-i Baḥrayn*, ed. 'Abd al-Ḥusayn Navā'ī (Tehran: Shāh Riżā Muqābil Dānishgāh, 1353 [1975]).
Sāvajī/*Kullīyāt*	Salmān Sāvajī, *Kullīyāt-i Salmān-i Sāvajī*, ed. 'Abbās 'Alī Vafā'ī (Tehran: Anjuman-i Āṡār va Mafākhir-i Farhangī, 1382 [2004]).
Shabānkāra'ī/*Majma'*	Muḥammad bin 'Alī bin Muḥammad Shabānkāra'ī, *Majma' al-Ansāb*, ed. Mīr Hāshim Muḥaddiṡ (Tehran: Mu'assasa-yi Intishārāt-i Amīr Kabīr, 1363 [1985]).
Shāmī/Lugal	Niẓām al-Dīn Shāmī, *Zafernâme*, ed. Necati Lugal (Ankara: Türk Tarih Kurumu Basımevi, 1949).
Shāmī/Tauer	Niẓām al-Dīn Shāmī, *Histoire des conquêtes de Tamerlan intitulée Ẓafar-nāma, par Niẓāmuddīn Šāmī, avec des additions empruntées au Zubdatu-t-Tawāriḫ-i Bāysunġurī de Ḥāfiẓ-i Abrū*, ed. Felix Tauer (Prague: Orientální ústav/Oriental Institute, 1937).
Shujā'ī/*Tārīkh*	Shams al-Dīn Shujā'ī, *Tārīkh al-Malik al-Nāṣir Muḥammad ibn Qalawūn al-Ṣāliḥī wa-Awlāduhu*, ed. Barbara Schäfer (Wiesbaden: Franz Steiner, 1978–85).
Storey/*Persian Literature*	Charles Ambrose Storey, *Persian Literature: A Bio-Bibliographical Survey* (London: Luzac & Co., 1927–).
TMEN	Gerhard Doerfer, *Türkische und Mongolische Elemente im Neupersischen* (Wiesbaden: Franz Steiner Verlag, 1963).
Vaṣṣāf/*Tārīkh*	'Abd Allāh b. Fażl Allāh Vaṣṣāf al-Ḥażrat, *Tārīkh-i Vaṣṣāf* [Lithograph ed. Bombay, 1269 (1853); reprint] (Tehran: Ibn-i Sīnā, 1338 [1959]).
Yazdī/*Ẓafar-nāma*	Sharaf al-Dīn 'Alī Yazdī, *Ẓafar-nāma*, ed. Muḥammad 'Abbāsī (Tehran: Amīr Kabīr, 1336 (1957–58).

1

Introduction and Sources for the History of the Jalayirids

In his chapter 'The Jalayirids, Muzaffarids and Sarbadārs' in volume six of the *Cambridge History of Iran*, Hans Robert Roemer characterised the period between the fall of the Mongol Ilkhanate and the arrival of Tīmūr in Iran as 'grim and unedifying', and mainly significant for its intellectual achievements, as well as for understanding Tīmūr's subsequent success in Iran.[1] The period of fifty years, from c. 1335 to 1385, certainly witnessed examples of sublime cultural production; this was the period of Ḥāfiẓ, and the refinement of painted manuscript illustration, to name two important examples. In addition, indeed, a student of the Timurids must certainly strive to understand Tīmūr's campaigns in Iran in the context of the political situation that preceded them. Yet, there is a general sense among scholars of the late-medieval Middle East (what Marshall Hodgson called the 'Later Middle Period', roughly 1250 to 1500) that the middle of the fourteenth century east of the Euphrates river is best understood as a tumultuous transition between two important dynastic cycles, those of the Ilkhans and the Timurids. Additionally, this was a period of political breakdown with little to offer for our understanding of either the Ilkhanate or the Timurid and Turkman sultanates that followed in the fifteenth century. While the half-century in question certainly did see its share of 'grim' and tumultuous political conflict, the historical significance of the events of the period can only be fully understood if we consider continuities with the Ilkhanid past, along with the reality of the dramatic end of stability and dynastic order that took place following the death of Abū Sa'īd Bahādur Khan in 1335.

We still know very little about the transition between the period of the Chinggisid Ilkhanate and the rulers that followed its collapse in the fourteenth century. Several amiral and local dynasties emerged following the death of Abū Sa'īd. This study takes as its subject one of these post-Ilkhanid dynasties. The Jalayirid sultans, descendants of the Mongolian tribe of Jalayir, ruled part of the former Ilkhanid domains in the middle of the fourteenth century. In the following chapters, the roots of the Jalayirids are traced from their origins in the historical record in the tribal society of the Mongol steppe, through their rise and claims to be the heirs to the Ilkhanate, and finally to the collapse of their authority and prestige in the world beyond their domains in the early fifteenth century. Although the Jalayirid period did see its share of violent conflict, the story of how the Jalayirids came to power is illustrative of the political dynamics that shaped much of the Mongol and post-Mongol period in the Middle East. The relationship between the most significant elements of the Ilkhanid ruling elite, the amirs and the court and household of the Chinggisid ruler, comes into clearer relief when the focus of historical inquiry is taken off the dynasty itself, and turned onto those non-royal elites who both supported and challenged the Ilkhanid political order.

The Jalayirid sultans sought to preserve the social and political order of the Ilkhanate, while claiming that they were the rightful heirs to the rulership of that order. Central to the Jalayirids' claims to the legacy of the Ilkhanate was their attempt to control the Ilkhanid heartland of Azarbayjan. This province, and its major city of Tabriz, represented the symbolic legacy and material wealth of the Ilkhanate, and became the focus of the Jalayirid political programme. Control of Azarbayjan meant control of a network of long-distance trade between China and the Latin West, which continued to be a source of economic prosperity through the eighth/fourteenth century. Azarbayjan also represented the centre of Ilkhanid court life, whether in the migration of the mobile court-camp of the ruler, or in the complexes of palatial, religious and civic buildings constructed around the city of Tabriz by members of the Ilkhanid royal family, as well as by members of the military and administrative elite.

In the years following the dissolution of the Ilkhanate after the death of Abū Sa'īd Bahādur Khan in 736/1335, the family descended from the Jalayir tribal amir Īlgā Noyan established themselves first as heirs to the traditional governors of the Ilkhanate's southwestern march lands, an area that was home to large numbers of Oyrat tribesmen in Arab Iraq and Diyarbakr, and later as rulers in the Ilkhanid imperial centre in Azarbayjan. At the height of their rule, under Sultan Shaykh Uvays (r. 757/1356–776/1374), the Jalayirids attempted to portray themselves as heirs to the Ilkhanid political legacy, and continuators of the Ilkhanate, albeit on a smaller territorial scale. Although the Jalayirids could not claim to be direct heirs of the last Ilkhanid ruler, they nevertheless could and did attempt to legitimise their claims to the Ilkhanid legacy through their family ties to the Ilkhanid royal house, as well as their role as upholders of Islamic and Mongol dynastic justice, an ideological combination that had been part of the political programme of the later Ilkhanid rulers themselves.

In this endeavour, the Jalayirid sultans, beginning with Shaykh Uvays, could count on representatives of the old Ilkhanid administrative and bureaucratic elite. The continuation of the patterns of rule of the old order, which the Jalayirids sought to uphold, was in the interest of those who had served the Ilkhanate in Tabriz. Members of the Ilkhanid administrative elite helped to construct the political programme and dynastic history of the Jalayirids, which linked them to the Ilkhanid past. As a result, the Jalayirids, ruling from their two capitals in Tabriz and Baghdad, came to represent a continuation of the Ilkhanid political past, through control of the territorial heartland of the Ilkhanate in Azarbayjan. This 'Ilkhanid political ideal' only began to break down when Tīmūr and his descendants attempted to reconstitute a larger polity on the model of Chinggis Qan's world empire, of which the Ilkhanid domains were only one part. A shift in political gravity from Azarbayjan to Khurasan and Transoxiana under the Timurids in the ninth/fifteenth century marked the end of the Ilkhanate as a principle for future political organisation. Deprived of Tabriz first by Tīmūr, and later by the Qarāquyūnlū confederation, the Jalayirid dynasty receded after the death of Sulṭān Aḥmad Jalayir in 813/1410.

At the heart of the history of the Jalayirids is the question of the relationship of 'tribal' to dynastic authority in the Mongol and Islamic contexts in this period. To what extent did a 'tribal' identity, however defined, matter in the period after the expansion of the Mongol empire in the thirteenth century, and the establishment of Chinggisid authority over the non-Mongol populations of the Oxus-to-Euphrates region? The Jalayirids rose to prominence in a period in which the dynasties ruled by descendants of Chinggis Qan disappeared in Yüan China and Chaghatayid central Asia, as well as in the Ilkhanate. The tribal ancestors of the Jalayirid sultans had constituted part of the foundation of Chinggis Qan's empire. Yet, the Jalayirids of the fourteenth century were not tribal chiefs. Instead, they were products of a military elite that owed its structure and hierarchy to the Ilkhanid dynastic state. The amirs within this hierarchy owed their status and position not to their tribes, but to their relationship to the khan and the royal family. In addition, members of the Ilkhanid military elite, like the Jalayirids, were often the sons of royal princesses, who had been married to tribal amirs to secure political alliances. Thus, the status enjoyed by one branch of Jalayir tribal amirs within the Ilkhanid imperial hierarchy put them in a position to establish a new dynastic dispensation in the eighth/fourteenth century. As this study illustrates, the Jalayirid sultans owed their success not to their tribal origins or identities, but to the particular historical circumstances of the role played by their ancestors in the life of the Ilkhanate. They sought to link themselves as closely as possible with the resources, symbols and historical rhetoric of the Chinggisid Ilkhans and the *ulūs* ('patrimonial commonwealth') that they created in the thirteenth and fourteenth centuries.

This study is organised into chapters tracing the historical past of the Jalayirid dynasty through individual ancestors in the context of the political formation and expansion of Chinggis Qan's empire in inner Asia; the foundation of the Ilkhanate by Hülegü Khan and his descendants; and the aftermath of the Ilkhanate's collapse. The post-Chinggisid period is examined in chapters dealing with the reign of Shaykh Ḥasan b. Amīr Ḥusayn; the reign of Sultan Shaykh Uvays b. Shaykh Ḥasan; the ideological strategies deployed to legitimate Shaykh Uvays's reign; and, finally, the reigns of Shaykh Uvays's sons, Sulṭān Ḥusayn and Sulṭān Aḥmad, and the end of Jalayirid authority in the former Ilkhanid lands.

Sources and Secondary Literature for the Jalayirids

Before turning to a chronological examination of the Jalayir tribe and its incorporation into the Mongol Ilkhanate, a discussion of sources for the history of the Jalayirids is in order. In what follows, an attempt has been made to identify the most important primary sources, and to place them into the social and political context of their composition, as far as is known. Then, an overview of secondary literature that has most directly informed this study is provided.

The earliest source which deals with the Jalayir tribe in relation to Chinggis Qan and the rise of the Mongol empire is the anonymous *Yuan chao bi shi*, or *Secret History of the Mongols*, a part-mythological, part-historical account of the ancestry and life of Temüjin, the future Chinggis Qan, stretching in time from the primordial past twenty-two generations before Temüjin's birth, until the reign of his son and successor, Ögödey.[2] The *Secret History* is unique as the only extant source composed by the Mongols themselves. Although it was originally written in Mongolian, the version which we have is a transliteration in Chinese characters. Three major English translations exist,[3] which often need to be consulted together in order to arrive at the clearest interpretation of events.

The *Secret History* provides an important source for the early Mongol view of Temüjin's rise to power within the context of tribal society on the steppe in the late sixth/twelfth and early seventh/thirteenth centuries. For the purposes of this study, it is valuable as a kind of ethnographic map of the Mongol tribes and the relationships of their members to Chinggis

Qan in the formative years of the Mongol empire. However, since it ends during the reign of Ögödey Qa'an, the *Secret History* provides no information on the establishment of the Ilkhanate, the appanage state founded in the Middle East by Chinggis Qan's grandson, Hülegü.

For the study of the Jalayir tribe in the Ilkhanate and the period of rule by the independent Jalayirid dynasty to the year 813/1410, narrative histories written in Persian provide the most important sources of information. Histories written for Ilkhanid rulers, which can be understood as representing the official dynastic view of the past, began in the early eighth/fourteenth century. Perhaps the most important monument of Persian historiography was the *Jāmi' al-Tavārīkh*, written by Rashīd al-Dīn Fażl Allāh Hamadānī (d. 718/1318).[4] This universal history is a collection of several sections on the history of the world and its peoples, including the Oghuz Turks, Chinese, Franks, Jews and Indians. Of importance for the Jalayir tribe and its relationship to the Ilkhanate is the section known as the *Tārīkh-i Ghāzānī*, commissioned by Ghazan Khan, completed during the reign of Öljeytü (r. 704/1304–716/1316), and devoted to the history of the Mongols and the Ilkhanate. Rashīd al-Dīn was the Ilkhanid vizier, sharing this position for a period with his rival, Sa'd al-Dīn Sāvajī. The *Tārīkh-i Ghāzānī* was written amid a series of centralising reforms initiated during the reign of Ghazan Khan, aimed at limiting the power of the tribal amirs and strengthening the central government. It is from this perspective that Rashīd al-Dīn provides an account of several branches of the Jalayir tribe within the Ilkhanate from the time of its establishment by Hülegü Khan in the late 650s/1250s. Particularly useful are the sections covering the years between 680/1282 and 694/1295, when four khans came to the throne, three of whom were deposed due to efforts by the amirs, including prominent members of the Jalayir tribe.

A second major work of the Ilkhanid historiographical tradition is the *Tajziyat al-Amṣār wa-Tazjiyat al-A'ṣār*, better known as *Tārīkh-i Vaṣṣāf* after its author, 'Abd Allāh ibn Fażl Allāh al-Shīrāzī Vaṣṣāf (d. c. 729 /1329).[5] In this history, Vaṣṣāf deals with events in Iran and Anatolia from the death of Möngke Qa'an in 657/1259 through to the year 712/1312, and including events in various provinces. Like the *Tārīkh-i Ghāzānī*, Vaṣṣāf's history is important for its account of the conflicts between the Ilkhanid dynasty and the amirs, as well as between branches of the Jalayir tribe itself in the late seventh/thirteenth century.

Another early eighth/fourteenth-century history is the *Rawżat Ūlī al-Albāb fī Tavārīkh al-Akābir wa-al-Ansāb*, completed in 718/1318 by Fakhr al-Dīn Abū Sulaymān Dāwūd Banākātī (d. 730/1330).[6] Banākātī's history is essentially a summary of Rashīd al-Dīn's *Tārīkh-i Ghāzānī*, with some extra information from Öljeytü's reign. Öljeytü's reign is more fully dealt with in the *Tārīkh-i Ūljāytū* of Abū al-Qāsim Qāshānī, completed after the year 718/1318.[7] This regnal history provides a great amount of detail in a straightforward style. Qāshānī's work is important for the information it provides about the Jalayir Amīr Ḥusayn Gūrgān, son of Āq Būqā, who married his father's wife, Öljetey Khatun, sister of the sultan Öljeytü.

The late Ilkhanid period produced the historian and financial director Ḥamd Allāh Mustawfī Qazvīnī (d. c. 740/1340).[8] Among his three major works was the *Ẓafar-nāma*, a work of verse emulating Firdawsī's *Shāh-nāma*, and covering events up to 734/1333–34. Charles Melville has pointed out the historiographic importance of the *Ẓafar-nāma*, as a source for the Timurid-era historian Ḥāfiẓ Abrū's *Ẕayl-i Jāmi' al-Tavārīkh*.[9] Qazvīnī also wrote a prose history, *Tārīkh-i Guzīda*, completed in 730 /1330. Although it depends in large part on older sources, it does contain some original information for Qazvīnī's own times. His third major work is the *Nuzhat al-Qulūb*, which provides important information on the geography and demography of the late Ilkhanid period.[10]

Within this category of official Ilkhanid historiography can be identified a subcategory of regional histories written from the perspective of the Ilkhanid western frontier in Anatolia. The earliest work from this category is *al-Avāmir al-'Alā'iyya fī al-Umūr al-'Alā'iyya* by Ibn Bībī (d. after 681/1282–83).[11] This history of the Saljūqs of Rūm from c. 584/1188 to 680/1281 was composed in a transitional period in which Anatolia was incorporated into the Ilkhanid polity, as Saljuqid authority was weakened by pressure from both the Mongols and the Mamluks. Ibn Bībī's mother was employed as court astrologer at Konya during the reign of the Saljūq sultan Kay Qubād I (d. 634/1237).[12] Following the Mongol conquest of Saljūq forces in Anatolia in 641/1243, and later, after the arrival of Hülegü Khan in Iran in the late 650s/1250s, the Mongols attempted to bring the Saljūq lands to the west under their control. As part of this programme of Mongol influence in Anatolia, 'Aṭā' Malik Juvaynī (d. 681/1283), Khurasanian administrative official, and author of the *Tārīkh-i Jahāngushāy*,[13] commissioned a history of the Saljūqs from Ibn Bībī. Charles Melville has suggested that the commission for *al-Avāmir al-'Alā'iyya* may have come around the year 676/1277–78, after the campaign of the Mamluk sultan Baybars in Anatolia and the collapse of the Saljūq state there. This event would have created the need for a work of history that asserted the ideas of justice, Muslim piety and ancient Iranian kingship as a means of connecting the Ilkhans more closely with Iran's imperial past, and thus asserting the authority of the Ilkhans in their rivalry with the Mamluks.[14] Ibn Bībī's history is important for the details it provides about the period of disorder after the Mamluk invasion and the uprisings carried out against Ilkhanid rule in Anatolia. These revolts involved several Jalayir amirs, and the eventual suppression of these revolts contributed to the elimination of certain Jalayir families, as well as the promotion of the family of the Ilgayid branch of the Jalayir, which would later found the Jalayirid dynasty.

A second major work from the Anatolian perspective is the *Musāmarat al-Akhbār wa-Musāyarat al-Akhyār*, written by Karīm al-Dīn Āqsarāyī (d. before 734/1333).[15] Almost three-quarters of this universal history deals with the history of the Mongols in Anatolia.[16] It was written for the amir Tīmūr Tāsh, the son of Amīr Chūpān, the premier military commander and political figure during the early reign of Abū Sa'īd (717/1317–727/1327). Āqsarāyī was a secretary and served as the administrator of religious endowments (*vaqf*) in Anatolia during the reign of Ghazan Khan.[17] When the young Abū Sa'īd came to the Ilkhanid throne in 717/1317, the family of Amīr Chūpān came to control the affairs of the state, and Tīmūr Tāsh b. Amīr Chūpān became governor of Anatolia. Āqsarāyī composed the *Musāmarat al-Akhbār* in 723/1323.[18] His accounts of the involvement of Jalayir amirs in the Mamluk invasion of Anatolia in 675/1277, as well as the involvement of other Jalayir amirs in the disorder there during the reign of Ghazan Khan, are important for the activities of several branches of the Jalayir tribe during the Ilkhanid period.

The histories mentioned above were all composed within the context of Ilkhanid dynastic rule in the region roughly between the Oxus and Euphrates rivers until the year 736/1335. Following the death of Abū Sa'īd in this year, the Ilkhanid territories began to fragment into regions controlled by amirs and local elites, due to the fact that no commonly recognised legitimate successor existed. Abū Sa'īd did not have any male offspring who may have ensured a smooth transition of political authority, and the continuation of the Ilkhanid dynasty. Although many descendants of the Ilkhanid rulers were alive, often available to serve as convenient puppets for powerful amirs, the pattern of succession had been settled on the descendants of Arghun Khan since his son Ghazan took the throne in 694/1295. Thus, even though several princes descended from Hülegü Khan emerged as possible candidates, there was no unanimous agreement on any of them among the various regional and tribal factions in the Ilkhanate.

In this situation, the pattern of history writing changed. With no universally recognised Ilkhanid ruler, historians wrote for patrons representing local dynasties that competed for claims to the Ilkhanid throne and its capital territory in Azarbayjan. These works fall chronologically and ideologically between the histories written for the Ilkhans and those written for Tīmūr and his descendants in the ninth/fifteenth century.

The single example of a history written for and about the Jalayirid dynasty is the *Tārīkh-i Shaykh Uvays*, composed by Abū Bakr al-Quṭbī al-Ahrī (or al-Aharī).[19] Writing around the year 761/1360, shortly after Shaykh Uvays's conquest of Azarbayjan, Ahrī provides a unique perspective on the history of the Ilkhanate, which anticipates the Jalayirids' eventual rise to power. The work is arranged according to the reigns of the Ilkhans and their successors. Shaykh Ḥasan's rule is not given an independent heading, and instead events between 736/1335 and 757/1356 are arranged according to the reigns of the puppet khans installed and recognised as sovereign by Shaykh Ḥasan, as well as those supported by his rivals. The Jalayirids are recognised as independent sultans only after the accession of Shaykh Uvays.[20] Although he relies on Rashīd al-Dīn for much of his information to 704/1304, Ahrī's history may be considered an independent source for the early years of the eighth/fourteenth century.[21]

An additional work of history dedicated to Shaykh Uvays, but devoted to an earlier period, is the *Ghāzān-nāma* of Nūr al-Dīn Azhdarī.[22] This poetic work, written between 1357 and 1362[23] by a talented physician and son of an Ilkhanid vizier,[24] deals with the ancestors and reign of Ghazan Khan. Azhdarī dedicated the *Ghāzān-nāma* to the 'king of kings of equity and religion (*shahanshāh-i bā-dād u dīn*), Shaykh Uvays'.[25]

Post-Ilkhanid historiography is also represented by the *Majma' al-Ansāb fī al-Tavārīkh* of Muḥammad b. 'Alī b. Muḥammad al-Shabānkāra'ī (d. 759/1358).[26] Writing originally in the service of the last Ilkhanid vizier, Ghiyāth al-Dīn Muḥammad Rashīdī, Shabānkāra'ī provides great detail about the critical years of transition after Abū Sa'īd's death. He wrote in praise of Shaykh Ḥasan Jalayir's Chinggisid puppet, Muḥammad Khan, whom he describes as the 'shadow of God'.[27] While the *Majma' al-Ansāb* does devote particular attention to the province of Fars, it nevertheless provides a great deal of information on Shaykh Ḥasan's establishment of political authority in Arab Iraq, and his attempt to capture the Ilkhanid imperial centre in Azarbayjan.

A final work of post-Ilkhanid historiography is the *Tārīkh-i Āl-i Muẓaffar* of Maḥmūd Kutubī.[28] The Muzaffarids were a local dynastic family that brought the provinces of Fars and Persian Iraq under their control in the period after 736/1335. In fact, the Muzaffarids had acted as local authorities in the regions of Kirman and Yazd in the later period of Ilkhanid rule, and also sought to bring Azarbayjan under their control throughout much of the eighth/fourteenth century. Kutubī's work, written in 823/1420 as an addition to a redaction of Ḥamd Allāh Mustawfī Qazvīnī's *Tārīkh-i Guzīda*,[29] provides a Muzaffarid perspective on the conflicts with the Jalayirids in Azarbayjan in the period before Tīmūr's first campaigns in Iran in the 780s/1380s.

The arrival of Tīmūr was the beginning of the end of the Ilkhanid dynastic tradition as the basis for political authority in Iran and Anatolia. Tīmūr's invasion and campaigns ushered in what is commonly known as the Timurid period (c. 1385–1506), in which authority came to rest with members of Tīmūr's family, and the centre of political gravity shifted from Azarbayjan to Khurasan and Transoxiana. The Timurid period was accompanied by a new historiographical tradition, which took Tīmūr and his family as its focus and object of glorification. Despite the fact that the Ilkhanate as a political ideal was no longer supported by Timurid historians, who tended to view the Ilkhanate as one part of a larger Chinggisid imperial polity which Tīmūr attempted to reconstruct,[30] these historians provide the majority of information on the Jalayirid dynasty, and for this reason their work is crucial to this study.

An important link between the Ilkhanid and Timurid historiographical traditions is the *Ẕayl-i Tārīkh-i Guzīda* of Zayn al-Dīn Qazvīnī, a continuation of the work of the author's father, Ḥamd Allāh Mustawfī Qazvīnī, up until the year 795/1393.[31] Although the *Ẕayl* was written for a Timurid audience, it was intended as a continuation of the *Tārīkh-i Guzīda*, and thus maintains a focus on Azarbayjan, the centre of the Ilkhanid realm, even after the arrival of Tīmūr and the transfer of political power to other centres. Because of the attention paid by Zayn al-Dīn to Azarbayjan in the period after 736/1335 (the work begins with the year 742/1341–42), the *Ẕayl* is an important source for the history of the Jalayirids, who conquered Azarbayjan in 759/1358.

Zayn al-Dīn Qazvīnī's work is also significant as a source for two later Timurid historians, Ḥāfiẓ Abrū[32] and Faṣīḥ Khvāfī.[33] Ḥāfiẓ Abrū wrote a number of historical works under the patronage of Tīmūr's son Shāhrukh at Herat.[34] His *Ẕayl-i Jāmi' al-Tavārīkh*, part of the larger *Majmū'a-yi Ḥāfiẓ Abrū*, is a continuation of Rashīd al-Dīn's history through to the end of the Ilkhanid period, until Tīmūr's arrival in Iran. Ḥāfiẓ Abrū relies on Zayn al-Dīn Qazvīnī for the basic structure of his account of the post-Ilkhanid period, which means that he tends to give precedence to events in Azarbayjan and the rule of the Jalayirids there.[35] Five short treatises on aspects of the eighth/fourteenth century in Khurasan and Mazandaran, also part of the *Majmū'a*, are collected in *Cinq opuscules de Ḥāfiẓ-i Abrū concernant l'histoire de l'Iran au temps de Tamerlan*, edited by Felix Tauer.[36] Of particular importance for this study is Ḥāfiẓ Abrū's account of Amīr Valī, the independent governor of Mazandaran, and rival of the Jalayirids in the period before Tīmūr, which is preserved in this edition. Faṣīḥ Khvāfī served at the courts of Bāysunqur Mīrzā and Shāhrukh, and presented his *Mujmal-i Tavārīkh-i Faṣīḥī* to Shāhrukh in 845/1442.[37] The sections of his history on the Jalayirid period follow Zayn al-Dīn and Ḥāfiẓ Abrū, but in a much simpler, less detailed style.

Other examples of Timurid history writing important for this study of the Jalayirids include the earliest history of the life and career of Tīmūr, the *Ẓafar-nāma* of Niẓām al-Dīn Shāmī, composed in 806/1404, prior to Tīmūr's death.[38] Shāmī provides a first-hand account of Tīmūr's conquest of Baghdad in 795/1393, and the flight of the Jalayirid Sulṭān Aḥmad. Additional relevant historical works composed under Tīmūr's successors include the *Muntakhab al-Tavārīkh-i Mu'īnī*, written by Mu'īn al-Dīn Naṭanzī for Shāhrukh in 817/1414.[39] In his 1957 edition, *Extraits du Muntakhab al-tavārīkh-i Mu'īnī (Anonyme d'Iskandar)*, Jean Aubin preserved sections of this work devoted to the descendants of Chinggis Qan, as well as the important ruling families in Iran after the Ilkhanate. The chapter devoted to the descendants of Shaykh Ḥasan Jalayir is especially important.[40] Appearing after Naṭanzī's *Muntakhab* chronologically was the *Ẓafar-nāma* of Sharaf al-Dīn 'Alī Yazdī, written c. 826/1422–23.[41] Yazdī's *Ẓafar-nāma* focuses on Tīmūr's military campaigns, and is a useful source for the periods of the Jalayirid Sulṭān Aḥmad's reign when he came into conflict with Tīmūr.

Later Timurid-era histories, which tend to rely on Yazdī and Ḥāfiẓ Abrū, include 'Abd al-Razzāq Samarqandī's *Maṭla'-i Sa'dayn va-Majma'-i Baḥrayn*, written for the Timurid Sulṭān Abū Sa'īd.[42] The first part of the title, translated as 'The Rising of the Two Fortunes', is a reference to the two Abū Sa'īds whose reigns provide the starting and ending points of the work, that is Abū Sa'īd Bahādur Khan (d. 736/1335) and Sulṭān Abū Sa'īd b. Muḥammad b. Mīrānshāh b. Tīmūr (d. 873/1469). One of the most well-known Timurid histories of the late ninth/fifteenth century is the *Rawżat al-Ṣafā'* of Mīr Muḥammad ibn Sayyid Burhān al-Dīn Khvāndshāh, better known as Mīrkhvānd.[43] Writing under the patronage of the minister and littérateur 'Alī Shīr Navā'ī at Herat, Mīrkhvānd devotes a large portion of this world history to the Ilkhanate and its aftermath in the eighth/fourteenth century. A final word should be added about Mīrkhvānd's grandson, Khvandamīr, whose *Ḥabīb al-Siyar fī Akhbār-i Afrād-i Bashar*, written under Safavid patronage in the late 920s/early 1520s, is a late example of the Persian world historical tradition begun by Rashīd al-Dīn, providing a great amount of detail for the seventh/thirteenth and eighth/fourteenth centuries.[44]

Although most of the historical writing in Persian was composed for the Timurid courts in Khurasan and Transoxiana, one contemporary work written in Anatolia is important for the eighth/fourteenth century. This is *Bazm u Razm*, written by ʻAzīz ibn Ārdashīr Astarābādī for Qāḍī Burhān al-Dīn, the ruler of Sivas.[45] After assuming a judgeship in Kayseri, Qāḍī Burhān al-Dīn had become vizier to Ḥukumdār ʻAlī Beg, the heir to the principality of Eretna in Anatolia. When Ḥukumdār ʻAlī Beg died, Burhān al-Dīn became regent to his young son, and the *qāḍī* emerged as the ruler of a principality in central Anatolia.[46] According to Astarābādī's own account in *Bazm u Razm*, he was employed at the court of the Jalayirid Sulṭān Aḥmad in Baghdad, but migrated to Anatolia and the service of Qāḍī Burhān al-Dīn after Tīmūr's invasion of Iran in 788/1386. *Bazm u Razm* provides an account of the first part of the reign of Sulṭān Aḥmad from a non-Timurid perspective.

Anatolia underwent a political transformation in the years between 784 /1382 and 804/1402. In this period, the authority of the Jalayirids, which represented a continuation of the pattern of Mongol rule in Anatolia from Azarbayjan begun in 641/1243, began to break down, as local amirs and beys such as Qarā Muḥammad of the Qarāquyūnlū,[47] Eretna (Aratnā),[48] Qāḍī Burhān al-Dīn[49] and Muṭahhartan[50] carved out independent spheres of influence. The Ottoman sultan Bāyezīd I greatly expanded his territory in Anatolia in the late eighth/fourteenth century, and provided a challenge to Tīmūr's claims to cities in eastern Anatolia, as well as a source of protection for the Jalayirid Sulṭān Aḥmad when he was driven from his capital at Baghdad. Because of the role played by Bāyezīd in the reign of Sulṭān Aḥmad, early Ottoman historiography treating this period provides an alternative narrative to the works of Timurid historians. The relationship between Sulṭān Aḥmad Jalayir and Sultan Bāyezīd can be traced to some of the earliest examples of Ottoman history writing produced during the period of the Conqueror, Meḥmed II (r. 855/1451–886/1481). These include the Persian *Bahjat al-Tavārīkh* composed by Shukr Allāh in the years 869/1465–873/1468.[51] In Shukr Allāh's history, the outline of later narratives written at Bāyezīd's court in Turkish on Sulṭān Aḥmad's time can be identified. Several of the 'royal calendars' (*taḳvīmler*) written around the same time also mention the Jalayirid sultan.[52] In addition, the Arabic history of Meḥmed II's chancellor and vizier, Ḳarāmānlı Meḥmed Pāşā, also provides a brief account of Sulṭān Aḥmad's arrival at the service of the Ottoman sultan.[53] Accounts are also found in histories written during the reign of Bāyezīd II (r. 886/1481–918/1512), which include the *Tevārīḫ-i Āl-i ʻOs̱mān* of ʻĀşıḳpāşāzāde (c. 887/1482).[54] This work, written in a popular style, including a question-and-answer format indicative of oral origins, provides a narrative different from that of Shukr Allāh. The narratives relating to Sulṭān Aḥmad found in *Bahjat al-Tavārīkh*, the royal calendars and 'Āşıḳpāşāzāde's *Tevārīḫ* are repeated and elaborated by historians of the early tenth/sixteenth century. The *Tevārīḫ-i Āl-i 'Os̱mān* of Rūḥī,[55] completed in 917/1511, before the death of Bāyezīd II, draws on Shukr Allāh's narrative. The *Kitâb-i Cihannümâ* of Neşrī,[56] also dedicated to Bāyezīd II, relies on this narrative, as well as on that found in 'Āşıḳpāşāzāde's *Tevārīḫ*. By the time of Sultan Süleymān, and historians such as Kemālpāşāzāde (d. 940/1534)[57] and Luṭfī Pāşā (d. 970/1562),[58] the main outline of the mid-ninth/fifteenth-century Ottoman accounts of the Jalayirids had been firmly established as part of the official histories, which tended to be organised by reign, with the period of Bāyezīd I typically occupying the fourth book or chapter.

Another major historiographical tradition important for the study of the Ilkhanid and Jalayirid periods comprises works written in Arabic in the Mamluk sultanate, the Ilkhanate's eastern neighbour. The long period of Mamluk rule in Egypt and Syria (648/1250–922/1517) produced a rich tradition of history writing, particularly in the form of annalistic chronicles and biographical dictionaries.[59] These Mamluk sources provide information on Iran and Anatolia in the Ilkhanid and post-Ilkhanid periods from an outside perspective.

Among eighth/fourteenth-century Mamluk chronicles, *al-Mukhtaṣar fī Ta'rīkh al-Bashar* by al-Malik al-Mu'ayyad 'Imād al-Dīn Abū al-Fidā'[60] provides information on affairs on the frontier between the Mamluk and Ilkhanid territories, particularly in Anatolia. Abū al-Fidā' was an Ayyubid prince[61] and governor in Hama in Syria under Sultan al-Nāṣir Muḥammad (3rd r. 709/1310–741/1341),[62] and thus was well informed on events close to Syria during the reign of Abū Sa'īd. Another Syrian chancery official, Ibn Faḍl Allāh al-'Umarī (d. 749/1349),[63] was also well informed about the Ilkhanate. The section of his encyclopaedic work *Masālik al-Abṣār fī Mamālik al-Amṣār* dealing with the Mongols has been published with a German translation by Klaus Lech.[64] Another Mamluk chronicle covering the Ilkhanate in the period after Abū Sa'īd's death is the *Ta'rīkh al-Malik al-Nāṣir Muḥammad b. Qalāwūn al-'āliḥī wa-Awlādihi*, by Shams al-Dīn b. al-Shujā'ī (d. after 756/1355).[65] This chronicle survives only as a fragment covering the years 737/1337–745/1345,[66] which includes accounts of Shaykh Ḥasan Jalayir in Iraq, as well as the conflicts between the Chubanids and the Sutayids on the Ilkhanid-Mamluk frontier. Biographies of the major political and religious figures of the eighth/fourteenth century are provided by Khalīl b. Aybak al-Ṣafadī (d. 764/1363) in his compilation *A'yān al-'Aṣr wa-A'wān al-Naṣr*.[67] Ṣafadī was one of the *awlād al-nās* (progeny of Mamluk amirs), and served in the chanceries of Damascus, Cairo and Aleppo.[68] The biographies of individuals from the Jalayirid, Chubanid, Sutayid and Ilkhanid families found in the *A'yān al-'Aṣr* demonstrate the relationships between these several influential groups and how they were related through marriage in a way that influenced Ilkhanid affairs, again with particular focus on the frontier with Mamluk Syria.

Mamluk chronicles from the ninth/fifteenth century are also significant for information on the Jalayirids through the beginning of the Timurid period in Iran. Taqī al-Dīn Aḥmad al-Maqrīzī's (d. 845/1442)[69] *Kitāb al-Sulūk li-Ma'rifat Duwal al-Mulūk* is a later Mamluk chronicle detailing the history of Egypt and Syria under the Ayyubids and Mamluks. Maqrīzī's history provides accounts from the period of Shaykh Ḥasan Jalayir's rule in Baghdad, as well as the reign of his son, Shaykh Uvays. A contemporary of Maqrīzī was Ibn Ḥajar al-'Asqalānī (d. 852/1449),[70] whose chronicle *Inbā' al-Ghumr fī Abnā' al-Umr* is important for the period of Sulṭān Aḥmad Jalayir and his conflicts with Tīmūr, as well as his relations with the Mamluks when he was forced out of Baghdad. Ibn Ḥajar also wrote a massive biographical dictionary, *al-Durar al-Kāmina fī A'yān al-Mi'a al-Thāmina*, which features over 5,000 entries on individuals who lived during the eighth/fourteenth century. Here his information on personalities of the Ilkhanid period tends to follow that of al-Ṣafadī.

Another biographical work devoted to the life of Tīmūr was written in Arabic in Mamluk Syria by Ibn 'Arabshāh (d. 854/1450).[71] His *'Ajā'ib al-Maqdūr fī Nawā'ib Tīmūr* is an unsympathetic account of Tīmūr, which includes information on Sulṭān Aḥmad Jalayir, and his son Sulṭān Ṭāhir, as well as on 'Abd al-'Azīz Astarābādī, author of *Bazm u Razm*. Ibn 'Arabshāh gives an account contrary to that given by Astarābādī himself concerning his migration from Jalayirid Baghdad to the court of Qāḍī Burhān al-Dīn in Sivas. Ibn 'Arabshāh and his family had been captured by Tīmūr during his conquest of Damascus in 803/1401, and were relocated to Samarqand. Because of this experience, Ibn 'Arabshāh had both first-hand knowledge of Tīmūr's empire and a personal hostility toward him.[72]

Finally, another ninth/fifteenth-century Mamluk historian, Abū al-Maḥāsin Yūsuf b. Taghrī Birdī (d. 874/1470),[73] must also be mentioned as a source for the Mamluks' relations with the Ilkhanate. Ibn Taghrī Birdī's *al-Nujūm al-Zāhira fī Mulūk Miṣr wa-al-Qāhira*, written after the year 857/1453, relies on earlier histories for its information on the eighth/fourteenth century. However, as Donald Little has pointed out, this did not prevent Ibn Taghrī Birdī from inserting his own interpretations, and thus this work represents a unique late Mamluk period perspective on earlier events.

Having introduced the relevant narrative historical sources in Persian, Turkish and Arabic, it should be mentioned that several Armenian histories also offer important perspectives on the period of Ilkhanid and Jalayirid rule. The Armenian historians Grigor of Akanc‘[74] and Kirakos of Ganjak[75] record the arrival of the Mongols and their dealings with the Armenian and Georgian ruling elite. Another Armenian historian, Hethum of Korykos, mentions the Jalayir as one of the seven principle ‘nations’ of the Mongols in his early eighth/fourteenth-century work *Flor des estoires de la terre d'orient*.[76] Colophons of Armenian manuscripts record the author, time and place in which the manuscripts were written, as well as a historical account of contemporary political and military events. A large number of these colophons have been translated and provide information about the later Ilkhans, Shaykh Ḥasan and his descendants, as well as Shaykh Ḥasan's main Chubanid rival, also known as Shaykh Ḥasan, and often referred to as Shaykh Ḥasan-i Kūchak.[77] An additional Armenian history, important for the late Jalayirid period, was written by Thomas of Metsop‘ (d. 851–52/1448).[78] Vladimir Minorsky has translated Thomas's account of the conflict between the Timurids and Qarāquyūnlū in Azarbayjan after the death of Tīmūr in 807/1405.[79] This account is significant for its treatment of the final years of the reign of Sulṭān Aḥmad Jalayir, and his death at the hands of the Qarāquyūnlū chief, Qarā Yūsuf, in 813/1410. Also of value for the early Ilkhanid period is the world history written in Syriac by Ibn al-‘Ibrī, also known as Bar Hebraeus (d. 1286).[80] Metropolitan of Aleppo, and later head of the Syriac Orthodox Church in Iran, Bar Hebraeus spent time at the Ilkhanid court as a physician, and provides many details of Mongol rule up until the year of his death.

In addition to narrative sources in the form of chronicles and biographical compilations, other literary and artistic artifacts provide information relevant to the history of the Jalayirids in the eighth/fourteenth century. These sources include administrative manuals, poetry, chancery documents and travel literature, as well as numismatic, artistic and architectural artifacts.

Muḥammad b. Hindūshāh Nakhjivānī's *Dastūr al-Kātib fī Ta‘yīn al-Marātib* was an administrative manual completed during the reign of Sultan Shaykh Uvays. The *Dastūr al-Kātib* provides guidance to secretaries on the appropriate form and style for chancery documents for a wide variety of occasions, from addressing sultans to muleteers. Of particular importance for understanding the political ideology of the Jalayirid dynasty is Nakhjivānī's introduction and dedication to the work. Nakhjivānī began writing the *Dastūr al-Kātib* under the direction of the vizier Ghiyāth al-Dīn Muḥammad at the end of the reign of Abū Sa‘īd, but completed it after Shaykh Uvays's conquest of Azarbayjan in 759 /1358. Nakhjivānī thus praises both the Ilkhanid sultan Abū Sa'īd and the Jalayirid sultan Shaykh Uvays, and attempts to link Shaykh Uvays to the Chinggisid Ilkhanid past as the legitimate continuator of the Ilkhanate in Azarbayjan. The *Dastūr al-Kātib* is also valuable for its information on chancery practice and protocol in the mid-eighth/fourteenth century. In this regard, it is supplemented by another work from the same period, 'Abd Allāh b. Muḥammad b. Kiyā al-Māzandarānī's *Risāla-yi Falakiyya*.[81] On the genre of administrative manuals, mention should also be made of the Ottoman period *inshā'* compilation *Mecmū'a-yi Münşe'āt-i Selāṭīn*, by Ferīdūn Aḥmed Bey (d. 991/1583).[82] Here are preserved several examples of letters purported to have been exchanged between the Ottoman sultan Orḫān and Shaykh Ḥasan Jalayir, Ottoman sultan Murād I and Shaykh Uvays Jalayir, and Ottoman sultan Bāyezīd I and Sulṭān Aḥmad Jalayir, as well as exchanges between Bāyezīd I and Tīmūr, which reference Sulṭān Aḥmad.

Poetry written at the Jalayirid court represents part of an official construction of the Jalayirid dynastic image. The poet Salmān Sāvajī (d. 778 /1376) served the Jalayirid royal family as court panegyrist, and composed *qaṣīda*s in praise of Shaykh Ḥasan, his wife Dilshād Khātūn, and their son Shaykh Uvays. Salmān's work, like that of Nakhjivānī, demonstrates an attempt to draw parallels between the Jalayirids and the Ilkhanid past, as well as to promote a more general notion of Chinggisid Mongol heritage as the source of Jalayirid dynastic sovereignty. Other poets of the period who wrote for Jalayirid sultans include Khvājū Kirmānī (d. 753/1352) and the renowned Ḥāfiẓ Shīrāzī (d. 791/1389). An important ninth/fifteenth-century source for the lives of poets during the period is the *Taẕkirat al-Shu'arā'* of Dawlatshāh Samarqandī (d. c. 900/1494),[83] in which biographical information on Salmān Sāvajī and his relations with the Jalayirids is treated. An additional work dedicated to poetics is the *Anīs al-'Ushshāq*, written by Sharaf al-Dīn Muḥammad b. Ḥasan Rāmī Tabrīzī.[84] This treatise on conventions of poetic praise of the beloved was dedicated to Shaykh Uvays, and includes an introduction devoted to the Jalayirid sultan. An examination of the titles and imagery ascribed to Shaykh Uvays in *Anīs al-'Ushshāq* provides an important indication of the foundations of Jalayirid political ideology.

In addition to these works produced at the Jalayirid court, designed to convey a conscious image of the dynasty, other documentary sources provide further information about social and economic life. In particular, the work of Gottfried Herrmann on Jalayirid documents dealing with Azarbayjan, and Ardabil in particular, reveals the relations between the sultans and the home region of the Ṣafaviyya Sufi order.[85] Ardabil was the hereditary territory of Sulṭān Aḥmad Jalayir, and was also under the religious influence of Shaykh Ṣadr al-Dīn (d. 794/1392), head of the order that would become the ruling dynasty of Iran in the tenth/sixteenth century. Documents drafted by the Jalayirid chancery also reveal information about Jalayirid fiscal policies, as well as forms and titles used by the sultans.

Finally, literature written by foreign travellers who recorded their observations of life in the Ilkhanid and Jalayirid territory is a rich source of cultural, economic and political information. The Maghribi traveller Ibn Baṭṭūṭa passed through the Ilkhanate during the reign of Abū Sa'īd, and observed life in cities such as Tabriz and Baghdad.[86] Later in the century, the Bavarian crusader Johannes Schiltberger recorded his observations on Tabriz, as well as reports regarding Tīmūr's conquest of Jalayirid Baghdad, and the death of Sulṭān Aḥmad.[87] Schiltberger had fought against Ottoman forces at Nicopolis under King Sigismund of Hungary, and was captured. He served under Sultan Bāyezīd I from 798/1396 to 804/1402, and under Tīmūr from 804/1402 to 807/1405. The Castilian envoy Ruy Gonzalez de Clavijo's account of economic life in Tabriz and Sultaniyya in the early ninth/fifteenth century also contributes to our understanding of the commercial importance of Azarbayjan to the Jalayirids and all other potential successors to the Ilkhanate.[88]

Having provided an overview of some of the most important primary source materials for the history of the Jalayirids, we turn now to consider secondary literature which has informed this study. The primary monograph on the Jalayirid dynasty is Shīrīn Bayānī's *Tārīkh-i Āl-i Jalāyir*. This work is essential for its survey of the political history of the Jalayirids, beginning with Shaykh Ḥasan, down to the last Jalayirid princes in Iraq in the ninth/fifteenth century, as well as for its discussion of the administration of the fiscal and military departments that the Jalayirids inherited from the Ilkhanate. Bayānī draws extensively on the works of Ahrī, Ḥāfiẓ Abrū, Zayn al-Dīn Qazvīnī and Nakhjivānī. She also devotes attention to social and artistic life under the Jalayirids. While this work provides an excellent survey of several aspects of Jalayirid history, it does not address the processes that led to the rise and subsequent legitimation of political authority of Mongol tribal descendants within the socio-political context of the Ilkhanate. Tracing the factors that led to this development is an important aspect of this study.

Works on the Jalayirid period in Arabic tend to follow the pattern set by Bayānī. Nūrī 'Abd al-Ḥamīd 'Ānī's 1986 work *Al-'Irāq fī al-'Ahd al-Jalā'irī* [89] gives a thorough treatment of Jalayirid rule in Iraq, including the Jazira and Diyarbakr, based on Arabic, Persian, Turkish and European language sources. The work is divided into chapters on the political background, the administration and its personnel, the military, geography and land use, the arts, commerce and finance. Sha'bān Rabī' Ṭurṭūr's *Al-Dawla al-Jalā'iriyya*,[90] published the following year, owes much to Bayānī in its organisation and content, also dealing with the history of the Jalayirid dynasty by ruler, then dealing with state institutions, poets, and the arts and sciences of the period. A less comprehensive work is Yumná Riḍwān's *Al-Dawla al-Jalā'iriyya*,[91] published in 1993, which relies almost exclusively on Arabic sources in its treatment of Jalayirid political history, foreign relations, administration, economy, society, culture and the arts. These studies, like Bayānī's work which they emulate, attempt to provide a comprehensive view of all aspects of political, social and economic life in the period of Jalayirid rule. They provide a good general, if somewhat static, overview.

The Jalayirids are the subject of several other shorter articles, including encyclopaedia entries[92] and part of a chapter in the *Cambridge History of Iran*.[93] This literature provides a good general overview of the Jalayirids and the political history of the post-Ilkhanid period, from 736/1335 to approximately the period of Tīmūr's campaigns in Iran (780s/1380s). These articles mention that the Jalayirid dynasty took its name from a tribe that had its origins near the Onon river in Mongolia, and was founded by descendants of this tribe.[94] John Masson Smith, Jr points out that Jalayirid genealogies usually begin with Īlgā (or Īlkā) Noyan, a follower of Hülegü Khan, and proceed through his descendants Āq Būqā and Amīr Ḥusayn to Shaykh Ḥasan, who was the founder of the dynasty.[95] Little attention is paid to other members of the Jalayir tribe who were prominent figures in the Ilkhanate, and the factors that led to the rise of Shaykh Ḥasan. The impression may be, then, that Shaykh Ḥasan was the chief among the Jalayir tribe in Iran and Anatolia, and was thus in a natural position to re-establish the Jalayir tribe when the Ilkhanid political structure broke down. However, this does not seem to have been the case, as will be shown in subsequent chapters. In fact, there were several prominent Jalayir families within the Ilkhanate during its first few decades. It was not Shaykh Ḥasan's role as a leader among his fellow tribesmen, but rather the position he held within the dynastic hierarchy of the Ilkhanid state, that served as the source of his influence and authority. It was thus not the tribe but the Ilkhanate which provided the social and political context in which Shaykh Ḥasan was able to lay the foundation for an independent dynasty in the eighth/fourteenth century. İsenbike Togan and Charles Melville have suggested that the end of the Ilkhanate resulted in a return to tribalism as the primary political medium after 736/1335.[96] However, it is very difficult to establish the form and degree to which the tribes reconstituted themselves in the eighth/fourteenth century. It seems rather an educated assumption, rather than a provable fact. What does seem clear is that, in the case of the Jalayir, tribal history and identity did not form the basis for political ideology. Rather, the political ideals of the Ilkhanate provided the basis for the legitimising ideology of the Jalayirids.

Roemer has highlighted the fact that after the murder of Ṭaghāy Tīmūr Khan in 754/1353, only the Jalayirids could claim Mongol descent among the various political factions vying for power after the Ilkhanate.[97] In fact, as Melville has noted, beginning with Shaykh Ḥasan's son Shaykh Uvays, the Jalayirids could claim descent from Hülegü through both parents, albeit through the maternal line on both sides.[98] The details of the relations between the Jalayirids and the Ilkhanid royal family, as well as their political and ideological implications, will be discussed in subsequent chapters.

In general, the post-Ilkhanid period has been neglected. The 'lords of the moment',[99] such as the Jalayirids, Karts, Muzaffarids and Chubanids, have largely been viewed as representatives of a chaotic interregnum between the Mongol and Timurid periods. Part of the reason for this may be the complexity of the political history. As one scholar put it, 'the years following the first clash between the two Hasans [Jalāyirī and Chūbānī] are among the most confusing in the history of the Il-Khanid empire'.[100] It is true that in the decades after 736/1335, several factions in regions throughout the Ilkhanid realm arose, and sorting out the 'who's who' of this period does pose a challenge. However, passing over the period, or dismissing it as irrelevant relative to the periods before and after, is to ignore a major historical issue, which is the transition in political ideology from that of the Ilkhanate to that which followed. In the Jalayirid dynasty, the issues that shaped this transition are evident. This study aims to identify the place of the Jalayir tribe within the Ilkhanid political system, and the ways in which the ideology that supported that system was appropriated and adapted by the Jalayirid sultans.

A great deal of scholarship has focused on the works of art and literature produced under the Jalayirids. Baghdad again became a centre for artistic patronage,[101] although not to the extent it had been in the past. The Jalayirids acquired a reputation as patrons of Persian poetry, including that of Salmān Sāvajī and Khvājū Kirmānī.[102] Wheeler Thackston has made available an English translation of one of the most important sources for the life and career of Salmān Sāvajī, the *Tazkirat al-Shu'arā'* of Dawlatshāh Samarqandī (d. c. 900/1494). In his work dedicated to the history and artistic legacy of the post-Ilkhan period in Iran and central

Asia, Thackston includes passages written by the ninth/fifteenth-century biographer of poets Dawlatshāh on the life of Salmān and his dealings with members of the Jalayirid dynasty, including Shaykh Ḥasan, his wife Dilshād Khātūn, and their son Shaykh Uvays.[103] Thackston also includes passages from Dawlatshāh's *Taẕkira* dealing with poetry written by Ḥāfiẓ to the Jalayirid Sulṭān Aḥmad, as well as Dawlatshāh's treatment of Sulṭān Aḥmad as a poet and artist in his own right.[104]

The Jalayirid court is perhaps most remembered for its patronage of miniature painting in Tabriz and Baghdad in the eighth/fourteenth century.[105] Bernard O'Kane has recently suggested that the mysterious *siyāh-qalam* paintings, featuring distinctive depictions of demons, dervishes and scenes of everyday life, have their origins in Jalayirid Tabriz, during the reign of Shaykh Uvays (r. 757/1356–776/1374).[106] O'Kane argues that the influence of this style of painting can also be found in later Jalayirid period artwork, pointing out that the pen and ink drawings found in the *dīvān* of Shaykh Uvays's son, Sulṭān Aḥmad (r. 784/1382–813/1410), seem to have been modelled on these *siyāh-qalam* paintings.[107] Art historians have identified a Jalayirid style,[108] and most agree that this style reached its most developed stage under Sulṭān Aḥmad. This sultan's own *dīvān*, or collection of poetry, is noteworthy for its marginal pen and ink illustrations (in a style known as *qalamsiyāhī*), consisting not of miniature illumination, but of decorative scenes not always connected with the poetic text. The *dīvān* and its place within the development of Jalayirid artistic patronage and production have been examined extensively by Deborah E. Klimburg-Salter. She argues that these illustrations fall within a period of experimental transition which saw the movement of the graphic image from the centre of the page to the margin.[109] Klimburg-Salter also contends that the prevalence of images of birds in the *dīvān* represents a conscious visual reference to the work of the Sufi poet Farīd al-Dīn ʿAṭṭār (d. 627/1230), the 'Conference of the Birds' (*Manṭiq al-Ṭayr*).[110]

Sulṭān Aḥmad was a connoisseur and active patron of painting. His workshops in Baghdad were active until Tīmūr's attack on the city in 803 /1401, and produced several well-known works of art.[111] Following the death of Tīmūr in 807/1405, Sulṭān Aḥmad attempted to regain control of Tabriz, and in the process continued to patronise painters in the city. One of the works thought to have been produced in Tabriz in the period between the death of Tīmūr and Sulṭān Aḥmad's own death in 813/1410 was a version of Niẓāmī's *Khusraw va Shīrīn*.[112] After the fall of Tabriz to the Qarāquyūnlū in 813/1410, artists who had worked in the Jalayirid ateliers there tended to migrate to Shiraz, where they sought the patronage of the Timurid prince Iskandar b. ʿUmar Shaykh. Klimburg-Salter traces the movement of the centre of artistic life in the late eighth/fourteenth century from the Jalayirid capitals of Baghdad and Tabriz to the Timurid cities of Shiraz and Herat, the latter being well-known as the home to a cultural fluorescence under the patronage of Sulṭān Ḥusayn Bāyqarā in the late ninth/fifteenth and early tenth/sixteenth centuries.[113]

Other works of visual art produced during the reign of Sulṭān Aḥmad have been the subject of art historians. Stefano Carboni has described a late eighth/fourteenth-century illustrated astrological treatise also attributed to the workshop of Sulṭān Aḥmad. This treatise features illustrations of the mansions of the moon, lunar-planetary conjunctions, and a treatise on the zodiac, a so-called 'Book of Nativities' (*Kitāb al-Mawālid*).[114] A more recent study has focused on illustrations contained in a 'book of marvels' copied for Sulṭān Aḥmad in 790/1388.[115] In addition to painting, Jalayirid calligraphy,[116] filigree bookbinding[117] and metalwork[118] have been the subject of art-historical studies.

Notes

1. H. R. Roemer, 'The Jalayirids, Muzaffarids and Sarbadārs', in Peter Jackson and Laurence Lockhart (eds), *The Cambridge History of Iran, Volume 6: The Timurid and Safavid Periods* (Cambridge: Cambridge University Press, 1986), 3.
2. Scholarship supplementing the study of the *Secret History of the Mongols* includes: Lajos Bese, 'Some Turkic Personal Names in the *Secret History of the Mongols*', *Acta Orientalia Academiae Scientiarum Hungaricae* 32:3 (1978): 353–69; J. A. Boyle, '*Iru* and *Maru* in the *Secret History of the Mongols*', *HJAS* 17 (1954): 403–10; Gari Ledyard, 'The Mongol Campaigns in Korea and the Dating of the *Secret History of the Mongols*', *CAJ* 9 (1964): 1–22; Hidehiro Okada, '*The Secret History of the Mongols*, a Pseudo-Historical Novel', *Journal of Asian and African Studies* [Tokyo] 5 (1972): 61–8; Nicholas Poppe, 'On Some Proper Names in the *Secret History*', in G. Décsy (ed.), *Eurasia Nostratica: Festschrift für Karl Heinrich Menges, Band I–II* (Wiesbaden: Otto Harrassowitz, 1977), 161–7; N. P. Shastina, 'Mongol and Turkic Ethnonyms in the *Secret History of the Mongols*', in Louis Ligeti (ed.), *Researches in Altaic Languages* (Budapest: Akadémia Kiadó, 1975), 231–44.
3. Francis Woodman Cleaves (ed. and trans.), *The Secret History of the Mongols* (Cambridge, MA: Harvard University Press, 1982); Urgunge Onon (trans.), *The Secret History of the Mongols: The Life and Times of Chinggis Khan* (Richmond: Curzon, 2001); Igor de Rachewiltz (trans.), *The Secret History of the Mongols: A Mongolian Epic Chronicle of the Thirteenth Century* (Leiden: Brill, 2004).

4. Storey/*Persian Literature*, 1:71–8 (no. 106). Scholarship on the life and work of Rashīd al-Dīn includes: Reuven Amitai-Preiss, 'New Material from the Mamluk Sources for the Biography of Rashid al-Din', in Julian Raby and Teresa Fitzherbert (eds), *The Court of the Il-khans, 1290–1340* (Oxford: Oxford University Press, 1994), 23–37; J. A. Boyle, 'Juvaynī and Rashīd al-Dīn as Sources on the History of the Mongols', in Bernard Lewis and P. M. Holt (eds), *Historians of the Middle East* (London: Oxford University Press, 1962), 133–7; J. A. Boyle, 'Rashīd al-Dīn: The First World Historian', *Iran* 9 (1971): 19–26; Karl Jahn, 'Rashīd al-Dīn as World Historian', in *Yádnáma-ye Jan Rypka* (The Hague and Paris: Mouton & Co., 1967), 79–87; Karl Jahn, 'The Still Missing Works of Rashīd al-Dīn', *CAJ* 9 (1964): 113–22; Zeki Velidi Togan, 'The Composition of the History of the Mongols by Rashīd al-Dīn', *CAJ* 8 (1963): 60–72.
5. Storey/*Persian Literature*, 1:267–70 (no. 344); Russell G. Kempiners, Jr, 'Vaṣṣāf's *Tajziyat al-Amṣār wa Tazjiyat al-A'ṣār* as a Source for the History of the Chaghadayid Khanate', *Journal of Asian History* 22 (1988): 160–87. Vaṣṣāf's history can be considered a continuation of the *Tārīkh-i Jahāngushāy* of the Khurasanian administrator 'Aṭā' Malik Juvaynī (d. 681 /1283). See Storey, 1:260–6 (no. 340).
6. Storey/*Persian Literature*, 1:79–80 (no. 109).
7. Storey/*Persian Literature*, 1:78–9 (no. 107); 1:267 (no. 342).
8. Storey/*Persian Literature*, 1:81–4 (no. 111).
9. Charles Melville, 'Ḥamd Allāh Mustawfī's *Ẓafarnāmah* and the Historiography of the Late Ilkhanid Period', in Kambiz Eslami (ed.), *Iran and Iranian Studies: Essays in Honor of Iraj Afshar* (Princeton: Zagros, 1998), 4.
10. Storey/*Persian Literature*, 2:129–31 (no. 190). On a seventh/thirteenth-century source for the *Nuzhat al-Qulūb*, see Angelo Arioli, 'Su una Fonte di Mustawfī Qazvīnī', in *La Bisaccia dello Sheikh: Omaggio ad Alessandro Bausani, Islamista nel Sessantesimo Compleanno* (Venice: Università degli Studi di Venezia, 1981), 29–41.
11. Storey/*Persian Literature*, 1:408–10 (no. 578).
12. Charles Melville, 'The Early Persian Historiography of Anatolia', in Judith Pfeiffer and Sholeh A. Quinn (eds), in collaboration with Ernest Tucker, *History and Historiography of Post-Mongol Central Asia and the Middle East: Studies in Honor of John E. Woods* (Wiesbaden: Harrassowitz, 2006), 138.
13. Storey/*Persian Literature*, 1:260–6 (no. 340).
14. Melville, 'The Early Persian Historiography of Anatolia', 140. Although most of *al-Avāmir al-'Alā'iyya* was written in the late seventh/thirteenth century, portions are taken from the *Saljūq-nāma* of Qa'anī. See A. C. S. Peacock, 'The Saljūq Campaign against the Crimea and the Expansionist Policy of the Early Reign of 'Alā' al-Dīn Kayqubād', *JRAS* 16:2 (2006): 135.

15. Storey/*Persian Literature*, 1:267 (no. 343); 1:410 (no. 580).
16. According to Charles Melville, 72.5 per cent of *Musāmarat al-Akhbār* is devoted to the history of the Mongols in Anatolia. See Melville, 'The Early Persian Historiography of Anatolia', 146.
17. Melville, 'The Early Persian Historiography of Anatolia', 145.
18. Melville, 'The Early Persian Historiography of Anatolia', 145.
19. İ. Aka, 'Aharī', *Encyclopaedia Iranica*, ed. Ehsan Yarshater (London and New York: Routledge and Kegan Paul, 1983), 1:634; Storey/*Persian Literature*, 1:243 (no. 321 [appendix no. 12]).
20. Ahrī/*TSU*, (Persian text), 182; (English translation), 81.
21. See Van Loon's introduction to his translation of *Tārīkh-i Shaykh Uvays*, 5.
22. Storey/*Persian Literature*, 1:271 (no. 346).
23. Denise Aigle, 'Mythico-Legendary Figures and History Between East and West', in *The Mongol Empire Between Myth and Realities* (Leiden: Brill, 2014), 31.
24. Nūr al-Dīn Azhdarī, *Ghāzān-nāma-yi Manẓūm*, ed. Maḥmūd Mudabbirī (Tehran: Bunyād-i Mawqūfāt-i Duktur Maḥmūd Afshār, 1380 [2001]), 13.
25. Azhdarī, *Ghāzān-nāma*, 19. Denise Aigle has pointed out that Azhdarī wrote the *Ghāzān-nāma* as a continuation of Firdawsī's *Shāh-nāma*, which served as a model for several historical works in the Ilkhanid and post-Ilkhanid periods. See Aigle, 'Mythico-Legendary Figures and History Between East and West', 26–31.
26. On Shabānkāra'ī and his history, see Jean Aubin, 'Un chroniqueur méconnu: Šabankara'i', *Studia Iranica* 10 (1981): 213–24; Denise Aigle, *Le Fārs sous la domination mongole: Politique et fiscalité (XIIIe–XIVe s.), Studia Iranica, Cahier 31* (Paris: Association pour l'Avancement des Études Iraniennes, 2005), 65–6; Storey/*Persian Literature*, 1:84–5 (no. 112).
27. Shabānkāra'ī commemorates Shaykh Ḥasan's protégé thus: 'On the 15th of Dhū al-Ḥijja 736 [25 July 1336], the greatest sultan, king of kings of the inhabited quarter, lord of the necks of the populace, shadow of God in both worlds (*sulṭān al-a'ẓam, shāhanshāh-i rub'-i maskūn, mālik-i riqāb al-umam, ẓill allāh fī al-arḍayn*) Muẓaffar al-Dunyā wa-al-Dīn Muḥammad—may God exalt his dignity—became established upon the throne of the sultanate, may he rule until Judgement Day.' See Shabānkāra'ī/*Majma'*, 305.
28. Storey/*Persian Literature*, 1:277–8 (no. 352).
29. Storey/*Persian Literature*, 1:277–8.
30. On Tīmūr's attempt to reconstruct the Chinggisid imperial polity through the installation of Chinggisid puppet khans in the Ilkhanate and the Golden Horde, as well as a khan from the line of Ögödey, see Beatrice Forbes Manz, 'Mongol History Rewritten and Relived', *Revue des Mondes Musulmans et de la Méditerranée, Série Histoire* 89–90 (2000): 138–9.
31. See Īraj Afshār's introduction to his edition of this work (Qazvīnī/*ZTG*),

5–12. Afshār characterises this work as one of the important contemporary documents for events related to the Jalayirid and Chubanid lines between the years 742/1341–42 and 794/1392 (although the last date mentioned in the text is 12 Rabīʻ I 795/26 January 1393), particularly in Azarbayjan and Arran (p. 5).

32. Storey/*Persian Literature*, 1:86–9 (no. 117).
33. Storey/*Persian Literature*, 1:90–1 (no. 120).
34. For a detailed discussion of the works and historiographical legacy of Ḥāfiẓ Abrū, see John E. Woods, 'The Rise of Timurid Historiography', *JNES* 46:2 (1987): 96–9. For an interpretation of Ḥāfiẓ Abrū's conception of the state and the function of the ruler, see A. K. S. Lambton, 'Early Timurid Theories of State: Ḥāfiẓ Abrū and Niẓām al-Dīn Šāmī', *Bulletin d'Études Orientales* 30 (1978): 1–9.
35. Ḥāfiẓ Abrū's dependence on Zayn al-Dīn Qazvīnī has been pointed out by Charles Melville in his article 'Ḥamd Allāh Mustawfī's *Ẓafarnāmah* and the Historiography of the Late Ilkhanid Period', 4. See also Woods, 'The Rise of Timurid Historiography', 97.
36. Ḥāfiẓ Abrū, *Cinq opuscules de Ḥāfiẓ-i Abrū concernant l'histoire de l'Iran au temps de Tamerlan*, ed. Felix Tauer (Prague: L'Académie Tchécoslovaque des sciences, 1959).
37. Edward Granville Browne, 'The *Mujmal* or "Compendium" of History and Biography of Faṣíḥí of Khwáf', *Le Muséon* ser. 3, 1:1 (1915): 50; Storey/*Persian Literature*, 1:90 (no. 120).
38. Woods, 'The Rise of Timurid Historiography', 83; Storey/*Persian Literature*, 1:278–9 (no. 354).
39. This work, previously known as the 'Iskandar Anonymous', is mentioned by Storey/*Persian Literature*, 1:86 (no. 115). See Woods, 'The Rise of Timurid Historiography', 89–93.
40. Woods, 'The Rise of Timurid Historiography', 89–93. In addition to Aubin's 1957 edition, a new edition of *Muntakhab al-Tavārīkh-i Muʻīnī* was edited by Parvīn Istakhrī and published in Tehran in 2004.
41. Woods, 'The Rise of Timurid Historiography', 85; Storey/*Persian Literature*, 1:283–8 (no. 356).
42. Storey/*Persian Literature*, 1:293–8 (no. 363).
43. Storey/*Persian Literature*, 1:92–101 (no. 123).
44. Storey/*Persian Literature*, 1:101–9 (no. 125). An English translation of *Ḥabīb al-Siyar* is available. See Khvāndamīr/Thackston.
45. Storey/*Persian Literature*, 1:410–11 (no. 581).
46. İsmail Hakkı Uzunçarşılı, *Anadolu Beylikleri ve Akkoyunlu, Karakoyunlu Devletleri* (Ankara: Türk Tarih Kurumu Basımevi, 1988), 162.
47. Faruk Sümer, *Kara Koyunlular (Başlangıçtan Cihan-Şah'a kadar)*, I. Cilt (Ankara: Türk Tarih Kurumu Basımevi, 1962), 45–54.
48. Uzunçarşılı, *Anadolu Beylikleri ve Akkoyunlu, Karakoyunlu Devletleri*, 155–61.

49. Uzunçarşılı, *Anadolu Beylikleri ve Akkoyunlu, Karakoyunlu Devletleri*, 162–8.
50. Yaşar Yücel, *Anadolu Beylikleri hakkında Araştırmalar: Eretna Devleti, Kadı Burhaneddin Ahmed ve Devleti, Mutahharten ve Erzincan Emirliği, II* (Ankara: Türk Tarih Kurumu Basımevi, 1989), 247–52.
51. Theodor Seif, 'Der Abschnitt über die Osmanen in Šükrüllāh's persischer Universalgeschichte', *Mitteilungen zur Osmanischen Geschichte* 2 (1923–25): 63–128. See Babinger/*GdO*, 19–20 (no. 8); Storey/*Persian Literature*, 1:91–2 (no. 122).
52. H. Nihal Atsız, 'Hicri 858 Yılına Ait Takvim', *Selçuklu Araştırmaları Dergisi* 4 (1975): 223–83; Osman Turan, *İstanbul'un Fethinden önce Yazılmış Tarihî Takvimler* (Ankara: Türk Tarih Kurumu Basımevi, 1954).
53. Ḳarāmānlı Nişāncı Meḥmed Pāşā, 'Tevārīḫ al-Salāṭīn al-'Os̱māniyye (Osmanlı Sultanları Tarihi)', trans. Konyalı İbrahim Hakkı, in *Osmanlı tarihleri: Osmanlı tarihinin anakaynakları olan eserlerin, mütehassıslar tarafından hazırlanan metin, tercüme veya sadeleştirilmiş şekilleri külliyatı* (Istanbul: Türkiye Yayınevi, 1949), 321–69. See Babinger/*GdO*, 24–6 (no. 11).
54. 'Āşıḳpāşāzāde, *Tevārīḫ-i Āl-i 'Os̱mān*, ed. 'Ālī Bey (Istanbul: Maṭba'a-yi 'Āmire, 1332 [1913–14]); 'Āşıḳpāşāzāde, *Âşıkpaşaoğlu Tarihi*, ed. H. Nihal Atsız (Istanbul: Milli Eğitim Bakanlığı Yayınları, 1992). See Babinger/*GdO*, 35–8 (no. 21).
55. Halil Erdoğan Cengiz and Yaşar Yücel, 'Rûhî Târîhi', in *Belgeler. Türk Tarih Belgeleri Dergisi*, 14/18 (1989–92); Franz Babinger, 'Rūḥī', trans. Christine Woodhead, *Encyclopaedia of Islam*, 2nd edn (Leiden: Brill, 1994), 8:594. See Babinger/*GdO*, 42–3 (no. 25).
56. Meḥmed Neşrī, *Kitâb-i Cihan-nümâ: Neşrî Tarihi*, ed. Faik Reşit Unat and Mehmed A. Köymen (Ankara: Türk Tarih Kurumu Basımevi, 1995). See Babinger/*GdO*, 38–9 (no. 22).
57. Babinger/*GdO*, 61–3 (no. 42).
58. Babinger/*GdO*, 80–1 (no. 64).
59. Athough the Mamluk chronicles and biographical dictionaries have long been mined for the rich detail they provide on the elite of Mamluk society, other forms of literature have generally been ignored by historians. Thomas Bauer has shown that poetry, *maqāmāt*, *inshā'* and other forms of literature, while often neglected by scholars of the Mamluk period, in fact were read widely and offer insight into aspects of Mamluk society and elite communication not available in the more strictly 'historical' sources. See Thomas Bauer, 'Mamluk Literature: Misunderstandings and New Approaches', *Mamlūk Studies Review* 9:2 (2005): 105–132; Thomas Bauer, 'Mamluk Literature as a Means of Communication', in Stephan Conermann (ed.), *Ubi sumus? Quo vademus? Mamluk Studies – State of the Art* (Göttingen: V&R Unipress, Bonn University Press, 2013), 23–56.

60. Brockelmann/*GAL*, 2:55–7.
61. Li Guo, 'Mamluk Historiographic Studies: The State of the Art', *Mamlūk Studies Review* 1 (1997): 29.
62. Donald P. Little, 'Historiography of the Ayyūbid and Mamlūk Epochs', in Carl F. Petry (ed.), *The Cambridge History of Egypt, Volume I: Islamic Egypt, 640–1517* (Cambridge: Cambridge University Press, 1998), 423.
63. Brockelmann/*GAL*, 2:177–8.
64. *Das Mongolische Weltreich: Al-'Umarī's Darstellung der mongolischen Reiche in seinem Werk Masālik al-Abṣār fī Mamālik al-Amṣār*, ed. and trans. Klaus Lech (Wiesbaden: Otto Harrassowitz, 1968).
65. Brockelmann/*GAL*, 2:35.
66. Little, 'Historiography of the Ayyūbid and Mamlūk Epochs', 427.
67. Brockelmann/*GAL*, 2:39–41.
68. Little,'Historiography of the Ayyūbid and Mamlūk Epochs', 431.
69. Brockelmann/*GAL*, 2:47–50.
70. Brockelmann/*GAL*, 2:80–4.
71. Brockelmann/*GAL*, 2:36–7; Babinger/*GdO*, 20–3 (no. 9).
72. On Ibn 'Arabshāh, see John E. Woods, 'Ebn 'Arabšāh', *Encyclopaedia Iranica*, ed. Ehsan Yarshater (London and New York: Routledge and Kegan Paul, 1996), 7:670; R. D. McChesney, 'A Note on the Life and Works of Ibn 'Arabshāh', in Judith Pfeiffer and Sholeh A. Quinn (eds), in collaboration with Ernest Tucker, *History and Historiography of Post-Mongol Central Asia and the Middle East: Studies in Honor of John E. Woods* (Wiesbaden: Harrassowitz, 2006), 205–49.
73. Brockelmann/*GAL*, 2:51–2.
74. Grigor of Akanc', 'History of the Nation of Archers', trans. Robert P. Blake and Richard N. Frye, *HJAS* 12:3/4 (1949): 269–399. An essential supplement is Francis Woodman Cleaves, 'The Mongolian Names and Terms in the History of the Nation of Archers by Grigor of Akanc'', *HJAS* 12:3/4 (1949): 400–43.
75. Kirakos Gandzakets'i's, *History of the Armenians*, trans. Robert Bedrosian (New York: Sources of the Armenian Tradition, 1986). J. A. Boyle has dealt with Kirakos's accounts of the Armenians' relations with the Mongols, in 'Kirakos of Ganjak on the Mongols', *CAJ* 7 (1962): 199–214, and 'The Journey of Het'um I, King of Little Armenia, to the Court of the Great Khan Möngke', *CAJ* 9 (1964): 175–89.
76. Sven Dörfer (ed.), *Die Geschichte der Mongolen des Hethum von Korykos (1307) in der Rückübersetzung durch Jean le Long, Traitiez des estas des conditions de quatorze royaumes de Asie (1351)* (Frankfurt am Main: Peter Lang, 1998), 237. According to Sven Dörfer, the editor of this work, Hethum of Korykos, from Cilician Armenia, dictated his history as 'Flor des estoires de la terre d'orient', in French, in 1307 in Poitiers on the command of Pope Clement V. The book was then translated into Latin by Nicolaus Faulcon as 'Flos Historiarum Terre Orientis'. It was retranslated into French

in 1351 by the monk Jean le Long d'Ypres, as 'Traitiez des estas et des conditions de quatorze royaumes de Asie'.

77. Avedis K. Sanjian (ed. and trans.), *Colophons of Armenian Manuscripts, 1301–1480: A Source for Middle Eastern History* (Cambridge, MA: Harvard University Press, 1969).
78. T'ovma Metsobets'i, *History of Tamerlane and His Successors*, trans. Robert Bedrosian (New York: Sources of the Armenian Tradition, 1987).
79. Vladimir Minorsky, 'Thomas of Metsop' on the Timurid-Turkman Wars', in *The Turks, Iran and the Caucasus in the Middle Ages* (London: Variorum Reprints, 1978), XI, 1–26.
80. Bar Hebraeus, *The Chronography of Gregory Abû'l Faraj, the Son of Aaron, the Hebrew Physician Commonly Known as Bar Hebraeus Being the First Part of his Political History of the World*, trans. Ernest A. Wallis Budge (Oxford: Oxford University Press, 1932).
81. 'Abd Allāh ibn Muḥammad ibn Kiyā al-Māzandarānī, *Die Resālä-ye Falakiyyä des 'Abdollāh Ibn Moḥammad Ibn Kiyā al-Māzandarānī: Ein persischer Leitfaden des staatlichen Rechnungswesens (um 1363)*, ed. Walther Hinz (Wiesbaden: Franz Steiner Verlag, 1952).
82. Ferīdūn Aḥmed Bey, *Mecmū'a-yi Münşe'āt-i Selāṭīn* (Istanbul: Dār al-Ṭibā'a al-'Āmira, 1848). See also Edward Granville Browne, *A Literary History of Persia, Volume 3: The Tartar Dominion (1265–1502)* (Cambridge: Cambridge University Press, 1956), 204–6; Babinger/*GdO*, 106–8 (no. 89).
83. Dawlatshāh/*Tazkira*.
84. Storey/*Persian Literature*, 3:250–1 (no. 426).
85. Gottfried Herrmann, *Persische Urkunden der Mongolenzeit* (Wiesbaden: Harrassowitz Verlag, 2004); Gottfried Herrmann and Gerhard Doerfer, 'Ein persisch-mongolischer Erlaß des Ğalāyeriden Šeyḫ Oveys', *CAJ* 19 (1975): 1–84; Gottfried Herrmann, 'Ein Erlaß des Ğalāyeriden Solṭān Ḥoseyn aus dem Jahr 780/1378', in *Erkenntnisse und Meinungen I herausgegeben von Gernot Wießner* (Wiesbaden: Otto Harrassowitz, 1973), 135–63.
86. Ibn Baṭṭūṭa, *Riḥlat Ibn Baṭṭūṭa: al-Musammā Tuḥfat al-Nuẓẓār fī Gharā'ib al-Amṣār wa-'Ajā'ib al-Asfār* (Miṣr: al-Maktaba al-Tijāriyya al-Kubrá, 1964); Ibn Baṭṭūṭa, *The Travels of Ibn Baṭṭūṭa,* A.D. *1325–1354*, trans. H. A. R. Gibb (Cambridge: Hakluyt Society at the University Press, 1971). See Brockelmann/*GAL*, 2:332–3.
87. Johannes Schiltberger, *The Bondage and Travels of Johann Schiltberger: A Native of Bavaria, in Europe, Asia, and Africa, 1396–1427*, ed. P. Bruun, trans. J. Buchan Telfer (New York: Burt Franklin, 1970; reprinted from London: Hakluyt Society, 1879).
88. Ruy Gonzalez de Clavijo, *Embassy to Tamerlane, 1403–1406*, trans. Guy Le Strange (London: George Routledge and Sons, 1928).
89. Nūrī 'Abd al-Ḥamīd 'Ānī, *Al-'Irāq fī al-'Ahd al-Jalā'irī: 738–814* H*/1337–1411 M: Dirāsa fī Awḍā'ihi al-Idāriyya wa-al-Iqtiṣādiyya* (Baghdad: Dār al-Shu'ūn al-Thaqāfiyya al-'Āmma, 1986).

90. Sha'bān Rabī' Ṭurṭūr, *Al-Dawla al-Jalā'iriyya* (Cairo: Dār al-Hidāya, 1987).
91. Yumná Riḍwān, *Al-Dawla al-Jalā'iriyya: wa-Ahamm Maẓāhir al-Ḥaḍāra fī al-'Irāq wa-Adhirbayjān khilāla al-Qarnayn al-Thāmin wa-al-Tāsi' ba'da al-Hijra* (Cairo: Maṭābi' al-Ahrām, 1993).
92. John Masson Smith, Jr, 'Djalayir, Djalayirid', *Encyclopaedia of Islam*, 2nd edn (Leiden: Brill, 1962), 2:401–2; Mükrimin Halil Yınanç, 'Celâyir', *İslam Ansiklopedisi* (Istanbul: Millî Eğitim Basımevi, 1945), 3:64–5; Muzaffer Ürekli, 'Celâyirliler', *Türkiye Diyanet Vakfı İslâm Ansiklopedisi* (Istanbul: Türkiye Diyanet Vakfı Vakıf Yayınları İşletmesi, 1993), 7:264–5.
93. Roemer, 'The Jalayirids, Muzaffarids and Sarbadārs', 1–41.
94. Smith, Jr, 'Djalayir, Djalayirid', 401; Yınanç, 'Celâyir', 64; Ürekli, 'Celâyirliler', 264; Roemer, 'The Jalayirids, Muzaffarids and Sarbadārs', 5.
95. Smith, Jr, 'Djalayir, Djalayirid', 401.
96. İsenbike Togan, *Flexibility and Limitation in Steppe Formations* (Leiden: Brill, 1998), 12–13; Charles Melville, *The Fall of Amir Chupan and the Decline of the Ilkhanate, 1327–1337: A Decade of Discord in Iran* (Bloomington: Indiana University, Research Institute for Inner Asian Studies, 1999), 72.
97. Roemer, 'The Jalayirids, Muzaffarids and Sarbadārs', 3.
98. Charles Melville, 'Abū Sa'īd and the Revolt of the Amirs in 1319', in Denise Aigle (ed.), *L'Iran face à la domination mongole* (Tehran: Institut Français de Recherche en Iran, 1997), 116.
99. This characterisation was made by René Grousset in his *The Empire of the Steppes: A History of Central Asia*, trans. Naomi Walford (New Brunswick, NJ, and London: Rutgers University Press, 1999), 391.
100. Luc Kwanten, *Imperial Nomads: A History of Central Asia, 500–1500* (Philadelphia: University of Pennsylvania Press, 1979), 245.
101. Ürekli, 'Celâyirliler', 264.
102. Roemer, 'The Jalayirids, Muzaffarids and Sarbadārs', 9.
103. Wheeler M. Thackston, *A Century of Princes: Sources on Timurid History and Art* (Cambridge, MA: The Aga Khan Program for Islamic Architecture, 1989), 11–12.
104. Thackston, *A Century of Princes*, 12–14.
105. Roemer, 'The Jalayirids, Muzaffarids and Sarbadārs', 9.
106. Bernard O'Kane, 'Siyah Qalam: The Jalayirid Connections', *Oriental Art* 49:2 (2003): 2.
107. O'Kane, 'Siyah Qalam', 3.
108. Stefano Carboni, 'Synthesis: Continuity and Innovation in Ilkhanid Art', in *The Legacy of Genghis Khan: Courtly Art and Culture in Western Asia, 1256–1353* (New Haven and London: Yale University Press, 2002), 223; Priscilla P. Soucek, 'Art in Iran: vii. Islamic, Pre-Safavid', *Encyclopaedia Iranica*, ed. Ehsan Yarshater (London and New York: Routledge and Kegan Paul, 1987), 2:611.

109. Deborah E. Klimburg-Salter, 'A Sufi Theme in Persian Painting: The Diwan of Sultan Ahmad Gala'ir in the Freer Gallery of Art, Washington, D.C.', *Kunst des Orients* 11 (1976–77): 57.
110. Klimburg-Salter, 'A Sufi Theme in Persian Painting', 65.
111. Works produced at Baghdad under Sulṭān Aḥmad Jalayir include *'Ajā'ib al-Makhlūqāt* (1388), *Kalīla wa Dimna* (1392), the *dīvān* of Khvājū Kirmānī (1396), and *Kitāb al-Buldan* (1399). See Klimburg-Salter, 'A Sufi Theme in Persian Painting', 70–3.
112. Klimburg-Salter, 'A Sufi Theme in Persian Painting', 73.
113. Klimburg-Salter, 'A Sufi Theme in Persian Painting', 74.
114. Stefano Carboni, 'Two Fragments of a Jalayirid Astrological Treatise in the Keir Collection and in the Oriental Institute in Sarajevo', *Islamic Art* 2 (1987): 149–50.
115. Anna Caiozzo, 'Une conception originale des cieux: planets et zodiaque d'une cosmographie jalayride', *Annales Islamologiques* 37 (2003): 59–78. Caiozzo examines a copy of the work *'Ajā'ib al-Makhlūqāt wa-Gharā'ib al-Mawjūdāt* by a certain Ṭūsī Salmānī, consisting of an illustrated cosmography, inspired by a seventh/thirteenth-century *'ajā'ib* work. Caiozzo argues that Salmānī's illustrations are unlike the illustrations in earlier versions.
116. Soucek, 'Art in Iran: vii. Islamic, Pre-Safavid', 611.
117. Alison Ohta, 'Filigree Bindings of the Mamluk Period', *Muqarnas* 21 (2004): 267–76.
118. Y. A. Godard, 'Bassin de cuivre au nom de Shaikh Uwais', *Athār-é Īrān: Annales du service archaeologique de Īrān* 1 (1936): 371–3.

2
Tribes and the Chinggisid Empire

The Jalayirid dynasty takes its name from Jalayir, the name of a Mongolian tribe from which it was descended. In order to understand the historical factors that led to members of the Jalayir establishing an Islamic sultanate in Iran and Iraq in the fourteenth century, we need first to examine some aspects of tribal society in inner Asia. Foremost, we need to address the question, what do we mean when we talk about 'tribes'? This chapter provides an overview of scholarship on inner Asian tribes, particularly those in Mongolia on the eve of the empire of Chinggis Qan. In addition, the impact of the Chinggisid empire on the tribes, and particularly on the Jalayir, is explored. The foundation of the empire resulted in a Jalayir diaspora, as members of this group were redistributed across Eurasia in accordance with new imperial political and social institutions.

Tribe and State Formation under the Mongols

Mongol society was tribally organised. That is, society was divided among several identity groups that are mentioned in sources like the *Secret History of the Mongols* and that have been characterised as tribes or clans by modern scholars. The literature on tribes in the fields of anthropology and history is vast, and the precise definition of 'tribe' is the subject of an ongoing scholarly debate. While it is impractical to try to sort out all of the various arguments of the literature about tribes since the nineteenth century, we need to address some key issues in order to deal with the specific case of the Jalayir tribe and the history of this group from the thirteenth to the fifteenth century. These issues include clarifying some of the major interpretations of the characteristics, functions and ideology of inner Asian tribes.

One of the most salient characteristics of tribes in inner Asia and elsewhere is that they are conceived of by their members as describing kinship relations. That is, tribes are groups defined by real or imagined blood relationships, in the same way that craft guilds are defined by one's profession, or citizenship is defined by one's national homeland. The fact that the ties of kinship within a tribe are not necessarily genetic has been understood by scholars of tribal societies for some time. Anthropologists have described tribes as 'ideal types' that are essentially imagined or constructed, and represent a 'state of mind' and model for organisation and action.[1] In general, while acknowledging the constructed or imagined nature of tribal identity, most scholars have maintained that the idea of kinship was central to tribal identity. An exception to this notion is the recent work of David Sneath on inner Asian states, which emphasises the importance of recognising groups, such as the Jalayir and other Mongol tribes, not in terms of kinship at all, but as 'aristocratic orders', in which elite families ruled over subjects who were not thought to be related.[2] In his book *The Headless State*, Sneath traces the history of western scholarship on tribal societies of inner Asia to demonstrate that the category of kin-based tribe was conceived as a preliminary stage in the natural development of human societies, for which the European nation state was the ultimate outcome. This scholarly baggage has continued and has, according to Sneath, led to apparent paradoxes when tribal steppe societies formed large imperial states on the steppe. However, if we conceive of groups like the Jalayir, Sulduz and Merkit not as large family groups but as a ruling nobility and its subject population, such imperial states seem less mysterious. While there do seem to be some problems with Sneath's interpretation,[3] his suggestion that the names of the Mongol tribes, found in sources like the *Secret History of the Mongols*, described individuals' identities within a complex political hierarchy is useful when we begin to examine the history of the Jalayir tribe, and particularly the ancestors of the Jalayirid sultans of the fourteenth century.

It would, however, be a mistake to completely discount kinship as a significant feature of tribal society. Even though tribal elites may not have thought of themselves as related by blood to their subjects, as Peter Golden has pointed out, kinship terminology provided at least the vocabulary of tribal society.[4] Crucial to maintaining tribal relationships was genealogy, which affirmed and legitimised kinship. Every Mongol kinship group had a male ancestor as a focal point of veneration.[5] Genealogies, while defining the limits of a tribe through reference to common ancestors, were not static or absolute. Rather, they provided the ideological means for many groups of nomads to smoothly incorporate and adopt outside groups into their own ranks, without making any essential structural changes.[6] Tribal genealogy thus was not fixed and closed, but rather frequently amended. Such amendments were reflections of changes in economic and political circumstances that necessitated the fusion of multiple tribal groups.[7] It is in this sense that tribes, including the Mongolian tribes such as the Jalayir, must be considered political groups, whose shared memory of kinship affiliation was the result of specific historical circumstances.

Another characteristic of inner Asian tribes, in addition to the centrality of an ideology of kinship legitimised by genealogy, was the flexibility of tribal structures. In terms of organisation, tribes were characterised by an openness and fluidity that allowed for the incorporation of outside kin groups and clients, as well as for the segmentation and division of the tribe. Eurasian nomadic tribes were open to all who were willing to subordinate themselves to its chief and who shared common interests with its tribesmen.[8]

These characteristics of kin-based ideology and fluidity of organisation served certain economic and political functions. Economically, the nature of the nomadic economy, based on movable and divisible animal stock, lent itself to the mobility and segmentary nature of tribal social organisation.[9] Politically, flexible tribal structures allowed for protection of groups threatened by other tribes, or by sedentary polities. In fact, the economic and the political functions of tribal organisation were closely related, and could contribute to the formation of what are often referred to as 'supra-tribal' states, or steppe empires. A common interpretation of the formation of supra-tribal empires like the Xiongnu, Türk and Uyghur confederations included the challenges posed by confrontation with sedentary, agrarian states to the south of the steppe. The need for protection in the face of the 'outside world' (to borrow a phrase from Anatoly Khazanov) was motivation and cause for tribes to enter into more complex, hierarchical organisations. Such formations were extensions of the pattern of social protection that were afforded by all tribes. Tribal formations presupposed the existence of another society, which was threatening in some way.[10] The formation of larger, supra-tribal confederations proved to be an effective way to defend against other large states, as well as to extract wealth from agrarian societies.[11] In an alternative interpretation, Nicola Di Cosmo has challenged the idea that supra-tribal empires emerge only as the result of encounters with sedentary neighbours. Di Cosmo has argued that the instability and relative poverty of the inner Asian steppe economy led to chronic low-level violence and social upheaval on the steppe.[12] The 'crisis' of this upheaval led to increased militarisation and the formation of new political organisations, based around allegiance to a supra-tribal leader.[13]

In general, most interpretations of inner Asian tribal and supra-tribal organisation recognise tribes as socio-political units, maintained by an ideology of common family ancestry, functioning to allow nomadic populations to best take advantage of the pastoral economy and defend themselves against common enemies. The flexibility and open nature of tribes allowed for the incorporation of outside groups, which could be legitimised through the construction of genealogies. Thus, it seems most useful to think of tribes not as static, rigid and egalitarian extended families, but rather as political units that defined relationships of social power among nomads, and provided the framework for allegiance to a ruling elite that legitimised its authority by appeals to a common history and kinship.

The Tribes of Mongolia on the Eve of the Empire of Chinggis Qan

There is little historical record of the tribes that became part of the Chinggisid Mongol empire before the twelfth century. The Mongols used a number of words to describe social and political categories. These include *irgen* (people),[14] *yasun* (bone),[15] *oboq/obogh* (clan-lineage)[16] and *aymagh* (tribe).[17] It is difficult to provide precise definitions for these categories, and to apply more theoretical categories to groups mentioned in historical sources, such as the *Secret History of the Mongols*. Scholars have disagreed about the political and social organisation of Mongol tribes such as the Jalayir. One of the major disagreements in historical discourse on Mongol tribes is over the degree of social stratification or egalitarianism among members of the tribes. One view is that before Chinggis Qan, the Mongolian socio-political structure was quite simple, with few 'aristocratic and feudal features'.[18] In other words, the tribes, while having individual political leadership, were generally equal and independent of one another. Another view emphasises the divisions within society, which gave rise to elite ruling lineages to which the other tribes were subordinate.[19]

A more nuanced approach is that of İsenbike Togan, who has identified two types of tribes in the pre-Chinggis Qan period. In one group were those that had multiple chiefs and favoured decentralisation and sharing of political power, including the Qongqirat, Ikeres and Mangqut. Another group displayed some political and administrative centralisation and hereditary leaders (*khāns*), including the Kereyit and Nayman.[20] Togan's work on the Mongolian tribes indicates that there was variation in the degree of social and political hierarchy among different groups, and that this variation helps to explain the success that Chinggis Qan achieved in bringing together various tribes under his leadership.

The tribal order of Mongolia underwent a dramatic change in the late twelfth century as the core of a supra-tribal empire began to form around Temüjin, later known as Chinggis Qan. Political power came to be concentrated in Temüjin's hands, while other elite families either transferred their allegiance to him, voluntarily or by force, or were destroyed completely. The causes of this strengthening of central political authority have been attributed to both ecological/economic and political reasons. One theory is that amidst heightened competition between the nomadic and sedentary societies on the edge of the steppe in the late sixth/twelfth century, smaller nomad groups responded by reorganising into larger groups with definite political leaderships.[21] The polity formed by Chinggis Qan can be viewed as part of these developments. Togan has argued that it was the larger, centralised tribes, such as the Kereyit and Nayman, that began to threaten the smaller, decentralised groups in the sixth/twelfth century. It was in this context that Chinggis Qan was able to emerge as an alternative source of political leadership.[22]

It is likely that a combination of factors made it appealing for smaller tribes to pledge allegiance to Temüjin's leadership early on. Temüjin's first followers were individuals, who swore allegiance to him as *nöker*s, or personal followers.[23] After he had attracted a significant number of *nöker*s, Temüjin's successes in battle and raids contributed to a bandwagon effect, making it more appealing for the Mongol nomads, individually, and increasingly as larger groups, to join Temüjin and submit to his authority. In 602/1206, Temüjin was confirmed as supreme leader of all the Mongol tribes, as Chinggis Qan, or universal ruler.[24]

What was the impact of Temüjin's consolidation of power on tribes like the Jalayir? The major consequence was that it altered the contours of the political hierarchy. Chinggis Qan and his relatives, rather than any other powerful families, could impose his political will because of the military support he could command. From the point of view of Chinggis Qan's subjects, one's social status became tied to one's proximity to the household of Chinggis Qan himself. The most important institution for achieving a status of privilege and authority was Chinggis Qan's household bodyguard, the *keshig*.

The *keshig* was composed of units of day guards, night guards and quiver-bearers (*qorchi*s), who were the only individuals allowed to carry their bows in the qan's presence.[25] As Thomas Allsen has shown, the *keshig* developed out of the qan's household, and became the main pool for recruiting personnel for the imperial administration.[26] The *keshig* was a springboard to power and influence for the qan's tribal subjects. Many powerful Mongol commanders (*noyan*s), including those of the Jalayir, began their careers in the *keshig*, either of Chinggis Qan or members of his family.

Another important development within Mongolian society during

Chinggis Qan's time was the establishment of new, decimally organised military units. Chinggis Qan organised his subjects into units of ten thousand, one thousand, one hundred and ten. At the head of the larger units were commanders appointed by Chinggis Qan himself, and not traditional tribal leaders.[27] Decimal military organisation was not new. Earlier steppe empires going back to the Xiongnu had used it as well.[28] However, unlike earlier imperial elites, Chinggis Qan chose to ignore his own tribe, the Qiyat, and instead rely on his trusted personal retinue.[29] Instead of deferring to the elite in his own tribe, Chinggis Qan channelled political authority through himself and his sons.

The promotion of individuals from all different tribal backgrounds ensured that one's tribal identity no longer provided the primary principle for political action.[30] Decimal unit commanders could bypass the channels of tribal authority, and instead act solely in the service of Chinggis Qan and his personal retinue. The effect of this development was the establishment of the person of Chinggis Qan – and, after him, his direct descendants – as the sole source of commonly recognised political authority in the generations to come. In this way, Chinggis Qan addressed the challenge that had traditionally faced supra-tribal leaders: the tension between the ruler and the tribal chiefs.[31] In the newly founded Chinggisid empire, the institutions of the *nöker*s, the *keshig* and the decimal military units ensured that loyalty to Chinggis Qan and his descendants was the path to power and prestige.

In addition to bringing tribal subjects more closely under his control, Chinggis Qan also sought to eliminate alternative centres of power. Tribes like the Kereyit, Nayman and Merkit, which had strong dynastic ruling hierarchies, were dismantled in a way that less politically stratified tribes like the Qongqirat, Sulduz and Jalayir were not.[32] However, a question that this study will attempt to address is the degree of continuity in tribal identity among the Jalayir as a result of the reorganisation of society and political culture during Chinggis Qan's time. İsenbike Togan has argued that in the seventh/thirteenth century, as the Mongol army of conquest came to identify with the interests of the empire, 'tribalism', the once dynamic social element, was pushed to the background as a 'reserve identity'.[33] However, in the eighth/fourteenth century, a retribalisation took place, as kinship re-emerged as a political factor.[34] While it is true that tribal loyalties are observable within the Chinggisid dynastic state in the seventh/thirteenth and eighth/fourteenth centuries, it is important also to recognise the ways in which tribes like the Jalayir had been fundamentally changed. Individuals maintained their tribal identities, but came to act within a different set of social and political parameters. These parameters were determined by the historic processes that shaped the Mongol empire and its successor states. For the descendants of the Jalayir tribe that founded a dynasty in Iraq and Azarbayjan in the eighth/fourteenth century, the tribe was replaced by the Chinggisid dynastic state as the source of political ideology and the context in which political action was taken.

Background to Mongol Expansion into the Islamic World

By the early 610s/mid-1210s, the Mongolian tribes were fully under Chinggis Qan's control, and the nature of his military and political project changed. Having absorbed the peoples of the Mongolian steppe into a united military structure, Chinggis Qan could now project these forces more fully into the sedentary regions to the southeast and southwest. For the nomadic tribal peoples of the steppe, going back as far as the Xiongnu confederation in the second century BCE, the sedentary, agrarian societies of China, Transoxiana and Persia had represented sources of material wealth which could be acquired through raids and larger-scale military operations. Although exchange always flowed between the agrarian and nomadic ecological zones, a successful nomadic chief could become extremely powerful by forcing the terms of this exchange through the threat of violence. However, raiding was not the only or even always the most efficient means of exploiting the sedentary economy. Control of the Eurasian trade routes, especially the so-called 'silk road', the transcontinental network of markets, depots and middlemen that connected China and the Mediterranean, had long been the goal of steppe leaders. It is likely that Chinggis Qan also planned his expansion strategy with this in mind.[35]

Clearly, the spark that ignited the Mongol invasion of the Islamic world was related to economic issues. When members of a Mongol trade caravan were killed by the Khwarazmian governor at Utrar in 615/1218, Chinggis Qan launched an attack on the empire of the Khwārazmshāh, the largest and most powerful state in the eastern Islamic world. This initial campaign, which lasted until 620/1223, began the process of the establishment of Mongol political influence in the region roughly from the Jaxartes (Syr Darya) river in the east to the Euphrates river in the west. The administrative structure consisted mainly of imperial officials known as *basqāq*s or *dārūghachī*s, backed by troop garrisons.[36] These officials were representatives of the great qan (Chinggis Qan until 624/1227; Ögödey Qa'an until 639/1241, and so on), in the citied regions of Eurasia. Transoxiana and Khurasan were represented by these imperial officials, while in western Iran, in the regions of Azarbayjan, Mughan and Arran, a less organised military governorship took hold. By the 660s/1260s, these regions had become independent political entities in the form of personal appanages of Chinggisid princely families. However, in the initial phases of Mongol conquest in the 620s/1220s, an attempt was made to bring these areas, with their urban commercial centres, under the control of a centralised imperial administration.

The spread of Mongol soldiers and their families into regions of China, Transoxiana and Iran meant an increase in the territorial and material wealth for Chinggis Qan's family as well as for the soldiers themselves. Chinggis Qan, his siblings, children and other close relatives embodied sovereignty for the new Mongol imperial enterprise. They were known as the *altān urūgh*, or 'golden family', and it would be through the lineage of Chinggis Qan's sons that legitimate political authority would inhere, even after de facto Chinggisid power had collapsed. The acquisition of geographic, material and human resources as a result of the early Mongol conquests was considered an addition to Chinggis Qan's personal household wealth, which would be distributed as inheritance to members of the *altān urūgh* after his death.

People, as well as territories, were divided primarily among Chinggis Qan's four principal sons (that is, those sons born to Chinggis Qan's wife Börte), and constituted their personal *ulūs*. The concept of *ulūs* was related to the household retinue, but constituted an expanded version that also included specific territory, as well as the people who resided in the towns and countryside there. The hereditary territory of this primary dispensation consisted mainly of the steppe lands extending from the Mongols' original pastures in eastern Mongolia to as far west as could be conquered. Chinggis Qan's sons received their share based on their ages. Thus, the youngest son, Tolui, inherited the Mongol homeland, while the older sons inherited territories further to the west.[37] Each son also received an allocation of troops. This aspect will be addressed in greater detail below, with special attention paid to the distribution of Jalayir individuals among the various princely appanages.

The sedentary, agricultural zone south of the steppe was, for the most part, not included as personal inheritance for the princes, but instead remained under the control of the great qan's representatives as part of the central administration. Conflict between two different spheres of authority – that of the princely appanages and that of the central administration – resulted in civil war by the middle of the seventh/thirteenth century. The basic cause of the conflict was rooted in the concept of political legitimacy prevalent among tribal-nomadic societies: the notion that sovereignty resided in the extended family of a leader. Ideally, succession was determined not by a strict pattern of lineal descent, but by the merits displayed by any member of that family by successfully keeping his predecessor's followers through military and economic success.

Chinggis Qan chose as his successor his third son, Ögödey. When Ögödey died in 639/1241, sovereignty did not pass automatically to his son Güyük, but was held temporarily by Ögödey's wife Töregene. It was not until an assembly (*quriltay*) could be held and the prominent members of the royal family agreed on the succession that Güyük was enthroned in 644/1246. When he died less than two years later, a challenge was made to Ögödeyid control of the great qanate and the central administration of the empire by an alliance of representatives of two other princely lines: those of Chinggis Qan's sons Jochi and Tolui. The Jochids were led by Batu Khan, Jochi's son and heir to his family's *ulūs* on the western steppe. The Toluids were led by Tolui's widow Sorqaqtani Beki, and her eldest son Möngke. The Jochid-Toluid alliance resisted continued Ögödeyid control of the empire, and by 649/1251 had succeeded in all but destroying the Ögödeyid family and weakening their allies, the family of Chinggis Qan's second son Chaghatay. Möngke became great qan, and power within the empire was shared in practice by Möngke in the east and Batu in the west.

It was during Möngke's reign (648/1251–657/1259) that the groundwork was laid for a fundamental change in the structure of political authority in the sedentary agrarian zone. The citied regions of Chinese and

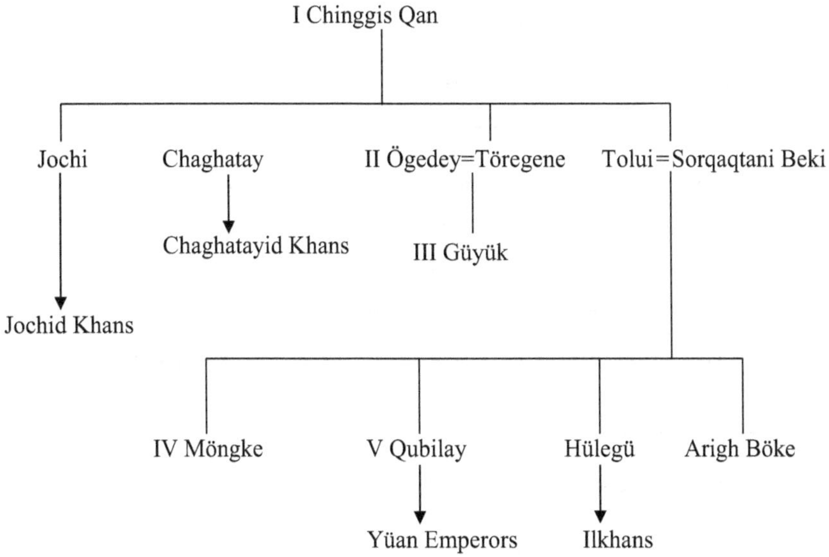

Roman numerals indicate succession to the great qanate

Figure 2.1 The *altān urūgh*: Chinggis Qan and his descendants.

Perso-Islamic civilisation, which until that time had been administered by imperial representatives who reported to the great qan in Qaraqorum, were assigned as hereditary appanages by Möngke Qa'an to his brothers in a secondary dispensation of political authority. It was secondary in the sense that these regions had not been included in Chinggis Qan's original disbursement of princely *ulūs*es, but were assigned later as part of a division of Toluid family holdings. Möngke sent his brother Qubilay to China and another brother Hülegü to Iran in an attempt to extend Toluid power into the sedentary agrarian zone and virtually surround the descendants of Chaghatay who ruled Transoxiana and Semirechye.[38] The purpose was to consolidate the power of the empire of the Toluids as a family, that is, Sorqaqtani Beki and her sons, but also to remove China and Iran from the central administration, and put them on par with other princely appanages. That is, China and Iran became the commonwealth of two separate branches of the Chinggisid royal family in the Toluid line, and eventually came to constitute separate and independent polities. China became the *ulūs* of the descendants of Qubilay, and, due to Qubilay's succession as great qan, also the seat of the empire as a whole. Iran – or, more precisely, the region between the Oxus and the Euphrates – became the *ulūs* of the descendants of Hülegü, also known as the Ilkhanate.

The term *īlkhān* was a title first used to refer to Möngke Qa'an's brother Hülegü following his conquest of the Abbasid caliphate and establishment of a political administration in the territory between the Oxus and the

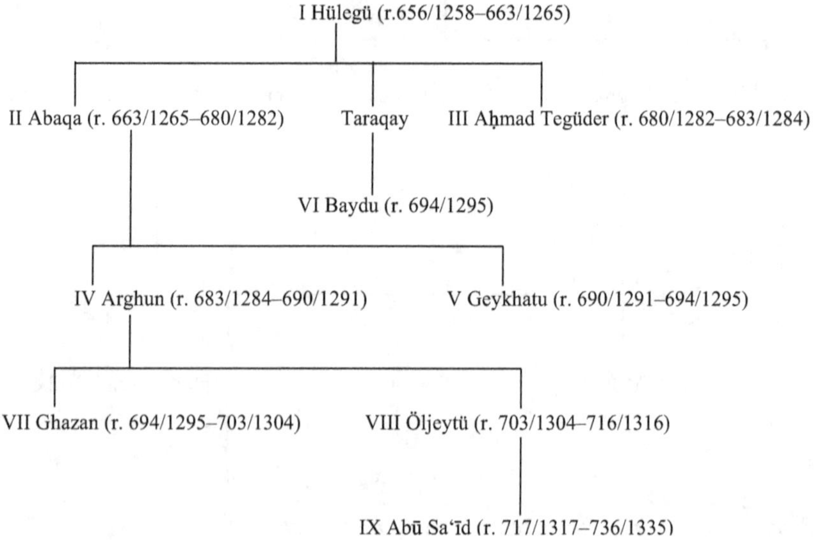

Figure 2.2 Ilkhan rulers.

Euphrates. Several theories have been offered as to the precise meaning of this title. Definitions have included 'tribal ruler', 'royal ruler' and even 'ruler of the Ili' (the river that flows into Lake Balkhash).[39] The generally accepted meaning is something like 'peaceful, subordinate or obedient ruler', reflecting a subservient position in relation to the great qan.[40] The polity, or *ulūs*, established by Hülegü was a branch of the Toluid-controlled Mongol empire, which had its capital in China. However, this title seems to have been given to Hülegü after he had established himself in Iran, and not at the time of his dispatch by Möngke.[41] The title *īlkhān* first appeared on the coins minted by Hülegü in Iran in the year 658/1259–60,[42] and the Mongol court in China continued to bestow titles on Ilkhan rulers until the end of Qubilay's reign (693/1294). Hülegü was formally invested by the Chinese court in 660/1262, when envoys arrived to recognise him as the ruler of the lands west of the Oxus river to the furthest reaches of Egypt and Syria.[43] Increasingly after Möngke's death, Hülegü and his successors attempted to convert their status from that of a representative of the great qan to the head of an independent *ulūs*. During the reign of his brother Qubilay as great qan, the formal bestowal of titles served to confirm and legitimise Hülegü's independence, particularly vis-à-vis the Jochid khans to the north, who claimed Azarbayjan as their own.[44]

The establishment of the Ilkhan *ulūs* had several effects on the history of the region, including an initial antagonism and exploitative attitude among the Mongol elite toward the agrarian population,[45] a new wave of Mongol and Turkic-speaking people into Iran, and a shift in overland trade patterns after the conquest of Baghdad and establishment of a new urban capital at Tabriz.[46] The effect of the establishment of the Ilkhanate on Mongol tribal society, and the Jalayir tribe in particular, will be addressed in Chapter 3.

The Jalayir Diaspora

Having outlined the dynastic history of the Chinggisids, including the division of the empire and the civil war that followed, we proceed now to explore the impact of these events on the Jalayir tribe in this period. Although the experience of the Jalayir was not identical to that of other tribes, we can identify a general trend that seems to hold for other tribes as well. That is, Jalayir individuals and their families were scattered across Eurasia as part of the military campaigns and imperial administrative apparatus under Chinggis Qan and his descendants. The Jalayir tribe, while continuing as a family identity, did not remain a coherent political category after this process began. Jalayir individuals did not act within the bounds of a Jalayir political organisation, but rather within the framework of the *ulūs*es ruled by members of the Chinggisid family. We can speak, then, of a Jalayir diaspora, in which individuals were sent to various corners of the empire, under the command of different Chinggisid princes.

Here we will discuss some prominent Jalayir amirs and officials who are mentioned in historical sources – particularly Rashīd al-Dīn's *Jāmi' al-Tavārīkh* – who served Chinggisids in China, Transoxiana and the steppe. The Jalayir who served in the Ilkhanate in Iran will be discussed separately in Chapter 3. As will be shown, the Chinggisid empire transformed the social and political relationships of the Jalayir, ensuring that loyalties and interests would come to rest not necessarily with fellow Jalayir tribesmen, but with the Chinggisid royal family.

Perhaps the most prominent Jalayir individual of the early period of the Mongol empire was Muqālī, who became the supreme commander and virtual ruler of northern China by the time of his death in 1223. Muqālī had been given to Chinggis Qan as a personal servant by his father, and served in the Mongol campaigns to break the power of the steppe confederations of the Tatar, Kereyit and Nayman in the early 1200s.[47] At the *quriltay* of 1206, Muqālī was named *tümen* commander, that is, commander of 10,000.[48] Muqālī served in the Mongol campaigns in China in the 1210s, and in 1217 Chinggis Qan named him commander-in-chief of all of northern China, and granted him the hereditary titles of grand preceptor (*taishi*) and prince-of-state (*güi-ong*).[49] In Persian sources, he was known as Muqālī Guyang, derived from this Chinese title. In his *tümen* unit, Muqālī commanded two *hazāra*s (units of 1,000) of Jalayir troops, as well as Onggut, Qushiqul, Uru'ut and others. He was also assigned units of Khitan and Jürchen auxiliaries (*charīk*).[50] Muqālī's son, Bo'ol, succeeded him in his role of *güi-ong* in northern China.[51]

In addition to Muqālī, other Jalayir individuals are mentioned in the *Secret History of the Mongols* as allies of Temüjin early on. These include Seche Domoq and his sons Harqay and Bala. Following the Mongol invasion of Khwarazm in the early 1220s, Bala was sent in pursuit of the fleeing Khwārazmshāh Jalāl al-Dīn.[52] Rashīd al-Dīn also mentions that their relatives included a certain Ughān, a *hazāra* commander posted to Kirman in Iran.[53] These were some of the first Jalayir tribesmen who came to the Muslim lands west of the Jaxartes river.

Members of the Jalayir and other tribes were also assigned to the service of the various sons and grandsons of Chinggis Qan. Both territory and personnel were distributed to these princes as part of their share in the empire. One of the most important of the princely households during the early period of the Mongol empire was that of Chinggis Qan's third son and heir to the imperial throne, Ögödey. The sons of one of Chinggis Qan's Jalayir attendants named Qadā'an passed into Ögödey's service as part of his inheritance. One of these sons, Īlūgā, had been Ögödey's tutor (*atabeg*) during his childhood, and also commanded one of Ögödey's personal *hazāra* units.[54] Īlūgā's son, Dānishmand, is also mentioned as the envoy of Qaydu to the court of the Ilkhan Abaqa (r. 663/1265–680/1282). Qaydu was an Ögödeyid who held the dominant power in the central Asian Chaghatayid *ulūs* during the last third of the seventh/thirteenth century.[55] This seems to indicate that Dānishmand continued to serve the Ögödeyids after the accession of Möngke Qa'an in 649/1251 and the subsequent purge of many Ögödeyid princes.

Īlūgā's brother, Īlchīdāy, also served Ögödey and his family, and was mentioned by Rashīd al-Dīn in his account of the civil war between the Ögödeyids and the Toluids after 1248. Īlchīdāy objected to Möngke Qa'an's accession to the imperial throne by saying:

> You all decided and said that as long as there remains a piece of flesh from the children of Ögödey Qa'an, [even] *if he is wrapped in grass a cow would not eat that grass, and if he is wrapped in fat a dog would not eat that fat*, we would accept him as qan, and another would not sit on the throne. How is it that you do otherwise?[56]

The lines in italics are spoken by Ögödey in the *Secret History of the Mongols*, during Chinggis Qan's consultation with his sons about who should succeed him.[57] Although one might assume that the appearance of this text in Rashīd al-Dīn's history is evidence that he had access to the *Secret History*, Thomas Allsen has shown that this was not necessarily the case.[58] Rashīd al-Dīn worked from a collection of chronicles and other historical documents, known as the *Altan Debter*, or 'Golden Register', which is no longer extant. Although the *Secret History* and the *Altan Debter* contained parallel passages, they were different texts. However, both preserve the Ögödeyid point of view that succession should have rightly continued with them, no matter how weak or unskilled their candidate may have been.

Rashīd al-Dīn was writing in a context in which the Toluids had become the ruling family, and thus needed to account for the abrogation of the previous agreement made between Chinggis Qan and his sons. What is important to note for our purposes in examining the history of the Jalayir is that Īlūgā and Īlchīdāy's fortunes were tied to the fortunes of Ögödey's personal household. These Jalayir brothers served Ögödey as a result of their personal relationship to him. In addition, Īlchīdāy's interests continued to lie with Ögödey's descendants, the inheritors of his personal share of human and territorial resources (*ulūs* or *yūrt*).[59] When the position of this *ulūs* was threatened by the internal political struggles within the empire, Īlchīdāy objected to the new rise of Toluid authority as a usurpation of Ögödeyid claims to the imperial throne, and with them his own status within the imperial system.

While Īlūgā and Īlchīdāy sought to defend the Ögödeyids' right to rule, another Jalayir, Mingāsār Noyan, benefited from the Toluid ascendancy. Mingāsār served as chief judge (*yārghūchī*)[60] under Möngke Qa'an, as well as grand chancellor (*chīngsāng*),[61] and oversaw the trials of the Ögödeyids and their supporters after Möngke's accession in 649/1251. Mingāsār owed his position to an earlier military assignment with Tolui Khan and Möngke on campaign against the Qipchaqs during the initial Mongol conquests. He later served with Möngke on campaign in southern China.[62] After Möngke became qan, he sent Mingāsār Noyan with 2,000 horsemen to meet the sons of Güyük and demand that they present themselves and their armies at Möngke's court.[63] Mingāsār tried Oghul Ghaymish, the wife of Güyük Qan, and Qādāgāch Khātūn, the mother of Ögödey's son Shīrāmun.[64] Mingāsār's attachment to Möngke Qa'an resulted in the appointment of his son Hindūqūr Noyan to Iran as a commander of a unit of 10,000.[65] The establishment of the independent appanage meant that Hindūqūr Noyan entered the service of the Ilkhans.

In addition to connections to the princely lines of Ögödey and Möngke, Jalayir amirs were also assigned to the *ūlūs* of Chaghatay, whose hereditary appanage extended from the western Mongolian steppes to the Oxus river. One of these Jalayir amirs was Qūshūq Noyan Jalayir, although we know little about his life and relationship to the Chaghatayid rulers.[66] Another was Mūngka Noyan Jalayir, commander of one of the four *hazāra*s Chinggis Qan left to Chaghatay. Mūngka Noyan's son, Yīsūr Noyan, became an amir in the army of Barāq, khan of the Chaghatayid *ulūs* from 664/1266–667/1269. In the case of Yīsūr Noyan, we see an example of how a tribal amir could cross between princely appanage states. Yīsūr Noyan was sent to the Khurasan frontier by Dū'a Khan (r. 681/1282–706/1306). He was captured there by the Ilkhanids and passed into the service of the Oyrat amir Ḥājī.[67]

Finally, at least two Jalayir amirs were in the service of the family of Arigh Böke, the fourth son of Tolui and Sorqaqtani Beki, and challenger to Qubilay's claim to the qanate. The Jalayir Jāngqī Kūrgān and Abūghān both served Arigh Böke's son Malik Tīmūr.[68]

The Chinggisid empire changed Mongol society as much as it changed the societies that were conquered by the Mongols. Tribes like the Jalayir constituted the social and political order of the steppe. This order came to an end in the early thirteenth century. The major consequence was that most tribes were dismantled as political organisations in a process of redistribution of land and personnel among Chinggis Qan's family as the Mongol empire expanded. Individuals maintained their tribal identities and memories of their genealogies that traced the ties of kinship that went back many generations. However, by the middle of the thirteenth century, to be a Jalayir said more about one's family's past than about one's political identity. Political allegiances had come to be defined by one's place within the Chinggisid imperial order, which meant which Chinggisid prince one served. Thus, members of the Jalayir tribe served Chinggis Qan in China, Ögödey and his descendants, the Toluids and the Chaghatayids. A number of Jalayir families also came to Iran to serve the *ulūs* founded by Chinggis Qan's grandson Hülegü in the 1250s. The following chapter is devoted to this aspect of the Jalayir diaspora, and examines how the ancestors of the Jalayirid dynasty began their rise to power in the late thirteenth century.

Notes

1. Philip S. Khoury and Joseph Kostiner, 'Introduction: Tribes and the Complexities of State Formation in the Middle East', in Philip S. Khoury and Joseph Kostiner (eds), *Tribes and State Formation in the Middle East* (Berkeley: University of California Press, 1990), 4; Richard Tapper, 'Anthropologists, Historians, and Tribespeople on Tribe and State Formation in the Middle East', in Khoury and Kostiner (eds), *Tribes and State Formation in the Middle East*, 56.
2. David Sneath, *The Headless State: Aristocratic Orders, Kinship Society and Misrepresentations of Nomadic Inner Asia* (New York: Columbia University Press, 2007).
3. See the review of *The Headless State* by Peter Golden, in *Journal of Asian Studies* 68 (2009): 293–6; David Sneath's rejoinder to this review in *Journal of Asian Studies* 69 (2010): 658–60; and Golden's response to Sneath's rejoinder in the same issue, 660–3. See also the review of Thomas Barfield, in *Comparative Studies in Society and History* 51 (2009): 942–3.
4. Peter Golden, review of David Sneath, *The Headless State*, in *Journal of Asiatic Studies* 68 (2009): 295.
5. Sechin Jagchid and Paul Hyer, *Mongolia's Culture and Society* (Boulder: Westview, 1979), 247.
6. Anatoly M. Khazanov, *Nomads and the Outside World* (Madison: University of Wisconsin Press, 1994), 143.

7. Lawrence Krader, *Peoples of Central Asia* (Bloomington: Indiana University Press, 1963), 156.
8. Rudi Paul Lindner, 'What Was a Nomadic Tribe?', *Comparative Studies in Society and History* 24:4 (October 1982): 701.
9. Khazanov, *Nomads and the Outside World*, 139; G. E. Markov, 'Problems of Social Change among the Asiatic Nomads', in Wolfgang Weissleder, *The Nomadic Alternative: Modes and Models of Interaction in the African-Asian Deserts and Steppes* (The Hague: Mouton, 1978), 307.
10. Lindner, 'What Was a Nomadic Tribe?', 710.
11. Joseph Fletcher, 'The Mongols: Ecological and Social Perspectives', *HJAS* 46:1 (1986): 16.
12. Nicola Di Cosmo, 'State Formation and Periodization in Inner Asian History', *Journal of World History* 10 (1999): 14.
13. Di Cosmo, 'State Formation and Periodization in Inner Asian History', 17–19.
14. Paul D. Buell, *Historical Dictionary of the Mongol World Empire* (Lanham, MD, and Oxford: The Scarecrow Press, 2003), 166.
15. B. I. Vladimirtsov, *The Life of Chingis-Khan,* trans. Prince D. S. Mirsky (London: George Routledge and Sons, 1930), 1.
16. Jagchid and Hyer, *Mongolia's Culture and Society*, 264; Luc Kwanten, *Imperial Nomads: A History of Central Asia, 500–1500* (Philadelphia: University of Pennsylvania Press, 1979), 189.
17. Jagchid and Hyer, *Mongolia's Culture and Society*, 264.
18. Kwanten, *Imperial Nomads*, 188.
19. Lawrence Krader, 'The Origin of the State among the Nomads of Asia', in *Pastoral Production and Society: Proceedings of the International Meeting on Nomadic Pastoralism* (Cambridge: Cambridge University Press, 1979), 227–8.
20. İsenbike Togan, *Flexibility and Limitation in Steppe Formations* (Leiden: Brill, 1998), 10.
21. Paul Buell, 'Tribe, Qan, and Ulus in Early Mongol China: Some Prolegomena to Yüan History', PhD dissertation, University of Washington, 1977, 19, 26.
22. Togan, *Flexibility and Limitation*, 11.
23. Krader, 'The Origin of the State among the Nomads of Asia', 228–9.
24. Paul Ratchnevsky, *Genghis Khan: His Life and Legacy*, ed. and trans. Thomas Nivison Haining (Oxford and Cambridge, MA: Blackwell, 1991), 89.
25. Timothy May, *The Mongol Art of War: Chinggis Khan and the Mongol Military System* (Yardley: Westholme, 2007), 35.
26. Thomas T. Allsen, 'Guard and Government in the Reign of the Grand Qan Möngke, 1251–59', *HJAS* 46:2 (1986): 507–13.
27. Ratchnevsky, *Genghis Khan*, 176.
28. Thomas J. Barfield, *The Perilous Frontier* (Cambridge: Blackwell, 1989), 197.

29. Barfield, *The Perilous Frontier*, 191, 197.
30. The reorganisation of Mongol society under Chinggis Qan and his successors also gave rise to new tribal identities. Jean Aubin has shown how the origin of the Qarā'unas as a new 'ethnicity' on the central Asian frontier with India in the thirteenth century was a result of the creation of a new military unit, comprising representatives from different Mongol tribes from each of the four princely *ulūs*es. See Jean Aubin, 'L'Ethnogénèse de qaraunas', *Turcica* 1 (1969): 74–8.
31. John E. Woods, *The Aqquyunlu: Clan, Confederation, Empire* (Salt Lake City: University of Utah Press, 1999), 11.
32. Togan, *Flexibility and Limitation*, 11–12, 137.
33. Togan, *Flexibility and Limitation*, 12.
34. Togan, *Flexibility and Limitation*, 13.
35. Paul Buell has characterised Chinggis Qan's campaigns in 616/1219–617/1220 in Transoxiana not as an accidental and sudden event, but as the logical continuation of a decade and a half of Mongol infiltration into the region. This infiltration, brought about through the process of political unification of the Mongol tribes around Chinggis Qan and the accompanying expansion of the newly formed Mongol polity, brought the nomads in closer contact with the sedentary societies of central Asia. With this contact came new interests in the affairs of that region including the control of overland trade between central Asia and China. See Paul D. Buell, 'Early Mongol Expansion in Western Siberia and Turkestan (1207–1219): A Reconstruction', *CAJ* 36 (1992): 30.
36. On the Mongol *basqāq*s, see V. V. Barthold, *Turkestan Down to the Mongol Invasion*, trans. H. A. R. Gibb (London: Luzac, 1928), 468; John of Plano Carpini in Christopher Dawson (ed.), *Mission to Asia* (Toronto: Toronto University Press, 1998), 40; István Vásáry, 'The Origin of the Institution of *Basqaq*s', *Acta Orientalia Academiae Scientiarum Hung. Tomus* 32:2 (1978): 205. On the related term *dārūghachī*, see *TMEN*, 1:319–23 (no. 193); Francis Woodman Cleaves, '*DARUΓA* and *GEREGE*', *HJAS* 16 (1953): 237–59. Gerhard Doerfer equates *bāsqāq* and *dārūgha*, as does Thomas Allsen. See *TMEN*, 2:241 (no. 691); Thomas T. Allsen, *Mongol Imperialism: The Politics of the Great Qan Möngke in China, Russia, and the Islamic Lands, 1251–1259* (Berkeley: University of California Press, 1987), 46.
37. 'Alā' al-Dīn 'Aṭā Malik Juvaynī, *Tārīkh-i Jahān-gushāy*, ed. Muḥammad ibn 'Abd al-Wahhāb Qazvīnī, 4th edn (Tehran: Intishārāt-i Arghavān, 1370 [1991]), 1:31–2; originally published in E. J. W. Gibb Memorial Series 16 (Leiden: Brill, 1912). See also Boyle's English translation: 'Alā' al-Dīn 'Aṭā Malik Juvaynī, *Genghis Khan: The History of the World Conqueror*, trans. J. A. Boyle (Seattle: University of Washington Press, 1997), 42–3.
38. See Allsen, *Mongol Imperialism*, 45–51.
39. *TMEN*, 2:208.
40. *TMEN*, 2:208; Allsen, *Mongol Imperialism*, 48; Reuven Amitai-Preiss,

'Evidence for the Early Use of the Title *īlkhān* among the Mongols', *JRAS* 3:1 (1991): 353.

41. Amitai-Preiss, 'Evidence for the Early Use of the Title *īlkhān* among the Mongols', 354.
42. Amitai-Preiss, 'Evidence for the Early Use of the Title *īlkhān* among the Mongols', 353.
43. Thomas T. Allsen, 'Changing Forms of Legitimation in Mongol Iran', in Gary Seaman and Daniel Marks (eds), *Rulers from the Steppe: State Formation on the Eurasian Periphery* (Los Angeles: Ethnographics Press, University of Southern California, 1991), 227.
44. Peter Jackson, 'The Dissolution of the Mongol Empire', *CAJ* 22 (1978): 235.
45. I. P. Petrushevsky, 'The Socio-Economic Condition of Iran under the Ilkhans', in J. A. Boyle (ed.), *The Cambridge History of Iran, Volume 5: The Saljuq and Mongol Periods* (Cambridge: Cambridge University Press, 1968), 491.
46. Janet L. Abu-Lughod, *Before European Hegemony: The World System* A.D. *1250–1350* (Oxford: Oxford University Press, 1989), 120.
47. Igor de Rachewiltz, Hok-lam Chan, Hsiao Ch'i-ch'ing and Peter W. Geier (eds), *In the Service of the Khan: Eminent Personalities of the Early Mongol-Yüan Period (1200–1300)* (Wiesbaden: Harrassowitz Verlag, 1993), 3–4.
48. De Rachewiltz et al., *In the Service of the Khan*, 4.
49. De Rachewiltz et al., *In the Service of the Khan*, 5.
50. Rashīd al-Dīn/*Jāmi'*, 459.
51. De Rachewiltz et al., *In the Service of the Khan*, 8.
52. *The Secret History of the Mongols*, §257, §264.
53. Rashīd al-Dīn/*Jāmi'*, 71.
54. Rashīd al-Dīn/*Jāmi'*, 68.
55. Michal Biran, *Qaidu and the Rise of the Independent Mongol State in Central Asia* (Richmond: Curzon, 1997), 32.
56. Rashīd al-Dīn/*Jāmi'*, 69.
57. *The Secret History of the Mongols*, §255.
58. Thomas T. Allsen, *Culture and Conquest in Mongol Eurasia* (Cambridge: Cambridge University Press, 2001), 90.
59. Juvaynī writes that 'in the time of the reign of Chingiz Khan, the area of the country expanded. He assigned to everyone their place of residence (*mawżi'-i iqāmat*) which they call *yūrt*.' See Juvaynī, *Tārīkh-i Jahān-gushāy*, 31.
60. On the office of *yārghūchī* and aspects of the Mongol legal system, see Valentin A. Riasanovsky, *Fundamental Principles of Mongol Law* (Bloomington: Indiana University Press, 1965).
61. Denise Aigle, *Le Fārs sous la domination mongole: Politique et fiscalité (XIIIe–XIVe s.), Studia Iranica, Cahier 31* (Paris: Association pour l'Avancement des Études Iraniennes, 2005), 85.
62. Rashīd al-Dīn/*Jāmi'*, 70.
63. Bar Hebraeus, *The Chronography of Gregory Abû'l Faraj, the Son of Aaron,*

the Hebrew Physician Commonly Known as Bar Hebraeus Being the First Part of his Political History of the World, trans. Ernest A. Wallis Budge (Oxford: Oxford University Press, 1932), 417.

64. When Oghul Ghaymish was brought before the tribunal (*yārghū*), Mingāsār stripped her naked. She was tried and then wrapped in felt and cast into the river. See Rashīd al-Dīn/*Jāmi'*, 839.
65. Rashīd al-Dīn/*Jāmi'*, 70.
66. One of the few references to Qūshūq Noyan credits him with bringing the secretarial skills of a Khitan named Vazīr to the attention of Chaghatay. See Rashīd al-Dīn/*Jāmi'*, 773–4.
67. Rashīd al-Dīn/*Jāmi'*, 606–7.
68. Rashīd al-Dīn/*Jāmi'*, 943.

3

The Jalayirs and the Early Ilkhanate

The military governorships that the Mongols had established in Khurasan and Azarbayjan were replaced by the Ilkhanate in the 1250s. Unlike the former governorships, which were responsible directly to the great qan in Qaraqorum, the Ilkhanate was a new princely *ulūs*, or appanage state, under the rule of Hülegü Khan, the brother of Möngke Qa'an. Hülegü's primary missions were to eliminate the Nizārī Ismā'īlīs, or Assassins, who had made an attempt on Möngke's life, and the Abbasid caliphate in Baghdad. Hülegü's forces were successful in both of these missions, and by 1260 the lands between the Oxus and the Euphrates were under Hülegü's control. As in the other princely *ulūs*es, which were mentioned in Chapter 2, members of the Jalayir and other Mongol tribes provided the manpower for Hülegü's army, and became the new amirs, or military elite, in Iran.

In the early years of the Ilkhanate, tensions developed between the khans (Hülegü and his descendants) and the amirs. In general, the khans sought to centre political power and wealth in their own hands, through a central government staffed mainly by native Persians. The amirs, in general, tended to resist this tendency toward centralisation, which threatened their own independence, power and wealth. Resistance among the amirs took the form of supporting alternative members of the Hülegüids, members of the Ilkhanid royal family, for the throne. Several Jalayir tribal families played a role in this struggle, which became particularly intense between 1282 and 1295.

This chapter examines the details of this struggle, which led ultimately to a centralisation process that eliminated all but one Jalayir family from political influence in the Ilkhanate. These Jalayirs were the descendants of Īlgā Noyan, a trusted commander of Hülegü during the Mongol invasion of the 1250s. By the end of the thirteenth century, the Ilgayid Jalayirs had become powerful amirs within the Ilkhanate, due to their ties to the royal family.

Īlgā Noyan and the Early Ilkhanate

The Jalayirid sultans of the fourteenth century were descended from Īlgā Noyan, who came to Iran in the army of Hülegü. He took part in the assault on Baghdad in January of 1258, leading a contingent of Mongol troops from the south of the city along the Tigris.[1] On the day that the Abbasid caliph al-Musta'ṣim bi-llāh was executed, Īlgā and his grandson, Qarā Būqā, were charged with undertaking reconstruction operations in Baghdad.[2] Two years later, following the Mongols' defeat by the Mamluks at 'Ayn Jalut, Īlgā Noyan led the remaining Mongol forces out of Syria, and headed north to Diyarbakr.[3] Here Īlgā was shot from his horse during the Mongol siege of Mayyafariqin (modern Silvan), but was carried off the field by two of his men.[4] In the winter of 1262–63, Īlgā appeared again in an Ilkhanid campaign against the Mongols of the Golden Horde at the Terek river in the Caucasus,[5] a sign that the once united Mongol empire had split into independent and mutually hostile khanates.

Īlgā Noyan served Hülegü until the khan's death in 663/1265. When Abaqa came to the royal court camp (*urdū*) in Jumādá I/March of that year, unaware that his father had died, Īlgā Noyan met him to break the news. Rashīd al-Dīn writes:

> Because Īlgā Noyan was commander-in-chief (*amīr-i ūrdūhā*) and followed the path of affection in the service of the Ilkhan for a long time, he gave Abaqa Khan food and drink. In private he informed him of the circumstances of his father.[6]

Abaqa succeeded Hülegü as Ilkhan. During his reign, Īlgā Noyan became the most respected senior amir.[7] An illustration of his position in the Ilkhanid hierarchy is given in an account of a diplomatic mission from the Chaghatayid *ulūs*. The vizier Mas'ūd Beg came in the winter of 665 /1266–67 to obtain an accounting of the Chaghatayid property (*īnchū*) in Iran.[8] At Abaqa's court, only Īlgā Noyan sat closer to the khan than the visiting dignitary Mas'ūd Beg.[9]

Īlgā's prominence in the new Ilkhanid appanage state, and the subsequent prominence of his sons, seems attributable to his close relationship with Hülegü and his role in many of the military campaigns which established the territorial limits of the Ilkhanate. In Baghdad, Syria, Diyarbakr and the Caucasus, Īlgā was one of the principal military leaders in conflicts with the Ilkhans' neighbours and rivals, the Mamluks and the Jochids.

The Jalayir and Tribal Factionalism (1282–95)

Īlgā Noyan was one of the many prominent amirs among the Ilkhanid elite. These amirs provided the military support that the khans required to maintain their authority. However, the amirs could also challenge a khan and assert his own independence by backing other Hülegüid princes. The tension between the centralisation of royal authority and the independent power of the amirs became acute following the death of Abaqa Khan in 1282.

Much of the account that follows is based on Rashīd al-Dīn's *Jāmi' al-Tavārīkh*, and the ideological background to this history should be kept in mind. In the struggle between royal centralisation and the dispersal of power among the amirs, Rashīd al-Dīn most certainly favoured the former. It is possible, then, to read his account of this period, some thirty years earlier, as a kind of warning against factionalism among the elite, which would lead to civil war and the breakdown of order. This history is crucial, however, for the details it provides about the personnel within the Ilkhanid elite, and particularly their tribal affiliations. In other words, if we want to know what role tribal identity played in the internal politics of the Ilkhanate, Rashīd al-Dīn is an indispensable source.

When Abaqa Khan died in 680/1282, his brother Aḥmad Tegüder was in Georgia, and immediately set out for the royal court at Maragha. He was met by some of the most powerful Ilkhanid amirs, including Shīktūr Noyan and Būqā of the Jalayir tribe.[10] Shīktūr was Īlgā Noyan's second son. Like his father, he served in the earliest Ilkhanid military campaigns in Syria in 657/1259.[11] In 658/1260 he accompanied emissaries from Mongolia to Hülegü in Anatolia to announce the death of Möngke Qa'an.[12] He later served in the left wing of the Ilkhanid army on campaign against the Chaghatayid khan Barāq in 668/1270.[13] By 680/1282, he was a respected senior amir.

Būqā was the son of Ūgulāy Qūrchī Jalayir, who had come to Iran with Hülegü as a scout (*qarāvul*).[14] Ūgulāy died when Būqā was still a child and Būqā was raised at the court of Abaqa Khan. Here he served as a grand counsellor (*'aẓīm-īnāq*), as well as keeper of the royal treasury (*khazā'in-i nārīn*)[15] and keeper of pelts (*khizāna-yi pustīn*).[16] In addition, Būqā served in the capacity of *tamghāchī*, keeper of the red imperial seal (*āl tamghā*) under Abaqa.[17]

After the period of mourning for Abaqa, the princes, ladies and amirs who were present at the court at Maragha deliberated over who should succeed him.[18] They were divided between support for Aḥmad Tegüder and Arghun, who served in Khurasan and had yet to arrive at the assembly.

Among the Jalayir amirs, Shīktūr Noyan supported Aḥmad Tegüder, while his brother, Āq Būqā, as well as Būqā and Būqā's brother Arūq, supported Arghun.[19] In the end, Arghun was convinced to step aside, for most of the amirs were in favour of Aḥmad Tegüder.[20] Arghun was forced to acquiesce, and on 26 Muḥarram 681/6 May 1282 all of the amirs agreed to confer rulership upon Aḥmad Tegüder.[21] The enthronement followed over a month later, on the summer solstice, 13 Rabīʻ I 681/21 June 1282. An oath (*mūchalgā*)[22] was given, and Aḥmad Tegüder was seated on the throne by the amirs Qūnqūrtāy and Shīktūr Noyan Jalayir.[23]

Shīktūr Noyan certainly held a prominent rank within the Ilkhanate at this time. Āq Būqā also achieved a high status under Aḥmad Tegüder, despite his initial support of Arghun. He became an intimate (*īnāq*) of the new khan,[24] a relationship that prompted resentment from Būqā.[25] Būqā continued to resist Aḥmad Tegüder's rule, although he was forced to leave Arghun's household in Khurasan and join the royal court in Azarbayjan.[26]

The tensions between Aḥmad Tegüder and Arghun, which reflected broader factionalism among the amirs, broke into open conflict in Ṣafar 683/May 1284. Armies representing the two sides clashed at Āq Khvāja in a battle that marked the beginning of Aḥmad Tegüder's fall.[27] Būqā continued to serve Aḥmad Tegüder as *tamghāchī* and chief military commander. Uncertain by this time of the loyalty of his men, Aḥmad Tegüder ordered his amirs to submit written oaths swearing that they would not transgress the command of Būqā.[28] Although Būqā was the khan's most trusted amir, he began to harbour resentment toward Aḥmad Tegüder.[29] At the same time, according to Rashīd al-Dīn, Aḥmad Tegüder began to ignore Būqā in favour of his Jalayir rival Āq Būqā, son of Īlgā. For these reasons, Būqā became more inclined to support Aḥmad Tegüder's brother Arghun.[30]

Less than a month later, Arghun surrendered to Aḥmad Tegüder, who chose not to execute his cousin. Būqā Jalayir, with the help of his brother and two other Jalayir kinsmen, engineered a coup that freed Arghun and began a purge of Aḥmad Tegüder's supporters. Āq Būqā Jalayir, Būqā's main rival, was also captured. A *quriltay* was then held to name Aḥmad Tegüder's successor. According to Rashīd al-Dīn, Būqā made the case for Arghun's enthronement:

> The qan who is the ruler of the inhabited quarter of the world and *āqā* of the entire family of Chinggis Qan, gave rulership of the lands of Iran after his own brother Hülegü Khan to his eldest son Abaqa Khan, who was the most perfect and intelligent. After him, by way of inheritance, it should go to his beloved son, the true successor Arghun. If meddlers (*fażūlān*) had not interfered, the

crown and throne would have gone to the sons, and none of this turmoil (*fitna*) would have happened. God knows where this all will end.[31]

These words, of course, belong to Rashīd al-Dīn and not to Būqā, and reflect Rashīd al-Dīn's own interested view that rulership in the Ilkhanate belonged to Arghun, the father of his patrons Ghazan and Öljeytü.

With Aḥmad Tegüder deposed, and eventually executed, and his own candidate on the throne, Būqā Jalayir was at the height of his power. Both Rashīd al-Dīn and his contemporary Vaṣṣāf make it clear that Arghun owed his throne to Būqā.[32] Būqā's influence was reflected in the fact that he controlled both the military and the financial administration. He was in charge of the army and the affairs of the royal household. Būqā also became the Ilkhanid grand vizier, and executed the *ṣāḥib-dīvān*, Shams al-Dīn, and replaced him with three individuals of his own choosing.[33]

Būqā's authority was recognised by Qubilay Qan in China, to whom the Ilkhans were still technically subordinate. Qubilay's representative arrived at the Ilkhanid court in 1286, with a decree (*yārlīgh*) recognising Arghun as khan and Būqā as chancellor (*chīngsāng*).[34] Būqā's power was formally recognised as virtually unlimited, for he was exempted from being tried for up to nine crimes.[35] He used his influence to protect his family as well. In 685/1286, his brother Arūq killed three men in Baghdad, including the personnel (*īnchū*) of Arghun Khan's brother Geykhatu. Būqā offered his brother sanctuary at the royal court, and refuge from retribution from Geykhatu.[36]

Arūq eventually returned to Baghdad, where, according to Rashīd al-Dīn, he behaved less like an amir than like a king, withholding tax receipts from the central treasury.[37] These abuses by Būqā and Arūq bred resentment among the other amirs and officials.[38] Rashīd al-Dīn puts the following indictment of Būqā in the mouth of the future grand vizier Ṣadr al-Din Zanjānī:

> Būqā has arranged rulership for himself. Without an order from the *pādishāh* or counsel with the amirs he does whatever he wants, and he dispenses wealth the way he wants. No one knows Arghun is the *pādishāh*, rather it's Būqā. Things have finally gotten to the point that whenever an envoy goes with a decree or passport (*yārlīgh va pā'iza*) to Tabriz, Amīr 'Alī, who is the governor (*vālī*) of that place, doesn't pay any attention unless [the document] has the red seal of Būqā (*āl tamghā-yi būqā*), and he turns back empty-handed.[39]

Arghun Khan was not pleased with these reports, and punished Būqā by removing the financial registry from his possession and dismissing his deputies and dependants from the royal council.[40] Realising that he had completely fallen out of favour with Arghun, Būqā paid off a number of Jalayir amirs in order to secure their loyalty, and again attempted to bring an Ilkhanid prince to the throne. These efforts failed, however, and Būqā was eventually executed, his mutilated corpse displayed publicly, in January 1289.[41] Trials of his relatives and dependants followed, and most of them were also executed.[42]

Būqā Jalayir's rise and fall reflects the tension between the amirs and princes in the Ilkhanate. Rashīd al-Dīn attributed his fall to the corrupt use of his authority to protect his brother, who acted ever more independently in Baghdad. The other amirs, as well as Arghun Khan, sought to bring Būqā under control. When he attempted to overthrow Arghun, as he had with Aḥmad Tegüder, other amirs stepped in to stop him. Būqā's fall was the end of the Ugulayid branch of the Jalayir in the Ilkhanate, which meant that the Ilgayids, including Shīktūr, Āq Būqā and Ṭughān, would gain prominence.

Challenges to the central authority of the khans did not end with Būqā's downfall, however. In the 1290s, the Ilkhanate's northwestern frontier in Anatolia became the site for a number of rebellions among the tribal amirs, including several from the Jalayir tribe. The political situation in Anatolia and the elimination of these rebellions by the central Ilkhanid authority are examined below.

Jalayir Amirs and the Anatolian Frontier

The Mongol presence in Anatolia began in 641/1243 with the victory of Bāyjū Noyan, the imperial military governor of western Iran, at Köse Dagh. Bāyjū defeated the army of the Saljūq sultan Kay Khusraw II (r. 634/1237–644/1246) and opened up eastern Anatolia to the Mongols. A second wave of Mongols migrated westward after 654/1256, when Bāyjū was forced to cede his control over Azarbayjan to the new Ilkhan ruler Hülegü Khan.[43] While Hülegü was successful in securing the relatively accessible plain of Diyarbakr, the higher country between the Euphrates and Kırşehir was a region of political fluidity for those political powers that sought to control it: the Ilkhans from Azarbayjan, the Mamluks from Cairo and Syria, and the Saljūq and Armenian rulers whose loyalty was sought by the larger imperial powers.

Zeki Velidi Togan has highlighted the importance of Anatolia to the Ilkhanid empire in an article discussing references made by Rashīd al-Dīn in his letters.[44] The authenticity of these letters has been the subject of much debate among scholars.[45] Without addressing the issue of whether or not the letters are authentic, it is worth mentioning some general aspects of Togan's work that suggest the importance of Anatolia to Rashīd al-Dīn and the Ilkhanate. Togan cites Ibn Bībī's report that the city of Erzincan was incorporated into the personal property (*injü=īnchū*) of Abaqa Khan.[46] When one also considers that over a third of Rashīd al-Dīn's personal property was located in Anatolia,[47] the importance of this western province to the Ilkhanid ruling elite is clear. The reason seems to have been the significance of Anatolia for overland trade, which passed through Ilkhanid territory in northern Iran on its way west. Öljeytü, under whom Rashīd al-Dīn served as vizier, constructed a new imperial capital at Sultaniyya, southeast of Tabriz, in the early eighth/fourteenth century.[48] As Togan points out, Sultaniyya marked the central point along the Ilkhanid imperial highway (*shāh-rāh*), extending from the Oxus to the Mediterranean. A large portion of the western half of this route (*shāh-rāh-i gharbī*) passed through Anatolia, via Erzurum, Erzincan and Konya.[49] Anatolia was more than just a frontier march; it was an integral part of the Ilkhanid economic system.

Following Abaqa Khan's accession in 663/1265, a son of Īlgā Jalayir, named Tūqū (or Ṭūghū), had been appointed to the province of Rūm as a secretary (*bītikchī*), along with Tūdā'ūn of the Sulduz tribe.[50] They were soon called upon by Abaqa to help put down the rebellion of Sharaf al-Dīn Mas'ūd b. Khaṭīr, who had challenged the authority of the Mongols' Saljūq protectorate from his bases in Niğde and Develi.[51]

Although the suppression of the revolt of Sharaf al-Dīn Mas'ūd helped to consolidate the position of the Saljuqid governor Mu'īn al-Dīn Sulaymān, known as the *parvāna*, in Anatolia, it had also demonstrated that the *parvāna* was dependent on Ilkhanid military support to maintain that position. In an attempt to achieve a greater degree of autonomy, the *parvāna* sent emissaries to the Mamluk sultan Baybars, encouraging him to invade Anatolia. Baybars, who had seized the sultanate after the Battle of 'Ayn Jalut in 658/1260, and who had laid the foundation of the sultanate through his campaigns against the Syrian crusader states, was eager to extend his northern frontier into Anatolia. As the Mamluk forces headed north in late 675/early 1277, Tūqū and Tūdā'ūn left their winter residence at Kırşehir to join the amir Qūtū, who was to arrive from Niğde.[52] However, when Tūqū reached the plain of Abulustayn (Elbistan), Qūtū was not there, and Baybars' forces soundly defeated the Mongols on 9 Dhū al-Qa'da 675/14 April 1277.[53] Baybars went on to Kayseri, where the *khuṭba* and *sikka* were given in his name.[54] Both Tūqū and Tūdā'ūn, as well as Ūrūghtū Jalayir, were killed at this battle.[55]

Mamluk supremacy in Anatolia did not last long. Baybars retreated when he realised that Abaqa himself was preparing an expedition to deal with the Mamluks and the *parvāna*, who had not been at Abulustayn to aid the Mongol troops.[56] The Ilkhanid amirs Samāghar and Kuhūrgāy soon replaced Tūqū and Tūdā'ūn as governors in this region.

Eastern Anatolia remained a stronghold for the Ilkhans under Jalayir and Sulduz governors, the ancestors of the Jalayirid and Chubanid dynasties of the eighth/fourteenth century. Īlgā Noyan's son Āq Būqā, who had become a favourite of Aḥmad Tegüder, served on the fringes of the Ilkhanid political scene in Anatolia during the reign of Arghun Khan and Būqā Jalayir. Here, Āq Būqā became attached to prince Geykhatu, Arghun's brother.[57] His time in Anatolia with Geykhatu meant that his status rose after Geykhatu became khan in 690/1291, leading to his appointment as chief amir (*mīr-i mīrān*).[58] During Geykhatu's reign, Āq Būqā Jalayir played a prominent role in the administrative affairs of the Ilkhanate. He became the patron (*murabbī*) of Ṣadr al-Dīn Zanjānī, Geykhatu's grand vizier. He also carried out the execution of his own brother Ṭughān, who had supported Baydu to succeed Arghun Khan, and had conspired with several other amirs against Arghun's vizier, Sa'd al-Dawla.[59] As one of Geykhatu Khan's trusted amirs, Āq Būqā was sent to Tabriz in 693/1294 to introduce the new Chinese-inspired paper currency, known as *chao* (*chāw*).[60] However, this fiscal experiment was short-lived, as its introduction led to utter chaos and a standstill of economic activity in Tabriz.[61]

Geykhatu ruled as khan from 690/1291 until 694/1295. He returned to Anatolia following the investigations into his brother's death in 690 /1291, and spent most of his reign in that region.[62] Geykhatu placed Iran under the command of Āq Būqā's brother, Shīktūr Noyan, as his deputy in Iran,[63] while Āq Būqā remained at Geykhatu's court in the west. During his reign, Geykhatu seems to have dispensed with the title '*īlkhān*' on his coins, omitting at times even the name of the great qan Qubilay.[64] Such a policy indicates an attempt to establish the full independence of the *ulūs* of Hülegü by severing the nominal ties of allegiance to the eastern court of the great qan, which had been at the foundation of the Ilkhanate's political identity since its establishment.

Despite these symbolic declarations of independent sovereignty, Geykhatu faced a challenge to his authority similar to that which Aḥmad Tegüder had faced a decade earlier. As lateral successors – that is, brothers of the previous khan – they were both threatened by the existence of the former khan's sons as rallying points for political opposition. For Geykhatu, this threat was represented not only by Arghun's son Ghazan, who had inherited his father's personal appanage in Khurasan, but also by his cousin Baydu, the grandson of Hülegü through his son Ṭaraqāy. Several disaffected amirs, led by Ṭaghāchār, gathered around Baydu in

Baghdad and launched a rebellion in 694/1295. When Ṭaghāchār moved against the army of Geykhatu Khan, Āq Būqā warned him that such an action was unlawful (*khilāf-i yāsā*). Ṭaghāchār responded, saying:

> Until today, Āq Būqā was commander of the entire country on the order of Geykhatu Khan. Now, by the virtue of Baydu's decree, leadership belongs to me.[65]

Āq Būqā's forces were overwhelmed, and Geykhatu was eventually captured and executed.[66]

Baydu's reign lasted only four months before he was toppled by Ghazan. By the time of Ghazan's accession in 694/1295, most of the sons of Īlgā Noyan Jalayir had disappeared from the political scene. Shīktūr Noyan seems to have died around this time, while Āq Būqā, Ṭughān, Ūrūghtū and Tūqū had all been killed between 675/1277 and 694/1295. Īlgā's family had represented a major component of the early Ilkhanate's military and administrative elite. However, by the early period of Ghazan's reign, representatives of other branches of the Jalayir tribe attempted to establish independent authority on the western frontier.

While Rūm had been Geykhatu's personal appanage, Ghazan had inherited Khurasan and thus had fewer personal ties to the west. It is perhaps this weakness in terms of dependants and allies in Anatolia that prompted or allowed for a series of uprisings in the region between 695/1296 and 698/1299. These uprisings involved several Jalayir amirs who, unlike the Ilgayids and Ugulayids, did not have close ties to the royal family, but who used the opportunity presented by their post in the west to carve out their own local influence.

One of these Jalayir amirs was Āyna Beg. His father, Qipchaq, was a relative of the family of Ūgulāy Qūrchī Jalayir. His brother, Ishāk Tughlī, was an amir in Aḥmad Tegüder Khan's army, and fought at the battle of Āq Khvāja in 683/1284 between Aḥmad Tegüder and Arghun.[67] However, he is not mentioned after this point, and it is likely that he was killed in 683/1284 during the purge of Aḥmad Tegüder's supporters, led by Būqā Jalayir. Āyna Beg survived this purge, and is mentioned as having being sent by Ghazan Khan to Anatolia to intercept a rebel named Īldār. After his forces seized Īldār near Erzurum,[68] Āyna Beg himself turned against Ghazan. He joined a faction of amirs who attacked Ghazan's army at Baylaqan in February or March 1296.[69] The next day, Ghazan's troops rallied, and Āyna Beg was captured. He was brought to Tabriz, where he was publicly executed.[70]

The following year, another Jalayir amir named Bāltū raised another rebellion. Bāltū had served in Anatolia along with his father, Tāyjī, from the period of Abaqa's reign (663/1265–680/1282).[71] As in the case of Āyna Beg, Bāltū's rebellion began as part of a campaign to put down the rebellion of another amir. This amir was Ṭaghāchār, who had sided with Baydu against Ghazan in the civil war of 1295.[72] After Baydu was defeated, Ṭaghāchār left Azarbayjan for Anatolia, taking refuge in Tokat.[73] Ṭaghāchār was eventually captured and executed by Bāltū's forces, but Bāltū then repeatedly ignored Ghazan's demands that he return.[74] Bāltū himself was defeated at Malatya,[75] and later captured in May of 1297.[76] Like Āyna Beg, Bāltū was publicly executed in Tabriz later that year.[77] In addition, the Saljūq sultan Mas'ūd II was suspected of having conspired with Bāltū. Ghazan had Mas'ūd deposed, and replaced by his nephew, 'Alā' al-Dīn Kay Qubād III.

This Saljūq coup still did not end the unrest in Anatolia. In the winter of 1298–99, a number of amirs, led by Sulaymish, who had led the coup against Mas'ūd II, revolted against Ghazan's appointed governors. Among the rebels was the Jalayir amir Iqbāl. By the spring of 1299, Ghazan's new commander in Anatolia, Amīr Chūpān Sulduz, had defeated Sulaymish and captured Iqbāl. This event marked a turning point in the Ilkhanid military administration in Anatolia.[78] Particularly after the death of the Saljūq sultan Mas'ūd II in 702/1303, Rūm came to be governed almost as an autonomous principality under Amīr Chūpān.[79] During the early reign of the young Abū Sa'īd Bahādur Khan (717/1317–727/1327), Amīr Chūpān became the Ilkhanid commander-in-chief and virtual sovereign.

The years between 1282 and 1300 were characterised by internal struggles in the Ilkhanate. The conflicts between Aḥmad Tegüder and Arghun, and between Geykhatu, Baydu and Ghazan, reflected not only the competing interests of the Ilkhanid royal family, but also those of the amirs who backed them. As we have seen in this chapter, an amir in the Ilkhanate who could help his candidate on to the throne could become extremely powerful, as Būqā Jalayir had been. Būqā was aided by other Jalayir tribesmen, but he was also opposed by other Jalayir, most notably Āq Būqā, the son of Īlgā Noyan. The Jalayir certainly did not act as a cohesive group during this period of civil war in the Ilkhanate. Conflict occurred not between tribes, but between supporters of different royal princes. After Ghazan Khan came to power in 1295, the amirs who had opposed Ghazan, and thus did not have a royal patron after Ghazan's succession, attempted to rebel. Several Jalayir tribesmen took part in these rebellions in Anatolia in the first years of Ghazan's reign.

By the turn of the fourteenth century, Amīr Chūpān Sulduz had begun to consolidate his authority in Anatolia, in the name of Ghazan Khan. This was part of a wider programme of centralisation under Ghazan Khan.

The khan and the non-Mongol administrative elite attempted to remove power from the hands of the amirs, and place it in the hands of the central government. This process involved a series of reforms, which included the regularisation of the financial administration, the collection of taxes, the revocation of individuals' privileges granted by previous rulers, and the increase in the authority of the khan as religious leader, through mass conversion to Islam and the formulation of an ideology that presented the khan as the *pādishāh-i islām*, and an ideal Muslim sovereign.

There were fewer challenges to the central authority of the khan from the amirs after 1300. Jalayir families that had opposed Ghazan had been eliminated, and the line of Īlgā Noyan was the one Jalayir family that had any political influence. As the following chapter illustrates, the son and grandson of Āq Būqā became closely tied to the Ilkhanid royal house during this period of political centralisation in the early fourteenth century.

Notes

1. Rashīd al-Dīn/*Jāmi'*, 1008. Īlgā Noyan, Kīt Būqā and Qūdūsūn are also all mentioned among Hülegü's amirs in Rashīd al-Dīn's genealogical work *Shu'ab-i Panjgāna*. Īlgā Noyan is among the first names listed in the account of the amirs in Hülegü's time. Īlgā is described as follows: 'Īlgā Noyan from the Jalayir was a great amir. He came here from that province (*vilāyat*) with Hülegü.' Kīt Būqā is listed two names below Īlgā in the same column: 'Kīt Būqā from the Nayman tribe was an amir of the army and extremely respected. He conquered Syria and Damascus (*shām va dimashq*), and after that was killed in battle with Egypt (*dar jang-i miṣr*).' Qūdūsūn (or Qudusūn, as his name is written in the *Shu'ab-i Panjgāna* manuscript) 'was a respected amir and was among the amirs who conquered Baghdad'. See Rashīd al-Dīn/*Shu'ab*, 139b–140a.
2. Rashīd al-Dīn/*Jāmi'*, 1,019.
3. Rashīd al-Dīn/*Jāmi'*, 1,034.
4. Rashīd al-Dīn/*Jāmi'*, 1,036.
5. Rashīd al-Dīn/*Jāmi'*, 1,046.
6. Rashīd al-Dīn/*Jāmi'*, 1,059.
7. Īlgā is listed among the top amirs during Abaqa's time in the *Shu'ab-i Panjgāna*. He is described as 'a greatly respected amir' (*amīrī-yi bas mu'tabar*). See Rashīd al-Dīn/*Shu'ab*, 144b.
8. On the issue of extra-territorial possessions of the Chinggisid princes, see Thomas T. Allsen, 'Sharing Out the Empire: Apportioning Lands under the Mongols', in Anatoly M. Khazanov and André Wink (eds), *Nomads in the Sedentary World* (Richmond: Curzon, 2001), 173; Paul D. Buell, 'Tribe,

Qan, and Ulus in Early Mongol China: Some Prolegomena to Yüan History', PhD dissertation, University of Washington, 1977, 125.

9. Rashīd al-Dīn/*Jāmi'*, 1,063.
10. Rashīd al-Dīn/*Jāmi'*, 1,124. Rashīd al-Dīn listed Shīktūr Noyan among the top amirs during Aḥmad Tegüder's reign in the *Shu'ab-i Panjgāna*. However, Rashīd al-Dīn also mentioned that Shīktūr did not pay much attention to him (*ziyādat-i iltifātī namī-kard*). See Rashīd al-Dīn/*Shu'ab*, 141b.
11. Rashīd al-Dīn/*Jāmi'*, 1,025–6.
12. Rashīd al-Dīn/*Jāmi'*, 1,028.
13. Rashīd al-Dīn/*Jāmi'*, 1,085.
14. For an overview of Būqā's career, see Jean Aubin, *Émirs Mongols et vizirs Persans dans les remous de l'acculturation* (Paris: Association pour l'Avancement des Études Iraniennes, 1995), 30.
15. Rashīd al-Dīn/*Jāmi'*, 1,110.
16. Rashīd al-Dīn/*Jāmi'*, 70.
17. Rashīd al-Dīn/*Jāmi'*, 1,110. The *āl tamghā* was probably adopted by the Mongols from Uyghur chancery practices. It was used for general imperial decrees, while the *altūn tamghā* (gold seal) was used specifically for financial documents or decrees. See Gerhard Doerfer, 'Āl Tamġā', *Encyclopaedia Iranica*, ed. Ehsan Yarshater (London and New York: Routledge and Kegan Paul, 1983), 1:766–8.
18. Rashīd al-Dīn/*Jāmi'*, 1,125.
19. Jean Aubin has described Būqā as leading a movement to return to Mongol tradition in the events surrounding the succession in 1284. See Aubin, *Émirs Mongols et vizirs Persans*, 38.
20. Rashīd al-Dīn/*Jāmi'*, 1,125.
21. Rashīd al-Dīn/*Jāmi'*, 1,125.
22. For the meaning of *mūchalgā*, see *TMEN*, 1:502–5 (no. 370).
23. Rashīd al-Dīn/*Jāmi'*, 1,126.
24. Rashīd al-Dīn/*Jāmi'*, 1,145.
25. Rashīd al-Dīn/*Jāmi'*, 1,140.
26. Rashīd al-Dīn/*Jāmi'*, 1,129; Rashīd al-Dīn/*Shu'ab*, 141b.
27. Rashīd al-Dīn/*Jāmi'*, 1,138.
28. Rashīd al-Dīn/*Jāmi'*, 1,138.
29. Rashīd al-Dīn records a clash between Aḥmad Tegüder and Būqā; see Rashīd al-Dīn/*Jāmi'*, 1,140.
30. Rashīd al-Dīn/*Jāmi'*, 1,140.
31. Rashīd al-Dīn/*Jāmi'*, 1,145.
32. Vaṣṣāf writes that since Arghun considered that he had become sultan thanks to Būqā's efforts, he conferred on him all but the name of khan. See Vaṣṣāf/*Tārīkh*, 230; Vaṣṣāf, *Taḥrīr-i Tārīkh-i Vaṣṣāf*, ed. 'Abd al-Muḥammad Āyatī (Tehran: Mu'assasa-yi Muṭāla'at va Taḥqīqāt-i Farhangī [Pizhūhishgāh], 1372 [1993]), 129.

33. For the period of Būqā's power at the head of the administration, see Aubin, *Émirs Mongols et vizirs Persans*, 38–41.
34. Rashīd al-Dīn/*Jāmi'*, 1,161; Vaṣṣāf/*Tārīkh*, 229. Vaṣṣāf writes that the title *chīngsāng* came 'from his majesty' (*az ḥażrat*), that is, Qubilay Qan. On the meaning of this Chinese title, and for an analysis of this incident, see Thomas T. Allsen, 'Notes on Chinese Titles in Mongol Iran', *Mongolian Studies* 14 (1991): 28–30.
35. Vaṣṣāf/*Tārīkh*, 229.
36. Rashīd al-Dīn/*Jāmi'*, 1,162–3.
37. Rashīd al-Dīn/*Jāmi'*, 1,166.
38. Vaṣṣāf/*Tārīkh*, 230.
39. Rashīd al-Dīn/*Jāmi'*, 1,167.
40. Rashīd al-Dīn/*Jāmi'*, 1,167–8.
41. Rashīd al-Dīn/*Jāmi'*, 1,171; Vaṣṣāf/*Tārīkh*, 233.
42. Vaṣṣāf/*Tārīkh*, 233. Būqā's son, Ābāchī, was raised by his fellow Jalayir tribesman Ṭughān, a son of Īlgā Noyan. Ṭughān wanted to free him, and brought him before Arghun to have him show allegiance (*hūljāmīshī*). Arghun was still angry about Būqā's betrayal, however, and ordered Ṭughān to purge his family. Ābāchī and his brothers Malik, Tarkhān Tīmūr and Qutlugh Tīmūr were killed. See Rashīd al-Dīn/*Jāmi'*, 1,171.
43. Claude Cahen, *Pre-Ottoman Turkey: A General Survey of the Material and Spiritual Culture and History c. 1071–1330*, trans. J. Jones-Williams (New York: Taplinger, 1968), 275.
44. Zeki Velidi Togan, 'References to Economic and Cultural Life in Anatolia in the Letters of Rashīd al-Dīn', trans. Gary Leiser, in Judith Pfeiffer and Sholeh A. Quinn (eds), in collaboration with Ernest Tucker, *History and Historiography of Post-Mongol Central Asia and the Middle East: Studies in Honor of John E. Woods* (Wiesbaden: Harrassowitz, 2006), 84–111.
45. For the main arguments concerning the authenticity of the letters of Rashīd al-Dīn, see Reuben Levy, 'The Letters of Rashīd al-Dīn Faḍl Allāh', *JRAS* (1946): 74–8; A. H. Morton, 'The Letters of Rashīd al-Dīn: Īlkhānid Fact or Timurid Fiction', in Reuven Amitai-Preiss and David O. Morgan (eds), *The Mongol Empire and its Legacy* (Leiden: Brill, 1999), 155–99; Abolala Soudavar, 'In Defense of Rašīd-od-dīn and his Letters', *Studia Iranica* 32 (2003): 77–120. Gary Leiser thoroughly summarises the entire debate in the introduction to his translation of Togan's article; see Togan, 'References to Economic and Cultural Life in Anatolia in the Letters of Rashīd al-Dīn', 84–7.
46. Togan, 'References to Economic and Cultural Life in Anatolia in the Letters of Rashīd al-Dīn', 90.
47. Togan, 'References to Economic and Cultural Life in Anatolia in the Letters of Rashīd al-Dīn', 100.
48. On the founding of Sultaniyya, see Dāvūd ibn Muḥammad Banākatī,

Tārīkh-i Banākatī: Rawżat Ūlā al-Albāb fī Maʻrifat al-Tavārīkh wa-al-Ansāb, ed. Jaʻfar Shiʻār (Tehran, 1348 [1969]), 475; Qazvīnī/*TG*, 607.

49. Togan, 'References to Economic and Cultural Life in Anatolia in the Letters of Rashīd al-Dīn', 101.
50. Rashīd al-Dīn/*Jāmiʻ*, 1,060. Tūdā'ūn was the grandfather of Amīr Chūpān, eponym of the fourteenth-century Chubanid dynasty.
51. Ibn Bībī/Houtsma, 314; Ibn Bībī/Erzi, 666–7; Paul Wittek, 'Niğde', *Encyclopaedia of Islam*, 2nd edn (Leiden: Brill, 1993), 8:15–16. The Khatirids had governed the district of Niğde under the Saljūqs. Following the death of the Saljūq sultan Rukn al-Dīn Qilij Arslān in 663/1265, which marked the rise in power of the *parvāna*, Muʻīn al-Dīn Sulaymān, Sharaf al-Dīn Masʻūd b. Khaṭīr attempted to assert his own influence over the new sultan, the young Kay Khusraw III. His actions brought reprisals from the Mongols after the *parvāna*'s report of the situation.
52. Karīm al-Dīn Maḥmūd al-Āqsarāyī, *Musāmarat al-Akhbār va Musāyarat al-Akhyār*, ed. Osman Turan (Ankara: Türk Tarih Kurumu, 1993), 113.
53. Āqsarāyī, *Musāmarat al-Akhbār*, 113; Rashīd al-Dīn/*Jāmiʻ*, 1,101.
54. Ibn Bībī/Houtsma, 317; Rashīd al-Dīn/*Jāmiʻ*, 1,101.
55. Ibn Bībī/Houtsma, 317; Āqsarāyī, *Musāmarat al-Akhbār*, 114; Rashīd al-Dīn/*Jāmiʻ*, 68.
56. Cahen, *Pre-Ottoman Turkey*, 289. Ibn Bībī reports that Baybars turned back to Egypt because he had not been joined by the *parvāna* or any of the other Saljūq amirs, his animals were dying due to lack of forage, and because he feared an attack from the Ilkhanids. See Ibn Bībī/Houtsma, 317–18.
57. Rashīd al-Dīn/*Jāmiʻ*, 1,178.
58. Vaṣṣāf/*Tārīkh*, 264–5.
59. Rashīd al-Dīn/*Jāmiʻ*, 1,181–3. For an account of Ṭughān's final days, see also Āqsarāyī, *Musāmarat al-Akhbār*, 167–70.
60. Rashīd al-Dīn/*Jāmiʻ*, 1,198.
61. See Karl Jahn, 'Čao', *Encyclopaedia of Islam*, 2nd edn (Leiden: Brill, 1961), 2:14; Karl Jahn, 'Das iranische Papiergeld', *Archiv Orientalni* 10 (1938): 308–40. For an account of the *chao* experiment, see Bar Hebraeus, *The Chronography of Gregory Abû'l Faraj, the Son of Aaron, the Hebrew Physician Commonly Known as Bar Hebraeus Being the First Part of his Political History of the World*, trans. Ernest A. Wallis Budge (Oxford: Oxford University Press, 1932), 496–7.
62. Rashīd al-Dīn/*Jāmiʻ*, 1,192.
63. Rashīd al-Dīn/*Jāmiʻ*, 1,192; Vaṣṣāf/*Tārīkh*, 260.
64. Thomas T. Allsen, 'Changing Forms of Legitimation in Mongol Iran', in Gary Seaman and Daniel Marks (eds), *Rulers from the Steppe: State Formation on the Eurasian Periphery* (Los Angeles: Ethnographics Press, University of Southern California, 1991), 230.
65. Vaṣṣāf/*Tārīkh*, 278.
66. According to Vaṣṣāf, Āq Būqā was executed on Baydu's order; see Vaṣṣāf/

Tārīkh, 282. According to Rashīd al-Dīn, Āq Būqā escaped this initial purge and continued to oppose Baydu, fighting alongside Ghazan. However, later that year he was captured and killed in battle near Hashtrūd; see Rashīd al-Dīn/*Jāmi'*, 1,202.

67. Rashīd al-Dīn/*Jāmi'*, 1,136.
68. Rashīd al-Dīn/*Jāmi'*, 1,261.
69. Rashīd al-Dīn/*Jāmi'*, 1,263.
70. Rashīd al-Dīn/*Jāmi'*, 1,267.
71. Rashīd al-Dīn/*Jāmi'*, 1,270.
72. Rashīd al-Dīn/*Jāmi'*, 1,265.
73. Āqsarāyī, *Musāmarat al-Akhbār*, 190–2.
74. Rashīd al-Dīn/*Jāmi'*, 1,270.
75. Rashīd al-Dīn/*Jāmi'*, 1,271.
76. Rashīd al-Dīn/*Jāmi'*, 1,277.
77. Rashīd al-Dīn/*Jāmi'*, 1,282.
78. Rudi Paul Lindner has pointed out the correlation between the suppression of Sulaymish's revolt and the proliferation of mints striking silver coins in Anatolia in the year 699/1299, probably an effort by Ghazan Khan to win support from the Turkmans there who had joined with Sulaymish, by letting them benefit from the profits from the silver coinage. See Rudi Paul Lindner, 'How Mongol Were the Early Ottomans?', in Reuven Amitai-Preiss and David O. Morgan (eds), *The Mongol Empire and its Legacy* (Leiden: Brill, 1999), 287.
79. René Grousset, *The Empire of the Steppes: A History of Central Asia*, trans. Naomi Walford (New Brunswick, NJ, and London: Rutgers University Press, 1999), 387.

4

From Tribal Amirs to Royal In-laws

In the preceding chapter, an attempt was made to trace the ways in which several Jalayir tribal families participated in the formation of the Ilkhanate and subsequent political events up until approximately the year 1300 CE. Most branches of the Jalayir tribe, whose members had attained prominent positions in the political hierarchy, had been eliminated by the end of the seventh/thirteenth century. These included the family of the vizier Būqā, as well as a number of Jalayir amirs who had led revolts in Anatolia against Ghazan Khan in the first years after his accession in 694/1295. By the beginning of the eighth/fourteenth century, only the Ilgayid branch of the Jalayir retained a strong position in the Ilkhanate. During the reigns of the last three Ilkhan rulers, the descendants of Īlgā would ensure their influence in the post-Ilkhanid period through their status as royal in-laws. By marrying into the Ilkhanid royal family, the Ilgayids not only achieved a proximity to the channels of political power, but also established an important aspect of their legitimising ideology which would be developed during the reign of the Jalayirid sultan Shakh Uvays (r. 757/1356–776/1374).

The purpose of this chapter is to examine the relationship between the Ilgayid Jalayirs and the Ilkhanid dynasty during the last forty years of effective Hülegüid rule (694/1295–736/1335), and to analyse the factors which enabled the Jalayirid amir Shaykh Ḥasan to establish a personal base of political power after this period, and lay the groundwork for the establishment of an independent Jalayirid sultanate. These factors include the Jalayirs' role as royal in-laws (*gūrgān, güregen*) at a time when attempts were made to limit the influence of the amirs and centralise authority in the Ilkhanate; the position of Shaykh Ḥasan Jalayir as military governor in Anatolia; and the establishment of Shaykh Ḥasan's control of Arab Iraq and that region's Oyrat tribal military elite.

One of the most significant aspects of the reign of Ghazan Khan (694/1295–703/1304) was his programme of religious and economic reforms.[1] In an attempt to consolidate his power after coming to the throne, Ghazan issued a series of decrees designed to give the royal court and its cadre of fiscal administrators more control over economic affairs. Ghazan's programme was an attempt to reorganise what, from the point of view of the administrators, had been a weakening of the political and economic authority of the khan and a dispersal of wealth and resources among the amirs. In the fifteen or so years after Abaqa's death in 680/1282, factions of amirs had played a major role in determining who would accede to the royal throne, leaving the khan beholden to his military backers and weakening his authority. A sign of the authority of the amirs was the fact that a Mongol, Būqā Jalayir, had become the vizier, a position commonly held by individuals from the non-military classes and the non-Mongol population.[2]

Ghazan's reforms covered a wide range of issues, but can be categorised generally as addressing religious and economic concerns. Ghazan and all of his amirs converted to Islam as a group in 694/1295.[3] It has been a matter of debate in modern scholarship, as well as in Ghazan's own time,[4] whether his conversion was a sincere act of faith or a political calculation. While the complex issue of religious conversion will not be addressed here,[5] it seems clear that one aspect of Ghazan's acceptance of Islam was an attempt to align the Ilkhan amirs with him as members of a single religious community, and thus limit the threat of political opposition.

In terms of the state economy, Ghazan's reforms aimed to regularise tax collection, monetary measure and land tenure. These measures were designed to centralise control over sources of income in the imperial court, and eliminate multiple claims to land or property by amirs or other members of the local elite who may have been granted rights to them in the past. The architect of these reforms was Ghazan's vizier Rashīd al-Dīn, who represented those in the administrative corps who sought a return to an order based on a prosperous state supported mainly by agrarian sources of wealth and preserved by justice enforced by a powerful, independent ruler. This vision of the proper political order, which looked to past rulers such as the Sasanian king Anūshirvān, or the Abbasid caliph Hārūn al-Rashīd, as models for right government, contrasted with the traditional Mongol vision of the political economy, which relied upon wealth in the form of movable animal stock and tax on commercial traffic, which would be redistributed by a khan to his supporters (*nöker*s).

In the seventh/thirteenth century this conception of legitimate authority was combined with an ideology of Chinggisid royalism, whereby political legitimacy derived from one's patrilineal descent from Chinggis Qan. It was understood in the Ilkhanate, as well as in the Chaghatay khanate, Golden Horde and Yüan empire, that only a member of the Chinggisid royal family had the right to rule. Within each of these Mongol states, a secondary legitimising principle existed as well. In the Ilkhanate, this secondary legitimising principle was one's descent from Hülegü Khan, and it was generally accepted by both the amirs and the administrators that only a Hülegüid – that is, a member of the Ilkhanid royal family – had the right to rule. During Ghazan Khan's time, under the tutelage of Rashīd al-Dīn, the concept of Hülegüid legitimacy became combined with the concept of a strong, just, Islamic ruler in the pre-Mongol mould. Such a ruler's obligation was not to redistribute wealth to his *söker*s in exchange for political support, but rather to consolidate wealth and authority in order to maintain order and justice in his realm. As a result of this ideology and the practical reforms that accompanied it, the amirs began to play less of an independent role in the eighth/fourteenth century. This did not mean, however, that the non-Chinggisid military elite were not influential in this period. The amirs consolidated their own power within the context of the existing royal structure. There were fewer open challenges to the authority of the Ilkhans after Ghazan Khan than there were before him.

For the Jalayir (and, more specifically, the Ilgayid branch of the Jalayir), their proximity to the Ilkhanid royal family, and eventual incorporation into it, allowed them to emerge as contenders to inherit the Ilkhanid political legacy after 736/1335. In this period the Ilgayid Jalayirs became incorporated through marriage into the Ilkhanid royal family, and thus put themselves in close contact with the newly centralising Ilkhanate. The descendants of Īlgā Noyan Jalayir became powerful in the early fourteenth century as a result of these processes. Their interests became those of the Ilkhanid dynasty and the centralised state that was the aspiration of administrators like Rashīd al-Dīn. In other words, they became part of not a Jalayir tribal order, but the Ilkhanid dynastic order. This process is the subject of what follows in this chapter.

Amīr Ḥusayn Gūrgān, 694/1295–722/1322

Āq Būqā Jalayir was killed in 694/1295 after Geykhatu Khan was overthrown by his cousin Baydu. Āq Būqā had been closely associated with Geykhatu Khan before and during his reign (690/1291–694/1295), and when the coup that toppled him was carried out, Āq Būqā was one of the first amirs to be purged. Had Baydu continued to reign as khan, it is likely that Āq Būqā's family would not have been heard from again. However, the continuation of his family, and ultimately the rise of the Jalayirid dynasty, was tied directly to the rise of Ghazan and his overthrow of Baydu later in 1295. Āq Būqā had been married to Ghazan's sister, Öljetey

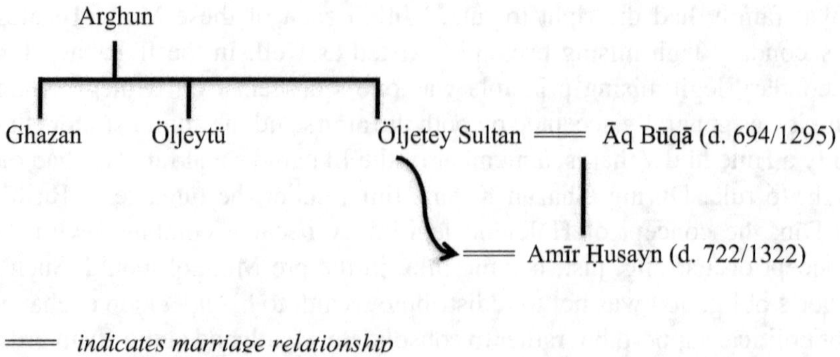

Figure 4.1 The Jalayir *güregen* relationship.

Sultan (Ūljatāy Sulṭān), and after Ghazan took the throne, he gave his sister to Āq Būqā's son, Amīr Ḥusayn.[6] Through this match Amīr Ḥusayn acquired the title *gūrgān* (*güregen*), or royal son-in-law.[7]

Little is known about Amīr Ḥusayn's life during the reign of Ghazan. However, after the accession of Öljeytü in 1304, Amīr Ḥusayn seems to have acquired a prominent status within the Ilkhanid ruling elite. He appears in the sources as one of the four *keshig* amirs under Öljeytü, along with Qutlughshāh, Amīr Chūpān and Pūlād Chīngsāng.[8] Vaṣṣāf records that when Öljeytü came to the throne, he put Amīr Ḥusayn in charge of overseeing the crown lands. A document dating from 704/1305 confirms that Amīr Ḥusayn had conducted an inspection of crown properties in the vicinity of Tabriz and Ardabil.[9] In addition to his administrative duties, Amīr Ḥusayn also took part in the major military campaign in Gilan in 1307–08.[10]

Amīr Ḥusayn seems to have enjoyed a great deal of favour from Öljeytü, as reflected in his provincial command appointment in the years after the Gilan campaign. Amīr Ḥusayn was assigned to Arran in 712 /1312–13, while Öljeytü personally led a campaign to secure the Syrian frontier with the Mamluks.[11] Arran was a major royal pasture region between the Kur and Aras rivers, in modern-day Azerbaijan. The Ilkhanid royal court made seasonal migrations from high-altitude summer pasture (*yāylāq*) in Persian Azarbayjan, near Tabriz, to lower-lying winter pasture (*qishlāq*) in the north, in Qarabagh and Arran. Here, Amīr Ḥusayn had the opportunity to host the khan in his own home near Tabriz,[12] as well as host, on at least one occasion, a banquet for a visiting Jochid envoy.[13] Thus, Amīr Ḥusayn's appointment to Arran meant proximity and access to Öljeytü Khan and the royal court, a privilege not afforded to amirs in more remote provinces.

Family ties helped to secure and reinforce this access to the royal court. Amīr Ḥusayn's daughter, Suyurghatmish, was married to Öljeytü. At the same time, Amīr Ḥusayn's wife, Öljetey Sultan, was the khan's sister. The marriage to Öljetey Sultan is particularly significant when we consider the statement by the historian Ahrī that Öljeytü virtually shared rulership with his sister.[14] Ahrī stresses that Öljeytü was very fond of Amīr Ḥusayn, both because he was a *güregen*, and because he was of eminent birth and always in his company.[15] Some of Ahrī's account can surely be considered designed to glorify the ancestor of his own Jalayirid patron, Sultan Shaykh Uvays. However, other sources confirm that Amīr Ḥusayn did enjoy a close and favourable relationship with Öljeytü. In addition, Amīr Ḥusayn also had a close relationship with Öljeytü's vizier, Khwāja Tāj al-Dīn 'Alī Shāh, who had previously attended to Amīr Ḥusayn in his own household.[16] His personal connections with the vizier, the khan and the khan's influential sister all ensured high status and influence for Amīr Ḥusayn and his family within the Ilkhanate.

However, the status of Amīr Ḥusayn and the other amirs was always dependent on the favour of the Chinggisid khan. This dependence became painfully clear to Amīr Ḥusayn in 1316 when Öljeytü died. His son and successor, Abū Sa'īd, was still a child, and real power in the Ilkhanate fell to Amīr Chūpān of the Sulduz tribe. Like the Jalayirid amirs before, Amīr Chūpān consolidated a great deal of power in Anatolia during Öljeytü's reign, and was the only Ilkhanid governor who had any success in compelling the tribes on the western frontier to submit to the khan's authority.[17]

From Öljeytü's death in 1316 to his own downfall in 1327, Amīr Chūpān was the de facto ruler of the Ilkhanate,[18] a status confirmed by titles bestowed by emissaries from the Yüan dynasty and China.[19] Like Amīr Ḥusayn, Amīr Chūpān had married into the Ilkhanid royal family.[20] He also forged family ties with the Ilgayid Jalayirs, marrying his daughter Baghdād Khātūn to Amīr Ḥusayn's son Shaykh Ḥasan. This three-way connection between the Ilkhanid royal household, the Ilgayid Jalayirs and the Sulduz-Chubanids would constitute the nexus of political power in the Ilkhanate through the 1340s.

The rise of Amīr Chūpān meant the marginalisation of Amīr Ḥusayn Jalayir, who was removed from his post in Arran to the eastern frontier.[21] Here, he spent the last years of his life attempting to subdue Chaghatayid incursions. Amīr Ḥusayn no longer had access to the heart of government at the Ilkhanid royal court, where he was replaced by Amīr Chūpān and his son Dimashq Khwāja as the real power behind the young Abū Sa'īd Khan.[22]

When Amīr Ḥusayn died in 1322, his son Shaykh Ḥasan became the

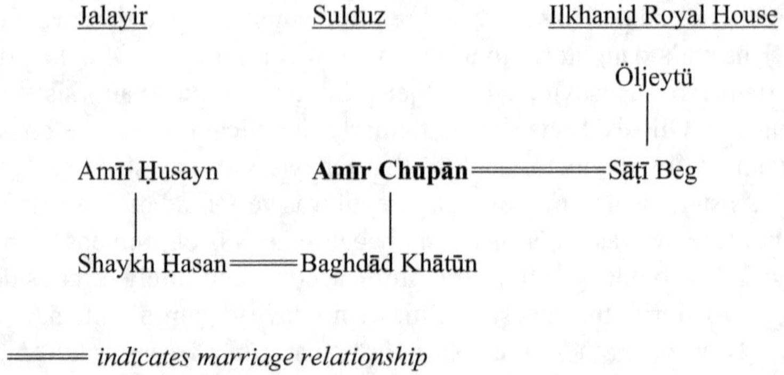

Figure 4.2 Amīr Chūpān at the centre of the Ilkhanid ruling elite.

head of the family of the Ilgayid Jalayirs. Shaykh Ḥasan was both a cousin of Abū Sa'īd and the son-in-law of Amīr Chūpān, the most powerful man in the Ilkhanate. Yet the sources tell us very little about Shaykh Ḥasan's life under Amīr Chūpān's rule. However, just five years later, Amīr Chūpān and his sons would be overthrown, and Shaykh Ḥasan would begin to lay the foundation of the independent Jalayirid dynasty. The remainder of this chapter is devoted to these developments, from the fall of Amīr Chūpān to the end of the reign of Abū Sa'īd.

Reaction against Amīr Chūpān's power came from the other Ilkhanid amirs and from a maturing Abū Sa'īd in 1327. The coup began when Dimashq Khwāja was accused of having an affair with Ṭughā Khātūn, a wife of the late Öljeytü Khan, and was executed.[23] Soon after, Amīr Chūpān was executed by the Kart malik of Herat. Amīr Chūpān's son, Tīmūr Tāsh, had fled to Damascus after his brother's execution, and was given refuge by the Mamluk sultan al-Nāṣir Muḥammad (3rd r. 1310–41). However, after Amīr Chūpān was killed, it was clear that the balance of power had shifted in Iran, and the Chubanids would find no refuge in the Mamluk sultanate. Tīmūr Tāsh was executed in Cairo in 1328.[24] Although

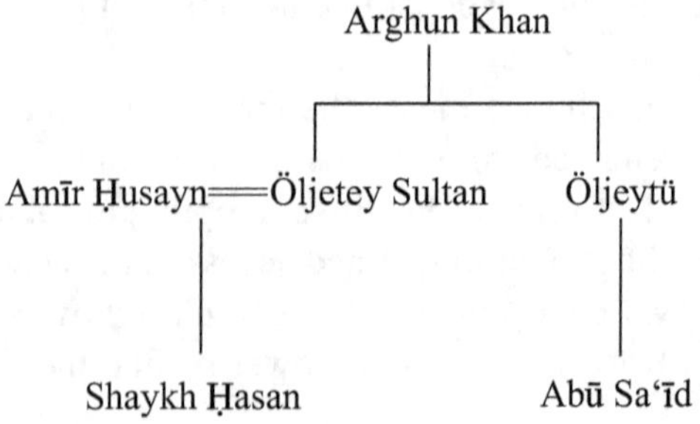

Figure 4.3 Shaykh Ḥasan Jalayir and the Ilkhanid royal house.

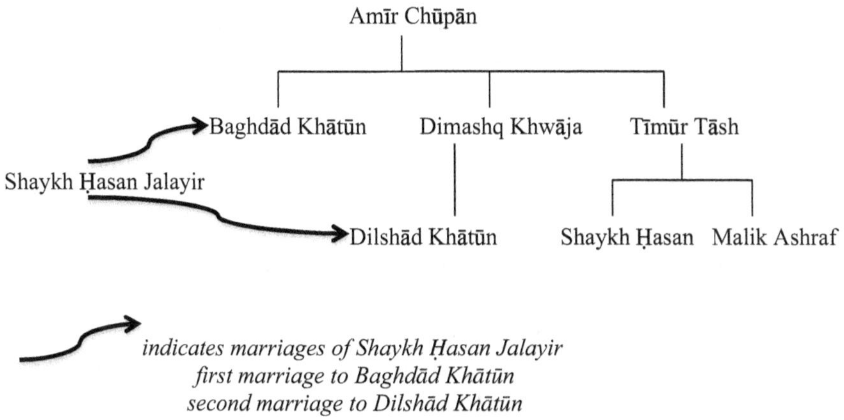

Figure 4.4 The Chubanids.

his head was sent to Abū Sa'īd,[25] the fact that he was not killed in Iran, combined with his own claims to have been the *mahdī*, or messiah in Islamic tradition, allowed for the rumour to spread that Tīmūr Tāsh was still alive. The consequences of this rumour will be discussed in the following chapter.

Shaykh Ḥasan Jalayir would eventually benefit from the fall of the Chubanids. However, he too suffered initially, when Abū Sa'īd forced him to give up his wife, Baghdād Khātūn, the daughter of Amīr Chūpān. The young Abū Sa'īd had long desired Baghdād Khātūn, but Amīr Chūpān had not allowed him to marry her, instead giving her to Shaykh Ḥasan. According to the Mamluk bibliographer Ṣafadī, Baghdād Khātūn controlled Abū Sa'īd with her beauty, and thus acquired great power.[26] Shabānkāra'ī writes that although the amirs, the vizier and other officials warned Abū Sa'īd that she had bad intentions and that women could not be trusted, they became inseparable.[27]

However much Baghdād Khātūn influenced Abū Sa'īd, it was clear that power had shifted back to the Ilkhanid house after 1327. Abū Sa'īd had come of age and was intent on preserving his personal authority against threats from the amirs. Shaykh Ḥasan Jalayir did not openly challenge his royal cousin, even after Abū Sa'īd took his wife from him. Instead, Shaykh Ḥasan replaced Tīmūr Tāsh in Anatolia, where he began acquiring his own power. His growing influence is evident in Mamluk records of messages sent to Egypt in 1328–29 from Shaykh Ḥasan, who was recognised as the khan's deputy (*nā'ib*).[28] The following year, Shaykh Ḥasan's envoys arrived in Egypt with greetings from the Mamluk sultan, independent of Abū Sa'īd's own messengers.[29] Shaykh Ḥasan is also named among the rulers of the day in the colophon of an Armenian manuscript dated 780 /1331, after Abū Saʻīd, and the Armenian and Georgian kings.[30]

Shaykh Ḥasan thus quickly established himself as a powerful local governor in Anatolia. As we have seen, the Anatolian frontier had traditionally been a place where Ilkhanid amirs could acquire personal power and launch rebellions against the central government. Shaykh Ḥasan's growing influence thus probably prompted Abū Saʻīd to take action against him. In 732/1331–32, a rumour was circulated in the royal household that Shaykh Ḥasan was conspiring with Baghdād Khātūn against the khan.[31] Only the intervention of Shaykh Ḥasan's mother, Öljetey Sultan, saved him from execution. Both of them were exiled to the Kemah fortress in Anatolia, while Baghdād Khātūn also suffered (*maflūk būd*) for her alleged part in the plot. However, after an inquiry, the rumour was judged to be false, and she returned to favour.[32] It seems that Shaykh Ḥasan was also cleared, for he resumed his role as chief amir in Anatolia around 732/1332.[33] He served with Abū Saʻīd's favour until the khan's death in 736/1335.[34]

Thus, by 1335, Shaykh Ḥasan Jalayir was at the top of the Ilkhanid military hierarchy. It is true that the fall of his father-in-law Amīr Chūpān and his family resulted in Abū Saʻīd Khan taking his wife Baghdād Khātūn. However, the fall of the Chubanids also meant that Shaykh Ḥasan became the chief amir, or *beylerbeyi*, of the Ilkhanate. His mother, the Chinggisid princess Öljetey Sultan, acted as his protector at court, while he received foreign envoys at his own household in Anatolia. Shaykh Ḥasan was enmeshed in the ruling household and dependent on the Ilkhanid royal house for his authority and status. However, the stability of the ruling hierarchy came to a crashing halt by the end of 1335 when Abū Saʻīd died without a suitable successor. The chaos that ensued would result in a scramble by Shaykh Ḥasan and several other members of the Ilkhanid ruling elite to preserve the Ilkhanid *ulūs*, with themselves at the top of the pile. As we will see in the next chapter, the period from 1335 to Shaykh Ḥasan's death in 1356 was a period of transition, as Shaykh Ḥasan struggled to assert himself as a protector of Ilkhanid sovereignty and eventually was resigned to the role of a local strongman in Baghdad.

Notes

1. See Bertold Spuler, *Die Mongolen in Iran: Politik, Verwaltung, und Kultur der Ilchanzeit, 1220–1350* (Berlin: Akademie-Verlag, 1955), 314–22.
2. As Jean Aubin has pointed out, Mongol amirs tended to take over the administration of the state following succession struggles. Būqā's vizierate was

followed by that of Shīktūr Noyan during Geykhatu's reign, and Nawrūz under Ghazan. See Jean Aubin, *Émirs Mongols et vizirs Persans dans les remous de l'acculturation* (Paris: Association pour l'Avancement des Études Iraniennes, 1995), 85.

3. Rashīd al-Dīn/*Jāmi'*, 1,255.
4. Rashīd al-Dīn's insistence on Ghazan's sincerity and complete impossibility of hypocrisy in his conversion perhaps implies some question of Ghazan's motives in his own time: 'It is not hidden from all the intelligent people that the Islam and faith of the *pādishāh* of Islam Ghāzān Khān was true and sincere, and free from the impurity of hypocrisy and laxity. For with his royal greatness and ability, and the perfection of his authoritative power, it is not imaginable that he was compelled or forced. With needlessness and independence, hypocrisy and suspicion are not possible.' See Rashīd al-Dīn/*Jāmi'*, 1,256. Charles Melville has pointed out that Rashīd al-Dīn was at pains to stress the sincerity of Ghazan's conversion. See Charles Melville, '*Pādishāh-i Islām*: The Conversion of Sultan Maḥmūd Ghāzān Khān', *Pembroke Papers* 1 (1990): 159.
5. For studies on conversion to Islam in the Mongol context, see Devin DeWeese, *Islamization and Native Religion in the Golden Horde* (University Park: Penn State Press, 1994); Judith Pfeiffer, 'Reflections on a "Double Rapprochement": Conversion to Islam among the Mongol Elite during the Early Ilkhanate', in Linda Komaroff (ed.), *Beyond the Legacy of Genghis Khan* (Leiden: Brill, 2006), 369–89; Judith Pfeiffer, 'Conversion Versions: Sultan Öljeytü's Conversion to Shi'ism (709/1309) in Muslim Narrative Sources', *Mongolian Studies* 22 (1999): 35–67.
6. It is not clear who Amīr Ḥusayn's mother was. There is no record of Āq Būqā's other wives. On the title *gūrgān*, see *TMEN*, 1:475–7 (no. 340).
7. Ahrī/*TSU*, (Persian text), 146; (English translation), 48.
8. Vaṣṣāf/*Tārīkh*, 468; Vaṣṣāf, *Taḥrīr-i Tārīkh-i Vaṣṣāf*, ed. 'Abd al-Muḥammad Āyatī (Tehran: Mu'assasa-yi Muṭāla'at va Taḥqīqāt-i Farhangī [Pizhūhishgāh], 1372 [1993]), 252; Abū al-Qāsim Qāshānī, *Tārīkh-i Ūljāytū*, ed. Mahin Hambly (Tehran, 1969), 8; Ḥāfiẓ Abrū/*ZJT*, 8. Shabānkāra'ī lists Amīr Ḥusayn third among the amirs after Amīr Chūpān and Pūlād. See Shabānkāra'ī/*Majma'*, 270.
9. Gottfried Herrmann, *Persische Urkunden der Mongolenzeit* (Wiesbaden: Harrassowitz Verlag, 2004), 84–5.
10. Ḥāfiẓ Abrū/*ZJT*, 16–17. On the Gilan campaign, see Charles Melville, 'The Īlkhān Öljeitü's Conquest of Gīlān (1307): Rumour and Reality', in Reuven Amitai-Preiss and David O. Morgan (eds), *The Mongol Empire and its Legacy* (Leiden: Brill, 1999), 73–125.
11. Vaṣṣāf/*Tārīkh*, 610.
12. Qāshānī, *Tārīkh-i Ūljāytū*, 83.
13. The banquet was a disaster, as the envoy insulted Amīr Ḥusayn's lineage. See Qāshānī, *Tārīkh-i Ūljāytū*, 175–6.

14. Ahrī/*TSU*, (Persian text), 148; (English translation), 50.
15. Ahrī/*TSU*, (Persian text), 149; (English translation), 51.
16. Qāshānī, *Tārīkh-i Ūljāytū*, 121.
17. Mehmed Fuad Köprülü, *Islam in Anatolia after the Turkish Invasion (Prolegomena)*, ed. and trans. Gary Leiser (Salt Lake City: University of Utah Press, 1993), 26.
18. See Charles Melville, *The Fall of Amir Chupan and the Decline of the Ilkhanate, 1327–1337: A Decade of Discord in Iran* (Bloomington: Indiana University, Research Institute for Inner Asian Studies, 1999); Charles Melville, 'Abū Sa'īd and the Revolt of the Amirs in 1319', in Denise Aigle (ed.), *L'Iran face à la domination mongole* (Tehran: Institut Français de Recherche en Iran, 1997), 89–120; Charles Melville, 'Wolf or Shepherd? Amir Chupan's Attitude to Government', in Julian Raby and Teresa Fitzherbert (eds), *The Court of the Ilkhans, 1290–1340* (Oxford: Oxford University Press, 1996), 79–93.
19. As Thomas Allsen has pointed out, in 724/1324 the Yüan emperor, after a recommendation from Abū Sa'īd, had issued an order to make Amīr Chūpān a 'commander unequalled in honour' and 'duke who assists the state'. Allsen has shown that these titles seem to be calques on the Islamic title *amīr al-umarā'*. See Thomas T. Allsen, 'Notes on Chinese Titles in Mongol Iran', *Mongolian Studies* 14 (1991): 33–4.
20. Amīr Chūpān married Öljeytü's daughter Dūlandī. When she died in 707 /1307–08, Amīr Chūpān was betrothed to his other daughter Sāṭī Beg. See Qāshānī, *Tārīkh-i Ūljāytū*, 7–8; Dāvūd ibn Muḥammad Banākatī, *Tārīkh-i Banākatī: Rawżat Ūlā al-Albāb fī Ma'rifat al-Tavārīkh wa-al-Ansāb*, ed. Ja'far Shi'ār (Tehran, 1348 [1969]), 473.
21. Amīr Ḥusayn may have been removed from Arran even before Öljeytü's death; Vaṣṣāf writes that he was in Baghdad at that time. See Vaṣṣāf/*Tārīkh*, 623.
22. Amīr Chūpān was grooming Dimashq Khwāja as his successor. An illustration of Dimashq Khwāja's position in the state is provided by Ibn Baṭṭūṭa, who arrived in Baghdad in 727/1327, coinciding with a visit by Abū Sa'īd to the city. He saw the khan and his vizier, Ghiyāth al-Dīn Muḥammad, on a boat on the Tigris. In front of them was Dimashq Khwāja who, Ibn Baṭṭūṭa wrote, held mastery over Abū Sa'īd (*al-mutaghallib 'alá abī sa'īd*). See Ibn Baṭṭūṭa, *Riḥlat Ibn Baṭṭūṭa: al-Musammā Tuḥfat al-Nuẓẓār fī Gharā'ib al-Amṣār wa-'Ajā'ib al-Asfār* (Miṣr: al-Maktaba al-Tijāriyya al-Kubrá, 1964), 1:143; Ibn Baṭṭūṭa, *The Travels of Ibn Baṭṭūṭa, A.D. 1325–1354*, trans. H. A. R. Gibb (Cambridge: Hakluyt Society at the University Press, 1971), 2:336–7.
23. Ibn Baṭṭūṭa, *Riḥla*, 1:144; Ibn Baṭṭūṭa, *The Travels of Ibn Baṭṭūṭa*, 2:337.
24. Ṣafadī/*A'yān*, 2:111–15.
25. Ṣafadī/*A'yān*, 2:115.
26. Ṣafadī/*A'yān*, 1:696.

27. Shabānkāra'ī/*Majma'*, 295: literally, 'he was with her in one garment, both stuck their heads out from one collar' (*bā vay dar yak jāma mī-būd har dū az yak garībān sar bīrūn karda*).
28. Maqrīzī/Ziyāda, 1:310.
29. Maqrīzī/Ziyāda, 1:320.
30. Avedis K. Sanjian (ed. and trans.), *Colophons of Armenian Manuscripts, 1301–1480: A Source for Middle Eastern History* (Cambridge, MA: Harvard University Press, 1969), 75.
31. Melville surmises that this accusation originated with rivals centred around Abū Sa'īd's mother, Ḥājī Khātūn. See Melville, *The Fall of Amir Chupan*, 35.
32. Ḥāfiẓ Abrū/*ZJT*, 142.
33. Ḥāfiẓ Abrū/*ZJT*, 142.
34. Ḥāfiẓ Abrū/*ZJT*, 142. In 1334, Abū Sa'īd appointed Mas'ūd Shāh, son of the Injuid governor of Fars, Maḥmūd Shāh, as Shaykh Ḥasan's deputy; see Ḥāfiẓ Abrū/*ZJT*, 143. Mas'ūd Shāh had been deported from Fars after his father's failed attempt to oust Abū Sa'īd's chosen governor there. Yet, he was soon released, and would remain an ally of Shaykh Ḥasan Jalayir in the years that followed. On the Injuids in Fars, see Shabānkāra'ī/*Majma'*, 296; J. A. Boyle, 'Īndjū', *Encyclopaedia of Islam*, 2nd edn (Leiden: Brill, 1971), 3:1,208.

5

Crisis and Transition (1335–56)

When Abū Sa'īd Bahādur Khan died on 13 Rabī' II 736/30 November 1335, in the words of Ḥāfiẓ Abrū, 'the kingdom without a sultan became like a body without a soul and a flock without a shepherd'.[1] With no clear heir to the throne, the Ilkhanid political order broke down. This had been an order based on the royal leadership of the Chinggisid dynasty descended from Hülegü, which by 1295 had settled in the line of Abaqa Khan. The centralising tendency that gained traction with Ghazan Khan and had reached its height under Abū Sa'īd had created strong ties between the Ilkhanid royal house and other military grandees, such as Shaykh Ḥasan, as well as administrative families such as that of Rashīd al-Dīn and Ghiyāth al-Dīn Muḥammad. The death of Abū Sa'īd put an end to the centralising dynamic of Ilkhanid politics. The period after 1335 was characterised by multiple power centres throughout the former Ilkhanid lands. An aspect of this development was the rise in power of the Oyrats, one of the few Mongolian tribes that still maintained its cohesion within the Ilkhanate in the fourteenth century. Although the Oyrats were initially led by their chief who attempted to take power after Abū Sa'īd's death, Shaykh Ḥasan ultimately became the lord of the Oyrat territories in Diyarbakr and northern Iraq. In this sense, Shaykh Ḥasan was a tribal chief; however, it was not the Jalayir, but the Oyrat tribe that came under his command in the 1340s. By the time of Shaykh Ḥasan's death in 1356, he was only one of several regional rulers, in control of the region from Khuzistan in the south to Diyarbakr in the north. However, he was unable to capture the real prize, which was Azarbayjan and its capital Tabriz.

This was also a period in which the notion of Chinggisid sovereignty seems to have lost some of its significance. Until the 1340s, amirs who attempted to claim the Ilkhanate for themselves generally offered their services to a Chinggisid puppet, who served to legitimise their bid for power. After the 1340s, however, local rulers had largely dispensed with Chinggisid pretenders and attempted to construct alternative ideological narratives. It would be Shaykh Ḥasan's son, Shaykh Uvays, who would develop this narrative most fully, after finally conquering Azarbayjan in the late 1350s.

The Death of Abū Sa'īd and Crisis in the Ilkhanate

Abū Sa'īd had no living male children. The only hope for the continuation of the dynasty was the unborn child of his wife Dilshād Khātūn. She was the daughter of Dimashq Khwāja b. Amīr Chūpān, and had become the favourite of Abū Sa'īd in the later years of his reign.[2] Her child would not be born until the following May, and in the intervening months various factions manoeuvred for position in the political vacuum.

One of these factions was led by Abū Sa'īd's vizier, Ghiyāth al-Dīn Muḥammad, the son of the vizier and historian Rashīd al-Dīn.[3] According to Shabānkāra'ī, at the time of Abū Sa'īd's death, the only grandees present at the *urdū* were Ghiyāth al-Dīn Muḥammad and the Injuid amir Sharaf al-Dīn Maḥmūd Shāh. The amir favoured a temporary ruler until all the amirs could convene and agree on a proper successor to Abū Sa'īd, and thus suggested that Öljeytü's daughter, Sāṭī Beg, act as regent in the interim.[4] However, Ghiyāth al-Dīn Muḥammad favoured a more permanent solution to what he regarded as an urgent problem, that is, a vacancy on the throne and an absence of royal authority in the Ilkhanate. Shabānkāra'ī demonstrates this point of view by quoting the vizier as saying:

> If we do this [enthrone Sāṭī Beg temporarily], an unspeakable uproar will arise. If rulership is not absolute (*mustaqill*), pain will reach the people of the country, and unlawful killing and plunder will be the price.[5]

Ghiyāth al-Dīn Muḥammad then revealed that Abū Sa'īd had designated as his successor a descendant of Tolui Khan, named Arpā, whom Abū Sa'īd had made a day labourer (*muyāvama'ī*), and who was currently working in the stables.[6] According to Ḥāfiẓ Abrū, Arpā was a descendant of Hülegü's brother, Arigh Böke, son of Tolui.[7] In the absence of a commonly recognised heir, Ghiyāth al-Dīn Muḥammad was free to designate Arpā as his own candidate to succeed Abū Sa'īd. The faction of Ghiyāth al-Dīn Muḥammad and Maḥmūd Shāh, along with Abū Sa'īd's mother and sister, Ḥājī Khātūn and Sāṭī Beg, conferred rulership on him the night that Abū Sa'īd died, and the next day, the *khuṭba* was given in his name, as Sultan Mu'izz al-Dunyā wa-al-Dīn Maḥmūd.[8] In an effort to enhance Arpā's legitimacy as the continuator of the Ilkhanid dynasty, he was married to Sāṭī Beg,[9] who, for the next several years, would become central to the political manoeuvring of the amirs. As an Ilkhanid princess, Sāṭī Beg represented the charisma of the Chinggisids, and thus became

Court faction:
Ghiyāth al-Dīn Muḥammad, supported Arpā, a descendant of Tolui
Sharaf al-Dīn Maḥmūd Shāh Īnjū, supported Sāṭī Beg, sister of Abū Sa'īd

Consensus eventually made for Arpā

Oyrat faction:
'Alī Pādshāh and Oyrat tribe, supported Mūsá, a descendant of Baydu

Figure 5.1 Factions following Abū Sa'īd's death.

an important symbolic figure as different parties attempted to claim that charisma for themselves.

The authority claimed by Arpā Khan and Ghiyāth al-Dīn Muḥammad was not recognised as legitimate throughout the Ilkhanid realm, however. In Anatolia, the amir Shaykh Ḥasan Jalayir refused to recognise Arpā Khan. Ghiyāth al-Dīn Muḥammad understood that this was a major obstacle to his plan, and warned the new khan that 'as long as [Shaykh Ḥasan's] opinion is not settled, nothing will be stable (*mumahhad*)'.[10]

Opposition to the regime of Ghiyāth al-Dīn and Arpā Khan also came from the Oyrat amirs who were led by 'Alī Pādshāh, Abū Sa'īd's maternal uncle.[11] 'Alī Pādshāh had two important advantages over the vizier and his Chinggisid protégé. First, he commanded the Oyrat tribal groups that resided in Mesopotamia, between Baghdad and Diyarbakr. The Oyrats were one of the few remaining cohesive tribal factions, and were mobilised frequently in the post-Ilkhan period. Second, 'Alī Pādshāh became the guardian of Dilshād Khātūn and her unborn child after she had fled to Baghdad after Abū Sa'īd's death.[12] It seems likely that 'Alī Pādshāh assumed that if she gave birth to a son, he would have an undisputed claim to the Ilkhanid throne. However, before the birth, 'Alī Pādshāh and the Oyrats raised their own Chinggisid protégé as their symbolic leader, a descendant of Baydu Khan named Mūsá.[13]

It is clear at this stage (c. 736/1336) that no military or political leader believed they could rule on their own terms without the prestige inherent in the family of Chinggis Qan. The fact that Arpā, a Chinggisid but not a Hülegüid, was enthroned raises the question of how important the secondary Ilkhanid dynastic dispensation was to the concept of legitimacy. Such a choice suggests that a more general Chinggisid descent was the primary requirement, although in Khurasan in the same period a descendant of Chinggis Qan's brother was recognised as khan. Such developments suggest that precise lineal proximity to the Ilkhans was not as important as a more broadly conceived Mongol prestige, where an appeal to the grandeur of the *altān urūgh* in its most general terms was the factor that lent legitimacy to political claims.[14]

The two contending factions of Arpā Khan and Ghiyāth al-Dīn Muḥammad on one side, and Mūsá Khan and ʻAlī Pādshāh on the other, met in battle in the spring of 736/1336.[15] Although the forces of Arpā and Ghiyāth al-Dīn Muḥammad greatly outnumbered the Oyrats, ʻAlī Pādshāh emerged victorious after two of Arpā's amirs defected, and after concocting a ruse which convinced both Arpā and Ghiyāth al-Dīn Muḥammad that the other had been defeated.[16] Tribal affiliation may have played a role in the defection of Arpā's troops to ʻAlī Pādshāh's side. According to Shabānkāra'ī, before the battle, Arpā's amir Akrunj had pledged his allegiance to ʻAlī Pādshāh and told him:

> Come with me, for your soldiers are all from among the Uyghur tribes (*qabā'il-i uyghūr*), and are of the same race (*hamjins*) as my *tūmān*. When it is the day of battle, we all will separate from Arpā's army.[17]

The connection between the Oyrats, who made up ʻAlī Pādshāh's army, and the Uyghur mentioned here is not entirely clear. However, Shabānkāra'ī makes it clear in his account of Akrunj's appeal to ʻAlī Pādshāh that there was some kind of affinity between the men they commanded. As a consequence of the Oyrat victory, Ghiyāth al-Dīn Muḥammad and his brother Pīr Sulṭān were captured and brought before ʻAlī Pādshāh. Ḥāfiẓ Abrū reports that ʻAlī Pādshāh wanted to spare them, but the other amirs pressured him to execute these sons of Rashīd al-Dīn.[18] The family's quarter in Tabriz (*rab'-i rashīdī*) was thoroughly plundered by the mob (*rind va awbāsh*).[19] Arpā Khan was also eventually captured and executed.[20]

ʻAlī Pādshāh had emerged as the dominant figure in the western Ilkhanid lands. Nine days after the battle with Arpā Khan and Ghiyāth al-Dīn Muḥammad, Dilshād Khātūn gave birth to a daughter, and the hope for the continuation of the male Hülegüid line was ended. ʻAlī Pādshāh attempted to rule through his Chinggisid protégé Mūsá Khan and his vizier, Jamāl Ḥājī b. Tāj al-Dīn ʻAlī Shīrvānī, but opposition to his regime soon emerged, finding a focus in Anatolia with Shaykh Ḥasan Jalayir. In the following section, we will examine the rise of Shaykh Ḥasan, his assumption of control over Oyrat-dominated Arab Iraq, and the establishment of Baghdad as the base of Jalayirid power.

Shaykh Ḥasan Jalayir and the Regionalisation of the Post-Ilkhan Period

Opposition to the Oyrat regime of ʻAlī Pādshāh formed part of a wider struggle over control of the frontier zone between the western Ilkhanid provinces of Anatolia, Diyarbakr and Arab Iraq, and the Mamluk sultanate. At the heart of this conflict was the control over the traditional migration corridor of the Oyrats, between their summer pastures in eastern Anatolia and their winter pastures in the area around Mosul.[21] These provinces were politically significant for two reasons. As the western edge of the Ilkhanid domains, they had served as a buffer against the Mamluk sultanate of Syria and Egypt, the Ilkhans' traditional rivals in the west. In addition, as home to the Oyrats, organised around their own tribal leadership, the region offered potential as a source of loyal military manpower.

The main opposition to the rule of ʻAlī Pādshāh and Mūsá Khan came from the amir Ḥājī Ṭaghāy, whose family had served as governors of the Ilkhanid province of Diyarbakr. His father, Sūtāy Akhtājī, was the head of a *tūmān* of troops in Diyarbakr from the beginning of Öljeytü's reign until his death in 732/1331–32.[22] According to Ṣafadī, when he died, control of Diyarbakr passed to ʻAlī Pādshāh.[23] Ḥājī Ṭaghāy and his family, who had hereditary claims to Diyarbakr, found themselves threatened from two sides after the rise of ʻAlī Pādshāh. Not only did they face pressure from the Oyrats in Iraq,[24] who sought to control Diyarbakr after Sūtāy's death, but they also faced pressure from the Mamluks, who sought to establish a secure eastern frontier. ʻAlī Pādshāh had offered this possibility to the Mamluk sultan al-Nāṣir Muḥammad, promising to turn Baghdad over to him and act as his deputy there in return for Mamluk aid against the sons of Sūtāy and Arpā Khan.[25] Ḥājī Ṭaghāy thus sought assistance from Shaykh Ḥasan Jalayir in Anatolia, and was soon joined by several other major amirs who opposed the Oyrat regime. Shaykh Ḥasan summoned a Hülegüid prince named Muḥammad from Tabriz, and crowned him sultan. After entrusting Anatolia to his deputy Eretna (Aratnā),[26] Shaykh Ḥasan set out for Tabriz with his following of amirs and the army of Rūm to confront ʻAlī Pādshāh.[27]

Thus Shaykh Ḥasan joined the scramble for power in the post-Abū Saʻīd Ilkhanate. He was in a good position and it is understandable that he would attract a large number of followers. According to the Mamluk chancery official al-ʻUmarī (d. 749/1349), Shaykh Ḥasan was the '*biklārī bik* [*beglerbeg*], or *amīr al-umarā*'', the same position held by Qutlughshāh under Ghazan Khan, and Amīr Chūpān under Öljeytü.[28] We may assume that he had a large number of troops under his direct command in Anatolia, the ‘right hand’ of the Ilkhanid *ulūs*. Since the death of the Saljūq sultan Mas‘ūd II at Konya in 702/1303, and further after the death of Amīr Chūpān in 727/1327, Ilkhan amirs in Anatolia had come to act with greater autonomy.[29] Such an increased regional independence was a common phenomenon in other regions of the Ilkhanate, which began to come under the control of local amirs and elite families. In Persian Iraq (‘Irāq-i ‘Ajam), the Injuids held sway, while the Muzaffarids emerged in Yazd and Kirman. At the same time, Ilkhan Iran became more profoundly divided between two spheres of political activity. In the west, the royal migration corridor between Sultaniyya and Tabriz in the south and Qarabagh, Arran and Mughan in the north became the centre of political gravity, and the area which all of the political contenders aspired to control.

During the rule of the Ilkhans, the city of Tabriz became the centre of imperial government and international trade, and a site for monumental architecture. Because of its administrative, economic and symbolic importance as the centre of Ilkhanid political authority, Tabriz remained the most important city in western Iran until the transfer of the Safavid capital to Qazvin in 955/1548. At the time of the conquests of Hülegü in Iran in the 650s/1250s, Tabriz was already an important city in the Mongol imperial administration. It became the site of the new central mint in 650 /1252–53, making it the financial centre of the entire Mongol empire.[30] After Hülegü’s arrival, it seemed as if Maragha would replace Tabriz as the Mongol capital in Azarbayjan. Hülegü constructed an observatory at Maragha, as well as a castle on the island of Shāhī near the city, where he was buried. According to Ḥamd Allāh Mustawfī Qazvīnī, Maragha was the original capital (*dār al-mulk*) of Azarbayjan before Tabriz.[31] However, during the reign of Hülegü’s grandson Arghun (r. 683/1284–690/1291), Tabriz began to emerge as the primary Ilkhanid city. Arghun built an urban quarter to the west of the city of Tabriz, at a place known as Sham (or Shamb), beginning around 689/1290. The building project included two palaces and a Buddhist temple, as well as a canal to encourage others to build houses in the area.[32] This quarter became known as Arghūniyya, and set the precedent for subsequent building and urban development by members of the Ilkhanid ruling elite. Arghun’s son Ghazan resided in the palace of Arghūniyya, and also began construction of his own tomb in the district of Sham in 696/1297. Around his mausoleum, Ghazan built a number of other public buildings, which came to form the core of the new suburb (*shahrcha*) of Ghāzāniyya.[33] These structures included a mosque, two madrasas, a hospice (*dār al-siyāda*), an observatory, a library, a council chamber (*dīvān-khāna*) and several baths.[34] The famous traveller Ibn Baṭṭūṭa camped outside Tabriz at the suburb of Sham during the reign of Abū Sa'īd, and described its madrasa and *zāviya* where food was provided to travellers.[35]

The Ilkhan rulers were not the only patrons of urban development in Tabriz. On the heights northeast of the city at a place called Valīyān Kūh the vizier and historian Rashīd al-Dīn built his own quarter, known as the Rab'-i Rashīdī.[36] Rashīd al-Dīn's son, Ghiyāth al-Dīn Muḥammad, who served as the vizier to Abū Sa'īd, continued building in the Rab'-i Rashīdī.[37] Another important building project was the Dimashqiyya quarter, built by Baghdād Khātūn, the wife of Shaykh Ḥasan Jalayir and Abū Sa'īd. The area was named for Baghdād Khātūn's brother, Dimashq Khwāja, who died in 727/1327 amid the downfall of the Chubanid family. Little trace remains of the Dimashqiyya quarter, which, according to a tenth/sixteenth-century source, was situated on the east side of the city.[38] Three sons of the Jalayirid sultan Shaykh Uvays were buried in the Dimashqiyya.[39]

In addition to these four districts, which represented the efforts of the Ilkhanid political elite to contribute to the flourishing of the religious and civic life of Tabriz, as well as to glorify their own memories, other building projects were undertaken in the city in the eighth/fourteenth century. One of the most important for the defence of the city was the extension of the city walls by Ghazan Khan in 702/1302–03,[40] an indication that Tabriz was growing at the turn of the eighth/fourteenth century. One of the major reasons for the urban growth during Ghazan's reign was probably the economic prosperity of the city as a centre of long-distance trade. The location of Tabriz on the east-west route that passed from Khurasan, through Qazvin, and into Anatolia to the Black Sea and Mediterranean ensured its importance as a centre for commercial traffic. Parallel to this, the cities of Baghdad and Basra suffered, due to the increased importance of Tabriz, as well as the growth of a commercial route to Hormuz that bypassed these cities and instead passed to the east through Iran.[41] In addition to economic decline, Arab Iraq suffered in terms of agricultural production following the Mongol invasions. This decline, which had begun in Abbasid times, was accelerated by the interruption of intensive cultivation that was only possible through a highly organised and co-ordinated administrative structure. At the same time, such a drop in production undermined the financial basis for any such centrally organised state, as had existed under the Sasanians and early Abbasids.[42]

The subsequent contraction of the economy in Arab Iraq due to the decline of commercial traffic and agricultural production helps to explain attempts by the Jalayirid amir Shaykh Ḥasan and Sultan Shaykh Uvays to extend their authority beyond Iraq into Azarbayjan. The growth of trade in Tabriz is reflected in another one of Ghazan's building projects, the

Ghāzāniyya market. Ibn Baṭṭūṭa was impressed by the size of this bazaar, as well as the quality of the items for sale, particularly the jewellery.[43] The Castilian envoy Clavijo, who passed through Tabriz some sixty years later, also commented on the great amount of merchandise and large number of merchants in the city.[44] Johannes Schiltberger, a Bavarian crusader and captive of Tīmūr, wrote that the ruler of Tabriz was wealthier than the most powerful Christian king, because so many merchants came to Tabriz.[45] Thus, during the eighth/fourteenth century, Tabriz was important for its role in regional and long-distance trade, and in periods of political instability in Azarbayjan, especially in the years 736/1335–744/1343, 753/1352–759/1358, and 786/1384–809/1406, Tabriz became a target and a prize for sultans and amirs who sought to profit from this trade.

In the eighth/fourteenth century, Tabriz remained the focus of political and economic life in western Iran, even after the death of Abū Sa'īd and the collapse of the political unity of the Ilkhanate. The successors to the Ilkhans continued to build in the city. The most important building of the Jalayirid period in Tabriz was the palace complex known as the *dawlat-khāna*. Built by Shaykh Uvays after his conquest of Azarbayjan in 759/1358, the *dawlat-khāna* served as the royal residence and home to the central government administration. Clavijo described the *dawlat-khāna* as a great palace, surrounded by a wall, with twenty thousand rooms.[46] The Qarāquyūnlū sultan Jahānshāh later built what became known as the new *dawlat-khāna* at a place called Ṣāḥib-Ābād during his reign (843/1439–872/1467).[47]

An important consequence of the disintegration of political unity in the Ilkhanate after 736/1335 was that the eastern Ilkhanid territory, particularly Khurasan, became significantly removed from the horizon of the factions competing for Azarbayjan, and developed along its own course. Of primary importance in Khurasan were the Kart maliks at Herat, the Shi'i-Sufi-*'ayān* condominium at Sabzavar, known as the Sarbadārs,[48] and the Mongol military elite under the leadership of Ṭaghāy Tīmūr Khan. As will be shown below, the Khurasanians made occasional contact with the western leaders, but for the most part Khurasan and Azarbayjan remained distinct political spheres until the rise of the Safavids in the tenth/sixteenth century. Even Tīmūr and his descendants, who conquered all of Iran and most of Anatolia, could not retain control over the west, which remained effectively ruled by the Jalayirids, followed by the Qarāquyūnlū and Āqquyūnlū Turkman confederations.

Shaykh Ḥasan's confrontation with 'Alī Pādshāh and the Oyrats was the first step in the establishment of Jalayirid control over the western regions. For Shaykh Ḥasan, however, the main issue may not have been a matter of seizing power for himself, but rather of limiting the personal power of 'Alī Pādshāh and ensuring consensus among the amirs. Before confronting 'Alī Pādshāh in battle, Shaykh Ḥasan called on 'Alī Pādshāh to give up his power and allow a sultan to be named by all the amirs. He appealed to the custom of their ancestors, and their background in a common Ilkhanid *ulūs*. This sentiment is recorded in Shabānkāra'ī's *Majma' al-Ansāb*, as well as the *Ẕayl-i Jāmi' al-Tavārīkh* of Ḥāfiẓ Abrū. In Shabānkāra'ī's version, Shaykh Ḥasan insists:

> In the *yāsā* of Chinggis Qan, when it comes to the affairs of royalty (*kār-i khāniyat*), war is not permitted. Why did the army of the *pādishāh* all fall into the hands of discord and ruin on the pretense of opposition between the amirs? 'Alī Pāshā is an *āqā*. Be patient, for I will arrive. Let the *āqā*s and *īnī*s and ladies hold a *quriltay* and establish someone from his lineage, and by him let us bring the dignity (*jāvir*) of Tolui and Hülegü nearer.[49]

Ḥāfiẓ Abrū's version reflects the same concern for the tradition of consensus lest order break down:

> We have all been in one *ulūs* and we know one another. The customs of the fathers and ancestors is clear. It is better that we all agree and seat a ruler on the throne who is deserving of the sultanate, and that everyone stays on his own path and custom.
>
> *Like this strife, that one seeks that which*
> *Brings discord throughout the land*
> *In order that unlawful* (nā-ḥaqq) *blood does not flow and the country remains flourishing and inhabited,*
> *The condition we give to you*
> *Is to either heed my words or suffer.*[50]

In both versions, Shaykh Ḥasan urges the amirs to agree to a convention of political acclamation (*quriltay*) in order to put an end to armed conflict and elect a ruler peacefully. The *quriltay* was a tradition of nomadic steppe politics, and had precedent in the Mongol empire going back to the assembly that named Chinggis Qan the ruler of all Mongols in 602/1206, although more often than not a *quriltay* was a symbolic confirmation of a single dominant contender for the throne, rather than an election among several candidates, and served as an occasion for members of the royal family and the amirs to gather and assert their voice in the collective political enterprise. The fact that a major *quriltay* had not been held for either Arpā or Mūsá Khan meant that Shaykh Ḥasan, the *amīr-i ulūs*, had not consented to these choices for political leadership, and was asserting what he assumed to be his traditional right to take part in the process of enthroning the new khan.

Although their accounts of Shaykh Ḥasan's message to the Oyrats are similar, Shabānkāra'ī and Ḥāfiẓ Abrū provide differing interpretations of his actual motives. According to the *Majma' al-Ansāb*, Shaykh Ḥasan's words were designed to lull the Oyrats into a false sense of security that would allow him to prepare his army from among the troops in Anatolia and Georgia.[51] Ḥāfiẓ Abrū, however, ascribes the cause of the conflict between Shaykh Ḥasan and 'Alī Pādshāh to the Oyrat amirs, who replied that 'we have taken the kingdom by the power of our own hands . . . [Shaykh Ḥasan] cannot deceive us with these fables (*afsānhā*)'.[52] The Oyrat position was that their rule was justified merely by the military force they were able to command. Contrary to this was Shaykh Ḥasan's appeal to the tradition of consensus and election of the ruler by all members of the military elite.

With the Oyrats' refusal to compromise, both sides prepared for military conflict. In the ensuing battle at Qarā Durra, near Ālādāgh, on 14 Dhū al-Ḥijja 736/24 July 1336, Shaykh Ḥasan's forces, referred to by Ḥāfiẓ Abrū as the Anatolians (*rūmī*), and the supporters of Muḥammad Khan (*muḥammadīyān*), defeated 'Alī Pādshāh and the Oyrat army.[53] Shaykh Ḥasan and Muḥammad Khan occupied Tabriz, the Ilkhanate's urban capital. Shaykh Ḥasan married Dilshād Khātūn, the former wife of Abū Sa'īd, in retribution for Abū Sa'īd's seizure of Baghdād Khātūn nine years earlier.[54] He also began to rebuild Tabriz, and returned the family of Rashīd al-Dīn to the vizierate, naming Khwāja Shams al-Dīn Zakarīyā to this office.[55] Now in control of eastern Anatolia and Azarbayjan, Shaykh Ḥasan had assumed the paramount position in the dissolving Ilkhanate. The continuing decentralisation and regionalisation of political power would make it impossible for Shaykh Ḥasan to reconstitute the united Ilkhanid *ulūs* with Muḥammad as khan, Shams al-Dīn Zakarīyā as vizier, and himself as *amīr-i ulūs*. Without a strong, commonly recognised ruler, and with the related increase in the power of local leaders of various social strata, Shaykh Ḥasan could not unite the whole of the Ilkhanid military to his banner.

For most of the next twenty years, until his death in 757/1356, Shaykh Ḥasan would face a number of challenges from competing regional powers, the most important of which was that of Shaykh Ḥasan Chūbānī, also known as Ḥasan-i Kūchak. The aim of Shaykh Ḥasan Jalayir in this period was to control Azarbayjan, while at the same time retaining his influence in Arab Iraq and eastern Anatolia. As time went on, it became apparent that the ideal of preserving the unity of the Ilkhanate as a single *ulūs* under the rule of a single Chinggisid khan was no longer a realistic possibility. During the period 736/1336–757/1356, Shaykh Ḥasan conducted a number of experiments with various Chinggisid princes in an effort to continue the Ilkhanid dynastic tradition, while he retained his own position as *amīr-i ulūs*. The descendants of Chinggis Qan were no longer in any position to rule; at the same time, the tribal contingents which had formed the basis of Mongol political culture before Chinggis Qan had been dismantled.

With these changing circumstances, the identity of the Jalayir as a group had also changed. The end of effective Ilkhanid rule represented the third phase in a process of reorganisation of the tribal groups, including the Jalayir, within the Mongol empire. In the first phase, they had been dispersed among Chinggis Qan's imperial army on a world scale at the start of the seventh/thirteenth century. The creation of the princely *ulūs*es reprioritised the meaning of one's tribal identity, and represented a second phase of reorganisation. For the Jalayir of the Ilkhanate, they were amirs of the *ulūs* first, and only secondarily members of a common tribe, although this tribal affiliation was remembered. In the third phase, the end of a realistic hope for a viable Ilkhan *ulūs* left an opening for new conceptions of political relationships and hierarchy. The old tribal structure could not be reconstituted after being so profoundly disrupted by the phenomenon of the Mongol world empire.[56] At the same time, neither a Sunni caliph nor a Chinggisid khan could be called on to fill the political void; in neither case could a suitable candidate be agreed upon after the end of both of those dynastic lines, in 656/1258 and 736/1335 respectively. Thus, the rise of the Jalayirid dynasty in the eighth/fourteenth century did not represent a reconstitution of tribal identity as the operative political mode.[57] Instead, the Jalayirids were a ruling family whose paternal heritage (Jalayir tribalism) and maternal heritage (Chinggisid royalism) had been the two former bases for political hierarchy among the Mongols, but were no longer viable. Nevertheless, their practical military and political strength allowed them to dominate much of the western Ilkhanid lands. This de facto authority at a time of ideological uncertainty contributed to fluid and changing notions of what legitimate political authority meant in the eighth/fourteenth century. At the height of Jalayirid power (757/1356–776/1374), Shaykh Ḥasan's son Shaykh Uvays would assume independent authority, deriving from a variety of ideological sources. However, during the period before Shaykh Uvays claimed royal authority for himself, Shaykh Ḥasan and his contemporaries attempted to rule in the name of Chinggisid puppet khans.

We have already mentioned Shaykh Ḥasan's enthronement of Muḥammad Khan, a descendant of Hülegü through his son, Möngke Temür.[58] Following his victory over the Oyrats led by 'Alī Pādshāh and

Mūsá Khan, Shaykh Ḥasan issued decrees to the Ilkhanid provinces declaring that the right of rulership belonged to him. However, theoretically, Shaykh Ḥasan served Muḥammad Khan, whose titles included 'the greatest sultan, king of kings of the inhabited quarter, lord of the necks of the populace, shadow of God in both worlds (*sulṭān al-a'ẓam, shāhanshāh-i rub'-i maskūn, mālik-i riqāb al-umam, ẓill allāh fī al-arḍayn*)'.[59] The authority of Muḥammad Khan was not recognised everywhere throughout the Ilkhanate, despite his lofty titles. Shaykh Ḥasan faced further opposition from a number of factions, including the Mongol leadership in the northeastern Iranian province of Khurasan.[60] The Khurasanian army, led by Shaykh 'Alī b. 'Alī Qūshchī, agreed to invade Azarbayjan, and chose a descendant of Chinggis Qan's brother Otchigin (Ūtikīn),[61] named Ṭaghāy Tīmūr, as their khan. In the spring of 737/1337 the Khurasanian forces occupied Sultaniyya, and threatened to oust Shaykh Ḥasan and Muḥammad Khan from Azarbayjan.[62] Faced with this invasion, Shaykh Ḥasan renewed his alliance with Sāṭī Beg, the daughter of Öljeytü and former wife of the short-lived Arpā Khan.

After being defeated by the Khurasanians, Mūsá Khan and his Oyrat followers joined them, and together they attacked Shaykh Ḥasan in Dhū al-Qa'da 737/June 1337 at Maragha.[63] Ṭaghāy Tīmūr retreated during the battle, and Shaykh Ḥasan defeated the combined Khurasanian-Oyrat army.[64] Both Mūsá Khan and Shaykh 'Alī were executed on the Feast of the Sacrifice (*'īd al-aḍḥá*). Soon after, Shaykh Ḥasan executed the rebellious amirs Īsan Qutlugh and Akrunj.[65] Although Shaykh Ḥasan continued to serve in the name of Muḥammad Khan, there was no doubt that he was the real power behind the throne.[66]

This victory had two important consequences for the position of Shaykh Ḥasan, and for the former Ilkhanid territory in general. First, the Khurasanian and Oyrat leadership had been eliminated. The Oyrats, who remained primarily in Iraq, would eventually come under the control of the Jalayirids. Second, although Ṭaghāy Tīmūr survived, Khurasan became even more isolated from political events in the west. Shaykh Ḥasan had consolidated his power in Azarbayjan, albeit for only a brief period. The following year he would be driven out of Azarbayjan by a resurgence of the other great family of Ilkhanid in-laws, the Chubanids.

The Jalayirid–Chubanid Rivalry

The Jalayirid–Chubanid rivalry would be the major theme of the remaining years of Shaykh Ḥasan's life, and would only be resolved after the final destruction of the Chubanids by an invasion from the Golden Horde in 758/1357. With the containment of the Oyrats and the Khurasanians, the conflict between Shaykh Ḥasan Jalayir and Shaykh Ḥasan Chūbānī over control of Azarbayjan would dominate events in western Iran and would shape the development of the contemporary political ideology. One aspect of this conflict was the competition between these two amirs for legitimacy through the khans they raised and supported. These khans were descended from various Chinggisid lines, with one exception. The Jalayirid–Chubanid rivalry was not a tribal conflict, a latent Jalayir-Sulduz feud in an eighth/fourteenth-century form, but instead was an attempt by two Ilkhanid amirs to reconstitute the Ilkhanid *ulūs*, albeit on a smaller scale, and reclaim their place within a political structure where practical affairs and symbolic legitimacy were firmly under their control.

The re-emergence of the Chubanids was led by Shaykh Ḥasan Chūbānī, the son of Tīmūr Tāsh (d. 728/1328) and grandson of Amīr Chūpān (d. 727 /1327). As mentioned above, Amīr Chūpān had been the *amīr-i ulūs* and virtual sovereign of the Ilkhanate until Abū Saʿīd engineered his removal and execution. The decade-long weakness of the Chubanid family allowed for the rise of Shaykh Ḥasan Jalayir in Anatolia, and his conquest of Azarbayjan in 737/1337. However, around this time, Shaykh Ḥasan Chūbānī hatched a plot to reclaim his family's prominence, which contributed to his reputation as a master of trickery.[67] He produced a certain Turk named Qarā Jurī, who had been the slave of one of his father's deputies, and claimed that he was in fact his father Tīmūr Tāsh.[68] It should be recalled that Tīmūr Tāsh had taken refuge in the Mamluk sultanate during the coup against Amīr Chūpān and his family, but was eventually executed on the order of Sultan al-Nāṣir Muḥammad.[69] However, Shaykh Ḥasan Chūbānī claimed that his father had survived, and had returned from Egypt and the *ḥājj* pilgrimage to assume the right of the Chubanids in the Ilkhanate.[70] Shaykh Ḥasan Chūbānī sent a message to Shaykh Ḥasan Jalayir announcing the return of his 'father'. Shaykh Ḥasan Jalayir was sceptical, and sent Tīmūr Tāsh's former chamberlain to ascertain the truth of the matter. Shaykh Ḥasan Chūbānī deceived (*bi-firīft*) the chamberlain, so that when he returned to Shaykh Ḥasan Jalayir, he confirmed that it was the real Tīmūr Tāsh.[71] Ḥāfiẓ Abrū reports that with this news, all of the Chubanids parted from Shaykh Ḥasan Jalayir and joined Shaykh Ḥasan Chūbānī and the false Tīmūr Tāsh. They were also joined by the Oyrats, who turned against the Jalayirid amir. The loss of these important troop contingents was a disastrous blow to Shaykh Ḥasan Jalayir. In the face of the Chubanids' superior force at Ālādāgh on 27 Dhū al-Ḥijja 738/16 July 1338, Shaykh Ḥasan Jalayir retreated, and his forces were defeated. His Chinggisid protégé Muḥammad Khan fell into the hands of the enemy and was killed. At this point, Shaykh Ḥasan Chūbānī suspected that Qarā Jurī, the false Tīmūr Tāsh, was plotting against him. He exposed him as a 'Turkman beggar, not Tīmūr Tāsh',[72] and abandoned him. Qarā Jurī went to Tabriz, but was routed there by Shaykh Ḥasan Jalayir, and eventually went to Baghdad with the Oyrats.[73]

Shaykh Ḥasan Jalayir thus found himself in an extremely weak position. He had lost much of his military backing, as well as his Chinggisid puppet khan, and had been driven out of Azarbayjan. He fled first to Sultaniyya, then further east to Qazvin. He returned to Sultaniyya after reaching a truce with the Chubanids in 739/late 1338.[74] Not only had he been driven out of Azarbayjan, but he had also lost his original base of operations in Anatolia, which was held by Shaykh Ḥasan Chūbānī's brother, Malik Ashraf. The Chubanids thus occupied the entire northwestern region of the former Ilkhanate, while Qarā Jurī and the Oyrats controlled Baghdad and Arab Iraq.

Shaykh Ḥasan Jalayir desperately needed a fresh source of military manpower if he hoped to retake what he had lost in the western provinces. For this, he looked to the east and the Khurasanians. Shaykh Ḥasan Jalayir recognised Ṭaghāy Tīmūr as khan, and invited him and his forces to invade. It is likely that Shaykh Ḥasan thought that he could control Ṭaghāy Tīmūr the way he had controlled Muḥammad Khan. However, when the Khurasanians reached Sultaniyya in mid-739/early 1339, Shaykh Ḥasan's followers resented their high-handed behaviour and resisted their leadership.[75] Needless to say, this did not help his position vis-à-vis the Chubanids.

Meanwhile, Shaykh Ḥasan Chūbānī was attempting to establish his own legitimacy in Arran and Azarbayjan by recognising Sāṭī Beg as *pādishāh*. Although it was fairly common for women to rule in the Mongol political context, they were usually the wives of deceased khans, who presided as regents or place-holders until a new male candidate could be enthroned at a *quriltay*.[76] It appears that Sāṭī Beg was at first more than a place-holder, and was intended by Shaykh Ḥasan Chūbānī to rule in her own right, lending legitimacy to his amirate. Sāṭī Beg was not an obscure and distant cousin of the main line of Ilkhan rulers, as Arpā, Mūsá and Muḥammad had been. She was the daughter of Öljeytü Khan, had been betrothed to Amīr Chūpān, and had been married to Arpā Khan. To further bolster his claims to legitimate authority, Shaykh Ḥasan Chūbānī named descendants of the two most important administrative families to the vizierate, Rukn al-Dīn Shaykhī Rashīdī, and Ghiyāth al-Dīn Muḥammad 'Alīshāhī.[77] Having taken Azarbayjan and installed as his allies representatives of the Ilkhanate's ruling elite, Shaykh Ḥasan Chūbānī turned to the

Khurasanians, who had been invited west by Shaykh Ḥasan Jalayir, and were threatening Chubanid rule.

Instead of going to war, Shaykh Ḥasan Chūbānī concocted another ruse, this time against Ṭaghāy Tīmūr Khan. He promised to turn the province of Arab Iraq over to the khan, in addition to the full support of his Chubanid followers, provided Ṭaghāy Tīmūr opposed Shaykh Ḥasan Jalayir.[78] However, when Ṭaghāy Tīmūr and the Khurasanian amirs arrived in Sultaniyya in the summer of 739–40/1339, Shaykh Ḥasan Chūbānī turned the tables. He revealed to Shaykh Ḥasan Jalayir the Khurasanians' pledge to himself, along with his own assurance to the Jalayir amir that 'you are my *āqā*, lord and kinsman'.[79] That is, Shaykh Ḥasan Chūbānī, by revealing the promises made to himself by Ṭaghāy Tīmūr, created a rift between the Khurasanians and Jalayirids. Shocked by Ṭaghāy Tīmūr's treachery, Shaykh Ḥasan Jalayir soundly rebuked him. The following day, Ṭaghāy Tīmūr and the Khurasanians returned to the east.[80]

Thus, by the summer of 739–40/1339, Shaykh Ḥasan Jalayir had lost Anatolia, Azarbayjan, and any possibility of Khurasanian military support. However, he came to dominate the lowlands west of the Iranian plateau, including Diyarbakr, Arab Iraq and Khuzistan, with his capital at Baghdad.[81] While it is not clear exactly how he was able to control these areas, it is likely that he had secured the loyalty of the Oyrats, who had dominated this region in the late Ilkhanid period. The Oyrats had lost their chief, 'Alī Pādshāh, in 736/1336, followed by subsequent elite allies, Mūsá Khan in 737/1337 and Qarā Jurī, the false Tīmūr Tāsh, in 738/1338. By the time Shaykh Ḥasan Jalayir had given up on Khurasanian support, he found new hope in Arab Iraq with the Oyrats. Here he crowned a new Chinggisid khan, a descendant of Geykhatu Khan named Jahān Tīmūr.[82]

By the summer of 740–41/1340, Shaykh Ḥasan Jalayir was ready to challenge the Chubanids again for control of Azarbayjan. Shaykh Ḥasan Chūbānī had become concerned that Sāṭī Beg was plotting against him, and enthroned a new khan, a descendant of Hülegü through his son Samat, named Sulaymān. The new Sulaymān Khan married Sāṭī Beg, thus keeping her symbolic presence at the court, but limiting her freedom to take independent action against Shaykh Ḥasan Chūbānī. In Dhū al-Ḥijja 740/June 1340, the Chubanid forces met Shaykh Ḥasan Jalayir and the armies of Diyarbakr, Arab Iraq and Khuzistan at the Jaghātū river in Azarbayjan. Once again, the Chubanids were victorious.[83] Shaykh Ḥasan Jalayir and Jahān Tīmūr retreated to Baghdad, and Shaykh Ḥasan Chūbānī took up residence in Tabriz.

Despite this defeat, Shaykh Ḥasan Jalayir did not give up his attempts to take back Azarbayjan. Although he had acquired considerable territory in upper Mesopotamia, including several major cities, including Baghdad and Mosul, Azarbayjan and the city of Tabriz remained his ultimate goal. Having been defeated in battle against the Chubanids in the summer of 740–41/1340, Shaykh Ḥasan Jalayir attempted a different strategy the following year. He had already attempted to make an alliance with the Mongol ruler in the east, Ṭaghāy Tīmūr Khan. Now, Shaykh Ḥasan looked to the west, and the Mamluks, for an alliance against Shaykh Ḥasan and the Chubanids. The Mamluks would naturally be concerned with the growth of Chubanid power in Azarbayjan and Anatolia, particularly considering that Shaykh Ḥasan Chūbānī's father had been killed on the orders of the Mamluk sultan al-Nāṣir Muḥammad. Furthermore, the millenarian aspect of Tīmūr Tāsh's claims to be the *mahdī*,[84] and the potential for militant religious calls for action among the tribal populations of the Mamluk frontier (as had happened with the appearance of Qarā Jurī, the false Tīmūr Tāsh), would give the Mamluks an interest in breaking Chubanid power in Tabriz.

Shaykh Ḥasan Jalayir had already sent a message to Sultan al-Nāṣir Muḥammad in 740/1339–40, requesting the Mamluk army be sent to Baghdad, Mosul and Persian Iraq, and for the sultan to broker an alliance between Shaykh Ḥasan Jalayir and Ḥājī Ṭaghāy, the son of Sūtāy Akhtājī and claimant to the Oyrat territories on the Mamluk-Ilkhanid frontier.[85] Such a move would involve both the Mamluks and Ḥājī Ṭaghāy in Shaykh Ḥasan Jalayir's struggle to oust the Chubanids from Azarbayjan. Shaykh Ḥasan Jalayir was thus willing to sacrifice his amirate in Baghdad and Diyarbakr in exchange for Azarbayjan. Ḥājī Ṭaghāy would certainly have demanded his family's traditional territory in Diyarbakr, while al-Nāṣir Muḥammad would be assured of a secure eastern frontier.

When a Mamluk representative arrived in Sultaniyya in 741/1341 to demand pledges of allegiances from Shaykh Ḥasan Jalayir and Ḥājī Ṭaghāy, Shaykh Ḥasan Jalayir repeated his request for the Mamluk army to be sent to the eastern lands (*bilād al-sharq*).[86] As security, Ḥājī Ṭaghāy sent his son, Barhashīn, and Shaykh Ḥasan Jalayir delegated Ḥājī Ṭaghāy's nephew, Ibrāhīm Shāh, to travel to Syria and make a show of the Jalayirids' and Sutayids' commitment to an alliance with the Mamluks. In Dhū al-Ḥijja 741/May 1341, Barhashīn and Ibrāhīm Shāh were received by al-Nāṣir Muḥammad in Aleppo. Here, the *qāḍī*s of Baghdad, Mosul and Diyarbakr presented oaths from Barhashīn and Ibrahīm Shāh, as well as from the people of those provinces, that they would be obedient to the Mamluk sultan. They also reported that the *khuṭba* had been given in the sultan's name in Baghdad, Mosul and Diyarbakr.[87] The mission was a success, and al-Nāṣir Muḥammad gave the order that the Mamluk army should be dispatched to them.[88]

It seemed that Shaykh Ḥasan Jalayir's diplomatic efforts had paid off. He had agreed to exchange Arab Iraq and Diyarbakr for Mamluk military support against Shaykh Ḥasan Chūbānī. However, the agreement soon broke down due to a series of events in the summer of 741–42/1341. Differing accounts are given by Ahrī, Ḥāfiẓ Abrū and Maqrīzī. According to Ahrī, the Jalayirids and Chubanids met in battle, and both sides fell back, with Shaykh Ḥasan returning to Baghdad.[89] Ḥāfiẓ Abrū writes that Shaykh Ḥasan Jalayir actually withdrew when he mistook the migration of a large number of Turks and Tajiks with their animals for the Chubanid army.[90] If this was true, it is understandable that the Jalayirid historian Ahrī might suppress it. After the Jalayirids' retreat, Shaykh Ḥasan Chūbānī dealt with the Jalayirids' ally Ḥājī Ṭaghāy. The Chubanid amir attacked Ḥājī Ṭaghāy after offering to make peace with him. After isolating Ḥājī Ṭaghāy, Shaykh Ḥasan Chūbānī appointed Ibrāhīm Shāh, his nephew, over the Sutayids (*sūtāyīyān*) in Diyarbakr.[91]

The question remains, however, why did the Mamluk army not arrive to aid Shaykh Ḥasan Jalayir and Ḥājī Ṭaghāy? The answer may rest with a report that reached al-Nāṣir Muḥammad from the governor (*ṣāḥib*) of Mardin.[92] This was the Artuqid governor of that city, al-Mālik al-Ṣāliḥ (r. 712/1312–765/1364). According to Maqrīzī, the dispatch from Mardin informed the sultan not to bother sending an army to Tabriz, for Shaykh Ḥasan Jalayir had sworn his allegiance to the Chubanids, and that the Jalayirids and Chubanids had written to Ḥājī Ṭaghāy saying that they would henceforth watch over the Euphrates as far as Syria.[93] In other words, the alliance between Shaykh Ḥasan Jalayir and Ḥājī Ṭaghāy had been broken, and the Mamluks could no longer count on the assistance of the Jalayirids. However, this is not the account given by Persian histories, which report Shaykh Ḥasan had retreated to Baghdad, either as a result of or before doing battle with Shaykh Ḥasan Chūbānī. What can account for this discrepancy?

It seems likely that Shaykh Ḥasan Chūbānī engineered a diplomatic move of his own to neutralise the threat of a Mamluk invasion of Azarbayjan. Ḥāfiẓ Abrū reports that after Shaykh Ḥasan Chūbānī had attacked Ḥājī Ṭaghāy, and began winning the Kurds and Sutayids of Diyarbakr to his side, he arrived at Mardin, where he received comfort and offerings of gifts from al-Mālik al Ṣāliḥ.[94] Shortly after this, Ḥāfiẓ Abrū reports that Shaykh Ḥasan Chūbānī appointed Ibrāhīm Shāh as governor of Diyarbakr in the place of his uncle, Ḥājī Ṭaghāy.[95] According to Ṣafadī, Ibrāhīm Shāh had married the daughter of the Artuqid governor of Mardin, al-Mālik al-Ṣāliḥ.[96] It seems possible that, while in Mardin, Shaykh Ḥasan Chūbānī may have promised al-Mālik al-Ṣāliḥ a place for his son-in-law Ibrāhīm Shāh as Chubanid governor of Diyarbakr in return for the favour of al-Mālik al-Ṣāliḥ sending word to the Mamluk sultan al-Nāṣir Muḥammad that there was no longer any need for Mamluk military intervention against the Chubanids. In this way, Shaykh Ḥasan Chūbānī would have broken the alliance between Shaykh Ḥasan Jalayir and Ḥājī Ṭaghāy, and kept the Mamluks from attacking Azarbayjan. At the same time, the Artuqid al-Mālik al-Ṣāliḥ would ensure the continuation of his family's influence in Diyarbakr. The Mamluks' failure to launch an invasion was probably also connected to the death of Sultan al-Nāṣir Muḥammad. He had been suffering from illness for some time, which the report from Mardin seemed to exacerbate. Maqrīzī and Ibn Taghrī Birdī write that news of peace between the Chubanids and Jalayirids so upset the sultan that he was afflicted with bloody diarrhoea.[97] He died just a few days later.

This incident in 741/1341 is significant for our overall assessment of the development of the Jalayirid ruling family and its relationship to the Ilkhanid political legacy in the years after Abū Sa'īd's death. It seems clear that Shaykh Ḥasan Jalayir, although unchallenged as amir in Baghdad and the western Ilkhanid provinces of Arab Iraq and Diyarbakr, was willing to exchange his control over that region for military aid from the Mamluks. His goal was the defeat of Shaykh Ḥasan Chūbānī and the Chubanids, and the establishment of Jalayirid rule in Azarbayjan. The major Ilkhanid economic and political centre of Tabriz represented the seat of Ilkhanid political authority. As long as the Chubanids continued to rule there, they could continue to designate sultans like Sulaymān Khan to rule as heirs to the Ilkhans. With this privilege came power and prestige for the entire Chubanid family; several sons of Amīr Chūpān and Tīmūr Tāsh shared in the commonwealth that Shaykh Ḥasan Chūbānī had built. The Chubanids had reclaimed their position as the power behind the Ilkhanid throne, which had been established by Amīr Chūpān Sulduz and had ended in 727/1327 when Abū Sa'īd asserted his personal authority and the top military position in the state passed to Shaykh Ḥasan Jalayir. After being foiled in his attempts to forge alliances with the Khurasanians and the Mamluks, Shaykh Ḥasan Jalayir must have had to resign himself to his role as amir of a provincial capital, and not kingmaker for the heir to the Ilkhanid throne. He dismissed his Ilkhanid protégé, Jahān Tīmūr, in 740/1340 or 1341, and henceforth did not raise his own candidate for the sultanate.

For the remainder of Shaykh Ḥasan Jalayir's life, he ruled over Baghdad, clashing occasionally with the Chubanids. The leader of the Chubanids after 744/1343 was another son of Tīmūr Tāsh named Malik Ashraf. He earned a reputation as a capricious and cruel ruler, who brought Azarbayjan to ruin. He enthroned his own puppet khan, named Anūshirvān, who was not a Hülegüid but was described instead as being from the race of the *kāvīyān*.[98] The name *kāvīyān* refers to the figure of Kāvah from the *Shāh-nāma*, a blacksmith who led the people of Isfahan against Zahāk, under the banner of his apron, the *dirafsh-i kāvīyān*.[99] This reference and the name Anūshirvān itself suggest that Malik Ashraf sought to appeal to the tradition of pre-Islamic Iranian kingship as the ideological foundation of his rule in Azarbayjan. This was a sign that by the mid-740s/1340s, Chinggisid ancestry was no longer seen as a prerequisite for legitimate rule, a development that would allow Shaykh Ḥasan Jalayir's son Shaykh Uvays to establish a Jalayirid dynasty in Azarbayjan in the late 750s/1350s.

The decades of the 740s/1340s and 750s/1350s were particularly difficult in Baghdad, where years of warfare since 736/1335 had led to scarcity of food and high prices.[100] As a result, many people left Baghdad for Syria and Egypt in the mid-740s/1340s.[101] These hardships were made worse by the fact that plague broke out in Azarbayjan and Arab Iraq in 747/1347. Malik Ashraf attempted to escape the plague in Azarbayjan that year by sending his army to attack Baghdad. Faced with a Chubanid attack, Shaykh Ḥasan wanted to flee Baghdad, but he was convinced (or forced) to stay and fortify the city by his wife Dilshād Khātūn, and other members of the urban elite.[102]

Dilshād Khātūn's influence over her husband Shaykh Ḥasan Jalayir, demonstrated in the account above, was discussed by Ṣafadī in his *A'yān al-'Aṣr*. Ṣafadī wrote that Dilshād Khātūn had seduced Shaykh Ḥasan with her beauty, and controlled him completely. Ṣafadī referred to her as the governor (*al-ḥākima*) of Iraq, whom no one opposed.[103] Dilshād Khātūn's great influence over the government in Baghdad, and the fact that her father was Dimashq Khwāja b. Amīr Chūpān, leads one to question whether the territory between Baghdad and Diyarbakr could be considered an extension of the Chubanid state in the western Ilkhanid provinces. Ṣafadī mentions that it was rumoured after Dilshād Khātūn's death in 752 /1351 that Shaykh Ḥasan had poisoned her because he was worried she was too inclined toward her cousin, Malik Ashraf.[104]

While it is impossible to know whether Shaykh Ḥasan actually did murder his wife, there was evidence he remained wary of Chubanid intrigue. In 751/1350–51, he wrote to the Mamluk sultan al-Nāṣir Ḥasan warning him not to trust Chubanid envoys who brought greetings and salutations to Cairo, for Malik Ashraf had sent them as spies to learn the orders of the Mamluk army, and that he planned to take over Egypt and Syria.[105] Perhaps Shaykh Ḥasan only sought to disrupt a possible alliance between al-Nāṣir Ḥasan and Malik Ashraf, but the potential for Chubanid intrigue, both in Cairo and in Baghdad, probably seemed a dangerous possibility to Shaykh Ḥasan Jalayir, especially when his Chubanid rivals were also his in-laws.

Shaykh Ḥasan Jalayir lived for five years after the death of Dilshād Khātūn. He made no further attempts to capture Azarbayjan, nor did he promote any other Hülegüid puppet khans. Shaykh Ḥasan's capital of Baghdad had undergone war, scarcity and disease during his rule. Many people left the city for refuge in Mamluk Syria and Egypt. When Shaykh Ḥasan died, almost a century after Hülegü's conquest of Baghdad, the former caliphal capital was a shadow of its former glory. The Ilkhanate had raised Tabriz and Sultaniyya to the status of imperial cities and major commercial centres. However, Tabriz itself underwent hardships similar to those in Baghdad in the 740s/1340s and 750s/1350s, including the outbreak of plague. This was compounded by what the sources describe as the capricious and ruinous administration of Malik Ashraf. In the coming years, Tabriz would be conquered several times, including by Shaykh Ḥasan's son Shaykh Uvays, who founded a Jalayirid dynasty as heir to the Ilkhanate in the traditional imperial centre.

Shaykh Ḥasan Jalayir had failed to take back the heart of the Ilkhanid territory of Azarbayjan. Instead, he found himself in control of the Oyrat heartland. Until the end of his life, his goal would be to recapture Azarbayjan. However, the amirate he founded in Baghdad, as well as around Mosul and Diyarbakr, would lead to new political networks that would establish the upper Tigris region as a coherent political zone. Although Shaykh Ḥasan did not succeed in claiming Azarbayjan and the economic and political centre of the Ilkhanate, it can be argued that Shaykh Ḥasan, as successor to the traditional Oyrat migration corridor between Diyarbakr and Arab Iraq, was heir to the Sutayids in the frontier region between Iran and the Mamluk sultanate. While this provided Shaykh Ḥasan with a large territorial domain, and a significant military force composed mainly of Oyrat tribesmen, the Jalayirid amirate fell short of the prestige that accrued to the Chubanid lands to the north. Chubanid rule in Azarbayjan and its capital city of Tabriz by Malik Ashraf b. Tīmūr Tāsh was the focus of post-Ilkhanid historical writing in Persian after 736 /1335. That is, the prestige of the former Ilkhan imperial centre was the focus of history in the post-Abū Saʿīd period, rather than any one ruling family. Little mention of Shaykh Ḥasan Jalayir is made in Persian histories for the years after 744/1343. The Jalayirid amirate was given more attention by Mamluk historians writing in Arabic, for whom Baghdad and Diyarbakr retained their interest as part of the Mamluks' eastern frontier.

An attempt has been made in this chapter to analyse the factors that enabled Shaykh Ḥasan Jalayir to establish a basis for a Jalayirid dynastic state in the mid-eighth/fourteenth century. The emergence of the Jalayirids was not a consequence of 'retribalisation' of pre-Ilkhanid Jalayir groups, but rather a combination of circumstances related to the relationship of the Ilgayid branch of the Jalayir to the Ilkhanid royal family in the early eighth/fourteenth century. The marriage of Amīr Ḥusayn to princess Öljetey Sultan established close ties with the royal court in a period when attempts were being made by the central administration to limit the power and influence of the amirs. In addition, the establishment of a power base in Anatolia after the fall of Amīr Chūpān gave Amīr Ḥusayn's son Shaykh Ḥasan a distinct advantage when central authority collapsed after 736/1335. Shaykh Ḥasan's position as *amīr-i ulūs*, and his independent power base on the western frontier, enabled him to challenge rival regional power brokers and eventually assume control of Arab Iraq and the Oyrat tribal elements which formed the military elite in that region. Although Shaykh Ḥasan did not declare his own political independence,[106] instead ruling through a series of Chinggisid protégés, the base he established in Baghdad provided a launching pad for his son Shaykh Uvays's conquest of Azarbayjan and an attempt to reconstitute the Ilkhanate in the west, with its centre in Tabriz, under the independent authority of the Jalayirid sultans. The historical and ideological aspects of this development constitute the focus of the following two chapters.

Notes

1. Ḥāfiẓ Abrū/*ZJT*, 143.
2. Charles Melville, 'Delšād K̲ātūn', *Encyclopaedia Iranica*, ed. Ehsan Yarshater (London and New York: Routledge and Kegan Paul, 1996), 7:255; Ṣafadī/*A'yān*, 2:355.
3. Peter Jackson and Charles Melville, 'Ğīāt̲ al-Dīn Moḥammad', *Encyclopaedia Iranica*, ed. Ehsan Yarshater (London and New York: Routledge and Kegan Paul, 2001), 10:598.
4. Shabānkāra'ī/*Majma'*, 293.
5. Shabānkāra'ī/*Majma'*, 293.
6. Shabānkāra'ī/*Majma'*, 294.
7. Ḥāfiẓ Abrū/*ZJT*, 145.
8. Shabānkāra'ī/*Majma'*, 294; Ḥāfiẓ Abrū/*ZJT*, 145.
9. Ḥāfiẓ Abrū/*ZJT*, 147.
10. Shabānkāra'ī/*Majma'*, 299. Arpā countered, asking what the problem was (*chih ghamm*), since he and Ghiyāth al-Dīn Muḥammad controlled the original capital (*takht-gāh-i aṣlī*) and the royal army (*lashkar-i sulṭānī*).

11. 'Alī Pādshāh was the brother of Abū Sa'īd's mother, Ḥājī Khātūn Oyrat. See Dāvūd ibn Muḥammad Banākatī, *Tārīkh-i Banākatī: Rawżat Ūlā al-Albāb fī Ma'rifat al-Tavārīkh wa-al-Ansāb*, ed. Ja'far Shi'ār (Tehran, 1348 [1969]), 473.
12. Ḥāfiẓ Abrū/*ZJT*, 148.
13. Ḥāfiẓ Abrū/*ZJT*, 149. Shabānkāra'ī seems to indicate that Mūsá was not named khan officially until after 'Alī Pādshāh's defeat of Arpā Khan and the vizier Ghiyāth al-Dīn Muḥammad. He also mentions that Mūsá was in fact 'Alī Pādshāh's second choice for khan. The first, a silk maker (*sha'r-bāfī*) from Baghdad, introduced 'Alī Pādshāh to a boy who he said was descended from Baydu Khan. After discerning signs of 'princeliness' (*pādishāhzādagī*) in the lad, he enthroned him as Mūsá Khan. See Shabānkāra'ī/*Majma'*, 301–2.
14. Marshall Hodgson writes of the broad concept of 'Mongolism', an appeal to the greatness of Mongol imperial power, founded partly on a new consciousness of power on a world scale, as the prevalent political ideology between the Nile and the Oxus in the eighth/fourteenth and ninth/fifteenth centuries. See Marshall G. S. Hodgson, *The Venture of Islam, Volume 2: The Expansion of Islam in the Middle Periods* (Chicago: University of Chicago Press, 1974), 404–5.
15. Shabānkāra'ī records the date as 17 Ramaḍān 736/29 April 1336. Ḥāfiẓ Abrū has 27 Ramaḍān 736/9 May 1336.
16. Shabānkāra'ī/*Majma'*, 301; Ḥāfiẓ Abrū/*ZJT*, 149.
17. Shabānkāra'ī/*Majma'*, 300.
18. Ḥāfiẓ Abrū/*ZJT*, 149.
19. Ḥāfiẓ Abrū/*ZJT*, 151.
20. Ḥāfiẓ Abrū/*ZJT*, 151. Arpā Khan was turned over to the family of Maḥmūd Shāh Īnjū to be executed in retaliation for Maḥmūd Shāh's death.
21. Faruk Sümer, *Kara Koyunlular (Başlangıçtan Cihan-Şah'a kadar)*, I. Cilt (Ankara: Türk Tarih Kurumu Basımevi, 1962), 33.
22. Ṣafadī/*A'yān*, 2:487. In the correspondence erroneously attributed to Rashīd al-Dīn, Sūtāy is referred to as commander of the army of Diyarbakr, as well as in charge of the Ilkhanids' *tūmān-i yaka* (*yeke tümeni*), or the ruler's elite (*khāṣṣ*) army. See Rashīd al-Dīn Fażl Allāh Hamadānī, *Mukātabāt-i Rashīdī*, ed. Muḥammad Abarqūhī and Muḥammad Shafī' (Lahore: University of the Punjab Oriental Publications, 1945), 17: *amīr sutāy va ḥājī ṭaghay kih umarā-yi tūmān-i yaka'and.* See also Zeki Velidi Togan, 'References to Economic and Cultural Life in Anatolia in the Letters of Rashīd al-Dīn', trans. Gary Leiser, in Judith Pfeiffer and Sholeh A. Quinn (eds), in collaboration with Ernest Tucker, *History and Historiography of Post-Mongol Central Asia and the Middle East: Studies in Honor of John E. Woods* (Wiesbaden: Harrassowitz, 2006), 98.
23. Ṣafadī/*A'yān*, 2:487.

24. Claude Cahen has characterised Sūtāy's son, Ḥājī Ṭaghāy, as the chief Oyrat who represented the principal surviving military force of the Mongol regime in upper Mesopotamia in the 730s/1330s. See Claude Cahen, 'Contribution à l'histoire du Diyār Bakr au quatorzième siècle', *Journal Asiatique* 243 (1955): 76. However, his conflict with 'Alī Pādshāh and the Oyrats, according to Ḥāfiẓ Abrū, was based on the 'ancient hatred (*kīna*) which he held in his heart for Amīr 'Alī Pādishāh and the Oyrat tribe'. Because of this, he 'raised his head in opposition to them. He committed all of his efforts to eradicating that tribe.' See Ḥāfiẓ Abrū/*ZJT*, 152. Due to this conflict of Ḥājī Ṭaghāy with the Oyrat tribe, and based on this reason given by Ḥāfiẓ Abrū, it seems safe to say that Ḥājī Ṭaghāy, and hence his father Sūtāy, were not from the Oyrat tribe.
25. Maqrīzī/Ziyāda, 1:397.
26. İsmail Hakkı Uzunçarşılı, *Anadolu Beylikleri ve Akkoyunlu, Karakoyunlu Devletleri* (Ankara: Türk Tarih Kurumu Basımevi, 1988), 156.
27. Ḥāfiẓ Abrū/*ZJT*, 152.
28. *Das Mongolische Weltreich: Al-'Umarī's Darstellung der mongolischen Reiche in seinem Werk Masālik al-Abṣār fī Mamālik al-Amṣār*, ed. and trans. Klaus Lech (Wiesbaden: Otto Harrassowitz, 1968), 93 (Arabic text); 153 (German translation). Al-'Umarī writes that there were four *umarā' al-ulūs*, the *beglerbegi*, and three others, known as the *umarā' al-qūl* ('amirs of the centre'). For a description of the 'four bey system' in the context of the Golden Horde, see Beatrice Forbes Manz, 'The Clans of the Crimean Khanate, 1466–1532', *Harvard Ukrainian Studies* 2 (1978): 282–309; Halil İnalcık, 'The Khan and the Tribal Aristocracy: The Crimean Khanate under Sahib Giray I', *Harvard Ukrainian Studies* 3/4 (1979–80): 445–66; Uli Schamiloğlu, 'Tribal Politics and Social Organization in the Golden Horde', PhD dissertation, Columbia University, 1986.
29. René Grousset, *The Empire of the Steppes: A History of Central Asia*, trans. Naomi Walford (New Brunswick, NJ, and London: Rutgers University Press, 1999), 387. Grousset suggests that had it not been for the fall of Amīr Chūpān's family, they would have established an independent sultanate in Anatolia, which would have hindered the expansion to the Ottomans. See Grousset, *The Empire of the Steppes*, 388.
30. Judith Kolbas, *The Mongols in Iran: Chingiz Khan to Uljaytu 1220–1309* (London and New York: Routledge, 2006), 153.
31. Qazvīnī/*Nuzhat*, 75.
32. Muḥammad Javād Mashkūr, *Tārīkh-i Tabrīz tā Pāyān-i Qarn-i Nuhum-i Hijrī* (Tehran: Anjuman-i Āsār-i Millī, 1352 [1973]), 449.
33. Qazvīnī/*Nuzhat*, 76.
34. Mashkūr, *Tārīkh-i Tabrīz*, 472.
35. Ibn Baṭṭūṭa, *Riḥlat Ibn Baṭṭūṭa: al-Musammā Tuḥfat al-Nuẓẓār fī Gharā'ib al-Amṣār wa-'Ajā'ib al-Asfār* (Miṣr: al-Maktaba al-Tijāriyya al-Kubrá, 1964), 1:147; Ibn Baṭṭūṭa, *The Travels of Ibn Baṭṭūṭa,* A.D. *1325–1354*,

trans. H. A. R. Gibb (Cambridge: Hakluyt Society at the University Press, 1971), 2:344.

36. Qazvīnī/*Nuzhat*, 521.
37. Qazvīnī/*Nuzhat*, 76.
38. Mashkūr cites the *Rawḍat al-Jinān* of Ḥāfiẓ Ḥusayn Karbalā'ī. See Mashkūr, *Tārīkh-i Tabrīz*, 596.
39. Mashkūr, *Tārīkh-i Tabrīz*, 596.
40. Mashkūr, *Tārīkh-i Tabrīz*, 470.
41. Janet L. Abu-Lughod, *Before European Hegemony: The World System* A.D. *1250–1350* (Oxford: Oxford University Press, 1989), 197.
42. Hodgson, *The Venture of Islam*, 2:389–90.
43. Ibn Baṭṭūṭa, *Riḥla*, 1:147; Ibn Baṭṭūṭa, *The Travels of Ibn Baṭṭūṭa*, 2:344–5.
44. Ruy Gonzalez de Clavijo, *Embassy to Tamerlane, 1403–1406*, trans. Guy Le Strange (London: George Routledge & Sons Ltd, 1928), 152.
45. Johannes Schiltberger, *The Bondage and Travels of Johann Schiltberger: A Native of Bavaria, in Europe, Asia, and Africa, 1396–1427*, ed. P. Bruun, trans. J. Buchan Telfer (New York: Burt Franklin, 1970; reprinted from London: Hakluyt Society, 1879), 44.
46. Clavijo, *Embassy to Tamerlane*, 152.
47. Mashkūr, *Tārīkh-i Tabrīz*, 597.
48. The Sarbadārs did not formally declare themselves independent of the Ilkhanate, as evidenced by their coinage, until 748/1347–48. Until this time, they attempted only to assert their autonomy against the local military elite. See John Masson Smith, Jr, *The History of the Sarbadār Dynasty, 1336–1381* A.D. *and its Sources* (The Hague: Mouton, 1970), 68.
49. Shabānkāra'ī/*Majma'*, 303.
50. Ḥāfiẓ Abrū/*ZJT*, 152.
51. Shabānkāra'ī/*Majma'*, 303.
52. Ḥāfiẓ Abrū/*ZJT*, 152–3.
53. Ḥāfiẓ Abrū/*ZJT*, 153; Shujā'ī/*Tārīkh*, 1:6. According to the *Majma' al-Ansāb*, 'Alī Pādshāh was dispatched on the field by Shaykh Ḥasan's own son, Ilkān Noyan. See Shabānkāra'ī/*Majma'*, 304.
54. Ḥāfiẓ Abrū/*ZJT*, 153–4.
55. Ḥāfiẓ Abrū/*ZJT*, 154. Khwāja Shams al-Dīn Zakarīyā was the son-in-law and nephew of Ghiyāth al-Dīn Muḥammad b. Rashīd al-Dīn.
56. Beatrice Forbes Manz uses two criteria to distinguish tribal from non-tribal groupings: (1) possession of a corporate name and identity, and (2) existence of an internal political structure able to supply the leadership of a tribe from within it. See Beatrice Forbes Manz, 'The Ulus Chaghatay Before and After Temür's Rise to Power: The Transformation from Tribal Confederation to Army of Conquest', *CAJ* 27 (1983): 85. Although the corporate name of the Jalayir was remembered, it seems that the political structure that existed to supply the leadership was not that of the Jalayir tribe, but that of the Ilkhanid dynastic state.

57. İsenbike Togan has suggested that the eighth/fourteenth century witnessed a 'retribalization' following the expansive phase of the Mongol army of conquest. Tribalism, once the dynamic social element, was pushed to the background as a 'reserve identity' in the seventh/thirteenth century, as all tribes came to identify their interests with the larger imperial enterprise. See İsenbike Togan, *Flexibility and Limitation in Steppe Formations* (Leiden: Brill, 1998), 12–13. However, it is important to emphasise that the pre-imperial tribes were not reconstituted in their former structure, but took on new forms. Togan argues that in the post-Chinggisid era, the tribes, rather than displaying structural differences and fighting among themselves for different goals, became more uniform entities which attempted to establish themselves around a centre in the person of a khan. See Togan, *Flexibility and Limitation*, 146.
58. Ḥāfiẓ Abrū/*ZJT*, 152; Maqrīzī/Ziyāda, 1:404.
59. Shabānkāra'ī/*Majma'*, 305.
60. Ḥāfiẓ Abrū writes that the amir 'Alī Ja'far was the catalyst for the Khurasanian invasion of Azarbayjan; see Ḥāfiẓ Abrū/*ZJT*, 154. However, Maqrīzī writes that Mūsá had fled to Khurasan after 'Alī Pādshāh was killed, and had joined with Ṭaghāy Tīmūr against Shaykh Ḥasan and 'the sons of Dimur Dāsh [Tīmūr Tāsh]'; see Maqrīzī/Ziyāda, 1:431.
61. Temüge Otchigin was Chinggis Qan's youngest brother. See *The Secret History of the Mongols*, §60.
62. Ḥāfiẓ Abrū/*ZJT*, 155.
63. Ḥāfiẓ Abrū/*ZJT*, 156; Shujā'ī/*Tārīkh*, 1:23.
64. Ḥāfiẓ Abrū/*ZJT*, 156.
65. Ḥāfiẓ Abrū reports that Īsan Qutlugh and Akrunj had embraced sufism (*dar z̲ī taṣavvuf raftand*) and had returned to Shaykh Ḥasan through the intervention of the *shaykh al-islām* Sharaf al-Dīn Darkanīzī. Shaykh Ḥasan first gave them full amnesty, due to the ruin and confusion in the kingdom, but in 738/1337–38 at the winter residence of Mughan, they were both executed. See Ḥāfiẓ Abrū/*ZJT*, 156.
66. As Shujā'ī recorded, Muḥammad Khan remained on the throne, while Shaykh Ḥasan governed the country (*al-bilād*); see Shujā'ī/*Tārīkh*, 1:23.
67. Ibn Taghrī Birdī, writing in the Mamluk sultanate, recorded in his biography of Shaykh Ḥasan Chūbānī that he was a 'sly fox (*dāhiya*), a master of trickery, cunning and deceit'. See Abū al-Maḥāsin Yūsuf Ibn Taghrī Birdī, *al-Nujūm al-Zāhira fī Mulūk Miṣr wa-al-Qāhira* (Cairo: Maṭba'at Dār al-Kutub al-Miṣriyya, 1929–72), 10:107.
68. Ḥāfiẓ Abrū/*ZJT*, 156.
69. Ṣafadī/*A'yān*, 2:115.
70. Ḥāfiẓ Abrū/*ZJT*, 156. According to Shujā'ī, the rumour was that Tīmūr Tāsh had not been executed in Egypt, but had escaped after switching places with his prison guard (*taḥayyala 'alá al-sijjān īlá an khalaṣa*). See Shujā'ī/*Tārīkh*, 1:36.

71. Ṣafadī writes that Tīmūr Tāsh's women and children also believed in this deception; see Ṣafadī/*A'yān*, 2:115. Ḥāfiẓ Abrū reports that Shaykh Ḥasan Chūbānī gave his mother to the false Tīmūr Tāsh; see Ḥāfiẓ Abrū/*ZJT*, 156.
72. Ḥāfiẓ Abrū/*ZJT*, 158.
73. Ḥāfiẓ Abrū/*ZJT*, 158.
74. Ḥāfiẓ Abrū/*ZJT*, 159.
75. Ḥāfiẓ Abrū writes that it became clear that the khan and his amirs were not acting of their own accord, but were under the influence of the Khurasanian administrators, led by Khwāja 'Alā' al-Dīn Muḥammad. He began a programme of confiscating the property of the peasants and other officials in western Iran, including Shaykh Ḥasan Jalayir's own hereditary possessions he had held since the time of Ghazan and Öljeytü. See Ḥāfiẓ Abrū/*ZJT*, 159–60.
76. Women who ruled the Mongol great qanate included Töregene Khatun, who reigned after the death of her husband Ögödey Qa'an, 639/1241–644/1246; Oghul Ghaymish, after the death of her husband Güyük Qa'an, 646/1248–649/1251; and Sorqaqtani Beki, the wife of Tolui Khan, who acted as the head of Tolui's personal *ulūs*, 630/1233–649/1251, and played a major role in establishing her sons Möngke, Qubilay and Hülegü in high positions in the empire. In the Chaghatay khanate, Orghina Khatun ruled after the death of her husband Qara Hülegü, 650/1252–658/1260.
77. They were, as their names indicate, descendants of the Ilkhanid viziers Rashīd al-Dīn (d. 718/1318) and Tāj al-Dīn 'Alīshāh (d. 724/1324).
78. Ḥāfiẓ Abrū/*ZJT*, 160.
79. Shabānkāra'ī/*Majma'*, 311. According to Ḥāfiẓ Abrū, Shaykh Ḥasan Chūbānī promised that once Ṭaghāy Tīmūr attacked the Jalayirids, or 'Īlkānīs', he would have him marry Sāṭī Beg and the kingdom would be theirs. However, when he received Ṭaghāy Tīmūr's written promise, Shaykh Ḥasan Chūbānī turned it over to Shaykh Ḥasan Jalayir. See Ḥāfiẓ Abrū/*ZJT*, 161.
80. Ḥāfiẓ Abrū/*ZJT*, 161.
81. Ibn Baṭṭūṭa reports that Shaykh Ḥasan captured the city of Hilla from Aḥmad b. Rumaytha, son of Abū Numayy, the amir of Mecca, who had seized the city after the death of Abū Sa'īd. See Ibn Baṭṭūṭa, *Riḥla*, 1:139; Ibn Baṭṭūṭa, *The Travels of Ibn Baṭṭūṭa*, 2:325.
82. Ḥāfiẓ Abrū/*ZJT*, 162.
83. Ḥāfiẓ Abrū credits the Chubanid victory to the bravery of Pīr Ḥusayn Chūbānī and the strength of the Chubanid left wing against the right flank of the 'Baghdādīs'.
84. Ṣafadī/*A'yān*, 2:111; Ibn Ḥajar/*Durar*, 1:307.
85. Maqrīzī/Ziyāda, 1:489.
86. Maqrīzī/Ziyāda, 1:517.
87. Maqrīzī/Ziyāda, 1:519.
88. Maqrīzī/Ziyāda, 1:519.

89. Ahrī/*TSU*, (Persian text), 168; (English translation), 68.
90. Ḥāfiẓ Abrū/*ZJT*, 163.
91. Ḥāfiẓ Abrū/*ZJT*, 165.
92. Maqrīzī/Ziyāda, 1:521.
93. Maqrīzī/Ziyāda, 1:521.
94. Ḥāfiẓ Abrū/*ZJT*, 165.
95. Ḥāfiẓ Abrū/*ZJT*, 165.
96. Ṣafadī/*A'yān*, 1:64.
97. Maqrīzī/Ziyāda, 1:522; Ibn Taghrī Birdī, *al-Nujūm al-Zāhira*, 9:162.
98. Qazvīnī/*ZTG*, 35; Ḥāfiẓ Abrū/*ZJT*, 176.
99. 'Kāwah', *Encyclopaedia of Islam*, 2nd edn (Leiden: Brill, 1976), 4:775.
100. Ismā'īl b. 'Alī Abū al-Fidā', *al-Mukhtasar fī Akhbār al-Bashar*, ed. Muḥammad Zaynahum Muḥammad 'Azab (Cairo: Dār al-Ma'ārif, 1998), 166; Ṣafadī/*A'yān*, 2:192; Ibn Ḥajar/*Durar*, 2:9.
101. Ṣafadī/*A'yān*, 2:192.
102. Qazvīnī/*ZTG*, 42.
103. Ṣafadī/*A'yān*, 2:355.
104. Ṣafadī/*A'yān*, 2:356; Melville, 'Delšād K̲ātūn', 255.
105. Maqrīzī/Ziyāda, 2:821.
106. Shaykh Ḥasan continued to use only the title *ulūs beg* that he had held under Abū Sa'īd. See John Masson Smith, Jr, 'Djalayir, Djalayirid', *Encyclopaedia of Islam*, 2nd edn (Leiden: Brill, 1962), 2:401.

6

Shaykh Uvays and the Jalayirid Dynasty

This chapter examines the political history of the reign of the Jalayirid sultan Shaykh Uvays (757/1356–776/1374). This period witnessed several developments in the dynamics of power and authority in the former Ilkhanid realm. The most significant developments were the Jalayirid conquest of Azarbayjan, Shaykh Uvays's claiming of independent royal authority, and the elimination of the Chubanids as contenders for the Ilkhanid throne. The eighteen-year reign of Shaykh Uvays represents the height of the Jalayirid dynasty's political power, and a critical turning point between the disappearance of the Chinggisid Ilkhans and the rise to power of Tīmūr and his descendants at the end of the eighth/fourteenth century. While this chapter focuses primarily on a chronological analysis of political events during Shaykh Uvays's rule, the following chapter addresses the ideological aspects of his assertion of independent authority as heir to the Ilkhanid tradition.

Shaykh Uvays and the Jalayirid Re-conquest of Azarbayjan

Shaykh Uvays was born in 743/1342–43[1] to Shaykh Ḥasan and Dilshād Khātūn, the daughter of Dimashq Khwāja Chūbānī and Tūrsun Khātūn. Tūrsun Khātūn was the granddaughter of Aḥmad Tegüder Khan through his daughter Kūnjak Khātūn.[2] With the exception of some basic genealogical information and panegyric found in the Jalayirid chronicle *Tārīkh-i Shaykh Uvays*, all of the Persian narrative sources for the period of Shaykh Uvays's life were written by Timurid historians, including Zayn al-Dīn Qazvīnī, Ḥāfiẓ Abrū and Mu'īn al-Dīn Naṭanzī. These histories are supplemented by a number of non-narrative sources, including land grant documents, court poetry and a major *inshā'* manual.

Shaykh Ḥasan Jalayir died in Rajab 757/July 1356 and was succeeded by his son Shaykh Uvays. Ḥāfiẓ Abrū commemorated his accession with these lines:

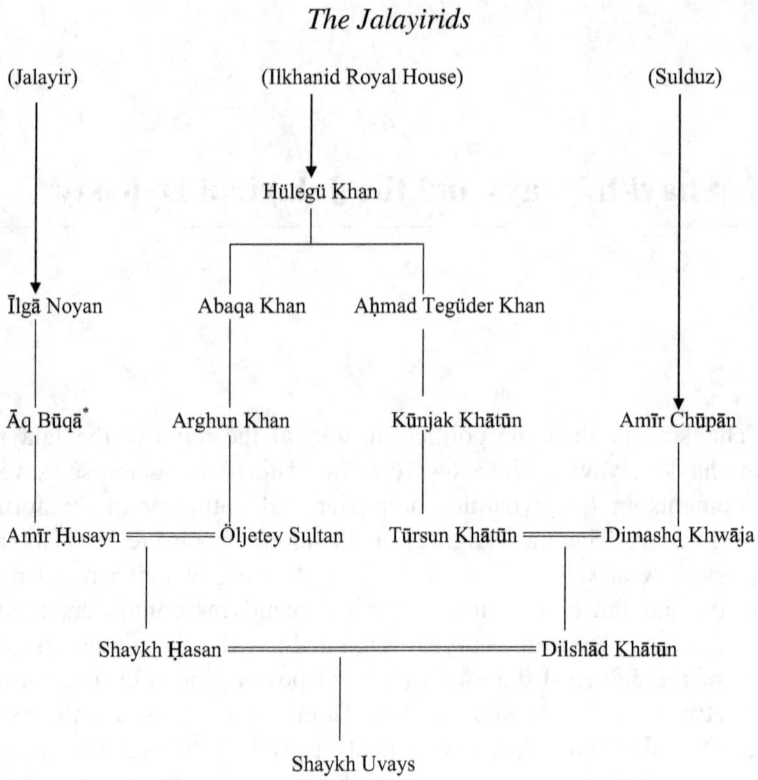

**Āq Būqā married Arghun Khan's daughter Öljetey Sultan. When he died in 694/1295, Öljetey Sultan married Āq Būqā's son Amīr Ḥusayn.*

Figure 6.1 The ancestry of Shaykh Uvays.

In the month of Rajab of the year 757
By the consent of the people and by the favour of the creator
The Khusraw of the face of the earth, by right
Sat upon the throne of sultans in the capital of Iraq
Lord of the sultans of the age, Shaykh Uvays
The absolute refuge and support of the kings of the world[3]

If Shaykh Uvays appears as a glorious ruler in Timurid historical memory, such a legacy seemed far from certain when he succeeded his father in 757/1356. At this time he ruled Arab Iraq, with nominal control over Diyarbakr, which remained a zone of conflicting political loyalties. Azarbayjan, eastern Anatolia and Persian Iraq remained under the control of the Chubanid Malik Ashraf b. Tīmūr Tāsh and his puppet ruler Anūshirvān. Malik Ashraf also sought to extend his influence in Diyarbakr, forming a union with the Artuqid governor of Mardin, al-Malik al-Ṣāliḥ (r. 712/1312–765/1364).[4] In this same year, Mubāriz al-Dīn Muḥammad Muẓaffarī deposed the Injuid governor in Fars, and took over that province.[5] The Muzaffarids came to control much of central and southwest Iran, and the cities of Yazd and Shiraz. Mubāriz al-Dīn Muḥammad took the title of caliph, with the *laqab* al-Mu'taḍid bi-Allāh, *nā'ib-i amīr al-mu'minīn*.[6]

The political situation changed abruptly in 758/1357 when the khan of the Jochid *ulūs*, Jānī Beg, invaded Azarbayjan and toppled the regime of Malik Ashraf Chūbānī. According to the narrative sources, the invasion was prompted by the maladministration of Malik Ashraf, which led many influential members of the population of Azarbayjan to seek refuge elsewhere.[7] Some of those who emigrated were prominent holy men, including the head of the young Ṣafaviyya order, Ṣadr al-Dīn Ardabīlī. Another of these shaykhs, Qāḍī Muḥyī al-Dīn Bardā'ī, travelled to the Jochid imperial capital at Saray (Sarāy Jīq), where he began preaching of the oppression of Malik Ashraf back in Tabriz.[8] Those present were so moved by the *qāḍī*'s account of Malik Ashraf's tyranny that they were driven to tears. Among those in his audience was the khan of the Golden Horde, Jānī Beg, who recognised the troubles in Azarbayjan as an opportunity for expansion of his empire. Since the time of Hülegü and the formation of the Chinggisid successor states in Iran and the Qipchaq steppe, the territory south of Darband had been a region of contention and conflict between the Ilkhans and their Jochid cousins. Jānī Beg realised that the growing dissatisfaction among the people, including the religious leadership in Tabriz, would enable him to finally conquer Azarbayjan and bring it into the Jochid political sphere. Indeed, this seems to have been the intention of Qāḍī Muḥyī al-Dīn Bardā'ī as well.

In 758/1357, Jānī Beg marched south toward Azarbayjan. Ahrī records an exchange of messages between Jānī Beg and Malik Ashraf, which provides an indication of one of the major sources of conflict in the Mongol successor states: the tension between the claims of the Chinggisid princes, and the independent political identities of the separate *ulūs*es. According to Ahrī, when Jānī Beg reached Shirvan, he sent the following message to Malik Ashraf:

> I am coming to take possession of the *ulūs* of Hülegü. You are the son of Chūbān whose name was in the *yarlīgh* of the four *ulūs*es. Today three *ulūs*es are under my command and I also wish to appoint you amir of the *ulūs*. Get up and come to meet me.[9]

Here in Ahrī's account, Jānī Beg promises to recognise Malik Ashraf's status as the grandson of Amīr Chūpān, the chief non-Chinggisid figure in the Ilkhanate during the time of Abū Sa'īd. However, as a member of the Chinggisid royal family, the Jochid khan was not willing to recognise the independent authority of Malik Ashraf or his puppet ruler.

Malik Ashraf's reported response reveals the point of view of the Chubanids and, certainly, the Jalayirids for whom Ahrī was writing:

> He [Jānī Beg] is the *pādishāh* of the *ulūs* of Berke, he has nothing to do with the *ulūs* of Abaqa [the Ilkhanate], for here the *pādishāh* is Ghazan and the amirate is mine.[10]

The clear message is that the Jochids have no business in the Ilkhanid territory, and that any claims they may make to Azarbayjan on the grounds of Chinggisid lineage are illegitimate.

The forces of Jānī Beg easily overran Azarbayjan and conquered Tabriz. Malik Ashraf was captured after fleeing to Khuy, and was paraded through the city of Tabriz, where people poured ashes on his head from the rooftops.[11] Jānī Beg sent him back to Jochid territory, but was convinced by Qāḍī Muḥyī al-Dīn and Kā'ūs, the Shīrvānshāh, that rebellion and disorder would only increase if Malik Ashraf was allowed to survive. Jānī Beg thus allowed Malik Ashraf to be killed on the road, and his head hung in the *maydān* in Tabriz.[12] With the Chubanid amir eliminated, and Azarbayjan under his control, Jānī Beg left his son Birdī Beg in the region with 50,000 men, and returned to Saray with Malik Ashraf's son, Tīmūr Tāsh, and daughter, Sulṭānbakht.[13]

Although Jānī Beg had successfully captured Azarbayjan, Jochid rule there was short-lived. Soon after Jānī Beg returned, he fell ill. Birdī Beg left Tabriz and eventually succeeded his father as khan.[14] The departure of the Jochids left a power vacuum that was filled by Akhī Jūq, a former amir of Malik Ashraf who had entered the service of Jānī Beg.[15] According to Zayn al-Dīn Qazvīnī, Akhī Jūq was able to attract a group of supporters by distributing jewels that he found sewn into a garment belonging to Malik Ashraf's sister. When Birdī Beg left Azarbayjan, Akhī Jūq marched to Tabriz, where he was welcomed by a large group of Malik Ashraf's followers.[16] The upheaval caused by the Jochid invasion created this opportunity for Akhī Jūq to seize power, although it is doubtful that many considered him as legitimate. Ahrī describes the period after the Jochid departure as the period of the 'cunning' of Akhī Jūq (*shaṭārat-i akhī jūq*).[17] This derogatory characterisation contrasts with the way Ahrī recorded the reigns of the previous Chubanids in Azarbayjan, whom he considered legitimate.[18] Part of the dissatisfaction toward Akhī Jūq seems to have been related to his continuation of Malik Ashraf's exploitative fiscal policies.[19]

The departure of the Jochids and the emergence of a former amir as ruler in Tabriz was enough to convince Shaykh Uvays that the time was ripe for the Jalayirids' return to Azarbayjan. In Ahrī's history, Shaykh Uvays's conquest of Azarbayjan is of tremendous significance, for it signals the real beginning of the reign of Shaykh Uvays.[20] This event is described in the following way in the *Tārīkh-i Shaykh Uvays*:

> There was a rumor of the imperial banners and an auspicious constellation which spread in the world, and that the sun of the sultanate would rise from Baghdad and this darkness of oppression of Azarbayjan would set. By the ray of light of its justice the world would be brightened, and the star of its mercy would illuminate the surface of hearts with color and fragrance. From the stronghold of the saints [Baghdad], the greatest king of kings, the ruler of Islam, Sultan Shaykh Uvays, set out to struggle and fight with the oppressors and the depraved.[21]

In the battle that took place in Sha'bān 759/August 1358[22] near Sītāy mountain, the Jalayirid forces defeated what remained of the Chubanid supporters.[23] Although Akhī Jūq escaped, Shaykh Uvays entered Tabriz and took up residence at the complex of Rashīd al-Dīn (*'imārat-i rashīdī*).[24] A decree issued by Shaykh Uvays in Dhū al-Qa'da 759/ October 1358, confirming the tax revenues to be paid to a dervish lodge in Azarbayjan, indicates that attention was paid to the fiscal administration of the region shortly after the conquest.[25] Shaykh Uvays pardoned many of the amirs, but executed forty-seven of the close allies of Malik Ashraf.[26]

The possibility of a Chubanid resurgence was one of the most dangerous political threats to Shaykh Uvays's authority. The Chubanids, or 'sons of Tīmūr Tāsh' as they were commonly called in Mamluk chronicles, were similar to the Jalayirids in terms of their origins and aims. They both shared similar family backgrounds, descending from Ilkhanid royal sons-in-law and Chinggisid princesses. Shaykh Uvays's mother was Dilshād Khātūn, daughter of the Chubanid amir Dimashq Khwāja b. Amīr Chūpān. Both the Jalayirids and Chubanids saw control of Azarbayjan as the key to their success, and almost all of the major battles fought between 736/ 1335 and 759/1358 took place in this region. Azarbayjan held significant material and symbolic attractions, as a centre of trade, capable of supporting large cavalry-based armies, and as the centre of the Ilkhanid royal domains. This last factor was certainly related to the first two, but it also carried with it a prestige of its own, as the two *amir-güregen* families – the Jalayirids and Chubanids – attempted to reconstitute the *ulūs* of Hülegü on their own terms.

Those individuals loyal to the Chubanids and their new leader, Akhī Jūq, were not completely eliminated in Shaykh Uvays's purge of the major

Chubanid amirs in Tabriz. Those who remained took refuge in Nakhjivan with Akhī Jūq, who had survived his army's defeat by the Jalayirids. Shaykh Uvays sent his amir 'Alī Pīltan to eradicate the *ashrafī*[27] holdouts there. However, we are told by Zayn al-Dīn Qazvīnī that 'Alī Pīltan moved slowly toward Nakhjivan out of the opposition and bad intent he harboured toward Shaykh Uvays.[28] The armies of Qarabagh and the Turkmans, who were supposed to join 'Alī Pīltan, discerned his 'negligence' (*tahāwun*), and instead joined Akhī Jūq.[29] 'Alī Pīltan was routed in the subsequent battle with Akhī Jūq on 27 Ṣafar 760/28 January 1359,[30] and it seemed as if the Jalayirid occupation of Azarbayjan was at an end. Because the Jalayirid army was dispersed and weakened under the winter conditions, Shaykh Uvays was forced to withdraw from Tabriz and return to Baghdad.[31] Thus, by the end of winter 760/1359, Akhī Jūq had returned to power in Azarbayjan as the representative of the remaining supporters of the Chubanid regime of Malik Ashraf. However, in the spring of 760/1359, Tabriz was conquered again, this time by the Muzaffarid ruler Mubāriz al-Dīn Muḥammad. After defeating Akhī Jūq near Sultaniyya, Mubāriz al-Dīn Muḥammad occupied Tabriz.[32]

Having driven out Akhī Jūq and Shaykh Uvays, it seemed as if the Muzaffarids were in a good position to unite Azarbayjan and central Iran under a single rule. Instead, Mubāriz al-Dīn Muḥammad Muẓaffarī quickly departed. Ahrī ascribes this departure to the approach of the Jalayirids led by Shaykh Uvays, and claims that when Mubāriz al-Dīn Muḥammad got word of the 'advance of the triumphant army arriving with joy and victory', he left and did not stop until he reached [Persian] Iraq.[33] Zayn al-Dīn Qazvīnī gives a similar account, but adds that the astronomers had warned the Muzaffarid sultan that this year he would be troubled by a tall, Turkish-looking youth, whom he understood to mean Shaykh Uvays.[34] When he fled, Shaykh Uvays returned to Tabriz. Muḥammad Muẓaffarī was seized and blinded when he returned to Isfahan.[35] Akhī Jūq was captured and executed, along with 'Alī Pīltan, who had conspired with them against Shaykh Uvays.[36]

Thus, by 761/1360, the Jalayirids under Shaykh Uvays had united Azarbayjan and Iraq and had eliminated the major threat to their power in the north: Akhī Jūq and the supporters of Malik Ashraf Chūbānī. However, the Chubanid threat remained as long as descendants from Amīr Chūpān through his son Tīmūr Tāsh survived. Malik Ashraf's son Tīmūr Tāsh, who had been taken to Saray by Jānī Beg after the Jochid invasion of Azarbayjan in 758/1357, attempted to take the province back himself in the spring of 761/1360. Tīmūr Tāsh left the Jochid *ulūs*, passing through Khwarazm to Shiraz, where he left his sister Sulṭānbakht. Tīmūr

Tāsh himself went to Ahlat and took refuge with the local governor, Khiżr Shāh.[37] Unwilling to harbour the Chubanid, Khiżr Shāh turned him over to Shaykh Uvays for execution.[38]

The death of Tīmūr Tāsh b. Malik Ashraf in 761/1360 marked the end of any Chubanid revival in Azarbayjan. The Jochid invasion, the execution of Malik Ashraf and the subsequent Muzaffarid invasion of Azarbayjan had all weakened the Chubanids and greatly facilitated Shaykh Uvays in conquering the region. With the dissolution of Chubanid power, Shaykh Uvays became recognised in Azarbayjan, as well as by foreign rulers,[39] as the political authority in both Baghdad and Tabriz. The following section examines the consolidation of Shaykh Uvays's authority through the confrontation and conciliation of individuals representing challenges to that authority in the period between 761/1360 and 768/1367.

Consolidation through Conciliation, 761/1360–768/1367

Our sources for the bulk of the reign of Sultan Shaykh Uvays do not include the history written in his name, Ahrī's *Tārīkh-i Shaykh Uvays*. Instead, for the period beginning after Shaykh Uvays's conquest of Azarbayjan, we must rely on other sources, including Zayn al-Dīn Qazvīnī's *Ẕayl-i Tārīkh-i Guzīda*, which was the source for Ḥāfiẓ Abrū's *Ẕayl-i Jāmi' al-Tavārīkh*, and Faṣīḥ Khvāfī's *Mujmal-i Faṣīḥī*.[40] Thus, the main sources for the life of Shaykh Uvays after the conquest of Azarbayjan and the elimination of the Chubanids were written for Timurid patrons, and were primarily dedicated to glorifying the life and conquests of Tīmūr. However, geographically, these histories focus their attention on the territory southwest of the Oxus, that is, the former Ilkhanid realm. Of the three works mentioned above, only Faṣīḥ Khvāfī includes information about Tīmūr's activities in the context of the Chaghatayid *ulūs*, before his first campaigns in Khurasan, beginning in 786/1384. However, Faṣīḥ Khvāfī also devotes attention to the Jalayirids, and it is clear that he utilised the works of Ḥāfiẓ Abrū and Zayn al-Dīn Qazvīnī. The reason for such attention to the activities of the Jalayirid sultan in the Ilkhanid lands in these Timurid histories is the fact that Zayn al-Dīn Qazvīnī's work is a continuation of the Ilkhanid chronicle *Tārīkh-i Guzīda*, written by his father Ḥamd Allāh Mustawfī Qazvīnī for the sultan Abū Sa'īd. For this reason, Zayn al-Dīn devotes his attention to the central Ilkhanid lands, particularly Azarbayjan. Thus, the *Ẕayl-i Tārīkh-i Guzīda* represents a transitional work, with a dual focus both on the lands of the Ilkhanate which were absorbed by Sultan Shaykh Uvays Jalayir, and on the Timurids. However, Tīmūr remains outside the scope of Zayn al-Dīn's history until his emergence within the Ilkhanid territory in the 780s/1380s. This structure was followed by Ḥāfiẓ Abrū and Faṣīḥ Khvāfī.

The fact that these histories were written by authors sponsored by the Timurids did not mean that they portrayed Shaykh Uvays negatively. He ruled in Azarbayjan and Iraq before Tīmūr arrived there, and so did not represent a threat to the Timurids' claims to these provinces. At the same time, however, we can know little about the specific ideological claims made by Shaykh Uvays himself from the Timurid histories. For Ḥāfiẓ Abrū, these details were secondary to Shaykh Uvays's role as the predecessor and placeholder for Tīmūr's inevitable conquests in the '*ulūs* of Hülegü'. Shaykh Uvays could thus be portrayed in a positive light by Ḥāfiẓ Abrū in a manner in which his son Sulṭān Aḥmad – whose reign corresponded with that of Tīmūr in the Ilkhanid lands, and thus represented a direct challenge to Timurid claims there – could not.[41]

The Revolt of Khwāja Mirjān in Baghdad

By putting an end to the family of Amīr Chūpān as a source of authority in Azarbayjan, Shaykh Uvays had accomplished what his father had not been able to: the establishment of Jalayirid authority in the seat of the former Ilkhanate. Shaykh Uvays was thus in a position to assume the role of a continuator of that dynasty. Although Azarbayjan had come under his control by 761/1360, local elites in other provinces attempted to test the limits of Shaykh Uvays's actual authority, and his ability to keep the enlarged Jalayirid realm intact. Perhaps the most critical was the rebellion of his governor in Baghdad, Khwāja Mirjān Khādim. The disobedience of a Jalayirid servant in the heart of the territory first taken by Shaykh Ḥasan was a significant challenge to Shaykh Uvays. Khwāja Mirjān seems to have co-ordinated his rebellion with Shaykh Uvays's campaign to the north, against the Shīrvānshāh Kā'ūs, in order to maximise the distance between the sultan's army and Baghdad. However, when Shaykh Uvays got word of Khwāja Mirjān's show of rebellion and open hostility toward him in the winter of 765/1363–64, he abandoned his Shirvan campaign and turned his attention to Baghdad.[42]

The reason for the rebellion is unclear. It does not seem to have been connected with any Chubanid or Oyrat resurgence, although one of Khwāja Mirjān's allies was Amīr Muḥammad Pīltan, a kinsman of 'Alī Pīltan, who had joined with Akhī Jūq.[43] Clearly there were elements among the amirs who opposed the sultan and sought to take advantage of his absence to take Baghdad for themselves. There is also evidence that Khwāja Mirjān and the rebels recognised the authority of the Mamluks in Baghdad at this time. According to Maqrīzī, Khwāja Mirjān gave the *khuṭba* and struck coins in the name of the Mamluk sultan al-Ashraf Sha'bān (r. 764/1363–778/1377), and took an oath of allegiance to him on behalf of the people of Baghdad.[44] Khwāja Mirjān also sent emissaries to the Mamluk court, who presented Mirjān's repudiation (*qad khala'a*) of Shaykh Uvays.[45]

Such independent action on the part of Khwāja Mirjān, and the recognition of Mamluk authority in Arab Iraq, soon drew the attention of Shaykh Uvays, who turned his military resources toward Baghdad from Shirvan. In addition to leading his own forces to Arab Iraq, Shaykh Uvays sought assistance from the Mamluk sultan al-Ashraf Sha'bān. Maqrīzī writes that the *qāḍī* of Tabrīz[46] sent a message to Sha'bān, informing him that Shaykh Uvays intended to put down the rebellion in Baghdad, and not to allow Khwāja Mirjān to take refuge in Mamluk territory in Syria or Egypt. The *qāḍī*'s message also called on the Mamluk sultan to march out with his own army and help the Jalayirid forces.[47]

Faced with the approach of the Jalayirid army, the rebels led by Khwāja Mirjān took defensive action in an attempt to halt the attack. Zayn al-Dīn Qazvīnī explains that since it was the beginning of spring 765/1364 when the army reached Baghdad, and there was an excess of water, Khwāja Mirjān was able to open the 'Awzaḥ dam,[48] flooding the plain of Baghdad.[49] The tactic succeeded in stalling Shaykh Uvays's troops, who were forced to commandeer boats from along the Tigris for an amphibious assault on the city.[50] When the army of Shaykh Uvays finally faced Khwāja Mirjān and his allied amirs, the amirs were routed and the opposition collapsed. The rebel amirs were executed or sent to Tabriz.[51] Khwāja Mirjān managed to escape temporarily, but was also eventually captured. Despite calls by the *'ulamā'* and notables of Baghdad for Khwāja Mirjān's execution, Shaykh Uvays pardoned him.[52]

This clemency on the part of Shaykh Uvays is curious. The fact that he executed a number of amirs, including Kay Khusraw, 'Alī Khwāja and Muḥammad Pīltan, suggests that he blamed the uprising more on these military commanders than on Khwāja Mirjān himself. Nevertheless, Shaykh Uvays stayed in Baghdad for eleven months in his father's former palace to ensure that rebellion did not quickly flare up again.[53] In the spring of 767/1366, Shaykh Uvays appointed Sulaymān Shāh Khāzin as the new governor of Baghdad and set out for Diyarbakr.[54] When Sulaymān Shāh died in 769/1367–68, Shaykh Uvays reinstated Khwāja Mirjān in his former post as governor.[55] Zayn al-Dīn Qazvīnī and Ḥāfiẓ Abrū write that Shaykh Uvays had forgiven his crime, and that Khwāja Mirjān served the last six years of his life as a worthy governor.[56]

Khwāja Mirjān's pardon and reinstatement just two years later indicate a desire on the part of Shaykh Uvays to establish his authority in Arab Iraq through a show of force, while at the same time making the governor Khwāja Mirjān more dependent on himself as the sultan and sole arbiter of justice there. Shaykh Uvays eliminated the amirs who gave support to the rebellion, yet did not give in to calls from the urban elite to eliminate Khwāja Mirjān. Thus, Shaykh Uvays isolated Khwāja Mirjān from any local support in Baghdad, by removing his amir allies, and leaving him among the *'ulamā'* and *a'yān* who were hostile to him. It is not surprising, then, that Khwāja Mirjān remained a loyal governor in Baghdad until his death in 775/1374, for he would have been solely dependent on the sultan against the local elite. In this way Shaykh Uvays ensured a relatively stable situation in Arab Iraq after 767/1366, which would enable him to be absent for long periods in Azarbayjan or elsewhere, without fear of disobedience from his governor there. Baghdad does seem to have thrived under Jalayirid rule, after a certain amount of neglect in the Ilkhanid period. Hülegü's sack of the city in 656/1258 did great immediate damage to the welfare of Baghdad. However, even in the years that followed, as the Ilkhanids worked to rebuild a flourishing state for themselves, Baghdad remained a secondary urban centre, peripheral to Tabriz and Sultaniyya, which became the primary focus of architectural patronage by the Ilkhans. With the emergence of the Jalayirids as the major power in the western Ilkhanid lands during the reign of Shaykh Uvays, Baghdad, which had become the Jalayirid centre during the lifetime of Shaykh Ḥasan, enjoyed a period of development and renewal.

The Emergence of the Qarāquyūnlū Turkmans under Bayrām Khwāja

Following the Khwāja Mirjān rebellion and Shaykh Uvays's extended stay in Baghdad from 765/1364 to 767/1366, the Jalayirid sultan turned his attention to Diyarbakr and the Qarāquyūnlū. Shaykh Uvays's campaign against the Qarāquyūnlū in 767/1366 represents one of the earliest mentions of this Turkman confederation in the historical sources, although neither Zayn al-Dīn Qazvīnī nor Ḥāfiẓ Abrū uses the name Qarāquyūnlū referring to the Turkmans in this context. The rebellion of Khwāja Mirjān had represented a threat to one half of Shaykh Uvays's territories inherited from his father, the Mesopotamian heartland of Arab Iraq. After bringing this region under control, Shaykh Uvays turned to the other half of Shaykh Ḥasan's territory: the upper Tigris region and Diyarbakr. This had been the main homeland of the Oyrat tribe in the Mongol period, and Shaykh

Ḥasan had emerged as the dominant amir over the Oyrats following the defeat of their chief, 'Alī Pādshāh, in 736/1336. Although the Oyrats maintained a presence in this region, in the mid-eighth/fourteenth century, in the northern regions of Diyarbakr, into eastern Anatolia, a confederation of Turkman tribesmen was emerging under the political leadership of their own chiefs. In the 760s/1360s, the leader of this group, which would become known as the Qarāquyūnlū, was a certain Bayrām Khwāja, whose brother Birdī Khwāja had come to power in Mosul.

Shaykh Uvays left Baghdad in the spring of 767/1366, and marched north along the Tigris. After taking Tikrit, he came to Mosul and seized Birdī Khwāja,[57] before continuing north toward Bayrām Khwāja. The Turkmans were defeated by Shaykh Uvays and the Jalayirid forces on the plain of Muş in the early summer of 767/1366. Following the battle, the Jalayirids plundered the Turkmans' population around Muş.[58] The aim of Shaykh Uvays's campaign against the Turkmans was very different from that of his campaign against Khwāja Mirjān in Baghdad, and thus it called for different tactics. In Baghdad, the sultan had to deal with a city which was his second capital, and which was an integral part of the Jalayirid realm. Shaykh Uvays sought to preserve Baghdad, as well as its governor, by treating him lightly, and thereby bringing him more closely under his direct control. However, the Turkmans in Diyarbakr and eastern Anatolia existed outside Shaykh Uvays's direct authority, and constituted a distinct political entity with its own leadership. Shaykh Uvays recognised the danger that a large, nomadic confederation on the fringe of Azarbayjan and Arab Iraq could pose to his authority in these provinces. He thus pursued a policy aimed at destroying the unity of the Turkmans by attacking members of their leading family (Birdī Khwāja and Bayrām Khwāja) and pillaging the Turkman population. In 767/1366, the balance of power favoured the Jalayirids, and Shaykh Uvays could afford a campaign of general destruction against the Turkmans. As discussed in Chapter 8, however, his successors were no longer able to subdue the Turkmans by force, and instead were obliged to conciliate them with official recognition of their possessions of land and people in Anatolia, and eventually to employ them as military auxiliaries in return for even further concessions.

Shirvan

Shaykh Uvays showed conciliation similar to that shown to Khwāja Mirjān when he faced the third major challenge in this consolidation phase of his reign. It has been mentioned above that Shaykh Uvays had intended to confront Kā'ūs Shīrvānī in 765/1363, before the rebellion of

Khwāja Mirjān forced him to give it up. The Shīrvānshāhs had long been semi-autonomous rulers in the region north of Azarbayjan. Their control of Darband, the primary but narrow pass from the Qipchaq steppe south into Iran, made them significant regional rulers. Although Shirvan was nominally a vassal of the Ilkhanate, and later of the Jalayirids, the relative independence of the Shīrvānshāhs, and their position as guardians of the traditional entryway of the Jochids into the Ilkhanid territories, required that they remain on friendly terms with whoever sat on the throne in Azarbayjan. Since Shaykh Uvays had come to the throne, Kā'ūs Shīrvānī had tested the resolve of the new Jalayirid sultan, and the limits of his authority. While Shaykh Uvays had been occupied with Khwāja Mirjān between 765/1364 and 767/1366, Kā'ūs twice invaded Tabriz and caused much of the population in Azarbayjan to leave the province.[59]

Shaykh Uvays returned to Tabriz in the summer of 767/1366 after his campaign against Bayrām Khwāja and the Turkmans. The following spring he sent his favourite, Bayrām Beg,[60] to Shirvan with a number of amirs and troops to bring Kā'ūs to heel. After a three-month siege of Kā'ūs's stronghold, the Jalayirids forced the Shīrvānshāh to surrender.[61] He was sent to the court of Shaykh Uvays, who kept him in confinement for another three months. However, he then pardoned Kā'ūs, and entrusted Shirvan to him again.[62] Zayn al-Dīn Qazvīnī and Ḥāfiẓ Abrū report that because of the favour and compassion the sultan showed to him, Kā'ūs readily subjugated all of Shirvan and Darband for Shaykh Uvays, and remained a faithful servant as long as he lived.[63] When Kā'ūs died in 774/1372–73, Shaykh Uvays confirmed his son, Hūshang, as his successor as Shīrvānshāh.[64] We are told that Hūshang had been attendant on Shaykh Uvays at the time of his father's death, indicating that the Jalayirid sultan had kept Hūshang away from Shirvan as an incentive for Kā'ūs's loyalty. As was the case with Khwāja Mirjān, Shaykh Uvays's clemency toward the previously rebellious Shīrvānshāh was coupled with the certainty that he would remain loyal after the sultan's show of force and eventual pardon. While Shaykh Uvays had left Khwāja Mirjān among those in Baghdad who opposed him, he held Kā'ūs's son hostage after returning Kā'ūs to his position in Shirvan. Both tactics allowed Shaykh Uvays to ensure servants remained loyal to his rule in the provinces without bloodshed. The moderation and clemency shown by Shaykh Uvays contributed to his reputation for compassion and justice in Timurid historiography. Naṭanzī described Shaykh Uvays as a

> ruler of extremely passionate heart, and just. In his time, the common people and the elite (*jumhūr-i 'avāmm va khavāṣṣ*) were quiet and content . . . at all

times, he was in the service of the tranquility of the populace, such that in the times of his government, all of Azarbayjan was the envy of paradise.[65]

Shaykh Uvays was able to increase the degree of his personal authority with regard to his provincial governors, and thus ensure the stability of his regime. However, when faced with the threat of the Turkman confederation, Shaykh Uvays was not willing to bring their leaders into the Jalayirid political structure, and instead attempted to destroy their leadership and eliminate the Turkman presence in Diyarbakr and eastern Anatolia. The Turkmans of the Qarāquyūnlū confederation would maintain a close but uneasy relationship with the Jalayirids into the Timurid period, and would eventually succeed the Jalayirid dynasty in Azarbayjan and Arab Iraq. However, in the period from 768/1367 to his death in 776/1374, Shaykh Uvays was at the height of his power after the period of conquest and consolidation. It was in these years that the royal power of the sultan in Tabriz reached the extent that had existed during the period of the later Ilkhanid rulers.

The Height of Sultanic Power in the Post-Ilkhanid Period (768/1367–776/1374)

The last seven years of Shaykh Uvays's reign was characterised by relative stability, without significant challenges to his authority as sultan within the borders of Azarbayjan, Arab Iraq and Diyarbakr. The period from 768/1367 to 776/1374 was characterised by three main developments, which are discussed below: Shaykh Uvays's campaigns against Amīr Valī in Mazandaran, the political marriages arranged between Shaykh Uvays's children and prominent political and religious figures, and the succession of deaths and disasters that affected the Jalayirid royal family, capped by the death of the sultan himself in 776/1374. The death of Shaykh Uvays initiated a new period in which sultanic power declined due to the rise of the authority of Amīr 'Ādil among several Jalayirid princes who each made their own claims for the authority Shaykh Uvays had established for the family. This trend was accelerated by the campaigns of Tīmūr and the Jalayirids' loss of Azarbayjan and, periodically, Baghdad as well.

The primary source for the life of Amīr Valī is the treatise (*risāla*) devoted to him by Ḥāfiẓ Abrū.[66] According to Ḥāfiẓ Abrū, Amīr Valī's father, Amīr Shaykh 'Alī Hindū, was the governor of Astarabad under Ṭaghāy Tīmūr Khan, a descendant of Chinggis Qan's brother, and the ruler of Khurasan after the death of Abū Sa'īd. Amīr Valī was well regarded by Ṭaghāy Tīmūr during his youth, and was educated and brought up by the khan.[67] He began to acquire his own following among those Mongol amirs opposed to the rise of the Sarbadārs at Sabzavar, an alliance of urban elites and followers of a Shi'i Sufi order.[68] After defeating the Sarbadār army, Amīr Valī established independent authority in the region southeast of the Caspian, from Astarabad to Damghan and Simnan.[69] Although Amīr Valī owed his allegiance in his youth to Ṭaghāy Tīmūr Khan, he did not recognise Ṭaghāy Tīmūr's son, Pādishāh Luqmān, as his nominal overlord. After initially summoning Pādishāh Luqmān to Astarabad, Amīr Valī turned him away and instead ruled in his own right. He also eliminated other members of the Taghay-Timurid family,[70] who represented the main source of Chinggisid authority in the eastern Ilkhanid provinces.

Amīr Valī's career in some ways mirrored that of Shaykh Ḥasan Jalayir. Both owed their positions to the Mongol khans whom their families had served. When the authority of the khans was weakened, they both were able to establish regional amirates for themselves in formerly Ilkhanid provinces. Amīr Valī, like Shaykh Ḥasan, did not declare himself a sultan or khan. However, it seems that, after he had defeated the Sarbadārs and brought Damghan and Simnan under his control, he set his sights further to the west, possibly to Azarbayjan. Ḥāfiẓ Abrū reports that at the end of 772/mid-1371, Amīr Valī assembled an army and set out for (Persian) Iraq.[71] This campaign prompted a response from Shaykh Uvays, who marched to meet Amīr Valī near Rayy. The threat to the Jalayirid state from Amīr Valī was different from those Shaykh Uvays faced in the period 761/1360–768/1367, as discussed above. Khwāja Mirjān and Kā'ūs Shīrvānī had been nominal servants of the Jalayirid sultan. The Turkmans under Bayrām Khwāja were also vassals of the sultan, and resided within the Jalayirid territory in Diyarbakr. Amīr Valī, on the other hand, was a foreign threat, and represented an extension of the eastern Ilkhanid military elite into the west, similar to the campaigns of Ṭaghāy Tīmūr Khan in 739/1339. However, unlike Ṭaghāy Tīmūr, who had been invited by Shaykh Ḥasan Jalayir to help him in his conflict with the Chubanids, Amīr Valī was an unwelcome threat to Shaykh Uvays's eastern frontier, and particularly to the cities of Rayy and Sultaniyya, which were vital to the commercial traffic bound for Tabriz.

In the battle that took place near Rayy, Amīr Valī's army defeated a smaller Jalayirid force and killed two major Jalayirid amirs.[72] The loss of these commanders led Shaykh Uvays to withdraw and give a temporary victory to Amīr Valī. However, the Jalayirids' counterattack forced Amīr Valī and his army to disperse, and Shaykh Uvays advanced to Simnan.[73] The sources report that the Jalayirid amirs did not favour pressing the advance beyond Simnan, and that Shaykh Uvays returned to Tabriz after entrusting Rayy to one of his own men.[74]

The Jalayirid amirs did not favour extending the sultan's authority into Mazandaran, a fact that supports the view that the former Ilkhanid provinces continued to maintain distinct political identities, as well as a division between Khurasan and Azarbayjan as separate centres of political authority. Such a division can perhaps be traced to the pre-Ilkhanid Mongol administration, which comprised an imperial representative in Khurasan, and another military governor in Azarbayjan. After a long period of political unity under the Ilkhanate, this separation re-emerged in the Jalayirid period. Despite his defeat in 772/1371, Amīr Valī maintained his authority in Astarabad, without any further pressure from Shaykh Uvays. The region of Rayy was established as the frontier zone between the Jalayirids and Amīr Valī.

The peripheral position of Rayy, away from the central authority of the Jalayirid sultan, perhaps contributed to the rise of the autonomy of Amīr 'Ādil, who would come to dominate politics in the Jalayirid realm after Shaykh Uvays's death. Amīr 'Ādil, who will be discussed further in Chapter 8, became the Jalayirid governor of Rayy around the year 775/1373.[75] Amīr Valī continued to threaten the Jalayirid eastern frontier, and in 774/1372–73 Shaykh Uvays prepared another campaign to confront him. However, the operation was called off due to the death of Shaykh Uvays's brother, as is discussed below. Shaykh Uvays did not carry out another campaign against Amīr Valī, although he planned to shortly before his own death in 776/1374.[76] Later, Amīr Valī looked to the Jalayirids for refuge and assistance against Tīmūr, who drove him from Astarabad and installed Ṭaghāy Tīmūr's son Pādishāh Luqmān in 786/1384.

The success of Shaykh Uvays against Amīr Valī and the establishment of Rayy as the Jalayirids' eastern frontier helped to establish the territorial limits of the sultan's authority. The reluctance of the amirs to remain in Simnan illustrates that Shaykh Uvays's authority was not absolute, but still subject to some degree of consensus by the amirs. However, the military elite was willing to recognise the Jalayirid sultan as the only source of royal authority in the western Ilkhanid lands, and did not oppose his assertion of independent authority.

Shaykh Uvays's growing power was also recognised by a representative of the Muzaffarids, another of the regional dynasties within the former Ilkhanid provinces. Descended from an elite 'Arab family from Khurasan, Mubāriz al-Dīn Muḥammad ibn Sharaf al-Dīn Muẓaffar was recognised as the Ilkhanid governor of Yazd by Abū Sa'īd in 719/1319–20. In the years that followed, he expanded his territory, taking Shiraz in 754/1353 and

Isfahan in 757/1356. That Mubāriz al-Dīn and his sons sought to incorporate Azarbayjan into their domains is evidenced by the several invasions they made to the north between 758/1357 and 776/1375. As mentioned above, after bringing all of Fars and Persian Iraq under his control, Mubāriz al-Dīn claimed the caliphate for himself.[77] He also attempted to take advantage of the disorder in Azarbayjan following the invasion of the Jochid Jānī Beg Khan, and thwarted the Chubanid-revivalist aspirations of Akhī Jūq in 758/1357. However, he soon had to withdraw after Shaykh Uvays's conquest the following year. Mubāriz al-Dīn was deposed and blinded by his sons, who henceforth shared political authority in the Muzaffarid state.[78]

In the years following Mubāriz al-Dīn's deposition and death, his sons and nephews competed for control over Fars and Persian Iraq from their bases in the cities of Shiraz, Isfahan, Yazd and Kirman. During the reign of Shaykh Uvays, Shāh Maḥmūd b. Mubāriz al-Dīn challenged his brother, Shāh Shujā', for leadership of the Muzaffarid family. The Jalayirids became involved in the internal struggles of the Muzaffarids when Shaykh Uvays gave his daughter in marriage to Shāh Maḥmūd's son in 771/1369–70.[79] The alliance between Shaykh Uvays and Shāh Maḥmūd Muẓaffarī had the effect of neutralising Shāh Shujā'. However, after Shaykh Uvays died in 776/1374, followed by Shāh Maḥmūd in 776/1375,[80] Shāh Shujā' was free to launch a campaign in an attempt to capture Azarbayjan for the Muzaffarids.

In the same year that Shaykh Uvays's daughter married into the Muzaffarid family (771/1369–70), Shaykh Uvays married his son Shaykh Ḥasan to the daughter of Qāḍī Shaykh 'Alī, the most prominent member of the *'ulamā'* in Tabriz.[81] This marriage was probably an attempt to strengthen the ties between the Jalayirids and the urban elite of Tabriz, with the uprising of Khwāja Mirjān in recent memory. Qāḍī Shaykh 'Alī naturally wanted his son-in-law Shaykh Ḥasan to succeed Shaykh Uvays as sultan. However, when Shaykh Uvays designated his son Sulṭān Ḥusayn as his successor, Qāḍī Shaykh 'Alī protested, saying that 'Shaykh Ḥasan is not bearing it. Since he is the elder brother, Sulṭān Ḥusayn would not be suited to the sultanate (*bi-salṭanat sulṭān ḥusayn dar nasāzad*).'[82] However, the amirs kept Shaykh Ḥasan confined, and executed him immediately after Shaykh Uvays's death was confirmed.[83] After the execution of his son-in-law, Qāḍī Shaykh 'Alī remained a prominent figure in Tabriz, and took part in a conspiracy against the new ruler Sulṭān Ḥusayn.

In addition to forging ties with the family of Qāḍī Shaykh 'Alī, Shaykh Uvays also associated with religious figures of a more antinomian inclination, including Fażl Allāh Astarābādī (d. 796/1394). Founder of the messianic Sufi movement known as the Ḥurūfiyya, Fażl Allāh came to Tabriz in the early 770s/1370s, after having travelled throughout Iran.[84] He came to believe, after a series of revelations, that he was the *mahdī*, the messiah who would bring order and justice to the world as he ushered in the end of time.[85] However, before he took up this mission (around the year 788/1386), Fażl Allāh was primarily known as a talented dream interpreter, and *ṣāḥib-i ta'vil* ('master of esoteric interpretation').[86]

Ḥurūfī sources maintain that Shaykh Uvays himself, along with several viziers, had contact with Fażl Allāh.[87] These sources also say that Fażl Allāh presented a *ṭāqiya*, a hat worn by Sufi dervishes, to Shaykh Uvays,[88] perhaps symbolising the sultan's inclinations or sympathies for followers of the mystic path. While in Tabriz, Fażl Allāh also married the daughter of one of Shaykh Uvays's viziers, Khwāja Bāyazīd Dāmghānī.[89] Fażl Allāh is not mentioned in the standard accounts of the reign of Shaykh Uvays written by Timurid historians. Neither is Khwāja Bāyazīd, although it is likely he was a member of the family of ministers from Damghan who had served the Chubanids in Tabriz before the Jalayirid conquest of the city.[90] In the time of Shaykh Uvays, Fażl Allāh did not yet think of himself as a prophetic figure. Instead, as Shahzad Bashir has claimed, it is likely he served more as an advisor to the elite of Jalayirid Tabriz through his dream interpretation.[91] The encounter between Fażl Allāh Astarābādī and Shaykh Uvays indicates both a desire for access to circles of political power on the part of Fażl Allāh, as well as a policy of recognition and accommodation of Sufi circles on the part of Shaykh Uvays.

The final years of Shaykh Uvays's reign were marked by a string of natural disasters and deaths among the royal family and ruling elite. The plague returned to Tabriz in 771/1369,[92] killing around 300,000, according to Zayn al-Dīn Qazvīnī.[93] The following year, a great flood inundated Tabriz, ruining most of the buildings there.[94] These two devastating events were followed by a flood in Baghdad in 776/1374, which killed around 40,000 people.[95] The precise consequences of these events are difficult to gauge, beyond the destruction and loss of life that occurred. However, the fact that these disasters primarily affected the urban populations of the sultanate's two major cities suggests that, with respect to the state elite, the non-amir urban notables, *'ulamā'* and administrative classes were affected to a greater degree than the military elites, whose activities were more closely connected with the mobile court-camp of the sultan, as well as their own herds. Such a consequence may have contributed to a decline among those who benefited from the stability and order of a commonly recognised sovereign who could act as a mediator among factions who would otherwise engage in violent conflict to settle disputes. At the same time, such a decline would lead to an increase in the influence of competing factions of amirs who came to dominate the sultanate, and weaken the authority of Shaykh Uvays's successor, Sulṭān Ḥusayn, in the years that followed.

The last years of Shaykh Uvays's reign also witnessed the deaths of many prominent figures within the sultanate. In 769/1367–68, the sultan's brother, Amīr Qāsim, died of consumption (*zaḥmat-i diqq*) and was buried near his father, Shaykh Ḥasan, in Najaf.[96] In the same year, Bayrām Beg, mentioned above in connection with the subjugation of Shirvan, died as a result of excessive drink. We are told that Bayrām Beg was beloved by Shaykh Uvays (*maḥbūb-i sulṭān*), who wore a black woollen cloak in mourning for his friend.[97] Ḥājī Māmā Khātūn, described by Zayn al-Dīn Qazvīnī as 'beloved by the sultan and the mother of his children', died in 770/1368–69.[98] Four years later, in 774/1372–73, Shaykh Uvays prepared his second campaign against Amīr Valī in Mazandaran. However, as he readied the army in Ujan, his intoxicated brother Amīr Zāhid fell off the roof of the palace[99] and died, causing the sultan to call off his campaign.[100]

In addition to these deaths within the royal family, two of the sultan's governors, Khwāja Mirjān and Kā'ūs Shīrvānī, both mentioned above, passed away shortly before Shaykh Uvays himself. There is a sense in the sources where all of these deaths are recorded, and where they comprise much of the information provided about the final years of Shaykh Uvays's reign, that this period represented the end of a generation within the Jalayirid sultanate, corresponding with the end of the reign itself. In the period after 776/1374, the sultanate under Sulṭān Ḥusayn would move away from the centralisation of Shaykh Uvays's period, and the conflicts of a new generation of royal princes and factions of amirs would contribute to a decentralisation of political authority. However, at the same time, the symbolic authority of the Jalayirid royal family continued, as several sons of Shaykh Uvays claimed that authority for themselves, or for the amirs that supported them.

The Jalayirids and Italian Merchants in Azarbayjan

A final issue relating to the reign of Shaykh Uvays and the Jalayirids' relationship to Azarbayjan in this period was the sultan's attempt to re-establish Tabriz as the commercial centre it had been under the Ilkhans. Azarbayjan had suffered economically during the period of Chubanid rule under Malik Ashraf in the 740s/1340s and 750s/1350s. The Chubanid regime turned against the Latin Christian merchants who had traded in Tabriz since the 680s/1280s. Genoa and Venice had sent the most merchants from the Latin West to the Ilkhanate in the seventh/thirteenth and eighth/fourteenth centuries. The result was that trade with Italian merchants dropped off almost completely after the death of Abū Saʿīd in 736/1335.[101] As a result of persecution of the foreigners in Tabriz, Genoese merchants abandoned the route through Iran for their trade with China. Instead, they followed a northern route, from Caffa in the Crimea, to Tana (Azov), to Saray on the Volga, and then around the north side of the Caspian Sea to Urgench.[102] The year 740–41/1340 seems to have been the beginning of the Chubanids' closing Tabriz to Italian merchants. While the Genoese trader Marco Morosini had sent his agents to Sultaniyya in 739–40/1339,[103] Genoa declared a boycott of the Chubanid lands in two decrees, issued in 740–41/1340 and 742–43/1342.[104] Jean Richard has written that Iran was closed to the Genoese in 743–44/1343.[105] Thus, if we take the years between 740–41/1340 and 743–44/1343 as the height of mutual hostility between the Chubanids and Genoa, it can be concluded that Shaykh Ḥasan Chūbānī was responsible for the cutting-off of trade with the Latin West.

After Shaykh Ḥasan Chūbānī's death, the economic repercussions of this policy began to be felt, prompting Malik Ashraf to send an emissary to propose peace with Genoa, and to return Genoese goods that had been seized.[106] However, this overture did not succeed in bringing the Genoese back to Tabriz.[107] The reluctance of Genoa to trade in Chubanid Tabriz may have been influenced by Malik Ashraf's reputation as an unpredictable and despotic ruler, who could have seized Genoese commercial property.

After he took control of Tabriz in 759/1358, the Jalayirid sultan Shaykh Uvays attempted to revive trade with both Genoa and Venice. The Genoese did not return,[108] perhaps because the Tana-Saray-Urgench route had proven secure and lucrative, under the protection of the Jochid khans. This may have also been due to conflict between the Genoese and Shaykh Uvays himself. According to Clavijo, writing thirty years after the sultan's death, tension arose between the Genoese merchants and Shaykh Uvays when the Genoese began to construct a castle outside Tabriz on land they purchased from the sultan.[109] Accustomed to operating out of their own strongholds on the Black Sea coast, the Genoese were extending this practice to the Jalayirid city. However, Shaykh Uvays informed them that it was not customary for merchants to build castles, before ordering them to be executed.[110]

Shaykh Uvays's attempts to lure the Venetians were also unsuccessful. In order to re-establish contact between the republic and Tabriz, Shaykh Uvays named an envoy to Venice in 770–71/1369.[111] The Venetians in

Trabzond on the Black Sea coast responded to the sultan that they had waited for two years to be granted passage for their caravan, and were clearly reluctant to believe the Jalayirid sultan's assurance. Shaykh Uvays wrote to the Venetian *bailo* in Trabzond again in 774–75/1373, in an attempt to convince the Venetian merchants that the caravan routes from the Black Sea to Tabriz were open and secure. The sultan gave his assurances that he would punish anyone who would impede or pillage the caravans. However, Venice did not respond to these overtures, unconvinced of the promises of Shaykh Uvays.[112]

It is not clear whether the disappearance of the Italian merchants had a negative effect on the economic prosperity of Tabriz. On the one hand, the Genoese and Venetians had been the main agents of commercial exchange with the Black Sea and Mediterranean economies in Iran. A shift to a northerly route, passing through the Jochid *ulūs*, would have hurt the Jalayirid economy. However, Tabriz continued to flourish in subsequent years. This can possibly be attributed to a shift in the silk trade in the late eighth/fourteenth century, as more caravans began carrying silk overland from Tabriz to Ottoman Bursa.[113] The European observers Schiltberger and Clavijo both commented on the many merchants and the high volume of trade in Tabriz around the turn of the ninth/fifteenth century, after the trade with the Italian states had slowed. Even though Shaykh Uvays failed to reopen trade channels with Genoa and Venice, Jalayirid Tabriz, as well as Sultaniyya, continued to prosper.

The Death of Shaykh Uvays

Sultan Shaykh Uvays died in Jumādá I 776/October 1374. His death is surrounded with a legend in both the Timurid and the Mamluk historiographical traditions, in which Shaykh Uvays foresaw his own death in a dream a few months before his actual demise. According to Zayn al-Dīn Qazvīnī, the sultan became aware of his fate three months before he died, and in the time that remained prepared a burial shroud and coffin, and put his affairs in order.[114] The Timurid historian Naṭanzī gives a similar account, writing that Shaykh Uvays became aware that he was going to die, and constructed a tomb for himself at a place called Kajījān-i Tabrīz.[115] Maqrīzī, also writing in the ninth/fifteenth century, reported that 'while sleeping he saw the pronouncement of his own death (*li-manām rāhu na'ayat ilayhi nafsihi*)'. Shaykh Uvays then turned the kingdom over to his son Sulṭān Ḥusayn, and began to devote himself to God (*aqbala yata'abbad*).[116]

Shaykh Uvays's tomb is located six kilometres southeast of Tabriz at a village called Pīna Shalvār, at the Shādī-ābād cemetery (Gūristān-i

Shādī-ābād-i Mashā'ikh).[117] The place is known locally as Zīva-Gulī,[118] and was the final resting place for a large number of sufis and holy men.[119] The inscription on Shaykh Uvays's tombstone reads:

> The late great sultan and the inspired and felicitous *khāqān* (*al-sulṭān al-a'ẓam al-maghfūr wa-al-khāqān al-mulham al-masrūr*), asker of the forgiveness of God (*al-rājī 'afw allāh*), the forgiven and strengthener of the religion of God (*al-maghfūr wa mu'izz-i dīn allāh*), the victorious Shaykh Uvays Bahādur Khan, may the mercy and blessing of God be upon him, was transported from this world (*dār al-'amal*) to the garden of paradise (*firdaws al-jinān*) on the 2nd of Jumādá I, 776 [10 October 1374].[120]

The preceding sections of this chapter have focused on providing an analysis of the military and political developments that contributed to the establishment of the rule of Shaykh Uvays Jalayir as sultan in the western provinces of the former Ilkhanate. By the end of his reign, the Jalayirid dynasty could claim to be the heir to the Chinggisid Ilkhan dynasty, something that was not achieved by Shaykh Ḥasan during the period of his rule as amir of Baghdad between 736/1336 and 757/1356. The Jalayirid conquest of Azarbayjan in 759/1358 contributed greatly to the material and territorial gains of Shaykh Uvays. However, the military successes that he achieved were connected with and supplemented by an elaboration of an ideological programme expressed through the literature and public artifacts produced during his reign by individuals whose positions depended on the continuity of the Ilkhanate, or an Ilkhanate-modelled system of administration and political patronage. In the following chapter, an analysis is carried out of the historical, literary and material artifacts produced under Shaykh Uvays, which helped to develop the notion of the Jalayirid dynasty, represented by Sultan Shaykh Uvays, as the heir to the Ilkhanid political tradition, in which the ruler acted as defender of Islam, upholder of royal justice, and the embodiment of the dynastic legacy of Chinggis Qan.

Notes

1. This is according to Naṭanzī, who gives his age as thirty-four at his death in 777/1375–76. However, his death is commonly accepted as 2 Jumādá I 776/9 October 1374. See Naṭanzī/Aubin, 167.
2. Ahrī/*TSU*, (Persian text), 184; (English translation), 83.
3. Ḥāfiẓ Abrū/*ZJT*, 184. These lines are attributed to Salmān Sāvajī. See Sāvajī/*Kullīyāt*, xx–xxi.
4. Malik Ashraf married the daughter of al-Malik al-Ṣāliḥ in a lavish ceremony in Tabriz. However, she was not to his liking, and he ignored her after their first night together. See Ḥāfiẓ Abrū/*ZJT*, 184.

5. Qazvīnī/*ZTG*, 57.
6. Ahrī/*TSU*, (Persian text), 176; (English translation), 76.
7. Ahrī/*TSU*, (Persian text), 176–7; (English translation), 76; Qazvīnī/*ZTG*, 57; Ḥāfiẓ Abrū/*ZJT*, 184; Samarqandī/*Maṭla'*, 1:289.
8. Qazvīnī/*ZTG*, 57–8; Ḥāfiẓ Abrū/*ZJT*, 184–5.
9. Ahrī/*TSU*, (Persian text), 177; (English translation), 76–7.
10. Ahrī/*TSU*, (Persian text), 177; (English translation), 77. The reference here is to Malik Ashraf's puppet, Ghazan II. Little is known about this apparent successor to Anūshirvān, although several coins struck in his name are known from the years 757/1356 and 758/1357. See Stephen Album, *Checklist of Islamic Coins*, 2nd edn (Santa Rosa: S. Album, 1998), 110. My thanks to Stephen Album for the reference.
11. Ahrī/*TSU*, (Persian text), 178; (English translation), 78; Qazvīnī/*ZTG*, 62; Ḥāfiẓ Abrū/*ZJT*, 187.
12. Qazvīnī/*ZTG*, 63; Ḥāfiẓ Abrū/*ZJT*, 188.
13. Ahrī/*TSU*, (Persian text), 179; (English translation), 78. Ahrī does not mention the Chubanid hostages. See also Qazvīnī/*ZTG*, 64; Ḥāfiẓ Abrū/*ZJT*, 188.
14. Qazvīnī/*ZTG*, 64–5; Ḥāfiẓ Abrū/*ZJT*, 189.
15. Ḥāfiẓ Abrū mentions that Akhī Jūq was among the troops of Malik Ashraf. See Ḥāfiẓ Abrū/*ZJT*, 186. Shīrīn Bayānī describes him as the governor of Tabriz and deputy (*nā'ib*) of Jānī Beg. See Shīrīn Bayānī, *Tārīkh-i Āl-i Jalāyir* (Tehran: Intishārāt-i Dānishgāh-i Tihrān, 1962), 34.
16. Qazvīnī/*ZTG*, 64; Ḥāfiẓ Abrū/*ZJT*, 188–9; Ahrī/*TSU*, (Persian text), 179; (English translation), 79.
17. Ahrī/*TSU*, (Persian text), 180; (English translation), 79.
18. Cf. Ahrī's reference to the amirate of Malik Ashraf (*imārat-i malik ashraf*), in Ahrī/*TSU*, (Persian text), 171; (English translation), 72.
19. Qazvīnī/*ZTG*, 65: 'He was tormenting the people with unnecessary confiscation and exactions'; Ḥāfiẓ Abrū/*ZJT*, 189.
20. In Ahrī's periodisation, the 'sultanate of Shaykh Uvays' begins not when he succeeds his father in Baghdad, but after the defeat of the Chubanids and the conquest of Azarbayjan. See Ahrī/*TSU*, (Persian text), 182; (English translation), 81.
21. Ahrī/*TSU*, (Persian text), 180; (English translation), 79–80.
22. Van Loon notes that the year of the battle has been left out of the manuscript of Ahrī's history, with only the last day of the month (*salkh*) of Sha'bān indicated. Thus, the date is end of Sha'bān 759/early August 1358; see Ahrī/*TSU*, (Persian text), 181; (English translation), 80. Zayn al-Dīn Qazvīnī, and thus also Ḥāfiẓ Abrū, have the end of Shawwāl 759/early October 1358. However, Sha'bān (August) must be correct, since at a later point in Zayn al-Dīn's narrative he records the execution of the Ashrafī amirs in Tabriz as taking place on 28 Ramaḍān of that year (3 September 1358). See Qazvīnī/*ZTG*, 66–7; Ḥāfiẓ Abrū/*ZJT*, 189.

23. Ahrī/*TSU*, (Persian text), 181; (English translation), 80; Qazvīnī/*ZTG*, 67; Ḥāfiẓ Abrū/*ZJT*, 189. According to Zayn al-Dīn Qazvīnī, who is followed by later Timurid historians, Shaykh Uvays's Oyrat troops, who comprised the left wing of his army, were in disagreement with each other and dispersed, leaving only the right wing to battle the Ashrafīs. See also Samarqandī/*Maṭla'*, 1:293; Mīrkhvānd/*Rawża*, 5:570.
24. Qazvīnī/*ZTG*, 67; Ḥāfiẓ Abrū/*ZJT*, 189; Mīrkhvānd/*Rawża*, 5:571.
25. Gottfried Herrmann and Gerhard Doerfer, 'Ein persisch-mongolischer Erlaß des Ğalāyeriden Šeyḫ Oveys', *CAJ* 19 (1975): 1–84.
26. Qazvīnī/*ZTG*, 67; Ḥāfiẓ Abrū/*ZJT*, 190; Samarqandī/*Maṭla'*, 1:294; Mīrkhvānd/*Rawża*, 5:571; Bayānī, *Tārīkh-i Āl-i Jalāyir*, 34–5.
27. Both Ahrī and Zayn al-Dīn Qazvīnī describe Akhī Jūq's followers as '*ashrafī*s', implying that they were the former supporters of Malik Ashraf Chūbānī. See Ahrī/*TSU*, (Persian text), 183; (English translation), 82; Qazvīnī/*ZTG*, 65; Ḥāfiẓ Abrū/*ZJT*, 190.
28. Qazvīnī/*ZTG*, 67; Ḥāfiẓ Abrū/*ZJT*, 190; Samarqandī/*Maṭla'*, 1:294.
29. Qazvīnī/*ZTG*, 67; Ḥāfiẓ Abrū/*ZJT*, 190; Samarqandī/*Maṭla'*, 1:294.
30. Ahrī/*TSU*, (Persian text), 183; (English translation), 82.
31. Qazvīnī/*ZTG*, 68; Ḥāfiẓ Abrū/*ZJT*, 190; Samarqandī/*Maṭla'*, 1:294; Mīrkhvānd/*Rawża*, 5:571.
32. Qazvīnī/*ZTG*, 69; Ḥāfiẓ Abrū/*ZJT*, 190.
33. Ahrī/*TSU*, (Persian text), 183; (English translation), 82.
34. Qazvīnī/*ZTG*, 69. See also Ḥāfiẓ Abrū/*ZJT*, 190.
35. Ahrī and Zayn al-Dīn write that Muḥammad Muẓaffarī was blinded by his sons; see Ahrī/*TSU*, (Persian text), 184; (English translation), 82; Qazvīnī/*ZTG*, 69. Ḥāfiẓ Abrū writes that he was blinded by his commanders (*sarān*); see Ḥāfiẓ Abrū/*ZJT*, 191.
36. Qazvīnī/*ZTG*, 70; Ḥāfiẓ Abrū/*ZJT*, 191. Ahrī writes, 'no one against whom Uvays harbored enmity in his heart escaped. They were seized by the servants of this highness and doomed to death'; see Ahrī/*TSU*, (Persian text), 184; (English translation), 83.
37. Qazvīnī/*ZTG*, 71; Ḥāfiẓ Abrū/*ZJT*, 191; Faṣīḥ Khvāfī/*Mujmal*, 93; Samarqandī/*Maṭla'*, 1:312.
38. Qazvīnī/*ZTG*, 71; Ḥāfiẓ Abrū/*ZJT*, 191; Faṣīḥ Khvāfī/*Mujmal*, 93; Samarqandī/*Maṭla'*, 1:312.
39. A letter purportedly sent by the Ottoman sultan Murād I to Shaykh Uvays in 762/1361 is preserved in Ferīdūn Aḥmed Bey, *Mecmū'a-yi Münşe'āt-i Selāṭīn* (Istanbul: Dār al-Ṭibā'a al-'Āmira, 1848), 89–90. In the letter, the sultan explains that until then no one had come from the Ottoman court due to the difficulties caused by the blockages of the roads through Anatolia, and that he was sending two individuals to be attendant at Shaykh Uvays's court, as well as a servant (or eunuch: *khādim*), ten beardless Rūmī slaves, and three pieces of red broadcloth (*chūqa-yi surkh*).
40. Ḥāfiẓ Abrū's dependence on Zayn al-Dīn Qazvīnī has been pointed out by

Charles Melville in his article 'Ḥamd Allāh Mustawfī's *Ẓafarnāmah* and the Historiography of the Late Ilkhanid Period', in Kambiz Eslami (ed.), *Iran and Iranian Studies: Essays in Honor of Iraj Afshar* (Princeton: Zagros, 1998), 4.

41. The positive historical image of Shaykh Uvays was continued in the Ottoman context as well. As Cornell Fleischer has pointed out, in Muṣṭafá 'Ālī's treatment of the Mongol successor states in his *Fuṣūl-i Ḥall ve 'Aḳd*, Shaykh Uvays is praised as a ruler who used his wealth to patronise art and learning, which served to glorify his memory. This positive image of the Jalayirid sultan was incorporated into Muṣṭafá 'Ālī's discourse on the degradation of Ottoman institutions in the late tenth/sixteenth century, and served a primarily rhetorical function in 'Ālī's criticism of the situation in his own time. See Cornell H. Fleischer, *Bureaucrat and Intellectual in the Ottoman Empire: The Historian Mustafa Ali (1541–1600)* (Princeton: Princeton University Press, 1986), 282, n. 22.
42. Qazvīnī/*ZTG*, 74; Naṭanzī/Aubin, 167; Ḥāfiẓ Abrū/*ZJT*, 192; Faṣīḥ Khvāfī/*Mujmal*, 96. Faṣīḥ Khvāfī refers to Khvāja Mirjān as Khvāja Jawhar Khādim, although he does refer to Khvāja Mirjān as the successor to Sulaymān Shāh Khāzin in Baghdad in 770/1368–69. See Faṣīḥ Khvāfī/*Mujmal*, 101. Ḥāfiẓ Abrū describes Khvāja Mirjān as the *vālī* of Baghdad in *Ẕayl-i Jāmi' al-Tavārīkh*, 192; Naṭanzī describes him as an *atabeg* (*nisbat bi-ū rāh-i atābīkī dāsht*) and governor (*ḥākim*) of Baghdad.
43. Ḥāfiẓ Abrū/*ZJT*, 193.
44. Maqrīzī/Ziyāda, 4:287.
45. Maqrīzī/Ziyāda, 4:287.
46. This was Qāḍī Shaykh 'Alī, whom Shaykh Uvays had entrusted with the administration of Tabriz when he set out for Baghdad. See Qazvīnī/*ZTG*, 74.
47. Maqrīzī/Ziyāda, 4:288.
48. Ḥāfiẓ Abrū has 'Quraysh Dam' (*band-i quraysh*). See Ḥāfiẓ Abrū/*ZJT*, 192.
49. Qazvīnī/*ZTG*, 74; Ḥāfiẓ Abrū/*ZJT*, 192.
50. Qazvīnī/*ZTG*, 75–6; Ḥāfiẓ Abrū/*ZJT*, 192–3. Zayn al-Dīn Qazvīnī and Ḥāfiẓ Abrū mention Shaykh Uvays's son and successor Sulṭān Ḥusayn for the first time in the context of the plans for the assault on Baghdad.
51. Qazvīnī/*ZTG*, 77; Ḥāfiẓ Abrū/*ZJT*, 193.
52. Qazvīnī/*ZTG*, 77; Naṭanzī/Aubin, 167; Ḥāfiẓ Abrū/*ZJT*, 193; Faṣīḥ Khvāfī/*Mujmal*, 96. Maqrīzī writes that Khvāja Mirjān was blinded (*saml 'aynayhi*), a detail not mentioned by the Persian sources. See Maqrīzī/Ziyāda, 4:293.
53. Qazvīnī/*ZTG*, 78; Ḥāfiẓ Abrū/*ZJT*, 194.
54. Qazvīnī/*ZTG*, 79; Ḥāfiẓ Abrū/*ZJT*, 194.
55. Qazvīnī/*ZTG*, 83; Ḥāfiẓ Abrū/*ZJT*, 195; Faṣīḥ Khvāfī/*Mujmal*, 101.
56. Qazvīnī/*ZTG*, 83; Ḥāfiẓ Abrū/*ZJT*, 195.
57. Qazvīnī/*ZTG*, 79; Ḥāfiẓ Abrū/*ZJT*, 194; Faruk Sümer, *Kara Koyunlular*

(Başlangıçtan Cihan-Şah'a kadar), I. Cilt (Ankara: Türk Tarih Kurumu Basımevi, 1962), 41.

58. Zayn al-Dīn writes that Shaykh Uvays plundered all of Bayrām Khvāja's *īl va ulūs*, which can be translated generally as 'population and land'. See Qazvīnī/*ZTG*, 79. Ḥāfiẓ Abrū adds 'tents' (*khāna*) to his description of the targets of the pillage of the Jalayirids; see Ḥāfiẓ Abrū/*ZJT*, 194.
59. Qazvīnī/*ZTG*, 81; Ḥāfiẓ Abrū/*ZJT*, 194; Faṣīḥ Khvāfī, *Mujmal-i Faṣīḥī*, 100.
60. Bayrām Beg b. Sulṭān Shāh is described by Ḥāfiẓ Abrū as the beloved of the sultan. A conflict between Bayrām Beg and two amirs in the royal council session (*majlis*) in 761/1360 prompted Shaykh Uvays to send Bayrām Beg to Baghdad for a time. This separation was the subject of Salmān Sāvajī's *Firāq-nāma*. See Ḥāfiẓ Abrū/*ZJT*, 191–2; Jan Rypka, *History of Iranian Literature* (Dordrecht: D. Reidl, 1968), 262.
61. Qazvīnī/*ZTG*, 81; Ḥāfiẓ Abrū/*ZJT*, 194–5; Faṣīḥ Khvāfī/*Mujmal*, 100.
62. Qazvīnī/*ZTG*, 82; Ḥāfiẓ Abrū/*ZJT*, 195; Faṣīḥ Khvāfī/*Mujmal*, 100.
63. Qazvīnī/*ZTG*, 82; Ḥāfiẓ Abrū/*ZJT*, 195.
64. Qazvīnī/*ZTG*, 90; Ḥāfiẓ Abrū/*ZJT*, 196–7; Faṣīḥ Khvāfī/*Mujmal*, 106. The close association between Shaykh Uvays and his vassal the Shīrvānshāh is illustrated by a manuscript of work known as the *Farhād-nāma*, composed between 1369 and 1372 by one Muḥammad b. Muḥammad b. al-'Arif al-Ardabīlī. A poetic work in Persian, the *Farhād-nāma*, as described by Filiz Çağman and Zeren Tanındı, contains two *masnavīs*, the first dedicated to Shaykh Uvays, and the second dedicated to the Shīrvānshāh Hūshang. See Filiz Çağman and Zeren Tanındı, 'Selections from Jalayirid Books in the Libraries of Istanbul', *Muqarnas* 28 (2011): 224–5.
65. Naṭanzī/Aubin, 163–6.
66. This *risāla* was published by Felix Tauer in 1959 under the title *Cinq opuscules de Ḥāfiẓ-i Abrū concernant l'histoire de l'Iran au temps de Tamerlan*, and was part of Ḥāfiẓ Abrū's larger work, the *Majmū'a-yi Ḥāfiẓ Abrū*. See Charles Ambrose Storey, *Persian Literature: A Bio-Bibliographical Survey* (London: Luzac & Co., 1927–), 1:86.
67. Ḥāfiẓ Abrū, *Cinq opuscules de Ḥāfiẓ-i Abrū concernant l'histoire de l'Iran au temps de Tamerlan*, ed. Felix Tauer (Prague: L'Académie Tchécoslovaque des sciences, 1959), 9.
68. On the Sarbadārs, see Jean Aubin, 'Aux origins d'un movement populaire medieval le cheykhisme du Bayhaq et du Nichâpour', *Studia Iranica* 5 (1976): 213–24; Jean Aubin, 'La fin de l'état Sarbadār du Khorassan', *Journal Asiatique* (1974): 95–118; John Masson Smith, Jr, *The History of the Sarbadār Dynasty, 1336–1381 A.D. and its Sources* (The Hague: Mouton, 1970).
69. Ḥāfiẓ Abrū, *Cinq opuscules*, 11.
70. Ḥāfiẓ Abrū, *Cinq opuscules*, 11.
71. Ḥāfiẓ Abrū, *Cinq opuscules*, 11.

72. Qazvīnī/*ZTG*, 87; Ḥāfiẓ Abrū, *Cinq opuscules*, 11; Ḥāfiẓ Abrū/*ZJT*, 196; Faṣīḥ Khvāfī/*Mujmal*, 104.
73. Qazvīnī/*ZTG*, 87–8; Ḥāfiẓ Abrū, *Cinq opuscules*, 11; Ḥāfiẓ Abrū/*ZJT*, 196; Faṣīḥ Khvāfī/*Mujmal*, 104.
74. Qazvīnī/*ZTG*, 88; Ḥāfiẓ Abrū/*ZJT*, 196; Faṣīḥ Khvāfī/*Mujmal*, 104 (Faṣīḥ Khvāfī does not mention the reluctance of the amirs to stay in Simnan).
75. Qazvīnī/*ZTG*, 88; Ḥāfiẓ Abrū/*ZJT*, 196; Faṣīḥ Khvāfī/*Mujmal*, 105. A decree, probably issued by Shaykh Uvays in Rabīʻ I 775/August 1373, instructed a certain Shujāʻ al-Dīn ʻĀdil Bahādur to recognise the rights of the disciples of the Ṣafavī shaykh Ṣadr al-Dīn in the district of Garmrūd. In his commentary on this document, Gottfried Herrmann suggests that this Shujāʻ al-Dīn ʻĀdil Bahādur could possibly be identified with Amīr ʻĀdil. See Gottfried Herrmann, *Persische Urkunden der Mongolenzeit* (Wiesbaden: Harrassowitz Verlag, 2004), 171.
76. Qazvīnī/*ZTG*, 92; Ḥāfiẓ Abrū/*ZJT*, 197.
77. Ahrī/*TSU*, (Persian text), 176; (English translation), 76.
78. Peter Jackson, 'Muẓaffarids', *Encyclopaedia of Islam*, 2nd edn (Leiden: Brill, 1992), 7:820–2.
79. Qazvīnī/*ZTG*, 85–6; Ḥāfiẓ Abrū/*ZJT*, 195–6; Faṣīḥ Khvāfī/*Mujmal*, 101–2.
80. Shāh Maḥmūd died on 9 Shawwāl 776/13 March 1375. See Kutubī/*TAM*, 91.
81. Qazvīnī/*ZTG*, 86; Ḥāfiẓ Abrū/*ZJT*, 196. Qāḍī Shaykh ʻAlī is first mentioned by Zayn al-Dīn Qazvīnī when Shaykh Uvays entrusted Qāḍī Shaykh ʻAlī and the sultan's brother, Amīr Zāhid, with the city of Tabriz in 765/1364, when Shaykh Uvays went to Baghdad to put down Khvāja Mirjān's rebellion; see Qazvīnī/*ZTG*, 74. He is next mentioned with reference to his daughter's marriage to prince Shaykh Ḥasan b. Shaykh Uvays. In the period after Shaykh Uvays's reign, Qāḍī Shaykh ʻAlī was the most prominent member of the religious elite in Tabriz, and apparently built a madrasa in the city; see Qazvīnī/*ZTG*, 129–30, 134. Along with Amīr ʻĀdil, Qāḍī Shaykh ʻAlī guided the actions of Sulṭān Ḥusayn b. Shaykh Uvays, and was exiled to Damascus following a plot against Sulṭān Ḥusayn; see Ḥāfiẓ Abrū/*ZJT*, 205. Faṣīḥ Khvāfī reports that Qāḍī Shaykh ʻAlī paid one hundred *tūmān aqcha*s to avoid execution; see Faṣīḥ Khvāfī/*Mujmal*, 113.
82. Ḥāfiẓ Abrū/*ZJT*, 197.
83. Ḥāfiẓ Abrū/*ZJT*, 197.
84. Fażl Allāh's travels took him to Isfahan, Mecca, Khwarazm, Sabzavar and back to Isfahan before he came to Tabriz. See Shahzad Bashir, *Fazlallah Astarabadi and the Hurufis* (Oxford: Oneworld, 2005), 7–19.
85. Bashir, *Fazlallah Astarabadi and the Hurufis*, 27, 30.
86. H. Algar, 'Astarābādī, Fażlallāh', *Encyclopaedia Iranica*, ed. Ehsan Yarshater (London and New York: Routledge and Kegan Paul, 1987), 2:841; Shahzad Bashir, 'Deciphering the Cosmos from Creation to Apocalypse: The Hurufiyya Movement and Medieval Muslim Esotericism', in Abbas

Amanat and Magnus Bernhardsson (eds), *Imagining the End: Visions of Apocalypse from the Ancient Middle East to Modern America* (London: I. B. Tauris, 2002), 173; Bashir, *Fazlallah Astarabadi and the Hurufis*, 11.

87. Abdülbâki Gölpınarlı, *Hurûfîlik Metinleri Kataloğu* (Ankara: Türk Tarih Kurumu Basımevi, 1973), 6; Ya'qūb Āzhand, *Ḥurūfiyya dar Tārīkh* (Tehran: Nashr-i Nay, 1369 [1990]), 11; Algar, 'Astarābādī, Fażlallāh', 842; Bashir, 'Deciphering the Cosmos from Creation to Apocalypse', 173; Bashir, *Fazlallah Astarabadi and the Hurufis*, 19–20.
88. Gölpınarlı, *Hurûfîlik Metinleri Kataloğu*, 6; Āzhand, *Ḥurūfiyya dar Tārīkh*, 11; Algar, 'Astarābādī, Fażlallāh', 842; Bashir, 'Deciphering the Cosmos from Creation to Apocalypse', 173.
89. Bashir, *Fazlallah Astarabadi and the Hurufis*, 21.
90. Mas'ūd Dāmghānī, the son-in-law of former vizier Khvāja 'Abd al-Ḥayy, was named vizier by the Chubanid Malik Ashraf in 750/1349. See Qazvīnī/*ZTG*, 46.
91. Bashir, *Fazlallah Astarabadi and the Hurufis*, 20.
92. The plague first appeared in Tabriz in 747/1346–47. See Michael W. Dols, *The Black Death in the Middle East* (Princeton: Princeton University Press, 1977), 45.
93. Qazvīnī/*ZTG*, 86; Ḥāfiẓ Abrū/*ZJT*, 196; Faṣīḥ Khvāfī/*Mujmal*, 103.
94. Qazvīnī/*ZTG*, 87; Ḥāfiẓ Abrū/*ZJT*, 196; Faṣīḥ Khvāfī/*Mujmal*, 104.
95. Qazvīnī/*ZTG*, 92; Ḥāfiẓ Abrū/*ZJT*, 197; Faṣīḥ Khvāfī/*Mujmal*, 108.
96. Qazvīnī/*ZTG*, 83; Ḥāfiẓ Abrū/*ZJT*, 195; Faṣīḥ Khvāfī/*Mujmal*, 101.
97. Qazvīnī/*ZTG*, 83–4; Ḥāfiẓ Abrū/*ZJT*, 195.
98. Qazvīnī/*ZTG*, 85; Ḥāfiẓ Abrū/*ZJT*, 195.
99. This palace, or pavilion, at Ujan is referred to as '*kūshk*' by Zayn al-Dīn Qazvīnī and Ḥāfiẓ Abrū, and '*qaṣr*' by Faṣīḥ Khvāfī.
100. Qazvīnī/*ZTG*, 89; Ḥāfiẓ Abrū/*ZJT*, 196; Faṣīḥ Khvāfī/*Mujmal*, 104–5.
101. Luciano Petech, 'Les Marchands Italiens dans l'Empire Mongol', *Journal Asiatique* 250 (1962): 569; Michele Bernardini, 'Genoa', *Encyclopaedia Iranica*, ed. Ehsan Yarshater (London and New York: Routledge and Kegan Paul, 2001), 10:423.
102. Michel Balard, 'Les Gênois en Asie centrale et en extrême-orient au XIVe siècle: un cas exceptionnel?', in *Économies et sociétés au moyen age: mélanges offerts à Eduoard Perroy* (Paris: Publications de la Sorbonne 5, 1973), 686.
103. Petech, 'Les Marchands Italiens dans l'Empire Mongol', 569.
104. Bernardini, 'Genoa', 423.
105. Jean Richard, 'Buscarello de Ghizolfi', *Encyclopaedia Iranica*, ed. Ehsan Yarshater (London and New York: Routledge and Kegan Paul, 1990), 4:569.
106. Petech, 'Les Marchands Italiens dans l'Empire Mongol', 569; Bernardini, 'Genoa', 423.
107. Nevertheless, Genoese trade did not completely disappear, despite Genoa's

official boycott. In January 1344 (Sha'bān or Ramaḍān 744) a Genoese citizen named Tommasino Gentile was absolved of having violated the boycott. See Balard, 'Les Gênois en Asie centrale et en extrême-orient', 685.

108. Bernardini, 'Genoa', 423.
109. Ruy Gonzalez de Clavijo, *Embassy to Tamerlane, 1403–1406*, trans. Guy Le Strange (London: George Routledge and Sons, 1928), 151–2.
110. Clavijo, *Embassy to Tamerlane*, 152.
111. Petech, 'Les Marchands Italiens dans l'Empire Mongol', 569.
112. Muḥammad Javād Mashkūr, *Tārīkh-i Tabrīz tā Pāyān-i Qarn-i Nuhum-i Hijrī* (Tehran: Anjuman-i Āsār-i Millī, 1352 [1973]), 593; Petech, 'Les Marchands Italiens dans l'Empire Mongol', 570.
113. Halil İnalcık, 'The Question of the Closing of the Black Sea under the Ottomans', in *Essays in Ottoman History* (Istanbul: Eren, 1998), 428.
114. Qazvīnī/*ZTG*, 92.
115. Naṭanzī/Aubin, 167.
116. Maqrīzī/Ziyāda, 4:381.
117. Bayānī, *Tārīkh-i Āl-i Jalāyir*, 51; Mashkūr, *Tārīkh-i Tabrīz*, 591.
118. Mashkūr gives the meaning of this name as '*istakhr-i zāviya*' (dervish lodge lake, or *zaviye gölü*). See Mashkūr, *Tārīkh-i Tabrīz*, 592.
119. Mashkūr, *Tārīkh-i Tabrīz*, 591–2.
120. Bayānī, *Tārīkh-i Āl-i Jalāyir*, 53.

7

Dynastic Ideology during the Reign of Shaykh Uvays

By 1360, Sultan Shaykh Uvays had taken control of Azarbayjan, the first step in consolidating Jalayirid rule over the lands of the western Ilkhanate. In addition to this military conquest, and the consolidation of authority as described in the previous chapter, the ideological foundations of the Jalayirid sultanate were elaborated during the reign of Shaykh Uvays. In this period, the servants and supporters of Shaykh Uvays created a complex narrative and official image of the Jalayirid dynasty as the rightful successors to the Ilkhanids. Unlike previous Chubanid amirs like Malik Ashraf, as well as Shaykh Ḥasan Jalayir, who had ruled in the name of figurehead khans, Shaykh Uvays claimed a number of royal titles for himself, including sultan, khan and *ṣāḥib-qirān* (lord of the auspicious conjunction). This ideological programme was created by individuals who relied on the Jalayirid court for their livelihood, and had also served the Ilkhanids and had a professional interest in the continuation of the Ilkhanid political order. They stood to benefit from a royal patron who ruled from the wealthy province of Azarbayjan and who patronised the urban literate religious and administrative culture in Tabriz. This chapter explores some of the major aspects of Mongol imperial, Ilkhanid and Perso-Islamic ideologies of legitimate rulership that came to be incorporated into works of history, administrative protocol, poetry, architecture and art during the reign of Shaykh Uvays. What we find is an ideology of legitimate rulership that looked to the Ilkhanid past while at the same time acknowledging the unique nature of the Jalayirid sultan's identity as the ideal upholder of the values of the steppe, justice and Islam.

Shaykh Uvays as Heir to the Ilkhanate

An important aspect of the political identity of Shaykh Uvays as presented by individuals in the service of the Jalayirid court was the close connection of his family to the Ilkhans. An attempt to present Shaykh Uvays as the legitimate heir to the Ilkhanid dynastic tradition is found in the only surviving work of history written for and about the Jalayirid dynasty, the *Tārīkh-i Shaykh Uvays*, completed around 761/1360 by Abū Bakr al-Quṭbī al-Ahrī. This work is a universal history, from the beginning of the world down to the accession of Ahrī's patron Shaykh Uvays. Ahrī depends for much of his information on the monumental universal history of the Ilkhan vizier Rashīd al-Dīn (d. 718/1318). However, the final section of the work is valuable for its account of the post-Ilkhan political situation from a Jalayirid perspective.

Ahrī's organisation of his account of the post-Abū Sa'īd period is significant. The history is arranged by the reigns of the Ilkhans. For the years after the death of Abū Sa'īd, Ahrī continued to present a linear succession of sultans, and organised his information under the reigns of the Chinggisid protégés installed by the amirs who held actual power. Thus, while the Chinggisid puppet khans installed by Shaykh Ḥasan Jalayir are given headings, Shaykh Ḥasan himself is not recognised as a legitimate ruler. It was Shaykh Uvays, whose reign is given the heading 'the sultanate of the supreme Ruler, lord of the necks of the populace (*salṭanat-i pādishāh-i a'ẓam mālik-i riqāb-i umam*) Shaykh Uvays Bahādur Khan', who was recognised by Ahrī as the first legitimate Jalayirid sovereign.[1]

Thus, Ahrī's work is not a history of a Jalayirid dynasty per se, with Shaykh Uvays as the climax of a noble ruling family. Although Shaykh Uvays's father and grandfather are given great respect, it is the Chinggisid ruling family that provides the basis for Ahrī's presentation of his universal history. Shaykh Uvays is of course the pinnacle and culmination of his narrative; however, it is a narrative that conforms to a notion of the privileged place of Chinggisid lineage, even when those who held power could not claim this lineage for themselves.

Although Shaykh Uvays was not a Chinggisid though the lineage of his father, Ahrī emphasised his genealogical ties to female members of the Ilkhanid royal house. The final section of his *Tārīkh* is dedicated to Shaykh Uvays's 'noble lineage' (*naṣab-i sharīfash*).[2] Here Ahrī points out that Shaykh Uvays's mother Dilshād Khātūn's own mother was descended from the Ilkhan Aḥmad Tegüder. He also reminds his reader that Shaykh Uvays's paternal grandmother was Öljetey Sultan, the daughter of Arghun, another former Ilkhan ruler.[3] Thus, Shaykh Uvays could claim a place in the noble Ilkhanid family tree through two female lines, relationships not commonly considered sufficient to make one a legitimate Chinggisid prince. Ahrī had to be careful to situate Shaykh Uvays into a narrative which recognised the Chinggisid legitimising principle, despite the fact that he was not only not a Chinggisid, but also did not claim to rule in the name of a protégé or puppet khan as his father Shaykh Ḥasan had done. The ambivalence this created among those who served him and helped to cultivate his imperial image is reflected in Ahrī's work. Ahrī and others who were patronised by the Jalayirid court attempted to accommodate the non-Chinggisid Jalayirid dynasty as continuators of the Chinggisid and, more specifically, the Ilkhanid tradition.

In addition to his genealogical ties to the Ilkhanids, attempts were also made to present Shaykh Uvays as the logical successor to the last Ilkhan, Abū Sa'īd, despite the fact that Shaykh Uvays was not a direct descendant of Abū Sa'īd. The author of the manual of court protocol written for Shaykh Uvays, *Dastūr al-Kātib fī Ta'yīn al-Marātib*, Muḥammad b. Hindūshāh Nakhjivānī, devoted a portion of his dedication in this work to the praise and memory of the last Ilkhan ruler Abū Sa'īd and his grand vizier Ghiyāth al-Dīn Muḥammad.[4] Here Nakhjivānī describes how he was commissioned to write his book:

> In the days of the reign (*dawlat*) of the late fortunate sultan (*sulṭān-i sa'īd*) and pious praiseworthy ruler (*khāqān-i ḥamīd-i mabrūr*) 'Alā' al-Dunyā wa-al-Dīn Abū Sa'īd . . . the late august martyr (*ṣāḥib-i sa'īd-i shahīd-i maghfūr*) Khwāja Ghiyāth al-Ḥaqq wa-al-Dīn Muḥammad Rashīdī, may God cool his grave, and the other pillars of state and assistants of His Majesty repeatedly sent the order for the compilation of such a book.[5]

Nakhjivānī goes on to relate that he was able to complete his assignment in the service of the 'sultan of Islam [Shaykh Uvays] . . ., who occupies the position of heir and lieutenancy to Sultan Abu Sa'id (*dar maḥall-i vilāyat-i 'ahd va qā'im-maqāmī-yi sulṭān-i sa'īd abū sa'īd*)'.[6] Here Nakhjivānī clearly acknowledges the prominence of the Ilkhanate and its last ruler Abū Sa'īd. Although he dedicated his work to Shaykh Uvays,[7] he sought to connect the Jalayirid sultan's current rule directly to the former authority of Abū Sa'īd, with the suggestion that Shaykh Uvays was the inheritor of the Ilkhanid charisma which Abū Sa'īd had possessed. The rhetorical appeal to the recent Ilkhanid past illustrates the conservative impulse found among individuals like Nakhjivānī whose privileged social positions had been ensured by the Ilkhanid political order. A desire for the continuation of this order is found in Nakhjivānī's *Dastūr al-Kātib*.

A similar rhetorical project is at work in another work, written and dedicated to Shaykh Uvays in the early part of his reign. The *Ghāzān-nāma*, composed by Khwāja Nūr al-Dīn Azhdarī around the year 1361, is a poetic work in the style of the *Shāh-nāma* about the reign of the Ilkhan Ghāzān Khan. Azhdarī achieved notoriety as a physician after curing Shaykh Uvays of an illness that none of the other royal doctors had been able to treat. He dedicated his work about Ghāzān Khan to Shaykh Uvays in an opening section 'in praise of the *pādishāh-i islām* Shaykh Uvays'.[8] This title given to Shaykh Uvays, in a work on the first Ilkhanid *pādishāh-i islām*, suggests the connection and continuity between Ghāzān Khan and Azhdarī's Jalayirid patron.

Expression of the Jalayirid imperial image during the reign of Shaykh Uvays was also found on coins struck in his name.[9] The formulas found on these coins, similar to the organisation of Ahrī's history, suggest that Shaykh Uvays was able to assert his political authority in his own right in a way that his father had not. Shaykh Ḥasan Jalayir had struck some of his coins in the name of his Chinggisid protégés,[10] and others without the name of a sovereign at all. These coins included only the Muslim declaration of faith (*shahāda*) or other religious formula and the names of the first four caliphs.[11] However, Shaykh Uvays's coins bear several variations with his own name and titles. These include the formula 'the greatest [or, most just] sultan Shaykh Uvays Bahādur [Khan], may God preserve his rule and his sultanate' (*al-sulṭān* [*al-a'ẓam* or *al-'ādil*] *shaykh uvays bahādur* [*khān*] *khallada* [*allāh*] *mulkahu* [*wa salṭanatahu*]).[12] The formulas found on the coins echo those used by the later Ilkhans, particularly Abū Sa'īd. A typical coin struck in Azarbayjan during Abū Sa'īd's reign includes the formula:

> struck in [*ḍuriba fī*]
> the reign of the greatest sultan [*dawlat al-sulṭān al-a'ẓam*]
> the great Ilkhan Abū [*īlkhān al-mu'aẓẓam abū*]
> Sa'īd, may God preserve his rule [*sa'īd khallada allāh mulkahu*][13]

Another example, struck in Anatolia, uses the title 'master of the necks of the populace', which was also used by Ahrī to refer to Shaykh Uvays. The formula on this Anatolian coin was:

> Struck in the reign of the greatest sultan [*ḍuriba fī dawlat al-sulṭān al-a'ẓam*]
> Master of the necks of the populace [*mālik riqāb al-umam*]
> Ilkhan of the world Abū Sa'īd [*īlkhān al-'ālam abū sa'īd*]
> May God preserve his rule [*khallada allāh mulkahu*][14]

Although the names and formulas on most of Shaykh Uvays's coins reflect an Islamic religious tradition expressed in Arabic script, some coins were also struck using Mongol (Uyghur) script.[15] Such a measure surely reinforced the Mongol heritage of the Jalayirid court.

A final example of an attempt to identify Shaykh Uvays as the heir to the Ilkhanids, and even as an Ilkhanid himself, is an inscription on a copper water bowl made for the Jalayirid sultan. The inscription on the vessel reads:

Made on the order of the greatest sultan [*al-sulṭān al-aʿẓam*]
The great Ilkhan, the most just and noble khāqān [*al-īlkhān al-muʿaẓẓam al-khāqān al-aʿdal al-akram*]
Master of the necks of the populace [*mālik riqāb al-umam*]
Shadow of God on Earth [*ẓill allāh fī al-ʿālam*]
Strengthener of the world and religion [*muʿizz al-dunyā wa-al-dīn*]
Shaykh Uvays, may God preserve his realm and his power[16]

Here, Shaykh Uvays is referred to as 'the great Ilkhan', a clear illustration that in official circles within the Jalayirid court at Tabriz, an attempt was being made to portray Sultan Shaykh Uvays as the rightful heir to Abū Saʿīd.

Shaykh Uvays and the Legacy of Chinggis Qan

The historian Ahrī, the administrator Nakhjivānī, the poet Azhdarī and the anonymous creator of the copper water bowl all produced works that presented their patron, the Jalayirid sultan Shaykh Uvays, as the rightful successor to the line of the Ilkhans. In addition to these references to the descendants of Hülegü, other examples of official Jalayirid propaganda emphasise Shaykh Uvays's connections to the more distant Mongol imperial past. In official literature and public displays, the Jalayirids sought to invoke the memory of Chinggis Qan and to suggest a link between themselves and the Mongol conqueror.

In the dedication to the *Dastūr al-Kātib*, Nakhjivānī refers to Shaykh Uvays as 'the reviver of the customs of Chinggis Qanid fortune' (*muḥyī-yi marāsim-i dawlat-i jinkiz khānī*) and 'the refuge of the noble magnanimity of the qans' (*panāh-i ukrūma-yi makrama-yi qā'ānī*).[17] Both of these references seem designed to suggest Shaykh Uvays's connections to the former glories of the Mongol empire, ruled by the great qans of Qaraqorum. Nakhjivānī's use of the word 'reviver' (*muḥyī*) in the first reference suggests not only that the fortune of rulership had passed to Shaykh Uvays, but also that the 'customs' (or 'rites'; *marāsim*) of Chinggisid authority had lapsed, presumably following the death of Abū Saʿīd. The second reference suggests that Shaykh Uvays had inherited the legacy of Turko-Mongol (*qā'ānī*) rulership. Nakhjivānī's language suggests that the memory of Chinggis Qan remained an important aspect of Jalayirid authority, despite the fact that Shaykh Uvays himself was not a patrilineal descendant of Chinggis Qan.

A similar presentation of Shaykh Uvays as carrying on the legacy of Chinggis Qan can be found in an inscription in the Mirjāniyya madrasa in Baghdad. The madrasa was built by the Jalayirid governor of Baghdad

Khwāja Mirjān (d. 775/1374) and funded by an endowment from the mother of Shaykh Ḥasan, Öljetey Sultan.[18] Khwāja Mirjān was discussed in the previous chapter in the context of his rebellion against Shaykh Uvays in Baghdad in 765/1363. Earlier in his life Khwāja Mirjān had been a slave at the court of the Ilkhan ruler Öljeytü (r. 703/1304–716/1316), and was assigned to the governorate of Baghdad by Shaykh Ḥasan Jalayir in 755/1354.[19] He began the construction of his madrasa during Shaykh Ḥasan's lifetime, although it was completed after his death, and so features inscriptions dedicated to Shaykh Ḥasan as well as to his son Shaykh Uvays. One of these inscriptions describes Shaykh Uvays as 'the adorner of the emblem of the Chinggis Qanid fortune' (*muzayyin shi'ār al-dawla al-jinkiz khāniyya*).[20] Here we find an echo of Nakhjivānī's panegyric. The similarity in the language suggests that this was a standard theme in Jalayirid ideological rhetoric. Shaykh Uvays and those who served him attempted to present a link between the current sultan and the unquestioned authority of Chinggis Qan. The fact that we find this language on a public building as well as in a book written for court officials suggests the interests of the dynasty in making their ideological message available to large numbers of religious as well as administrative elites throughout the realm.

Shaykh Uvays as the Ideal Muslim Ruler

In addition to these references to the Jalayirid sultan as the rightful heir to the Ilkhanate and 'Chinggis Qanid fortune', the role of Shaykh Uvays as a Muslim ruler who upholds and defends the faith is also emphasised in the official literature. If we return to the work of Nakhjivānī, we find reference to Shaykh Uvays as the 'raiser of the banners of prophetic law' (*bar afrāzanda-yi rāyāt-i shar'-i nabawī*) and the 'lighter of the candle of the chosen religion [or, the religion of Muḥammad]' (*bar afrūzanda-yi sham'-i dīn-i muṣṭafawī*), as well as 'strengthened by the assistance of God, lord of the two worlds' (*mu'ayyad bi-ta'yīd allāh rabb al-'ālamīn*).[21] Such titles emphasise the role of Shaykh Uvays as an Islamic ruler whose authority is derived from God and who defends the religion of the Prophet. Since the period of Ghazan Khan, the Ilkhans had been not just khans in the image of Chinggis Qan, but Muslim rulers as well. They were sultans, *pādishāh*s of Islam.[22]

The Jalayirid sultan's role as a ruler who upholds right religion is also expressed in the *Anīs al-'Ushshāq*, a treatise on poetics written by Sharaf al-Dīn Muḥammad Rāmī Tabrīzī in the early years of Shaykh Uvays's reign. Rāmī dedicated his work to Shaykh Uvays, whom he described in his dedication as a defender and supporter of religion (*ḥāfiẓ-i bilād allāh*; *nāṣir-i 'ibād allāh*; *mu'ayyad min al-samā'*).[23] Such epithets do not necessarily connect the Jalayirids to the Ilkhanids, but they do suggest that Shaykh Uvays's identity as a Muslim ruler was another important aspect of the official legitimising ideology of the post-Ilkhanid period.

Among the inscriptions of the Mirjāniyya madrasa in Baghdad, we find an expression of Shaykh Uvays's role as protector of the Muslim community as well. Thus, in the entrance inscription, Shaykh Uvays is 'he who aids the world and religion, the helper of Islam and the Muslims' (*ghiyāth al-dunyā wa-al-dīn mughīth al-islām wa-al-muslimīn*),[24] and in the *miḥrāb* inscription he is 'the renewer of the customs of the Muslims' (*muḥyī marāsim al-milal al-muṣtafwiyya*).[25] These inscriptions, alongside the references to 'Chinggis Qanid fortune' as discussed above, reveal that Jalayirid authority was understood as derived from the dynasty's identity as both Mongol and Muslim.

Shaykh Uvays and the Ideal of Royal Justice

Finally, those who served and wrote in honour of Shaykh Uvays also worked to construct an image of their ruler as an eminently just monarch. The Jalayirid sultan was the perfect ruler because of his attention to matters of justice and the balancing of the interests and needs of all of his subjects. Shaykh Uvays's adherence to justice is expressed by Nakhjivānī when he refers to him as 'diffuser of the standards of equity' (*nāshir-i alwiya-yi nasfat*),[26] 'most just of the greatest of sultans' (*a'dal-i a'āẓim al-salāṭīn*), and 'custodian of approved action' (*vālī-yi vilāyat-i pasandīda-kirdarī*).[27] Alongside these are several descriptions in the *Dastūr al-Kātib* of the mercy and benevolence Shaykh Uvays shows to his subjects. He is the 'spreader of the carpet of mercy' (*bāsiṭ-i bisāṭ-i raḥmat*), the 'dissolver of the difficulties of worldly creatures' (*ḥallāl-i mushkīlat-i jahānīyānī*), 'succor of the distressed' (*ghiyāth-i malhūfīn*), 'aider of the oppressed' (*mughīth al-maẓlūmīn*), and the 'fortifier of the weak and the poor' (*muqawwī al-żu'afā' wa-al-masākīn*).[28] The Mongols were heirs to both Islamic and pre-Islamic notions of justice in Iran and Mesopotamia. Their predecessors the Abbasids had looked to both sacred law and royal law as part of their political ideology. In their articulation of this ideology, the caliphs had drawn on much older roots, in pre-Islamic Iranian and Hellenic traditions whereby the ruler served as dispenser and upholder of the law. Said Amir Arjomand has described this aspect of Abbasid ideology as 'Sasanian patrimonialism', which emphasised 'protection of the weak from the strong, removal of oppression, and administration of punishment for wrongdoing and for contraventions of customary norms of fairness'.[29] It is this vision of justice upheld by the ruler that is expressed in these examples from Nakhjivānī.

The Jalayirid sultan is praised for his justice in other examples as well. In his *Anīs al-'Ushshāq*, Rāmī describes Shaykh Uvays as a spreader of security, justice and beneficence (*bāsiṭ al-amn wa-al-amān*; *nāshir al-'adl wa-al-iḥsān*), and the shadow of God on Earth (*ẓill allāh fī al-arḍ*).[30] The musician 'Abd al-Qādir Marāghī, who was a renowned fixture at Jalayirid and Timurid courts, began his career in the service of Shaykh Uvays. In his autobiography, Marāghī referred to Shaykh Uvays as the *ṣāḥib-qirān*, and a *pādishāh* who dispenses justice, beneficence and generosity to the world.[31] The Mirjāniyya madrasa also displays expressions similar to those found in the works of Nakhjivānī, Rāmī and Marāghī. On the madrasa's entrance inscription is a testament to Shaykh Uvays's role as the 'spreader of justice in the world' (*nāshir al-'adl fī al-'ālam*).[32] On the left side of the *miḥrāb* is another inscription which characterises Shaykh Uvays as 'he who draws the hem of mercy upon the Arabs and the Turks' (*sāḥib dhayl al-raḥma 'alá al-a'rāb wa-al-atrāk*).[33] Such a specific reference to both of these groups was not only poetically elegant but also reflective of the diversity of the ethnic and linguistic population in Baghdad. This was a city that was home to a largely Arabic-speaking population, alongside the mostly Turkish amirs, a situation that had existed since the early Abbasid period.

Synthesis of Ideological Traditions: The Panegyric Poetry of Salmān Sāvajī

The aspects of the political ideology developed by the supporters and servants of Shaykh Uvays dealt with above were part of an attempt to present the Jalayirid sultan as the heir to the legacy of the Ilkhanate, through his connections to the Ilkhanid royal house, who upheld Islam and justice in his realm. All of these aspects are brought together in the work of the poet Salmān Sāvajī, who composed many verses praising the Jalayirids. In the section that follows, the life and work of Salmān Sāvajī are briefly examined in order to illustrate the way in which all of the ideological traditions discussed above were included in the writings of a single individual who received the patronage of the Jalayirids for helping to construct an image of legitimate rulership through elegant language.

Salmān Sāvajī was born around the year 709/1309–10 in Sāvah in Persian Iraq, to a family that had served the Ilkhan viziers in the business of accounting (*istīfā'ī*).[34] In his entry for Salmān, the biographer of poets

Dawlatshāh Samarqandī wrote that his family was always honoured by the sultans.[35] The career of Salmān's father benefited from the fact that it coincided with that of the most prominent native of Sāvah of the period, Sa'd al-Dīn Sāvajī, who served as vizier with Rashīd al-Dīn during the reigns of Ghazan and Öljeytü.[36] Salmān himself was trained in the business of the *dīvān* and chancery script (*'ilm-i siyāq va qūfī*),[37] but also began to gain notoriety as a poet at the end of Abū Sa'īd's reign. His patron was the vizier Ghiyāth al-Dīn Muḥammad, for whom he composed a *qaṣīda* known as *Badā'i' al-Asḥār* (or *Abḥār*).[38]

After Ghiyāth al-Dīn Muḥammad was killed in his conflict with 'Alī Pādshāh and the Oyrats in 736/1336, Salmān sought the patronage of Shaykh Ḥasan and his newly appointed vizier Shams al-Dīn Muḥammad Zakarīyā. After Shaykh Ḥasan was forced to abandon Azarbayjan in 740/1340 and settle permanently in Baghdad, Salmān followed him there, and soon became poet laureate (*malik al-shu'arā'*) of the Jalayirid court.[39] According to Dawlatshāh, Salmān was discovered by Shaykh Ḥasan Jalayir while the poet was making his way to Baghdad from his home town of Sāvah. Salmān composed a spontaneous verse about the amir and his slave who was fetching the arrows that he was shooting. Pleased with his work, Shaykh Ḥasan promoted Salmān, who became the darling (*qurrat al-'ayn*) of the Jalayirid family, and whose prestige reached the highest level during the reign of Shaykh Uvays.[40]

The vast majority of Salmān's odes (*qaṣā'id*, sing. *qaṣīda*) that survive are dedicated to prominent members of the Jalayirid dynasty and their ministers. In the following discussion of these *qaṣīda*s, attention has been paid to the attributes, titles and qualities ascribed specifically to the sultan, while less emphasis has been placed on the literary qualities of the odes. In other words, what is considered here are aspects of the official image and persona of Shaykh Uvays as expressed by the Jalayirid court poet, as a way of understanding what elements went into the creation of the Jalayirid dynastic image. Aspects relating to the artistic qualities of Salmān's work are not of primary concern here.

The panegyric of Salmān was probably not intended for a wide public audience; it is assumed here that his work was intended for the ears of the sultan and his entourage. However, it is likely that Salmān's odes were recited aloud in the restricted public forum of the royal court, which included members of the royal family, administrative officials, religious figures, and foreign travellers and envoys. What is suggested here is that given the dearth of narrative historical sources representing an official Jalayirid view of their own place in history and their relationship to the Ilkhanid past, the poetry written for the Jalayirid court, about the sultan, might help us to gauge more accurately what the Jalayirid view of their relationship to the Mongol political past might have been.

One of the most prevalent images in Salmān's *qaṣīda*s dedicated to Shaykh Uvays is that of the sun. The sultan is commonly referred to as the 'sun of the sultanate' (*āftāb-i salṭanat*),[41] or a similar variation, such as 'sun of the sky of the sultanate/power/rule' (*āftāb-i āsmān-i salṭanat*[42] or *āftāb-i āsmān-i mulk*[43]). Salmān employs other variations on this solar imagery, referring to Shaykh Uvays as 'lord of the sun of (royal) glory' (*dāvar-i khūrshīd-i farr*)[44] and the 'noble sun' (*khūrshīd-i karam*).[45] The sultan is also called the 'sun of justice protection' (*āftāb-i 'adl-parvar*),[46] suggesting that his ability to dispense and enforce justice spread like the rays of the sun throughout the kingdom. More will be said about Shaykh Uvays and the issue of justice in Salmān's *qaṣīda*s below.

Another major theme in Salmān's praise of Shaykh Uvays is frequent comparison to the historical and legendary pre-Islamic kings of Iran. In these comparisons, Salmān claims that Shaykh Uvays is equal to or surpasses these great rulers in whatever attribute they are most famous for. For example, Shaykh Uvays is likened to Anūshirvān in justice, Ardashīr in bravery, and Jamshīd in glory.[47]

Justice is a third major theme in Salmān's odes to Shaykh Uvays. The role of the ruler as a just and disinterested arbiter of the various competing interests in society was central to the concept of legitimate political authority in many pre-modern societies. Shaykh Uvays was not a lawgiver, in that he did not introduce a new code of justice as part of his political programme. Instead, he sought to uphold the Ilkhanid legal tradition, which had come to involve a combination of Islamic (*sharī'a*) and Mongol dynastic law (*yāsā*). The Islamic legal tradition involved more than just the theological debates and rulings of religious scholars and jurisconsults. The tradition of dynastic decree or arbitration, often referred to as *maẓālim*, was also part of the legal tradition in Islamic societies in the region ruled by the Ilkhanids.

Another common theme in Salmān's praise and characterisation of Shaykh Uvays is the sultan as the 'shadow of God' (*sāya-yi khudā*,[48] *sāya-yi ḥaqq*,[49] *ẓill-i ḥaqq*,[50] *sāya-yi parvardagār*[51]). This was a common title used by Islamic rulers since the time of the early Abbasid caliphs. It placed Shaykh Uvays well within the caliphal tradition, as a ruler whose right to rule depended on his role as a representative of God's will on earth. Variations on this title included 'shadow of God's grace' (*sāya-yi luṭf-i khudāvand*[52] or *sāya-yi luṭf-i ilahī*[53]) and 'divine shadow' (*sāya-yi khudā'ī*).[54]

In his verse in praise of Shaykh Uvays, Salmān made reference to

Shaykh Uvays's role as defender and supporter of Islam. These references range from the general 'upholder of religion' (*bar-dārā-yi dīn*)[55] and 'religion-protecting king' (*shāh-i dīn-parvar*)[56] to more specific references to Islamic tradition, such as 'supporter of the religion of the Prophet' (*nāṣir-i dīn-i nabī*).[57] In one instance, Salmān suggests that Shaykh Uvays draws upon both Shi'i and Sunni religious heritage to support his rule. Thus, he is the 'knower of the knowledge of 'Alī' (*'ālim-i 'ilm-i 'alī*) and 'equal in justice to [Caliph] 'Umar' (*'adīl-i 'adl-i 'umar*).[58] This reference to 'Alī among the attributes of the sultan illustrates the significance of Shi'i and 'Alid loyalties in the eighth/fourteenth century, particularly in the Jalayirids' domains in Arab Iraq. Shaykh Uvays's inheritance from his father included the cities of Najaf and Karbala, important centres of Shi'i veneration as the sites of the tombs of 'Alī and his son Ḥusayn. Shaykh Uvays's father and mother were both buried in Najaf, perhaps suggesting a personal devotion to 'Alī on the part of Shaykh Ḥasan and Dilshād Khātūn. In addition, the eighth/fourteenth century saw the rise of a number of Sufi *ṭarīqa*s demonstrating allegiance with, or at least sympathy for, the family of 'Alī and the Shi'i imamate. One of these was the Ḥurūfiyya, whose founder, Fażl Allāh Astarābādī, discussed briefly in the previous chapter, claimed descent from the seventh Shi'i imam, Mūsá al-Kāẓim. The Ṣafaviyya of Ardabil, although active in the mid-eighth/fourteenth century under Shaykh Ṣadr al-Dīn, had not yet taken on the overtly Shi'i aspects it would display in the ninth/fifteenth century.

The cultivation of an identity for Shaykh Uvays as a supporter and defender of Islam was not unique, but part of a general trend in the eighth/fourteenth century throughout the regions that had been conquered by the Mongols. In the Jochid *ulūs*, or Golden Horde, as well as in the Chaghatayid central Asia (the Ulus Chaghatay and Moghulistan), the political elite had converted to Islam by the mid-fourteenth century. Only in China did the Mongol rulers not become Muslims, but instead Sons of Heaven in the model of previous Chinese dynasties. The specifically Islamic symbols and language of authority found in the post-Ilkhanid period in Iran were thus part of a more general pattern of the Islamisation of Mongol khanates across Eurasia in the fourteenth century.

In addition to verses dedicated to Shaykh Uvays, Salmān also praised Shaykh Uvays's father, Shaykh Ḥasan, as well as his mother, Dilshād Khātūn (or Dilshād Shāh). An examination of Salmān's *qaṣīda*s in praise of these other two Jalayirid patrons, the parents of Shaykh Uvays, reveals similar language that combines claims to universal rule, references to famous Iranian kings of the historical and mythical past, and emphasis on the religious aspect of Jalayirid rule in Arab Iraq.

Shaykh Ḥasan is praised, like his son, as a conqueror (*khidīv-i jahān-gushā*)[59] and lord of the age (*dārā-yi 'ahd*,[60] *dārā-yi zamān*,[61] *khudāvand-i zamān*,[62] *sulṭān-i zamān* [63]). As with Shaykh Uvays, Salmān employs imagery of the sun, describing Shaykh Ḥasan as *āftāb-i mulk*,[64] *āftāb-i salṭanat* [65] and *shāh-i khurshīd-maḥall*.[66] Salmān also evokes the image of the person of Shaykh Ḥasan at the centre of the 'circle of kingship' (*nuqṭa-yi dā'ira-yi pādishāhī*)[67] and at the centre of the turning circle of heaven.[68] In addition, Shaykh Ḥasan is compared to the great kings of the past. He exhibits the 'traces of Jamshīd' (*jamshīd-āsār*),[69] and is a 'lord of the lineage of Farīdūn' (*dārā-yi afrīdūn-nasab*)[70] and 'Jamshīd worthy of Alexander' (*jamshīd-i iskandar-ḥasab*).[71] Such rhetoric placed Shaykh Ḥasan and his family in the tradition of the kings and heroes of the *Shāh-nāma*.

The pre-Islamic past is blended with the religious obligations of a Muslim ruler, who embodies all the best qualities of the Abrahamic-Quranic tradition. Thus, Shaykh Ḥasan is a ruler with the heart of Ḥaydar ('Alī) (*ḥaydar-dil*), the sunna of the most praised (Muḥammad) (*aḥmad-sunan*), the blood of Jesus (*'īsá-dam*) and the manner of Joseph (*yūsuf-shiyam*).[72] Here we see a blend of Shi'i and Sunni references, along with the pre-Islamic prophets Jesus and Joseph. Salmān seems to stress Shaykh Ḥasan's Shi'i leanings in one characterisation of the amir as 'a lord Ḥasan by name, Ḥusaynī by lineage and origin' (*dārā-yi ḥasan-nām ḥusaynī-yi nasab va aṣl*).[73] Such a line evokes not only the Jalayirid family lineage (Shaykh Ḥasan and his father Amīr Ḥusayn), but also the names of the two sons of 'Alī ibn Abī Ṭālib, the second and third Shi'i imams, Ḥasan and Ḥusayn. Perhaps this allusion appealed to elements among the Shi'i *'ulamā'* present at the court in Baghdad.[74] Salmān's play on these names connected the Jalayirid ruling family with Shi'i religious tradition as they found themselves ruling over two of the most important Shi'i holy sites of Najaf and Karbala.[75]

In addition to his praise of Shaykh Uvays and Shaykh Ḥasan, Salmān also wrote in honour of Dilshād Khātūn, the wife of Shaykh Ḥasan and mother of Shaykh Uvays. She was a descendant of the Chubanid amir Dimashq Khwāja, son of Amīr Chūpān and Tūrsun Khātūn, the grand-daughter of Aḥmad Tegüder Khan. As such, Dilshād represented the Ilkhanid royal house, as well as the Chubanid Sulduz family that had ruled the state de facto under Amīr Chūpān in the first years of Abū Sa'īd's reign. The union of Shaykh Ḥasan and Dilshād Khātūn produced Shaykh Uvays, progeny of all three major political families of the later Ilkhanate: the Jalayirids, Chubanids and Hülegüids. However, it was not just Dilshād's role as the mother of a future sultan that made her an important political figure. She also took an active role in the administration of the government in Baghdad.[76]

The image of Dilshād as a political leader, and not just the wife of Shaykh Ḥasan, is reflected in Salmān Sāvajī's *qaṣīda*s dedicated to her. She is the 'head and chief of the kings of the world' (*sar va sarvar-i shāhān-i jahān*;[77] also *sar-i salāṭīn*[78]) and 'lord of the sultans of the sea and plain' (*khudāygān-i salāṭīn-i baḥr va barr*).[79] Salmān even casts Dilshād in the role of a conqueror, praising 'Dilshād Shāh, a ruler veiled by the glory of the king, seized the kingdom of Sanjar and broke the crown of Heraclius' (*dilshād shāh shāhī k'az farr-i malik muqanna' bi-girift mulk-i sanjar bi-shikast tāj-i hirqil*).[80] In addition, just as Shaykh Uvays and Shaykh Ḥasan are compared to the great pre-Islamic kings of Iran, so Dilshād is compared to former queens, including Bilqīs, the Queen of Sheba, Qaydāfa, Queen of Barda, and Dārāb, the eldest daughter of Bahman in the *Shāh-nāma*.[81]

Finally, like her husband and son, Dilshād Khātūn is portrayed by Salmān as a supporter and defender of Islam. Thus, she is the 'supporter of prophetic law' (*nāṣir-i shar'-i payambar*) and 'guardian of the world and religion' (*'iṣmat-i dunyā va dīn*).[82] Salmān also describes Dilshād as the '*ka'ba* of the men of the state, [and] *qibla* of the lords of religion' (*ka'ba-yi arkān-i dawlat qibla-yi arbāb-i dīn*).[83] Here, as with Shaykh Ḥasan, the axis around which the heavens and circle of kingship turn, Dilshād too is imagined as a fixed central focus (*ka'ba*) around which turn the affairs of both the state and religion.

Salmān Sāvajī personally benefited from his close association with the Jalayirids, and acquired a vast amount of land and property from Dilshād Khātūn and Shaykh Uvays. However, Salmān's undoing was his unwillingness to continue his loyalty to the Jalayirids after Shaykh Uvays's son and successor, Sulṭān Ḥusayn, was driven out of Tabriz by the Muzaffarid prince Shāh Shujā' in 776/1375. Although Muzaffarid occupation in Tabriz was short-lived, Salmān's *qaṣīda*s in praise of Shāh Shujā' earned him the ire of Sulṭān Ḥusayn when he returned and restored Azarbayjan to Jalayirid control.

The preceding overview of the relationship of Salmān Sāvajī to the Jalayirid ruling family is intended to help understand the ideological foundations of their rule in the former Ilkhanid domains in the period after Abū Sa'īd, and especially during the reign of Shaykh Uvays. Praise for Shaykh Uvays and his parents, Shaykh Ḥasan and Dilshād Khātūn, emphasised the new dynasty's image as conquerors, world rulers and preservers of past traditions of both pre-Islamic Iranian kingship and Islam. The Jalayirids patronised Salmān not only for his talents as a poet, but also for the ways in which his verse reinforced the notion of Shaykh Uvays as a ruler very much in line with the legacy of Abū Sa'īd and the Ilkhanid state. While Salmān's verse was not necessarily for public consumption, its more narrow focus on the ruler and his court was designed to establish a political identity for the Jalayirids among the ruling class, and perhaps also among the literary and administrative elites who had served the Ilkhans, and could now hope to continue their livelihoods in the service of rulers who sought to present themselves as the rightful heirs to the Ilkhanid regime.

The preceding discussion has been an attempt to identify and analyse the ways in which legitimate political authority was conceived and expressed in the post-Ilkhanid Islamic world in the eighth/fourteenth century through an examination of the literary and material production of the court of the Jalayirid sultan Shaykh Uvays. The Jalayirid dynasty was descended from a Mongol tribal group that established itself among the ruling elite of the Ilkhanate from the earliest days of that state's existence. Although they were not patrilineal descendants of Chinggis Qan, their privileged place within the Ilkhan state, along with their matrilineal descent from two Ilkhanid rulers, seems to have allowed Shaykh Uvays to claim to uphold, if not the direct Chinggisid bloodline, then at least a more general notion of Mongol heritage. At the same time, an image of Shaykh Uvays as the dispenser and defender of justice in the name of Islam was also cultivated by those who produced literature at his court in Tabriz. Such an image had a long history in the Islamic world, and was one taken up by the Ilkhans, particularly Ghazan and Abū Sa'īd. The continuation of the rhetoric of a ruler who upheld Islamic and Chinggisid traditions indicates a conscious attempt on the part of the Jalayirid court, particularly after the re-conquest of the Ilkhanid heartland of Azarbayjan, to re-establish the Ilkhanate, albeit only in its western provinces and without a true prince of the blood. In an age when the symbolic authority of both the caliph and Chinggis Qan's family were no longer viable bases on which to arrange the political order, the expressions of the Jalayirid court under Shaykh Uvays represent an ongoing attempt to reformulate the meaning of legitimate authority among a ruling class which drew on both the glories of the conquests of Chinggis Qan and the expectations of the Muslim community to fashion its image and maintain its position.

The reign of Shaykh Uvays represented the height of royal authority in the years after Abū Sa'īd's death. The Jalayirid sultan seemed to have successfully established a dynastic state, founded on the principles upheld by the Ilkhans. The survival of this state would be challenged in the years following the death of Shaykh Uvays, first by a succession struggle among his sons, and then by the Chaghatayid amir and conqueror Tīmūr. As will be discussed in the following chapter, these challenges weakened the Jalayirid hold over Azarbayjan, Diyarbakr and Arab Iraq, and eventually led to the end of the dynasty in the early ninth/fifteenth century, as well as the end of the Ilkhanate as a compelling political concept.

Notes

1. Ahrī/*TSU*, (Persian text), 182; (English translation), 81.
2. Ahrī/*TSU*, (Persian text), 184; (English translation), 83.
3. Ahrī/*TSU*, (Persian text), 184; (English translation), 83.
4. Nakhjivānī/*Dastūr*, 25.
5. Nakhjivānī/*Dastūr*, 24–5.
6. Nakhjivānī/*Dastūr*, 25.
7. Nakhjivānī was a member of the Ilkhanid financial administration in the mid-eighth/fourteenth century. He was a close associate of the grand vizier Ghiyāth al-Dīn Muḥammad, who urged him to write a book of composition and correspondence protocol (*inshā'*) during the reign of Abū Sa'īd. However, he did not complete his *Dastūr al-Kātib* until many years after Abū Sa'īd's death, during the reign of Shaykh Uvays. See Nakhjivānī/*Dastūr*, ix, xi, 24–5.
8. Nūr al-Dīn Azhdarī, *Ghāẓān-nāma-yi Manẓūm*, ed. Maḥmūd Mudabbirī (Tehran: Bunyād-i Mawqūfāt-i Duktur Maḥmūd Afshār, 1380 [2001]), 19.
9. During the reign of Shaykh Uvays, coins were struck in his name throughout the Jalayirid sultanate, in provinces that were directly under his rule (Baghdad, Wasit, Khuy, Tabriz, Ardabil, Nakhjivan, Shirvan), as well as in Persian Iraq and Fars (Kashan, Isfahan, Shiraz). See Shīrīn Bayānī, *Tārīkh-i Āl-i Jalāyir* (Tehran: Intishārāt-i Dānishgāh-i Tihrān, 1962), 49.
10. Stephen Album, 'Studies in Ilkhanid History and Numismatics I: A Late Ilkhanid Hoard (743/1342)', *Iranian Studies* 13 (1984): 70–6, 84–7.
11. H. L. Rabino, 'Coins of the Jalā'ir, Ḳara Ḳoyūnlū, Mus͟ha'<u>sh</u>a', and Aḳ Ḳoyūnlū Dynasties', *Numismatic Chronicle* 6:10 (1950): 101.
12. Rabino, 'Coins of the Jalā'ir', 105; Bayānī, *Tārīkh-i Āl-i Jalāyir*, 49.
13. Sheila Blair, 'The Coins of the Later Ilkhanids: A Typological Analysis', *JESHO* 26 (1983): 300.
14. Blair, 'The Coins of the Later Ilkhanids', 299.
15. Ilkhanid coins, and those struck after 736/1335, would often exhibit the name of the ruler in Uyghur script. For example, coins struck in the name of the Chubanid puppet Sulaymān Khan, as well as those struck in the name of Shaykh Uvays, gave the ruler's name in this form. See Rabino, 'Coins of the Jalā'ir', 105; Norman D. Nicol, Raafat el-Nabarawy and Jere L. Bacharach, *Catalog of the Islamic Coins, Glass Weights, Dies and Medals in the Egyptian National Library, Cairo* (Malibu, CA: Undena, 1982), no. 4,712. There are also examples of coins struck in the name of Ghazan in which this

pattern is reversed, that is, the ruler's name is written in Arabic script, while the formula is in Uyghur script. See Blair, 'The Coins of the Later Ilkhanids', 296.

16. Y. A. Godard, 'Bassin de cuivre au nom de Shaikh Uwais', *Athār-é Īrān: Annales du service archaeologique de Īrān* 1 (1936): 371.
17. Nakhjivānī/*Dastūr*, 14.
18. Tariq Jawad al-Janabi, *Studies in Medieval Iraqi Architecture* (Baghdad: Republic of Iraq, Ministry of Culture and Information, 1982), 114.
19. Al-Janabi, *Studies in Medieval Iraqi Architecture*, 114.
20. Al-Janabi, *Studies in Medieval Iraqi Architecture*, 135–6.
21. Nakhjivānī/*Dastūr*, 14.
22. See Charles Melville, '*Pādishāh-i Islām*: The Conversion of Sultan Maḥmūd Ghāzān Khān', *Pembroke Papers* 1 (1990): 159–77.
23. Sharaf al-Dīn Muḥammad b. Ḥasan Rāmī, *Anīs al-'Ushshāq*, ed. Muḥsin Kiyānī (Tehran: Intishārāt-i Rawzna, 1376 [1997–98]), 39.
24. Vincenzo Strika and Jābir Khalīl, *The Islamic Architecture of Baghdad: The Results of a Joint Italian-Iraqi Survey* (Naples: Istituto Universitario Orientale, 1987), 48. Arabic text taken from Nāṣir al-Naqshbandī, 'al-Madrasa al-Mirjāniyya', *Sumer* 2 (1946): 48.
25. Al-Janabi, *Studies in Medieval Iraqi Architecture*, 135–6.
26. Nakhjivānī/*Dastūr*, 13.
27. Nakhjivānī/*Dastūr*, 14.
28. Nakhjivānī/*Dastūr*, 13–14.
29. Said Amir Arjomand, *The Shadow of God and the Hidden Imam: Religion, Political Order, and Societal Change in Shi'ite Iran from the Beginning to 1890* (Chicago and London: University of Chicago Press, 1984), 96.
30. Rāmī, *Anīs al-'Ushshāq*, 39.
31. Murat Bardakçı, *Maragalı Abdülkadir: XV. yy. bestecisi ve müzik nazariyatçısının hayat hikâyesiyle eserleri üzerine bir çalışma* (Istanbul: Pan Yayıncılık, 1986), 154.
32. Strika and Khalīl, *The Islamic Architecture of Baghdad*, 48.
33. Al-Janabi, *Studies in Medieval Iraqi Architecture*, 135–6.
34. Sāvajī/*Kullīyāt* (Vafā'ī's introduction), vi–vii.
35. Dawlatshāh/*Taẕkira*, 286.
36. Sāvajī/*Kullīyāt* (Vafā'ī's introduction), viii.
37. Dawlatshāh/*Taẕkira*, 286.
38. Sāvajī/*Kullīyāt* (Vafā'ī's introduction), xi.
39. Sāvajī/*Kullīyāt* (Vafā'ī's introduction), xii.
40. Dawlatshāh/*Taẕkira*, 287.
41. Sāvajī/*Kullīyāt*, 89, 92, 198.
42. Sāvajī/*Kullīyāt*, 174.
43. Sāvajī/*Kullīyāt*, 176.
44. Sāvajī/*Kullīyāt*, 63.
45. Sāvajī/*Kullīyāt*, 84.

46. Sāvajī/*Kullīyāt*, 105.
47. Sāvajī/*Kullīyāt*, 111.
48. Sāvajī/*Kullīyāt*, 21.
49. Sāvajī/*Kullīyāt*, 46.
50. Sāvajī/*Kullīyāt*, 82.
51. Sāvajī/*Kullīyāt*, 105.
52. Sāvajī/*Kullīyāt*, 145.
53. Sāvajī/*Kullīyāt*, 111.
54. Sāvajī/*Kullīyāt*, 21, 203.
55. Sāvajī/*Kullīyāt*, 77.
56. Sāvajī/*Kullīyāt*, 119.
57. Sāvajī/*Kullīyāt*, 40.
58. Sāvajī/*Kullīyāt*, 40.
59. Sāvajī/*Kullīyāt*, 10.
60. Sāvajī/*Kullīyāt*, 10, 86.
61. Sāvajī/*Kullīyāt*, 49.
62. Sāvajī/*Kullīyāt*, 49.
63. Sāvajī/*Kullīyāt*, 79.
64. Sāvajī/*Kullīyāt*, 10.
65. Sāvajī/*Kullīyāt*, 130.
66. Sāvajī/*Kullīyāt*, 107.
67. Sāvajī/*Kullīyāt*, 107.
68. 'The turning of heaven is like a circle round his grace' (*kih hast gardan-i gardūn z'bar-i minnatash chūn chanbarī*): Sāvajī/*Kullīyāt*, 205.
69. Sāvajī/*Kullīyāt*, 107.
70. Sāvajī/*Kullīyāt*, 153.
71. Sāvajī/*Kullīyāt*, 153.
72. Sāvajī/*Kullīyāt*, 153.
73. Sāvajī/*Kullīyāt*, 79.
74. Shaykh Ḥasan's supposed 'Alid loyalties have been noted by Roemer, due to the fact that he was buried in Najaf, site of the tomb of 'Alī. See H. R. Roemer, 'The Jalayirids, Muzaffarids and Sarbadārs', in Peter Jackson and Laurence Lockhart (eds), *The Cambridge History of Iran, Volume 6: The Timurid and Safavid Periods* (Cambridge: Cambridge University Press, 1986), 6, 9.
75. Sheila Blair has interpreted Shaykh Uvays's repair of the shrine of 'Alī in Najaf as both a memorial to his father, who was buried there, and an affirmation of his 'Alid loyalties. See Sheila Blair, 'Artists and Patronage in Late Fourteenth-Century Iran in the Light of Two Catalogues of Islamic Metalwork', *BSOAS* 48:1 (1985): 55.
76. See Ṣafadī/*A'yān*, 2:355.
77. Sāvajī/*Kullīyāt*, 30.
78. Sāvajī/*Kullīyāt*, 116.
79. Sāvajī/*Kullīyāt*, 36, 165.

80. Sāvajī/*Kullīyāt*, 137. The references here are to the Saljūq sultan Sanjar (d. 552/1157) and the Byzantine emperor Heraclius (d. 20/641).
81. Sāvajī/*Kullīyāt*, 6.
82. Sāvajī/*Kullīyāt*, 6.
83. Sāvajī/*Kullīyāt*, 6. In another example, Dilshād Khātūn is 'that lofty *ka'ba* and that *qibla* of excellence' (*ān kā'ba-yi a'ālī v'ān qibla-yi ma'ālī*). See Sāvajī/*Kullīyāt*, 137.

8

Challenges to the Jalayirid Order

The period following the death of Sultan Shaykh Uvays was one of disruption of the central authority he had attempted to establish in Tabriz. Between 776/1374 and 788/1386 the rule of the Jalayirid sultans was challenged by the power of the amirs, who rallied support around alternative Jalayirid princes. The most powerful amir in this period was Amīr ʻĀdil Āqā, who enjoyed support from the Oyrat tribesmen, and whose authority in Sultaniyya was confirmed by Tīmūr. Power in the sultanate became divided between Tabriz, Baghdad and Sultaniyya, each home to a Jalayirid contender for the throne. In addition, this period saw the rise in influence of the Qarāquyūnlū Turkmans on the northwestern frontier, and the beginning of their at times friendly, at times hostile relations with the Jalayirids.

The political situation was turned upside down after 788/1386, with the first campaigns of Tīmūr in Iran, which fundamentally altered the balance of power and challenged the Ilkhanid legacy as promoted by the Jalayirids. Tīmūr's arrival was not immediately devastating for the Jalayirid dynasty, however, and in fact Tīmūr's conquests served to restore the authority of the sultan by eliminating his rivals. The long reign of Sulṭān Aḥmad (r. 784/1382–813/1410) was characterised by a series of flights from Tīmūr's armies and subsequent attempts to regain control of Tabriz and Baghdad. Although Sulṭān Aḥmad was severely weakened by the Timurid campaigns, between 788/1386 and 813/1410 Jalayirid sovereignty remained important for political actors who sought to oppose or resist the Timurids. The Mamluk sultanate, the Ottoman beylik and the Qarāquyūnlū confederation all looked to the Jalayirid sultan as the embodiment of an alternative to Tīmūr in the late fourteenth century. For the Qarāquyūnlū leader Qarā Yūsuf in particular, Sulṭān Aḥmad became a link to the Ilkhanid legacy, which served as ideological capital with which to make claims to legitimate authority in Azarbayjan and Iraq in the early fifteenth century. Although the Jalayirid dynasty continued until the demise of Sulṭān Aḥmad's grandson, Sulṭān Ḥusayn, in 835/1432, the Qarāquyūnlū seizure of Tabriz following Sulṭān Aḥmad's death in 813/1410 signalled the end of the symbolic significance of Jalayirid sovereignty in the former Ilkhanid lands.

Breakdown of Central Authority (776/1374–788/1386)

The period from the death of Shaykh Uvays in 776/1374 until Sulṭān Aḥmad was driven from Tabriz by Tīmūr's forces in 788/1386 was one of political decentralisation, the growth of power of the amirs, and a weakening of the sultan's authority. Sulṭān Ḥusayn (r. 776/1374–784/1382) depended on his chief amir, 'Ādil Āqā, who held effective power in Tabriz and Sultaniyya. At the same time, Sulṭān Ḥusayn's brothers became rallying points for other amirs who opposed Amīr 'Ādil. In a sense, this was an indication that the notion of Jalayirid dynastic authority continued to be strong among the ruling elite after Shaykh Uvays's death. Any amir who wanted to establish himself sought the ideological cover of a Jalayirid prince to lend him legitimacy. At the same time, however, the Jalayirid state seemed on the verge of disintegration from within, particularly after Sulṭān Ḥusayn was killed by his brother, Sulṭān Aḥmad, in 1382, even while his other brothers Bāyazīd and Shaykh 'Alī maintained separate courts at Sultaniyya and Baghdad respectively. Amid the internal struggles for power among the Jalayirids was the steady growth in power of the Qarāquyūnlū Turkmans, led by Bayrām Khwāja, and subsequently by Qarā Yūsuf. The expansion of the territory and prestige enjoyed by the Qarāquyūnlū was linked to events in the Jalayirid sultanate in these years, as Amīr 'Ādil, and later Sulṭān Aḥmad, called on the Turkmans for military support in order to tip the balance of power to themselves in the struggles with the other amirs and princes.

Amīr 'Ādil Āqā (sometimes called 'Sāriq'; 'yellow, blond') began his rise to power at the end of the reign of Shaykh Uvays. In approximately 772/1370–71, Shaykh Uvays assigned him to the province of Rayy,[1] and it was here and in Sultaniyya that he would establish the base of his support. Although his assignment to Rayy is the first mention of Amīr 'Ādil in the sources, it seems that he quickly rose to prominence thereafter among the amirs of the Jalayirid realm. When Shaykh Uvays died in 776/1374, several amirs supported Sulṭān Ḥusayn in opposition to Amīr 'Ādil and another of Shaykh Uvays's sons, Shaykh 'Alī.[2] At the time of the sultan's death, both Amīr 'Ādil and Shaykh 'Alī were away from Tabriz, unable to assert themselves in the question of succession, and were obliged to offer their allegiance to Sulṭān Ḥusayn.[3] Although several important amirs were hostile to Amīr 'Ādil, he maintained his position of prominence. Amīr 'Ādil acted as Sulṭān Ḥusayn's protector when the Muzaffarid Shāh Shujā' occupied Tabriz in 777/1375, escorting the new sultan to Baghdad. This act allowed Amīr 'Ādil to keep Sulṭān Ḥusayn at a distance from those amirs who were hostile to himself. After the Muzaffarid threat had passed, however, and Amīr 'Ādil returned to his post in Sultaniyya, a group of conspirators attempted to move against him.

The timing of the conspiracy may have been prompted by Sulṭān Ḥusayn's bestowal of the city of Rayy to Amīr Valī, who, as discussed in Chapter 6, had served there as military governor under Shaykh Uvays.[4] Rayy had been under the authority of Amīr 'Ādil, and the reassignment of the city to Amīr Valī may have been perceived as a sign that Sulṭān Ḥusayn was willing to limit the scope of Amīr 'Ādil's authority. In 779/1378, a group of amirs gathered around Sulṭān Ḥusayn at his camp in Ujan. When Amīr 'Ādil arrived and presented himself at the royal pavilion, the amirs voiced their dissatisfaction with him, and announced that they no longer accepted his leadership.[5] Amīr 'Ādil was forced to return to Sultaniyya, and the amirs momentarily had their major rival out of the way. The role of Sulṭān Ḥusayn in these events is unclear. Ḥāfiẓ Abrū seems to indicate that he initially accepted the amirs' attempt to marginalise Amīr 'Ādil; however, he was soon forced to call on Amīr 'Ādil's aid after his treasury and possessions were plundered by the amirs.[6]

It thus became apparent that Amīr 'Ādil was the real power that held the sultanate together, and that the Jalayirid sultan's position in the royal capital at Tabriz could only be maintained by his backing and protection. This was due in part to the fact that Amīr 'Ādil commanded the loyalty of the Oyrats, one of the few autonomous Mongol tribal groups in the former Ilkhanid realm. Leading his own forces from Sultaniyya, and calling on the Oyrat army to the west, Amīr 'Ādil was able to overwhelm the rebellious amirs from two fronts. In his message to the Oyrats, he promised abundant property grants (*suyūrghāl*s)[7] to all who joined with Sulṭān Ḥusayn.[8] After the rebels were defeated, Sulṭān Ḥusayn sent his own letter to Amīr 'Ādil, assuring him that he had been opposed to the rebels, and that they should be punished.[9] Amīr 'Ādil executed four of the leaders of the uprising, while those who had remained loyal to the sultan were generously rewarded.[10] After this incident, there was no question that Amīr 'Ādil was the supreme authority behind the Jalayirid throne.[11]

Amīr 'Ādil's power increased even more following his successful defence against a second Muzaffarid invasion, led by Shāh Shujā' in 783/1381.[12] Based on Ḥāfiẓ Abrū's account, Shāh Shujā' this time seemed certain that he would be successful thanks to an alliance with Amīr 'Ādil. The Jalayirid commander had made overtures of friendship to the

Muzaffarids, sending gifts from Baghdad to Shiraz. Shāh Shujā‘ sent an envoy to Amīr ‘Ādil at Sultaniyya with the message:

> I have set out to subdue Tabriz. Now, if ‘Ādil Āqā is in agreement with me, and if his outward show of friendship is sincere, he must join with me and become obedient. If he has feigned the appearance of friendship, there must be war.[13]

However, the historian of the Muzaffarids, Maḥmūd Kutubī, does not suggest that there was any perceived alliance between Amīr ‘Ādil and the Muzaffarids, and writes only that Shāh Shujā‘ sought to punish Amīr ‘Ādil for exerting his own total authority over the region of Sultaniyya.[14] The battle that ensued outside Sultaniyya resulted in a Muzaffarid withdrawal, and Shāh Shujā‘ returned to Shiraz.[15] For Amīr ‘Ādil, his successful defence of the country against the Muzaffarids seems to have helped him even further in the consolidation of his own power. Ḥāfiẓ Abrū writes that Amīr ‘Ādil had achieved such a victory, and dealt with a matter of such difficulty, that his power (*tasalluṭ*) in the country increased.[16] Sulṭān Ḥusayn, on the other hand, had not faced the Muzaffarid attack. He had delayed in coming from Tabriz, and although he did take part in the main battle, he left Sultaniyya during the siege to meet his brother Sulṭān Aḥmad.[17] This situation reflected the relationship between the sultan and Amīr ‘Ādil throughout Sulṭān Ḥusayn's reign: authority in the Jalayirid realm was exerted by Amīr ‘Ādil through his control of the military, while Sulṭān Ḥusayn remained largely a symbolic figure.

Amīr ‘Ādil's military power was mirrored in the urban milieu by the influence of certain notable families, particularly the Kujujī shaykhs in Tabriz. Christoph Werner, Daniel Zakrzewski and Hans-Thomas Tillschneider have traced the close ties between the Kujujī family and the Jalayirid sultans, beginning with Shaykh Uvays, and have described Khwāja Shaykh Kujujī as both an urban notable and a representative of the Jalayirid dynasty.[18] In the conflict within the Jalayirid family after Shaykh Uvays's death, Khwāja Shaykh Kujujī sought to secure his prominence in Tabriz and provide some measure of stability for his family in the midst of the uncertain political situation by founding a mosque-madrasa-*khānqāh* complex in the city.[19] The endowment document, dated 782/1380, was witnessed by three of Shaykh Uvays's sons, including Sulṭān Ḥusayn, who referred to Kujujī in the document as ‘my father’ (*padaram*) and the ‘sultan of shaykhs of both worlds’ (*sulṭān al-mashāyikh fī ‘alamayn*).[20] According to Werner et al., Kujujī was a largely independent ruler in Tabriz, and portrayed himself in the tradition of a princely founder of the complex.[21] Between the power of Amīr ‘Ādil among the army, and Khwāja Shaykh Kujujī in Tabriz, the Jalayirid dynasty seemed to be more of an irrelevant or even destabilising element in the political life of Azarbayjan after Shaykh Uvays.

Little changed in this balance of power after Sulṭān Ḥusayn was murdered by his brother, Sulṭān Aḥmad, in Tabriz in 1382. Shaykh Uvays had made Sulṭān Aḥmad responsible for the region around Ardabil, a region closely tied to the Ṣafaviyya Sufi order under the leadership of Shaykh Ṣadr al-Dīn (d. 794/1392).[22] After a disagreement with his brother Sulṭān Ḥusayn, Sulṭān Aḥmad left Tabriz for Ardabil, and then went on to Arran and Mughan, where he prepared a military force. He then returned to attack Tabriz, a task made easier by the fact that Amīr ʿĀdil and all the Jalayirid forces were away from Azarbayjan, engaged in operations against Amīr Valī in Rayy.[23] Sulṭān Aḥmad entered Tabriz and the palace unopposed, and took the place of his brother on the royal throne. Sulṭān Ḥusayn managed to escape from the palace into the city, where he attempted to hide among the populace. However, he was quickly seized and executed.

Initially, Sulṭān Aḥmad seems not to have had the support of many of the amirs, who remained loyal to Amīr ʿĀdil. Instead, Sulṭān Aḥmad's followers were among the lower strata of society. According to Astarābādī, who served Sulṭān Aḥmad in Baghdad before joining the court of the ruler of Sivas, Qāḍī Burhān al-Dīn, Sulṭān Aḥmad systematically eliminated the 'great amirs and renowned chiefs (*ṣanādīd-i nāmdār*), who were the step-sons of favor (*rabīb-i niʿmat*) and the product of the dynasty (*ṣanīʿ-i tarbiyat-i ān khāndān*)', and gathered to himself 'a faction (*ṭāʾifa*) from among the followers of the army (*dhanāb-i mutajanda*) and the rabble of the people (*awbāsh al-nās*) who were marked by weakness of origin and ignorance of lineage', and who lacked intellect and bravery.[24] Of course, Astarābādī was clearly hostile to his former patron Sulṭān Aḥmad, and would not have been interested in glorifying his rise to power. However, it does seem likely that Sulṭān Aḥmad would have had to rely on non-elite supporters from among the population of Tabriz, considering that Amīr ʿĀdil commanded the loyalty of many of the Jalayirid amirs, and at the same time controlled Sulṭān Ḥusayn. Sulṭān Aḥmad could not have expected much enthusiastic support after killing his brother the sultan, and disrupting the political dynamic that put power back into the hands of the amirs in the period after Shaykh Uvays.

Sulṭān Aḥmad fled Tabriz when Amīr ʿĀdil marched against him following his assassination of Sulṭān Ḥusayn.[25] It was at this point that he attempted to appeal to his royal heritage in order to win some of the amirs to his side. He sent a message to Muḥammad Davātī, who was leading Amīr ʿĀdil's forces near the Aras river, and another to ʿAbbās Āqā and Misāfir Īradājī, the amirs whom Amīr ʿĀdil had deputised to occupy

Tabriz.[26] According to the Timurid historian Mīrkhvānd, Sulṭān Aḥmad asked, 'you are the *nöker*s of my father, why do you serve 'Ādil?'[27] His appeal to their loyalty to Shaykh Uvays, and thus the Jalayirid dynastic authority which had now devolved upon Sulṭān Aḥmad himself, convinced these amirs to turn against Amīr 'Ādil. They made their opposition known to Amīr 'Ādil, who was forced to leave Azarbayjan and return to Sultaniyya.[28] Sulṭān Aḥmad was able to return to Tabriz, but not before his own followers killed 'Abbās and Misāfir, out of fear that they would acquire privileged positions under Sulṭān Aḥmad.[29]

Amīr 'Ādil's supremacy among the amirs continued not only after Sulṭān Aḥmad came to power, but also even after Tīmūr's armies came to Iran. Details of Tīmūr's campaigns will be discussed below. At this point it is useful to note that initially Amīr 'Ādil was the beneficiary of Tīmūr's arrival. In 787/1385, Tīmūr captured Sultaniyya, and summoned Amīr 'Ādil, who had fled to Shiraz.[30] When Amīr 'Ādil complied, Tīmūr rewarded his obedience with *suyūrghāl* grants and confirmed his authority in Sultaniyya and Tabriz.[31] Tīmūr sought to incorporate Amīr 'Ādil into his own expanding military elite and marginalise the Jalayirid sultan in the process. Thus, the initial contact between Tīmūr and the Jalayirid realm continued the process of decentralisation and weakening of Jalayirid authority that had begun after Shaykh Uvays's death.

Despite the weakness of the sultanate in the period 776/1374–788/1386, the notion that legitimate authority resided in the Jalayirid dynasty persisted. Amīr 'Ādil did not attempt to seize the throne for himself, but executed his power in the name of Sulṭān Ḥusayn. The durability of the idea of Jalayirid sovereignty combined with a decentralisation of power meant that Jalayirid princes became rallying points of political conflict after the reign of Shaykh Uvays. In fact, this pattern reflected that of the Ilkhanid period, which was characterised by a balance between the centralising aspirations of the royal court and administrative authorities on the one hand, and the tendency for military power to be distributed among the amirs in the provinces on the other. Thus, the sons of Shaykh Uvays, as the Chinggisids had previously, all represented potential foci for the political aspirations of the military elite.

Sulṭān Ḥusayn was an attractive rallying point for the amirs when faced with the threat of invasion by the Muzaffarid Shāh Shujā' on two occasions. From all of our Timurid accounts, Sulṭān Ḥusayn was little more than a puppet of Amīr 'Ādil. According to Naṭanzī, he was desperately in love with his own image, and would cover his head, stare at his beautiful face in the mirror, and weep.[32] Yet, Sulṭān Ḥusayn's personality was preferable to the Muzaffarid invaders, and the amirs were ready to accept the nominal authority of the Jalayirid sultan, who could be more easily controlled and manipulated. Once the Muzaffarid threat had passed, other princes also offered opportunities for those opposed to the authority of Amīr ʻĀdil. Sulṭān Ḥusayn's brothers Shaykh ʻAlī, Sulṭān Aḥmad and Bāyazīd were all potential candidates for the Jalayirid throne.

Shaykh Uvays had assigned his son Shaykh ʻAlī to govern Baghdad before he died in 776/1374.[33] He was not chosen to succeed as sultan, despite the fact that he was older than Sulṭān Ḥusayn. Following the revolt of Khwāja Mirjān in the 760s/1360s, it is likely that Shaykh Uvays intended to prevent such uprisings in the future by leaving both Iraq and Azarbayjan in the hands of his two sons. Iraq had regained its political importance under the Jalayirids, after having become a secondary Ilkhanid province. Iraq had been the base of Shaykh Ḥasan's authority in the 740s/1340s and 750s/1350s when Azarbayjan was under Chubanid control. Under Shaykh Uvays and his successors, Baghdad remained the 'second city' in the Jalayirid realm, after Tabriz. By appointing Shaykh ʻAlī to the government of Iraq, he ensured that this province would remain under the authority of the Jalayirid royal house.

Shaykh ʻAlī seems to have governed Baghdad quietly during the first years of the reign of his brother Sulṭān Ḥusayn. However, he became the focus of an uprising in the year 780/1379,[34] directed against the son of the vizier Shams al-Dīn Zakarīyā, Vajīh al-Dīn Ismāʻīl.[35] The conspirators were from among the entourage of Shaykh ʻAlī and Vajīh al-Dīn Ismāʻīl and had the backing of the prince, who had come into conflict with Ismāʻīl.[36] They ambushed and killed Vajīh al-Dīn Ismāʻīl, sending the city of Baghdad into an uproar.[37]

The murder of the son of the vizier in Baghdad in the name of a Jalayirid prince posed a challenge to the established order of Sulṭān Ḥusayn, Shams al-Dīn Zakarīyā and Amīr ʻĀdil. When the sultan got word of the disorder in Baghdad, he appealed to his brother to remember that Iraq had been their family's original stronghold, from where they drew much of their power and support, and that he held his authority by virtue of royal mandate (*vaṣīyat-i pādishāhī*) and was not dependent on the amirs.[38] Essentially, Sulṭān Ḥusayn was urging his brother Shaykh ʻAlī to bring the situation in Baghdad under control before the violence spread.

However, the sultan's message was not enough to bring order to the region. Until the end of Sulṭān Ḥusayn's reign, the province of Arab Iraq remained in the hands of a rebel governor named Pīr ʻAlī Bādīk (or Bāvīk), who ruled in the name of prince Shaykh ʻAlī. Iraq and Azarbayjan, which had been united by Shaykh Uvays, and which constituted the foundation of the independent Jalayirid realm, were by 783/1381 divided between two branches of the Jalayirid house.

Amīr ʻĀdil also appealed to the authority of prince Shaykh ʻAlī in Baghdad following Sulṭān Aḥmad's coup in Tabriz in 784/1382. Amīr ʻĀdil sent envoys to Shaykh ʻAlī's court, urging him to march against his brother, Sulṭān Aḥmad.[39] Shaykh ʻAlī was more than just a symbolic challenge to Sulṭān Aḥmad, for he did lead an army to Azarbayjan, and when one of Sulṭān Aḥmad's amirs and his men defected to Shaykh ʻAlī, Sulṭān Aḥmad fled the field.[40] Shaykh ʻAlī thus was a rallying point for the military power of amirs such as Pīr ʻAlī Bādīk and Amīr ʻĀdil, as well as a formidable leader in his own right, who controlled the resources of Baghdad, long a Jalayirid stronghold.[41]

Finally, mention should be made of yet another Jalayirid prince, Shaykh Uvays's son Bāyazīd. Following Sulṭān Aḥmad's seizure of power in 784/1382, Bāyazīd escaped Tabriz and took refuge with Amīr ʻĀdil in Sultaniyya. Here, he served to replace Sulṭān Ḥusayn as Amīr ʻĀdil's Jalayirid puppet. Amīr ʻĀdil enthroned him as sultan in Sultaniyya,[42] in opposition to Sulṭān Aḥmad in Tabriz.

Thus, on the eve of Tīmūr's first campaigns in Iran, the Jalayirid dynasty was characterised by division among three main princely factions, corresponding to three geographical regions. Sulṭān Aḥmad claimed the sultanate in Tabriz, Amīr ʻĀdil acted as protector to Bāyazīd, who also had a claim to royal authority in Sultaniyya, and Shaykh ʻAlī continued to rule unopposed in Baghdad. The political unity achieved by Shaykh Uvays had split among his sons, who all shared in the claim to dynastic succession.

The disputes internal to the Jalayirid royal family were soon overshadowed by much larger external threat from the Ulus Chaghatay in the east, in the form of Tīmūr. Before dealing with the consequences of Tīmūr's invasions for the Jalayirids, however, mention should be made of another significant development to the west in the period between Shaykh Uvays's death in 776/1374 and Tīmūr's first Iranian campaign in 787/1385–86. This development was the growing power of the Qarāquyūnlū Turkmans, who became ever more involved in Jalayirid dynastic politics. In fact, the growth of Qarāquyūnlū power in this period was tied closely to the role they played in Jalayirid political conflict.

As discussed in the previous chapter, Shaykh Uvays had led a campaign against the Qarāquyūnlū chief Bayrām Khwāja in 767/1366. At the Battle of Muş, the Jalayirid forces defeated the Turkmans and required Bayrām Khwāja to pay tribute to the sultan.[43] However, just three years after his defeat at Muş, Bayrām Khwāja had taken Mosul.[44] After Shaykh Uvays's death, as the Jalayirid sultanate faced more immediate threats from the Muzaffarids, Bayrām Khwāja took the cities of Sürmelü, Ala-Kilise, Khuy and Nakhjivan, effectively severing the agreement he was forced to accept in 767/1366.[45]

Sulṭān Ḥusayn and Amīr ʻĀdil were able to turn their attention to the west after Shāh Shujāʻ abandoned Tabriz in 777/1376. At a *quriltay* at Ujan that year, the Jalayirid amirs pushed for a campaign against Bayrām Khwāja.[46] The army, led by Amīr ʻĀdil, headed first to Erciş, where Bayrām Khwāja's nephew Qarā Muḥammad had taken possession of the citadel. After securing a two-week truce with the Jalayirids, Qarā Muḥammad began digging a trench and fortifying the walls of his fortress. He also used this opportunity to send for aid from Bayrām Khwāja in Erzurum. However, when the Qarāquyūnlū reinforcements arrived, fifty of them were taken prisoner, and Qarā Muḥammad was forced to submit to the Jalayirid sultan.[47]

What is striking about this brief campaign is the leniency shown to the Qarāquyūnlū at every stage. Amīr ʻĀdil held back from besieging Qarā Muḥammad, even though he must have realised such a delay would enable him to seek help from Bayrām Khwāja. The fifty Turkmans who were captured and sent to the Jalayirid camp were not only spared, but also assigned patents and grants (*marsūm va suyūrghāl*) by the sultan.[48] Finally, even Qarā Muḥammad and Bayrām Khwāja were rewarded for their eventual submission, being assigned grants (*suyūrghāl*) after Qarā Muḥammad presented himself in Tabriz twenty days later.[49] Amīr ʻĀdil clearly did not want to direct too much energy to Anatolia, and was content with nominal vassalage from the Qarāquyūnlū. The autonomy enjoyed by the Qarāquyūnlū enabled Qarā Muḥammad to consolidate his power from Nakhjivan to Erzurum and around Lake Van, and eventually played a decisive role in the succession to the Jalayirid throne after Sulṭān Ḥusayn's death in 784/1382.

After Sulṭān Aḥmad seized the throne in Tabriz, he faced opposition from Amīr ʻĀdil, as well as from his brother, prince Shaykh ʻAlī, and his amir, Pīr ʻAlī Bādīk. As mentioned above, Sulṭān Aḥmad was routed by the army of Baghdad led by Shaykh ʻAlī. In need of military support, Sulṭān Aḥmad approached Qarā Muḥammad and the Qarāquyūnlū near Nakhjivan. According to Mīrkhvānd, the Qarāquyūnlū leader agreed to help Sulṭān Aḥmad on two conditions. The first was that Sulṭān Aḥmad and his men not interfere and allow the Turkmans to fight 'in their own way' (*bi-ṭarīq-i ʻādat-i khvaysh*). The second was that the Qarāquyūnlū would retain the spoils taken in battle.[50] Sulṭān Aḥmad had little choice but to agree to Qarā Muḥammad's conditions. In the short term, Sulṭān Aḥmad's alliance proved successful. The Qarāquyūnlū defeated the army of Baghdad and killed prince Shaykh ʿAlī and Pīr ʿAlī Bādīk, and Sulṭān Aḥmad took control of both Tabriz and Baghdad.[51] At the same time, the Qarāquyūnlū confederation, and in particular its chief Qarā Muḥammad, achieved unprecedented status. In addition to the abundant plunder taken by the Turkmans in the battle, the ties between the Qarāquyūnlū and the Jalayirids were formalised through marriage. Sulṭān Aḥmad gave his aunt Vafā Qutlugh to Qarā Muḥammad, while Sulṭān Aḥmad married Qarā Muḥammad's daughter.[52] The close ties between Sulṭān Aḥmad and the Qarāquyūnlū, and especially Qarā Muḥammad's son Qarā Yūsuf, would continue throughout the period of Tīmūr's campaigns in Iran, Iraq and Anatolia. We turn now to these campaigns and their impact on the Jalayirid realm.

Tīmūr was a product of the Ulus Chaghatay, half of the former Chaghatay khanate of central Asia, formed as the inheritance of Chinggis Qan's second son, Chaghatay. By 771/1370 the amir Tīmūr of the Barlas tribe had consolidated his power among the tribes of the Ulus, and ruled in the name of his own Chinggisid puppet khan. Tīmūr's vision for conquest extended beyond the Ulus Chaghatay, however, and in fact he sought to reconstitute the former Mongol empire of Chinggis Qan, encompassing not only central Asia, but also the Qipchaq steppe, Iran and China. Tīmūr's campaigns in the Jalayirid lands of western Iran and Iraq began in 786/1384, and would continue throughout the rest of his life. These years of war were devastating for the region, particularly for agriculture and for urban life in Baghdad. The Timurid invasions and conquests also disrupted the post-Ilkhanid political order that the Jalayirids had tried to control and create. As will be discussed in the following section, Tīmūr's conquests inadvertently restored the authority of the Jalayirid sultan against his internal rivals, but at the same time aimed to make the former Ilkhanid lands subject to Tīmūr's larger imperial project. Although the Jalayirid Sulṭān Aḥmad spent much of his reign on the run from Tīmūr, trying to win back Tabriz and Baghdad, Jalayirid sovereignty became a useful ideological tool for those opposed to Timurid power. Sulṭān Aḥmad and his family thus had a symbolic significance far greater than their actual power in the period between 788/1386 and 813/1410, when Sulṭān Aḥmad was killed by his Qarāquyūnlū rival Qarā Yūsuf.

One of the immediate impacts of Tīmūr's invasion of Iran was the appearance of a large number of amirs and soldiers from outside the region. This wave of new Chaghatayid amirs expected to share in the wealth of the territory they helped conquer, as part of their reward for service in Tīmūr's army of conquest. The Chaghatayid amirs also represented a new political force within the Jalayirid sultanate, as demonstrated by the events surrounding the downfall of Amīr ʿĀdil. In the summer of 788/1386, Amīr

'Ādil was summoned by Chaghatayid envoys who informed him that Tīmūr was returning to Iran after spending the winter in Samarqand. The day after Amīr 'Ādil reached Tīmūr's camp near Nihavand, Muḥammad Sulṭānshāh, the leading Chaghatayid amir in Tabriz, also joined the royal entourage. According to Ḥāfiẓ Abrū, Muḥammad Sulṭānshāh repeatedly condemned the conduct of Amīr 'Ādil to Tīmūr, who became troubled about him.[53] Things got worse for Amīr 'Ādil when Tīmūr's forces occupied Tabriz. Tīmūr came to Tabriz personally and demanded an inquiry into the finances of Azarbayjan. When it became clear that little remained in the treasury there, the blame fell to Amīr 'Ādil and his amirs, who were tortured and killed in Ramaḍān 788/September 1386.[54] Amīr 'Ādil's power in the Jalayirid lands was seen as a threat by the Chaghatayid amirs, who took the opportunity to undermine his authority when they could. The dynamics of power had changed rapidly following the arrival of Tīmūr and his men. Amīr 'Ādil was no longer the most powerful military leader in Iran, but instead one of many amirs, who needed to demonstrate his loyalty to Tīmūr in order to maintain his position. When he lost Tīmūr's confidence, he was easily removed. Amīr 'Ādil's downfall represents a major early indication that Tīmūr and his forces from outside the old Ilkhanid structure would have a significant transformative impact on the political landscape by altering the balance of power and channels of authority that the Jalayirids had inherited from the Ilkhanate and sought to preserve.

The dynamics of power changed particularly in Azarbayjan, the centre of royal authority for the Ilkhans as well as the Jalayirids. Tīmūr's incursions into Iran resulted in a new status for Azarbayjan. The former seat of Ilkhanid authority was important symbolically for Tīmūr, who saw the former *ulūs* of Hülegü as integral to his imperial vision. Yet, for Tīmūr and his successors, Azarbayjan was always difficult to control, and was never fully integrated into the Timurid realm, despite Tīmūr's success in driving Sulṭān Aḥmad Jalayir from the province. Thus, in the period from 788/1386 to 795/1393, while Tīmūr was not in Iran, and Sulṭān Aḥmad was in Baghdad, Azarbayjan was dominated by the local strongman Aghachkī (or A'jakī), who claimed to serve Tīmūr in the province.[55] However, Aghachkī was only one among several local amirs and *a'yān* who were left to manoeuvre among themselves in this period. It seems that Sulṭān Aḥmad was content in these years to remain in Baghdad, and did not make any attempts to claim Azarbayjan for himself. Azarbayjan became the setting for more local political struggles, and cannot be considered to have been under either Jalayirid or Timurid control in this period.

Other Jalayirid provinces were more directly ruled by the Timurids, and were eventually divided formally by Tīmūr among members of his family. In 805/1403 Tīmūr entrusted the province of Arab Iraq, and the responsibility for its restoration after so many years of devastation from his own campaigns, to his grandson, Abā Bakr.[56] In Sharaf al-Dīn 'Alī Yazdī's account of this occasion, Tīmūr addressed the other princes and amirs, and identified the independent action of the people of Baghdad as the cause of the region's ruin:

> Before this, the people of Baghdad gave themselves and their country over to the wind, as a consequence of raising their own army in opposition. On account of the discord and our revenge, the country declined once again. Because of the fact that in Iraq knowledge of the *sharī'a* has spread from Baghdad, and the schools of law from there became famous, one understands that the country should return to a state of flourishing, and that it should again become a seat of equity and justice.[57]

Tīmūr assigned Arab Iraq, Kurdistan and Diyarbakr, including authority over the Oyrat tribe, to Abā Bakr.[58] To his grandson 'Umar b. Mīrānshāh, he left the '*ulūs* of Hülegü Khan', including Azarbayjan, Anatolia and Syria.[59] Thus, by 805/1403, the Jalayirid lands had become divided between two Timurid princes, and incorporated into a new imperial structure, ruled from Samarqand.

Closely connected to Tīmūr's redistribution of Jalayirid territory among his grandsons was the ideological abrogation of the notion of Ilkhanid prestige, which had been central to Jalayirid claims to legitimate sovereignty. The descendants of Tīmūr comprised a new dynastic family, in the same way that Chinggis Qan's family provided the basis for the Mongol imperial dynasty of the seventh/thirteenth century. When Tīmūr's symbolic Chinggisid puppet khan Sulṭān Maḥmūd died in 805/1402, a successor was not enthroned, an omission suggesting that a representative of the Chinggisid royal family was no longer necessary to lend prestige and legitimacy to Tīmūr's imperial undertaking. Like Chinggis Qan's, Tīmūr's conquests were evidence of the fortune of his own family, who after his death would provide the source of legitimate political authority. A corollary to this notion is that the old Chinggisid royal lines, including that which ruled the Ilkhanate, were no longer viable sources of legitimate authority. For the Jalayirids, who strove after 736/1335 to establish themselves as the heirs to the Ilkhans as defenders of Islam and continuators of Chinggisid tradition, such a transformation in ideology was a threat to all of their political claims.

Sulṭān Aḥmad's Reign in the Period of Tīmūr's Campaigns (795/1393–807/1405)

The period from Tīmūr's occupation of Tabriz in 788/1386 until his death in 807/1405 was one of great instability for Sulṭān Aḥmad's rule in Azarbayjan and Arab Iraq. After establishing himself at Baghdad, the Jalayirid sultan was driven out of the city several times between 795/1393 and 806/1403, and was forced to seek alliances with other rulers, including the Mamluk sultan al-Ẓāhir Barqūq, the Ottoman sultan Bāyezīd I, and the Qarāquyūnlū Turkman leader Qarā Yūsuf. The details of Sulṭān Aḥmad's activities in this tumultuous period are sometimes difficult to piece together due to the fact that they are not the main focus of most of the available sources. However, an examination of Mamluk, Ottoman and Timurid sources reveals that although Sulṭān Aḥmad's power in Baghdad was weakened considerably by attacks from Tīmūr, as well as opposition from the local elite, the Jalayirid sultan represented a powerful symbol of opposition to Tīmūr, and thus a potential ally for several rulers in regions threatened by him. In the following section, Sulṭān Aḥmad's relations with the Mamluks, Ottomans and Qarāquyūnlū are examined in an attempt to provide a clear narrative of events in this period, and to situate the Jalayirid sultanate within the larger context of the changing political dynamics of the Nile-to-Oxus region at the end of the eighth/fourteenth century.

Although in the long term Tīmūr's conquests undermined the foundations of Jalayirid authority, they in fact also had the immediate effect of restoring the authority of the Jalayirid sultanate under Sulṭān Aḥmad. As has been mentioned above, after Shaykh Uvays's death, power had become dispersed among the amirs and several of Shaykh Uvays's sons. However, Tīmūr's execution of Amīr 'Ādil in 788/1386 removed the largest obstacle to royal authority within the Jalayirid realm. Sulṭān Aḥmad was able to act freely, and although he was driven out of Tabriz by the Timurids, he established himself in Baghdad as the sole claimant to the Jalayirid throne.[60] Between 788/1386 and 795/1393[61] Sulṭān Aḥmad ruled in Baghdad without any interference from Tīmūr. In this time, he acquired the reputation of a negligent and oppressive ruler. While we might expect such a characterisation as natural in the Timurid sources, this view is also shared by historians hostile to Tīmūr. Astarābādī records that during these years, Sulṭān Aḥmad was occupied with music and revelry, and did not give any attention to matters of state. As a result, economic life in Baghdad suffered.[62] Ibn 'Arabshāh, another writer hostile to Tīmūr, nonetheless also described Sulṭān Aḥmad's evil ways:

> When the sultan [Sulṭān Aḥmad] took over the kingdom of Iraq, he extended the hand of his wickedness and withdrew the wing of compassion and courtesy. He began to behave unjustly himself and tyrannize his subjects, and spend his days and nights in deviation and depravity.[63]

Aside from these general characterisations, we know little about the details of Sulṭān Aḥmad's period in Baghdad in these years. Our main sources for the period are the Timurid histories, which focus on Tīmūr's activities in Khwarazm, Moghulistan, and especially with Tuqtāmīsh Khan on the Qipchaq steppe. The culmination of these operations was Tīmūr's victory over the Jochid army at Qundurcha on the steppe in the summer of 793/1391. The Timurid sources leave a similar lacuna for Sulṭān Aḥmad's activities between the years 797/1395 and 802/1400, when Tīmūr was occupied elsewhere, most notably in Delhi. The years between these two periods of relative calm were marked by Tīmūr's second Iranian campaign, aimed at chastising the rulers there who had begun to assert their autonomy in his absence. Tīmūr set out from Samarqand in the summer of 794/1392, and reached Persian Iraq in early 795/1393. He proceeded to Luristan, Shiraz and Isfahan, defeating the Muzaffarid ruler Shāh Manṣūr, and ordering the execution of the entire Muzaffarid house.[64]

Attention fell next to Sulṭān Aḥmad in Baghdad. According to Niẓām al-Dīn Shāmī, Tīmūr attacked Sulṭān Aḥmad because he failed to show the proper signs of submission, and did not strike coins and give the *khuṭba* in Tīmūr's name.[65] However, according to the Mamluk historian al-Maqrīzī, whose account is followed by Ibn Taghrī Birdī, Sulṭān Aḥmad did in fact show the proper signs of submission, but was betrayed by the *a'yān* of Baghdad, who sent a message to Tīmūr inviting him to take the city.[66] They cited Sulṭān Aḥmad's killing of his amirs, his oppression of the general populace, and his tendency to drink and debauchery as the reasons why he was not an acceptable ruler.[67] Sulṭān Aḥmad fled Baghdad on 14 Shawwāl 795/23 August 1393 when Tīmūr's armies attacked.[68] Tīmūr's forces overtook Sulṭān Aḥmad at Karbala and routed them, taking his harem captive and plundering his baggage.[69] His son, 'Alā' al-Dawla, was captured and sent to Samarqand.[70] Sulṭān Aḥmad managed to escape with a group of his followers and fled toward Mamluk Syria.[71]

Sulṭān Aḥmad was honoured at al-Rahba by the amir Nu'ayr, chief of the Āl Faḍl bedouins on the Mamluk sultanate's Syrian frontier.[72] He then travelled on to Aleppo, where he was met by the Mamluk governor, Julbān Qarāsaqal, who accommodated him at the *maydān*.[73] Sultan Barqūq ordered Julbān to honour Sulṭān Aḥmad, and to put the royal *dīwān* at his disposal for whatever he needed.[74] Sulṭān Aḥmad also wrote a message to

Barqūq, putting in a good word for both Nu'ayr and Julbān, and requesting permission to come to Cairo. Barqūq took counsel from his amirs, who agreed that Sulṭān Aḥmad should be allowed to come.[75]

On 17 Rabī' I 796/20 January 1394, Sulṭān Aḥmad arrived at al-Raydaniyya outside Cairo, and he spent the next month and a half as Barqūq's honoured guest. The hospitality shown to Sulṭān Aḥmad was accompanied by grand public spectacles and ceremonies designed to demonstrate Sulṭān Aḥmad's dignity as a sovereign Muslim ruler, as well as to illustrate Barqūq's own majesty and beneficence as Sulṭān Aḥmad's protector against the threat from Tīmūr.

Upon Sulṭān Aḥmad's arrival at al-Raydaniyya, the highest-ranking amirs of Egypt greeted him before Barqūq came down from his throne (*masṭaba*) to receive him.[76] He did not allow Sulṭān Aḥmad to kiss his hand, but instead embraced him. According to al-Maqrīzī, they wept together, and Barqūq offered encouraging words, promising Sulṭān Aḥmad that he would someday regain his throne. As they sat together, Sulṭān Aḥmad was presented with several fine gifts, including a cloak and a horse from Barqūq's stable.[77] They then rode in procession toward the citadel, accompanied by the amirs and army.[78] Sulṭān Aḥmad proceeded to a residence that Barqūq had prepared for him at Birkat al-Fil, where the *ustādār* laid out a banquet, attended by all the amirs. After the amirs had departed, Barqūq sent 200,000 silver dirhams, 200 pieces of Skandari cloth, three horses, twenty mamluks and twenty slave girls.[79]

Sulṭān Aḥmad was thus introduced to the Mamluk political elite as the equal to Barqūq as a fellow Muslim sovereign. Such a diplomatic choice on the part of the Mamluk sultan served to elevate not only the status of Sulṭān Aḥmad, but Barqūq's own as well. Barqūq used the occasion of Sulṭān Aḥmad's arrival to illustrate his distinction, not merely as the most powerful member of the Mamluk military elite, but as a dynastic founder, whose authority transcended the Mamluk political order, and was on the same level as other dynastic rulers. The ceremonies that followed Sulṭān Aḥmad's initial reception provided further opportunity for Barqūq to distinguish both his guest and himself. On 19 Rabī' I/22 January, Sulṭān Aḥmad attended Barqūq's *khidma* at the *īwān* of the *dar al-'adl*.[80] Sulṭān Aḥmad was seated directly to the right of Barqūq, a place of honour normally reserved for the *amīr kabīr*.[81] Later in the week, Barqūq continued to show hospitality to Sulṭān Aḥmad by taking him on a hunting trip outside of Cairo.[82]

During Sulṭān Aḥmad's stay in Cairo, Tīmūr's envoy, Shaykh Sāvahī, arrived in Cairo. The message he delivered, as presented by Yazdī, offered a new interpretation of the balance of political power from Egypt to Iran:

> Before this, the powerful rulers were from the lineage of Jingīz Khān [Chinggis Qan]. They contended with the rulers of these countries. Because of that, trouble came to the people of Syria, and the inhabitants of that region. In the end, successive messengers and messages were sent from them, and the situation turned out well. That matter required the security and trust of the world and the people. When Abū Sa'īd died, and from the lineage of Jingīz Khān there was no ruler who had the power to implement his authority in Iran, rulers of various factions appeared. The world was thrown into confusion. Now, since the precedent of endless favor, the *mālik-i mulk*, may he be glorified and exalted, made all of the countries of Iran, as far as Arab Iraq, which neighbors that country, submitted to our command, sound thought and good wishes of the people require that, in accordance with neighborliness, the gates of correspondence and diplomacy be opened, and envoys from both sides come and go, so that the roads are secure and merchants of both sides are able to move in safety and security. This could certainly be the cause for flourishing in the country and tranquility for the subjects.[83]

In this Timurid view of Ilkhanid history, good relations with the Mamluks were only established when the Ilkhanid rulers opened up diplomatic channels with Syria and allowed merchants and envoys to pass freely. However, after Abū Sa'īd, the lack of a single strong ruler in Iran had led to disorder of the kind experienced in the first years of Mongol rule. Now that Tīmūr had established the singularity of his rule, the opportunity existed for a new opening of communication, as well as the free and secure flow of merchants between Iran, Syria and Egypt. Implied here is that Barqūq's protection of Sulṭān Aḥmad would be of little benefit to him, since the Jalayirids were only one of the many post-Abū Sa'īd factions that had upset the previously established balance. Indeed, Tīmūr's diplomatic overtures were probably aimed at eventually convincing Barqūq to turn over Sulṭān Aḥmad, who was now openly a rebel against Tīmūr. Barqūq had different ideas, however. When Tīmūr's envoy arrived in Cairo, Barqūq convinced Sulṭān Aḥmad to murder the shaykh. Yazdī compares this killing of an envoy – which, he writes, is not permitted on the bases of religious or common law (*az qawā'id-i shar'ī va siyāsī*), nor by royal or communal custom (*rusūm-i mulkī va millī*) – to the murder of Chinggis Qan's envoys by agents of Sultan Muḥammad Khwārazmshāh in 615/1218.[84]

The dynastic charisma represented by the Jalayirid house and embodied by Sulṭān Aḥmad was demonstrated by Barqūq's marriage on 9 Rabī' II/11 February to Tūndī Khātūn, daughter of Sulṭān Ḥusayn b. Shaykh Uvays.[85] As Ann Broadbridge has pointed out, this was the first time a Mamluk sultan had married a royal princess from an established dynasty since al-Nāṣir Muḥammad.[86] The marriage created closer ties between

Barqūq and Sulṭān Aḥmad, while also emphasising the significance of dynastic sovereignty to the nature of both of their identities as rulers. Following his marriage to Tūndī Khātūn, Barqūq held a large military parade at al-Rumayla, which Sulṭān Aḥmad attended. After the review, Barqūq visited the tombs of al-Shāfi'ī and Sayyida Nafīsa, and distributed alms to the poor. They rode back together to al-Rumayla, and then to al-Raydaniyya. The following day they set out for Damascus, on a campaign to confront Tīmūr.[87]

The campaign was soon cut short, however. On the road, they received news that Tīmūr had returned to his own country.[88] After spending more than a month in Damascus, Sulṭān Aḥmad departed for Baghdad, on 1 Sha'bān 796/1 June 1394. Barqūq presented Sulṭān Aḥmad with 500,000 dirhams, a horse, camels, armaments and a ceremonial sword. These gifts were accompanied by a *taqlīd* confirming Sulṭān Aḥmad as Barqūq's *nā'ib* in Baghdad.[89] The *taqlīd* signalled a change in the diplomatic relationship between the Mamluk and Jalayirid sultans. The protection and generosity that Sulṭān Aḥmad had found at the Mamluk court came at the price of submission to the ultimate authority of al-Ẓāhir Barqūq. In fact, however, there is little evidence that Sulṭān Aḥmad showed any regard for Barqūq's authority in Baghdad after he returned.

We know little about Sulṭān Aḥmad's rule in Baghdad in the period from 797/1395, when he returned from Mamluk Cairo, until 802/1400, when he abandoned the city a second time. Early Ottoman as well as Mamluk historical writing deal with this episode, yet differ on the specific reasons for Sulṭān Aḥmad's flight. According to several early Ottoman histories, Sulṭān Aḥmad and Qarā Yūsuf left their homeland because of the wickedness of Tīmūr,[90] and made their way to Egypt. They were held captive by the Mamluk sultan, but managed to escape through trickery and take refuge with Bāyezīd.[91]

While the Ottoman chroniclers cite the 'wickedness of Tīmūr' as the reason for Sulṭān Aḥmad's departure from Baghdad, the Mamluk historians al-Maqrīzī and Ibn Taghrī Birdī write that the *a'yān* of Baghdad had written to Tīmūr's governor at Shiraz that Sulṭān Aḥmad was oppressing the populace and had killed amirs,[92] and that Tīmūr should come and take the city.[93] Sulṭān Aḥmad fled again from Baghdad,[94] this time seeking assistance from Qarā Yūsuf, who was ruling Mosul. However, their combined forces were routed at Baghdad, and both of them headed for Syria.[95]

The Timurid account of these events is itself different from the Ottoman and Mamluk accounts. According to the Timurid historians, who among themselves differ on the details,[96] Sulṭān Aḥmad's departure from

Baghdad was prompted by his discovery of a conspiracy among his amirs and relatives, initiated by an amir named Shirvān. When Sulṭān Aḥmad learned of the conspiracy, he methodically had 2,000 of his amirs, intimates and relatives killed. In a state of paranoia, he slipped out of Baghdad and joined Qarā Yūsuf, chief of the Qarāquyūnlū Turkmans, and urged him to attack the city. However, apparently fearing further confrontation with Tīmūr in Iraq, Sulṭān Aḥmad instead left Baghdad again and accompanied Qarā Yūsuf to Syria.[97]

Mamluk histories provide the best account of events after Sulṭān Aḥmad and Qarā Yūsuf arrived in Syria. As they approached Aleppo with a large group of Turkman followers, they were confronted at al-Sajur by Damurdāsh (or Tīmurtāsh) al-Muḥammadī, governor of Aleppo, and Dūqmāq, governor of Hama.[98] A battle took place on 24 Shawwāl 802 (18 June 1400),[99] and the army of Aleppo was defeated by the Turkmans. Dūqmāq and a group of other amirs were captured,[100] and Dūqmāq later had to ransom himself for 100,000 dirhams.[101] Sulṭān Aḥmad and Qarā Yūsuf sent a message to the Mamluk sultan al-Nāṣir Faraj that they had not come to make war. Rather, they sought refuge and aid, such as had been previously offered to Sulṭān Aḥmad by his father Barqūq. Their message was ignored, and Faraj ordered the governor of Damascus to capture them and send them to Cairo.[102] Unable to find sanctuary in Syria, Sulṭān Aḥmad and Qarā Yūsuf went north to Anatolia,[103] where they were defeated by the Mamluk governor of Bahasna.[104]

Sulṭān Aḥmad and Qarā Yūsuf apparently parted ways after the battle at Bahasna,[105] and Sulṭān Aḥmad soon encountered Tīmūr's forces, who intercepted his baggage train (*aghrūq*). Although Sulṭān Aḥmad escaped, his older sister, Sulṭān Dilshād, as well as his wives and daughters, were captured and taken prisoner.[106] Sulṭān Aḥmad continued west into the Ottoman domains, until he joined Sultan Bāyezīd at Aqsaray. Bāyezīd granted the revenue from Kütahya as *tīmār* to Sulṭān Aḥmad and he settled there.[107] Later, Qarā Yūsuf also arrived in Anatolia, and was also given refuge by Bāyezīd.[108]

As Tīmūr drove south from Sivas to ʻAyntab (Antep), Aleppo and Damascus in 803/1400, Sulṭān Aḥmad and Qarā Yūsuf urged Bāyezīd to extend his control east of the Euphrates in Anatolia.[109] They laid siege to the city of Erzincan,[110] which was under the control of the amir Muṭahhartan, who had pledged his allegiance to Tīmūr.[111] The Ottoman forces took the city, and Sulṭān Aḥmad acted as intermediary between Bāyezīd and Muṭahhartan. He left the amir in control of Erzincan, but sent his wives and children to Ottoman Bursa to ensure that Muṭahhartan would remain loyal.[112]

The accounts of this incident illustrate why the protection afforded to Sulṭān Aḥmad and Qarā Yūsuf by Bāyezīd became a major diplomatic issue between Tīmūr and the Ottoman sultan. In the correspondence between them, Tīmūr demanded that Bāyezīd desist from giving refuge to them, while Bāyezīd staunchly refused.[113] Here again Sulṭān Aḥmad Jalayir was valuable to a regional ruler as a symbol of opposition to Timurid claims to the former Ilkhanid lands. The Jalayirid sultan lent Bāyezīd prestige as the protector of the 'rightful' heir to authority in Tabriz.

Sulṭān Aḥmad Returns to Baghdad, and Returns Again to Bāyezīd (803–04/1401–02)

Despite his value to Bāyezīd, Sulṭān Aḥmad was not content to remain an honoured addition at the Ottoman court. In the spring of 803/1401, as Tīmūr began to pull out of Syria and return to the east, Sulṭān Aḥmad requested leave from the Ottoman sultan to return to Iraq. Bāyezīd granted his request, and sent him home loaded with gifts.[114] In Dhū al-Qaʻda/July, Tīmūr began a month-long siege of Baghdad. Sulṭān Aḥmad had left a fellow Jalayir tribesman named Faraj in charge of the city.[115] When he refused to give up the city to Tīmūr's men, saying he had explicit orders from Sulṭān Aḥmad to turn the city over to no one but Tīmūr himself, Tīmūr came to Baghdad and attacked. After a long siege in the blazing July heat, Tīmūr's forces finally breached the walls and poured into Baghdad. The city would pay for its resistance. Tīmūr ordered a massacre of the population, and for all the buildings, except the mosques, madrasas and *khānqāh*s, to be razed. The Bavarian knight Johannes Schiltberger, who was in the service of the Ottoman Sultan Bāyezīd I in 803/1401, recorded that Tīmūr not only burned the city, but also had the land ploughed and barley planted, so that no one would know that any houses had ever stood there.[116]

Sulṭān Aḥmad returned to Baghdad in the winter of 804/1401–02. The sources report that although the city was completely ruined, Sulṭān Aḥmad attempted to rebuild and encourage repopulation. Yazdī wrote that those who had scattered out of fear began to return and gather around Sulṭān Aḥmad.[117] Although Tīmūr had destroyed the city of Baghdad, Sulṭān Aḥmad continued to provide a focus of organisation for those who suffered from Tīmūr's punitive operations. Without a steady presence of Tīmūr's amirs in Baghdad, and as long as Sulṭān Aḥmad stayed alive, the potential for independent action and resistance to Tīmūr remained in Arab Iraq. At the same time, Sulṭān Aḥmad could offer no active military resistance to Tīmūr if he chose to attack.

In mid-804/early 1402, when he learned that the Jalayirid sultan had returned, Tīmūr did indeed attack. Tīmūr's grandson Abā Bakr b. Mīrānshāh and the amir Jahānshāh were sent to Baghdad and took Sulṭān Aḥmad by such surprise that, according to one account, he jumped into a boat dressed in only his shirt and fled down the Tigris. He met his son Sulṭān Ṭāhir and a number of *nöker*s, and together they travelled to Hilla.[118] Driven out of Baghdad for the second time in two years, Sulṭān Aḥmad returned to the protection of Sultan Bāyezīd, although it seems that he left his son Sulṭān Ṭāhir in Hilla.

However, by the summer of 804/1402, the Ottoman sultan could no longer offer any protection to Sulṭān Aḥmad. According to the histories of ʻĀşıḳpāşāzāde and Neşrī, Tīmūr was urged to invade Anatolia by several of the beys whose territories had been conquered by Bāyezīd.[119] In late Dhū al-Ḥijja 804/July 1402, Tīmūr's army defeated the Ottomans at Çubukovası, outside Ankara.[120] Bāyezīd was taken prisoner,[121] and Tīmūr sent expeditions across western Anatolia to stamp out any remaining resistance. One of these expeditions was led by prince Maḥmūd Sulṭān, who proceeded to Bursa. Here he captured Bāyezīd's son Muṣṭafá and the daughter of Sulṭān Aḥmad Jalayir.[122] The Ottoman defeat at Ankara marked the end of Bāyezīd's efforts to bring Anatolia under his control, and in the twenty-year period after the battle, the regional *beylik*s that he had attempted to eliminate returned, as Ottoman princes struggled among themselves.[123] For Sulṭān Aḥmad, the Ottoman defeat meant that he no longer had an ally in Anatolia to look to for protection when he was threatened in Iraq.

Sulṭān Aḥmad Returns to Baghdad, Faces Uprising by Sulṭān Ṭāhir, Driven Out by Qarā Yūsuf (805–06/1403)

After returning to Baghdad from Anatolia, Sulṭān Aḥmad went on to Hilla to meet Sulṭān Ṭāhir. He seized Sulṭān Ṭāhir's main advisor, Āghā Fīrūz, causing Sulṭān Ṭāhir to become suspicious of his father's intentions. After conspiring with others among Sulṭān Aḥmad's amirs, Sulṭān Ṭāhir led a revolt against his father.[124] This is the version of the incident recorded by Sharaf al-Dīn ʻAlī Yazdī. It seems possible also that the amirs in Iraq had lost confidence in Sulṭān Aḥmad and were already plotting with the Jalayirid prince to turn against him. In any case, both Sulṭān Aḥmad and the amirs had good reason to believe that Sulṭān Ṭāhir's loyalty to his father was less than total. It should be recalled that Sulṭān Aḥmad had imprisoned him at Alinjaq fortress for eleven years and, as Naṭanzī reported, 'because of what his father had done to him, he became savage in his nature. At the seduction of a group of pernicious people, he attacked his father.'[125]

Faced with the insurrection of Sulṭān Ṭāhir and his amirs, Sulṭān Aḥmad once again called on the aid of Qarā Yūsuf, who carried him across the Euphrates to safety, and provided an army to confront Sulṭān Ṭāhir. In the ensuing battle, the Turkman forces were victorious. As Sulṭān Ṭāhir retreated, he attempted to jump a stream (*jūyī*)[126] with his horse, but he fell and drowned under the weight of his horse and his armour.[127]

Sulṭān Aḥmad had survived the conspiracy from within his own family, but now he faced a different problem. He had invited the Qarāquyūnlū into Arab Iraq, and urged them to attack his son and top amirs. There was little to keep Qarā Yūsuf from taking Arab Iraq and Baghdad for himself. Qarā Yūsuf followed Sulṭān Aḥmad from Hilla to Baghdad, and took the city.[128] Sulṭān Aḥmad was driven out of Baghdad for the third time in as many years, this time by his former ally Qarā Yūsuf. According to the Timurid tradition, Sulṭān Aḥmad hid in the city, fearing for his life. He was found by a certain Qarā Ḥasan, who sneaked him out of Baghdad at night, carrying him on his shoulders. On the road, they came across a domestic servant (*ḥashamī*) who had a cow. Sulṭān Aḥmad mounted the cow and Qarā Ḥasan led him to Tikrit, where an Oyrat tribesman supplied Sulṭān Aḥmad with horses, money, weapons and clothing. At Tikrit, he was joined by several of his *nöker*s, who accompanied him on to Syria.[129] Thus, Sulṭān Aḥmad made a third journey seeking refuge and protection in the Mamluk sultanate. Much had changed since he had been welcomed with open arms by Sultan Barqūq ten years earlier. In the aftermath of Tīmūr's invasion of Syria, the Mamluk military elite was in upheaval. Sultan Barqūq's young son, al-Nāṣir Faraj, sat on the throne in Cairo, while in Syria several factions led by rival amirs competed for supremacy. Sulṭān Aḥmad and Qarā Yūsuf, who soon followed him in exile after being expelled himself from Baghdad by the Timurids in the autumn of 806/1403, thus found themselves in a precarious political situation in Syria. On the one hand, they represented a danger as rebels against Tīmūr; their presence might have provoked another devastating invasion. On the other hand, they also represented potential allies to the Syian amirs battling each other in this period.

Sulṭān Aḥmad arrived in Aleppo on 15 Ṣafar 806/3 September 1403.[130] He was initially ordered to be detained there by the sultan, but was later summoned to Cairo. As he proceeded to Egypt, Sulṭān Aḥmad was received in Damascus by its governor, amir Shaykh al-Maḥmūdī (the future Sultan al-Mu'ayyad Shaykh).[131] Shaykh had already received Qarā Yūsuf, who had arrived in Damascus after being driven out of Baghdad himself by the Timurids.[132] Shaykh had made Qarā Yūsuf one of his own amirs, no doubt pleased to count Qarā Yūsuf's Turkman followers among his own military forces. At the end of Jumādá II 806/January 1404, Shaykh received orders from Cairo to imprison both Sulṭān Aḥmad and Qarā Yūsuf.[133] Later, in Sha'bān/February–March, he was directed to execute them both. Shaykh did not comply, and instead requested verification of the order.[134] In opposition to the sultan's command, Shaykh kept Sulṭān Aḥmad and Qarā Yūsuf imprisoned in Damascus. It was here, according to Timurid sources, that they made a pact to divide Azarbayjan and Arab Iraq between themselves when they were released.[135]

Shaykh kept them incarcerated until events in Cairo drew him into conflict with the sultan, and prompted him to mobilise his forces in Syria. This confrontation was set in motion when the amir Yashbak al-Sha'bānī, who controlled most of the political affairs in Cairo, came into conflict with Sultan Faraj, when he attempted to remove Faraj's brother-in-law,[136] Īnāl Bāy b. Qajmās, from his position as *amīr ākhūr*.[137] In Ṣafar 807/August 1404, Yashbak's faction was defeated in battle by the supporters of the sultan. Yashbak fled to Syria, and was received by Shaykh in Damascus.[138] Before Yashbak's arrival, Shaykh had already released Qarā Yūsuf from prison, perhaps anticipating that his Turkman followers would prove useful in any future hostilities. After his arrival in Damascus, Yashbak convinced Shaykh to release Sulṭān Aḥmad as well,[139] a signal that the Mamluk sultan's authority no longer extended to Syria. Shaykh bestowed 100,000 silver dirhams and 300 horses upon each of them.[140] Sulṭān Aḥmad and Qarā Yūsuf were no longer the sultan's prisoners, but members of Shaykh's own retinue.

Sulṭān Aḥmad and Qarā Yūsuf accompanied Shaykh on his campaign against the Mamluk governor of Safad in Sha'bān 807/February 1405.[141] However, when Shaykh went on campaign against Sultan Faraj in Egypt in support of the amir Jakam, who declared himself sultan in Syria, Sulṭān Aḥmad stayed behind in Damascus. He took the opportunity to leave Damascus, on 16 Dhū al-Ḥijja 807/15 June 1405, and returned yet again to Baghdad.[142]

Sulṭān Aḥmad's refusal to fully submit to Tīmūr meant that parties threatened by the spread of Timurid domination at the end of the eighth/fourteenth century found him a symbol of opposition. Offering protection to the heir to the Ilkhanate positioned Barqūq, Bāyezīd and Qarā Yūsuf against Tīmūr and the Chaghatayid amirs. The fact that Sulṭān Aḥmad was often a refugee from his home in Baghdad between 795/1393 and 806/1403 meant that he was dependent on his protectors; when they removed their protection, or were defeated, Sulṭān Aḥmad had to seek another patron. Yet, despite Tīmūr's multiple campaigns into the former Ilkhanid lands, the western Ilkhanate proved harder for the Timurids to rule than Khurasan or Fars. The Qarāquyūnlū Turkmans, led by Qarā Yūsuf, and not the Timurids, became the successors to the Jalayirids in Azarbayjan and Arab Iraq. To understand how this occurred, we must examine two historical developments. The first is how Qarā Yūsuf became the closest ally of Sulṭān Aḥmad and acquired power and prestige on the basis of their relationship. The second is the conversion of this relationship into 'ideological capital' used by Qarā Yūsuf to present his family as the rightful heirs to the Jalayirid house, and thus, ultimately, to the Ilkhanate.

The Qarāquyūnlū Turkmans as Heirs to the Jalayirid-Ilkhanid Legacy

Sulṭān Aḥmad's alliance with Qarā Yūsuf began shortly after his seizure of the throne in 784/1382, when he faced opposition from his brother Shaykh 'Alī. Turkman military support helped Sulṭān Aḥmad defeat Shaykh 'Alī and take Baghdad for himself. However, Baghdad's loyalty to Sulṭān Aḥmad remained in question. Opposition among the *a'yān* of the city may account for Sulṭān Aḥmad's seemingly irrational purge of hundreds of amirs and members of his own household in 802/1400. According to Yazdī, a representative of Tīmūr had come to Baghdad and began secretly paying a number of Sulṭān Aḥmad's amirs and dependants. Sulṭān Aḥmad joined six of his loyal attendants across the Tigris under cover of darkness, and rode to join Qarā Yūsuf.[143] Sulṭān Aḥmad at first urged the Turkmans to attack Baghdad, but in the end he had a change of heart and paid them off handsomely not to carry it out.[144] It was at this time that Sulṭān Aḥmad made his second flight to Mamluk Syria, this time together with Qarā Yūsuf. As discussed above, they found that they were not welcome in Syria, and thus went to Bāyezīd's court in Anatolia instead.

Sulṭān Aḥmad was obliged to call on the help of the Qarāquyūnlū again in 805/1403 when, after returning from Anatolia, he faced Sulṭān Ṭāhir's uprising in Baghdad. As mentioned above, Qarā Yūsuf helped to put down the rebellion around Sulṭān Ṭāhir, but then took Baghdad for himself. Sulṭān Aḥmad fled to Syria for a third time, and Qarā Yūsuf followed at his heels, threatened himself by Tīmūr. Both came into the service of the Mamluk governor of Damascus, Shaykh al-Maḥmūdī, as discussed above. Tīmūr's death emboldened Sulṭān Aḥmad to leave Damascus and return to Baghdad in 807/1405. Qarā Yūsuf also took the opportunity to expand his authority through a combination of military power and promotion of an ideological programme that presented his family as the rightful heirs to the Jalayirids in Azarbayjan and Iraq. His close relationship with Sulṭān Aḥmad over the preceding years formed the basis of these claims. Later Timurid historians Mīrkhvānd and Khvāndamīr emphasise the importance of the relationship between Qarā Yūsuf and Sulṭān Aḥmad to the eventual Qarāquyūnlū assertion of authority over the Jalayirid realm. According to Mīrkhvānd, while they were confined together in Cairo, Qarā Yūsuf and Sulṭān Aḥmad had contact with each other (*miyān-i īshān ikhtilāṭ-i āmad va shud vāqi' mī-shud*).[145] During their period in Cairo, Qarā Yūsuf's son Pīr Budāq was born. Sulṭān Aḥmad reportedly accepted Pīr Budāq as his own son (*ū rā bi-farzandī qabūl kard*), providing the nurse of his own son for him and looking after them (*dāya-yi farzand nazd-i khūd nigāh dāshta bi-ta'ahhud-i īshān mashghūl shud*). Sulṭān Aḥmad seems to have assumed the role of godfather or uncle to Pīr Budāq. Qarā Yūsuf later exploited this relationship to achieve a legalistic appropriation of the Jalayirid sultanate for his own family.

In addition, Sulṭān Aḥmad and Qarā Yūsuf made a pact of friendship and an agreement on spheres of influence each would maintain once they left Egypt. They agreed that if they did manage to escape confinement, they would not attack each other (*agar az ān varṭa khalāṣī yāband qaṣd-i yakdīgar nakunand*), and that they would be united (*muddathā bā ham muttaḥid bāshand*). Tabriz would belong to Qarā Yūsuf and Baghdad would belong to Sulṭān Aḥmad, and neither one would interfere in the other's land (*tabrīz az qarā yūsuf va baghdād az Sulṭān Aḥmad bāshad va hīchyak muta'arriż-i mamlakat-i dīgarī nashavand*).[146] Sulṭān Aḥmad recognised the importance of maintaining an alliance with Qarā Yūsuf, and probably saw his concession of Azarbayjan as a necessary expedient to this end. He later attempted to regain Azarbayjan, in violation of this oath.

The relationship of Sulṭān Aḥmad to Pīr Budāq and the pact made with Qarā Yūsuf provide the basis for the explanation by the Timurid historians for why Qarā Yūsuf was subsequently justified in establishing Pīr Budāq as a legitimate ruler (*khān*) in Azarbayjan, and for eventually killing Sulṭān Aḥmad in 813/1410. First, Pīr Budāq's close relationship to Sulṭān Aḥmad, a virtual father-son relationship, was given by Qarā Yūsuf as the justification for enthroning Pīr Budāq as khan. Second, Sulṭān Aḥmad's violation of the pact he had made with Qarā Yūsuf made Qarā Yūsuf's defeat of the Jalayirid sultan, his appropriation of his patrimony and his execution a legitimate act as well. In the Timurid narrative of these events, the period of exile and captivity in Egypt of Sulṭān Aḥmad and Qarā Yūsuf was significant for later attempts by Qarā Yūsuf to assert his own family's authority in a way that recognised Jalayirid claims, while at the same time rationalising the transferal of authority to the new Qarāquyūnlū dispensation.

Although Sulṭān Aḥmad supposedly agreed that Qarā Yūsuf should rule in Azarbayjan, the Turkmans still had to take it from the Timurids. Qarā Yūsuf prevailed in this after defeating Abā Bakr Mīrzā in two major battles. The second decisive victory came in 810/1408, and Abā Bakr was driven into Sistan, where he was killed.[147] Before Abā Bakr's death Qarā Yūsuf was reluctant to take a royal title for himself. We are told that support for Qarā Yūsuf came not only from the Qarāquyūnlū Turkmans but also from the 'amirs of Iraq', those forces that had been attached to the Timurid princes Abā Bakr and 'Umar (Mīrānshāhī). According to Mīrkhvānd, the amirs insisted on supporting Qarā Yūsuf, even after he disavowed any claims to the sultanate in Azarbayjan and Iraq:

> I am from the Turkman people, my summer residence is Alataq and my winter residence is Diyarbakr and the banks of the Euphrates. The throne of the sultanate does not belong to us (*takht-i salṭanat nisbatī bi-mā nadārad*).[148]

Although the amirs agreed that they had an obligation to Abā Bakr, they also faulted him for driving his own brother ('Umar Mīrzā) from Azarbayjan, which Tīmūr had expressly willed to him.[149] With the support of the amirs of Iraq, Qarā Yūsuf was able to resist Abā Bakr's attempt to establish his authority in Azarbayjan and Arab Iraq. As Mīrkhvānd framed the issue, Abā Bakr may have been the grandson of the *ṣāḥib-qirān*, but this dynastic connection was not sufficient for him to rule. The Qarāquyūnlū chief and the military elite of Iraq were in a position to take power for themselves. Such a pattern echoes the rise to power of Shaykh Ḥasan Jalayir and the Oyrat tribesmen of Iraq in the 730s/1330s, when central authority was breaking down in the Ilkhanate. Azarbayjan, Arab Iraq and the region between Mosul and Erzincan would remain a coherent political unit under the Qarāquyūnlū as it had been under the Jalayirids. The reluctance of Qarā Yūsuf to challenge a descendant of Tīmūr, the *ṣāḥib-qirān*, can be read as part of Mīrkhvānd's narrative in the service of a descendant of another branch of the Timurid house, Sulṭān Ḥusayn Bāyqarā of Herat. From this perspective, the branch of Tīmūr's family descended from his son Mīrānshāh – including Abā Bakr, who had inherited the western Ilkhanid provinces – could be denigrated in the service of glorifying an alternative Timurid princely line.

After the defeat of Abā Bakr, Qarā Yūsuf was faced with the issue of legitimising his own political authority. He had defeated the Timurid prince, but Qarā Yūsuf had little in the way of lineage or family connections that could bolster his ideological claims to the former seat of the Ilkhanate. However, the symbolic significance of Azarbayjan as the former capital of the Ilkhanate had faded, along with the memory of the Ilkhanate itself. The period of Tīmūr's campaigns, through which he attempted to construct his own version of the Mongol world empire, had accelerated even further the trend toward regionalisation among the former Ilkhanid provinces that had begun after 736/1335. The Jalayirid sultans had been supported by those elites in Tabriz that had benefited from the Ilkhanid imperial system; however, for the twenty years or so between c. 790/1388 and 810/1408, Tabriz had been forced to carry on rather independently of any one dynastic authority. While this dynastic ambiguity existed, the notion of Tabriz as an imperial centre had less appeal, for it was doubtful whether it would play the role of imperial capital as an appanage in a larger Timurid empire. For those reasons, it seems as if Qarā Yūsuf did not feel compelled to connect his family and lineage to the Ilkhans the way the Jalayirids had done; rather, he sought to publicly demonstrate that his family members were the rightful heirs to the Jalayirid dynasty itself through Sulṭān Aḥmad's formal recognition of Qarā Yūsuf's son, Pīr Budāq.

These ideological considerations began shortly after Qarā Yūsuf's victory over Abā Bakr Mīrzā in 810/1408, when Qarā Yūsuf and his men returned to the summer pasture around Alataq and 'considered the matter of the *khuṭba* and *sikka*' (*dar bāb-i khuṭba va sikka andīshhā namūdand*).[150] Qarā Yūsuf was reluctant to recognise his own son as sultan,[151] and instead took a more indirect approach. In the course of sending *fatḥ-nāma*s and benedictions to the governors of neighbouring provinces after his victory, Qarā Yūsuf also sent a delegation to Sulṭān Aḥmad in Baghdad, which included gifts and a letter directly from Pīr Budāq. Sulṭān Aḥmad honoured the Qarāquyūnlū delegation and responded to Pīr Budāq's letter with affection, again referring to him as his son.[152] Sulṭān Aḥmad also sent Pīr Budāq a 'parasol and other royal items' (*chatr va dīgar-i asbāb-i salṭanat*).[153] When the Qarāquyūnlū envoys returned to Tabriz, Qarā Yūsuf immediately seated Pīr Budāq on the throne. The *khuṭba*, royal decrees and coins were all issued in his name.[154] Local rulers acknowledged the authority of Pīr Budāq Khan. However, the most important acknowledgement for Qarā Yūsuf would have to come from Sulṭān Aḥmad. Qarā Yūsuf sent a messenger to explain the situation:

> Since his majesty [Sulṭān Aḥmad] called Pīr Budāq his son anew, and sent a parasol and other royal articles for him, by virtue of the necessity of obedience, we consigned the government of Azarbayjan to him.[155]

Qarā Yūsuf used the letter of congratulations sent by Sulṭān Aḥmad to Pīr Budāq, in which he called him his son, along with the royal parasol he sent as a gift, as evidence of a formal transfer of authority from Sulṭān Aḥmad to Pīr Budāq, and thus the replacement of Jalayirid authority in Azarbayjan with that of a new dynastic dispensation, that of the Qarāquyūnlū Turkmans. If we accept the account of the pact made between Sulṭān Aḥmad and Qarā Yūsuf in Damascus, the enthronement of Pīr Budāq in Azarbayjan accords with that arrangement. The former Jalayirid provinces, which Tīmūr had bequeathed to the descendants of Mīrānshāh, were divided between a Qarāquyūnlū sphere in Azarbayjan and a Jalayirid sphere in Arab Iraq. The Turkmans loyal to Qarā Yūsuf held the Diyarbakr and Lake Van regions, also once claimed by Sultan Shaykh Uvays Jalayir.

Sulṭān Aḥmad's Death and the Demise of the Jalayirids

As long as Sulṭān Aḥmad remained in Baghdad, Qarā Yūsuf was content to honour the division between their sultanates. Sulṭān Aḥmad spent a great deal of money and effort rebuilding the fortifications of the city, which had been the target of a brutal siege and sacking by Tīmūr in 803/1401.[156] However, Sulṭān Aḥmad was not the only member of the Jalayirid house who could potentially challenge Qarā Yūsuf's newly laid claims to Azarbayjan. Sulṭān Aḥmad's son 'Alā' al-Dawla had been captured by Tīmūr and confined in Samarqand until Tīmūr's death in 807/1405. By 808/1406, a group of amirs from Iraq who were also in Samarqand promoted 'Alā' al-Dawla as their leader, and headed back to Azarbayjan.[157] While Naṭanzī reports that 'Alā' al-Dawla challenged his father, similar to his brother Sulṭān Ṭāhir,[158] a later tradition related by Mīrkhvānd and Khvāndamīr holds that 'Alā' al-Dawla went straight to Azarbayjan, where he ran afoul of Qarā Yūsuf. Both traditions record that Qarā Yūsuf imprisoned 'Alā' al-Dawla in the castle at Adilceviz.[159]

In the autumn of 812/1409, Sulṭān Aḥmad set out from Hamadan to attack Sultaniyya, presumably as a first operation in an attempt to conquer Azarbayjan. Although Qarā Yūsuf had conquered Tabriz and installed young Pīr Budāq on the throne there, he himself continued to follow the traditional Qarāquyūnlū migration between Alataq and Diyarbakr. Thus, Sulṭān Aḥmad calculated that an attack on Sultaniyya, to the south and east of Tabriz, could be carried out without an immediate reaction from Qarā Yūsuf and the Turkmans, and might provide him with a stronghold outside of Arab Iraq.

Sulṭān Aḥmad was forced to give up his siege of Sultaniyya, however, when he learned that an individual named Uvays, who claimed to be his son, was stirring up rebellion back in Baghdad. Sulṭān Aḥmad returned to put down the rebellion and spent the winter of 812/1409–10 in Baghdad. The next spring, Qarā Yūsuf was drawn even further away to the west, in order to quell an insurrection in Erzincan led by the local governor Muṭahhartan and the Āqquyūnlū chief Qarā 'Us̱mān.[160] The result of Qarā Yūsuf's campaign was that Mardin and Erzincan were both incorporated into the Qarāquyūnlū domains, as the rule of the Artuqids and Muṭahhartan came to an end.

With Qarā Yūsuf's attention in the west, Sulṭān Aḥmad made another attempt to capture Azarbayjan in the summer of 813/1410. He made an alliance with Shāhrukh and his brothers Iskandar Sulṭān and Khalīl Sulṭān,[161] as well as with the Shīrvānshāh Ibrāhīm al-Darbandī.[162] Meeting no resistance, the Jalayirid sultan made a triumphal entrance into Tabriz in August of that year.[163] Qarā Yūsuf had left his son Shāh Muḥammad to defend Azarbayjan, but he fled to Khuy when Sulṭān Aḥmad's forces approached. Qarā Yūsuf quickly set off back to Tabriz from Erzincan and faced off against the Jalayirid army in late Rabī' II 813/August 1410. According to al-Maqrīzī, the Jalayirid sultan commanded a force of 60,000 horsemen.[164] However, Sulṭān Aḥmad's army was routed by the Qarāquyūnlū near Shanba-yi Ghāzān, the suburb founded by Ghazan Khan outside Tabriz.[165] Sulṭān Aḥmad was knocked from his horse during the battle, and his weapons and clothes were taken by one of the Turkmans. Helpless, Sulṭān Aḥmad crawled into a drainage ditch in a nearby garden (*sulṭān bi-sūrākh-i bāghī kih āb az ānjā bīrūn mī-āmad khazīd*).[166]

Samarqandī reports that one of the lowly men (*liyām*) of Tabriz named Bahā' al-Dīn Jūlāh revealed him to Qarā Yūsuf.[167] Mīrkhvānd recounts a more colourful story of an old shoemaker (*pīrī kafsh-dūz*) who had climbed into a tree to watch the battle and had seen Sulṭān Aḥmad crawl into the ditch. When the shoemaker called out to the sultan, he told him to be quiet and not to give him up. That night he would make his escape and reward the shoemaker's silence with a *suyūrghāl* in the district of Ya'qūbiyya. When the shoemaker went home and told his wife, she told him that Ya'qūbiyya was too far away, and that they should report the sultan's whereabouts to Qarā Yūsuf. The shoemaker did so, and Qarā Yūsuf's men pulled Sulṭān Aḥmad out of the ditch. Wearing the clothes of a beggar, he was taken to Qarā Yūsuf's court. Here he was reminded by his old ally Qarā Yūsuf that he had made an oath not to attack him. Because he had broken the oath, Qarā Yūsuf forced Sulṭān Aḥmad to sign an order (*nīshānī*) to the effect that the remaining Jalayirid princes in Baghdad had to relinquish their claims there, and that henceforth Baghdad would be ruled by Qarā Yūsuf's son Shāh Muḥammad.[168]

For the second time, Qarā Yūsuf had employed legalistic means to transfer authority from the Jalayirids to his own family, this time forcing Sulṭān Aḥmad to write the order with his own hand.[169] The Jalayirid territories had passed to Pīr Budāq and Shāh Muḥammad, the sons of Qarā Yūsuf Qarāquyūnlū. Mīrkhvānd and Khvāndamīr report that Qarā Yūsuf did not want to kill Sulṭān Aḥmad, but that the amirs of Iraq, led by Bisṭām Jāgīr, wanted him executed. To make their case, the amirs addressed Sulṭān Aḥmad:

> You brought ruin to the dynasty of Shaykh Uvays (*khānidān-i sulṭān uvays*) and you killed those who were left after his reign (*dawlat*). No suitable deed has come from you, [and] we do not want to allow you to deceive Amīr Qarā Yūsuf.[170]

Qarā Yūsuf was convinced to allow Sulṭān Aḥmad to be killed. Even after the execution,[171] the amir Bisṭām reported to Qarā Yūsuf that the common people were insisting Sulṭān Aḥmad was still alive. In order to quell these rumours, Sulṭān Aḥmad's body was displayed to the public for three days at a madrasa in Tabriz. Sulṭān Aḥmad was buried next to his brother Sulṭān Ḥusayn in the Dimashqiyya complex in Tabriz.[172]

Following Sulṭān Aḥmad's execution, a purge began of the remaining princes. 'Alā' al-Dawla was dispatched at the Adilceviz castle, and a campaign was carried out by Shāh Muḥammad in Arab Iraq to eliminate the other surviving Jalayirids. Prince Maḥmūd b. Walad b. Shaykh 'Alī b. Shaykh Uvays held out in Baghdad against the Qarāquyūnlū until 814/1411, when Shāh Muḥammad's forces finally drove him out, and he took refuge in Khuzistan. Maḥmūd was eventually driven out of Khuzistan by supporters of his brother Uvays, a child who was under the control of his mother, Tūndī Sulṭān. This Shaykh 'Alid branch of the Jalayirid dynasty was thus marginalised in Khuzistan, and was essentially overrun by the Qarāquyūnlū. In fact, the defeat of Sulṭān Aḥmad in 813/1410 signalled the end of effective Jalayirid claims to the old centres of Tabriz and Baghdad. The Turkmans had inherited the traditional Jalayirid territories.

Notes

1. Qazvīnī/*ZTG*, 88; Ḥāfiẓ Abrū/*ZJT*, 196.
2. Ḥāfiẓ Abrū/*ZJT*, 198.
3. Ḥāfiẓ Abrū/*ZJT*, 198.
4. Shaykh Uvays had gone to war with Amīr Valī in 772/1370–71 after he rebelled. Shaykh Uvays eventually assigned Rayy to Amīr 'Ādil. After Sulṭān Ḥusayn came to the throne, Amīr Valī sent him one of his daughters as a sign of friendship. However, when Sulṭān Ḥusayn saw her and did not

find her appealing, he refused to marry her. However, he gave Rayy back to Amīr Valī as compensation; see Ḥāfiẓ Abrū/*ZJT*, 204.

5. Ḥāfiẓ Abrū/*ZJT*, 205.
6. Ḥāfiẓ Abrū/*ZJT*, 206.
7. The *suyūrghāl* (*soyurghal*) in the Ilkhanid context has been characterised most recently by Halil İnalcık as a grant guaranteeing absolute proprietorship, total exemptions and immunities on land revenue and peasant labour within a well-defined area, freed from the control of the state and its agents. See Halil İnalcık, 'Autonomous Enclaves in Islamic States: *Temlîks*, *Soyurghal*s, *Yurdluḳ-Ocaḳlıḳ*s, *Mâlikâne-Muḳāṭa'a*s and *Awqāf*', in Judith Pfeiffer and Sholeh A. Quinn (eds), in collaboration with Ernest Tucker, *History and Historiography of Post-Mongol Central Asia and the Middle East: Studies in Honor of John E. Woods* (Wiesbaden: Harrassowitz, 2006), 112.
8. Ḥāfiẓ Abrū/*ZJT*, 207.
9. Ḥāfiẓ Abrū/*ZJT*, 209.
10. Ḥāfiẓ Abrū/*ZJT*, 209.
11. Following the conspiracy of the amirs, Amīr 'Ādil took up residence at Sultaniyya, while Sulṭān Ḥusayn remained in Tabriz.
12. Ḥāfiẓ Abrū gives the date 783/1381–82. See Ḥāfiẓ Abrū/*ZJT*, 218. Maḥmūd Kutubī gives the year for the start of this campaign as 781/1379–80. See Kutubī/*TAM*, 96.
13. Ḥāfiẓ Abrū/*ZJT*, 218.
14. Kutubī/*TAM*, 96.
15. Ḥāfiẓ Abrū portrays this episode as a victory for Amīr 'Ādil, explaining that Shāh Shujā' sought a truce due to pressure from his own troops, who were low on equipment and provisions. See Ḥāfiẓ Abrū/*ZJT*, 219. However, Maḥmūd Kutubī writes that it was Amīr 'Ādil who asked for peace from Shāh Shujā', and that he paid off the Muzaffarids handsomely to go back to Fars. See Kutubī/*TAM*, 97. Perhaps realising that he could not count on assistance from Amīr 'Ādil, Shāh Shujā' concluded it would be futile to try to take Tabriz, and that he would have to be content only with a share of the treasure from Sultaniyya.
16. Ḥāfiẓ Abrū/*ZJT*, 220.
17. Ḥāfiẓ Abrū/*ZJT*, 218–19.
18. Christoph Werner, Daniel Zakrzewski and Hans-Thomas Tillschneider, *Die Kuǧuǧī-Stiftungen in Tabrīz: Ein Beitrag zur Geschichte der Ǧelāyiriden* (Wiesbaden: Dr. Ludwig Reichert Verlag, 2013), 35.
19. Werner et al., *Die Kuǧuǧī-Stiftungen in Tabrīz*, 16.
20. Werner et al., *Die Kuǧuǧī-Stiftungen in Tabrīz*, 100.
21. Werner et al., *Die Kuǧuǧī-Stiftungen in Tabrīz*, 38.
22. According to the eleventh/seventeenth-century Safavid genealogical history *Silsilat al-Nasab-i Ṣafaviyya*, Shaykh Ṣadr al-Dīn was responsible for the construction of a complex known as the Safavid *khaṭīra* in Ardabil during

his time as head of the order in the eighth/fourteenth century. Although the Ṣafaviyya was still a local religious order, and would not emerge as the ruling dynasty of Iran until the turn of the tenth/sixteenth century, under the leadership of Shaykh Ṣadr al-Dīn it was an influential organisation in Ardabil at the time when Sulṭān Aḥmad had his hereditary appanage there. See Ḥusayn ibn Abdāl Zāhidī, *Silsilat al-Nasab-i Ṣafaviyya, Nasabnāma-yi Pādishāhān bā 'Uzmat-i Ṣafavī* (Berlin: Chāpkhāna-yi Īrānshahr, 1343 [1924]), 39. Gottfried Herrmann has edited a decree from Sulṭān Ḥusayn to his brother Sulṭān Aḥmad in 780/1378, instructing Sulṭān Aḥmad and a certain Sharaf al-Dīn Maḥmūdī not to demand taxes from shops outside a Ṣafaviyya *zāviya* in Ardabil. The prestige of Shaykh Ṣadr al-Dīn is recognised in this decree, which refers to the shaykh as 'the spiritual guide of the general populace' (*murshid-i ṭavā'if al-amm*). See Gottfried Herrmann, 'Ein Erlaß des Ǧalāyeriden Solṭān Ḥoseyn aus dem Jahr 780/1378', in *Erkenntnisse und Meinungen I herausgegeben von Gernot Wießner* (Wiesbaden: Otto Harrassowitz, 1973), 135–63.

23. Qazvīnī/*ZTG*, 106; Ḥāfiẓ Abrū/*ZJT*, 220; Mīrkhvānd/*Rawża*, 5:587.
24. Astarābādī/*Bazm*, 16–17.
25. Mīrkhvānd/*Rawża*, 5:588.
26. Mīrkhvānd/*Rawża*, 5:588.
27. Mīrkhvānd/*Rawża*, 5:588.
28. Mīrkhvānd/*Rawża*, 5:588.
29. When Sulṭān Aḥmad's men, including Ḥamza, Yāghī Bāstī and Abū Sa'īd, reached Tabriz, 'Abbās, Misāfir and the *a'yān* of Tabriz came out of the city to formally receive them (*rasm-i istiqbāl*). Ḥamza told his men that since these individuals had submitted to Sulṭān Aḥmad, they would acquire authority (*ṣāḥib-i ikhtiyār khvāhand shud*), and so it was in their best interests to kill them. See Mīrkhvānd/*Rawża*, 5:588.
30. Shāmī/Tauer, 97; Shāmī/Lugal, 117.
31. Shāmī/Tauer, 97; Shāmī/Lugal, 117.
32. Naṭanzī/Aubin, 166.
33. Shabānkāra'ī/*Majma'*, 313. See also John Masson Smith, Jr, ''Alī b. Oways', *Encyclopaedia Iranica*, ed. Ehsan Yarshater (London and New York: Routledge and Kegan Paul, 1983), 1:853–4. A decree issued by prince Shaykh 'Alī has been edited by Gottfried Herrmann. The order, which confers three villages in the Ardabil region on the disciples of Shaykh Ṣadr al-Dīn Ṣafavī, was issued from Qarabagh in 766/1365, during the reign of Shaykh Uvays. See Gottfried Herrmann, *Persische Urkunden der Mongolenzeit* (Wiesbaden: Harrassowitz Verlag, 2004), 162–5.
34. Ḥāfiẓ Abrū and Mīrkhvānd give the year 780/1378–79 for the start of the uprising, while Zayn al-Dīn Qazvīnī gives the year 781/1379–80. See Qazvīnī/*ZTG*, 101; Ḥāfiẓ Abrū/*ZJT*, 209; Mīrkhvānd/*Rawża*, 5:582.
35. Vajīh al-Dīn Ismā'īl had been given authority in Baghdad in 776/1374 by Shaykh Uvays following the death of the previous governor, Khwāja Sarvar

Khāzin, 'from grief' (*az ghuṣṣa ranjūr shud va namānd*) after the city was devastated by a flood. See Ḥāfiẓ Abrū/*ZJT*, 197; Faṣīḥ Khvāfī/*Mujmal*, 108. Zayn al-Dīn Qazvīnī describes Vajīh al-Dīn Ismā'īl as '*ṣāḥib-qirān* of the time'; see Qazvīnī/*ZTG*, 101.

36. Qazvīnī/*ZTG*, 101; Ḥāfiẓ Abrū/*ZJT*, 209; Mīrkhvānd/*Rawża*, 5:582.
37. Ḥāfiẓ Abrū/*ZJT*, 211; Mīrkhvānd/*Rawża*, 5:583.
38. Mīrkhvānd/*Rawża*, 5:583.
39. Mīrkhvānd/*Rawża*, 5:589.
40. Mīrkhvānd/*Rawża*, 5:589.
41. In his autobiography, court musician 'Abd al-Qādir Marāghī referred to Shaykh 'Alī as *shāh-i 'ālam*, or 'king of the world'. The use of this title seems to indicate both that Marāghī was in the entourage of Shaykh 'Alī during the succession struggles following Sulṭān Ḥusayn's death, and that Shaykh 'Alī had pretensions to leadership of the Jalayirid house as the successor to Shaykh Uvays. See Murat Bardakçı, *Maragalı Abdülkadir: XV. yy. bestecisi ve müzik nazariyatçısının hayat hikâyesiyle eserleri üzerine bir çalışma* (Istanbul: Pan Yayıncılık, 1986), 28, 155.
42. Mīrkhvānd/*Rawża*, 5:587.
43. Faruk Sümer, *Kara Koyunlular (Başlangıçtan Cihan-Şah'a kadar)*, I. Cilt (Ankara: Türk Tarih Kurumu Basımevi, 1962), 42.
44. Sümer, *Kara Koyunlular*, 42.
45. Sümer, *Kara Koyunlular*, 43.
46. Ḥāfiẓ Abrū gives two dates for possibly two different *quriltay*s, in spring of 777/1376 and spring of 779/1378; he writes that the matter of Bayrām Khwāja was discussed at both. See Ḥāfiẓ Abrū/*ZJT*, 203. Mīrkhvānd gives only 777/1376 for the *quriltay*. See Mīrkhvānd/*Rawża*, 5:579.
47. Ḥāfiẓ Abrū/*ZJT*, 204; Mīrkhvānd/*Rawża*, 5:579.
48. Mīrkhvānd/*Rawża*, 5:579.
49. Ḥāfiẓ Abrū/*ZJT*, 204.
50. Mīrkhvānd/*Rawża*, 5:589.
51. Mīrkhvānd/*Rawża*, 5:589.
52. Mīrkhvānd/*Rawża*, 5:589.
53. Ḥāfiẓ Abrū/*ZJT*, 241.
54. Qazvīnī/*ZTG*, 122; Ḥāfiẓ Abrū/*ZJT*, 242.
55. Qazvīnī/*ZTG*, 148.
56. Beatrice Forbes Manz, *The Rise and Rule of Tamerlane* (Cambridge: Cambridge University Press, 1989), 142.
57. Yazdī/*Ẓafar-nāma*, 2:368.
58. Yazdī/*Ẓafar-nāma*, 2:369.
59. Yazdī/*Ẓafar-nāma*, 2:402.
60. Shaykh 'Alī, who had been proclaimed sultan by the elites of Baghdad when Sulṭān Aḥmad killed Sulṭān Ḥusayn, was killed in battle with Sulṭān Aḥmad's forces in 786/1384–85. See Ghiyāth/*Ta'rīkh*, 102–3.
61. Astarābādī/*Bazm*, 17.

62. According to Astarābādī, bills of exchange became worthless (*naqd-i hunar kāshid shud*) and a mockery was made of the market (*bāzār-i nafāq nifāq yāft*). It was these difficult conditions that, Astarābādī writes, prompted him to leave Baghdad and go to Anatolia, where he entered the service of Qāḍī Burhān al-Dīn in Sivas. See Astarābādī/*Bazm*, 17–18. This account, which Astarābādī gives about his own journey from the court of Sulṭān Aḥmad in Baghdad to Sivas, differs from the account given by Ibn ʻArabshāh, who writes that Qāḍī Burhān al-Dīn had heard of Astarābādī's talents, and had requested that Sulṭān Aḥmad give him leave to join his court. When Sulṭān Aḥmad refused, Astarābādī escaped and came to Sivas on his own. See Ibn ʻArabshāh/*ʻAjā'ib*, 121–2. See also the discussion by Mehmed Fuad Köprülü in his introduction to his 1928 edition of *Bazm u Razm*.
63. Ibn ʻArabshāh/*ʻAjā'ib*, 68.
64. Khvāndamīr/Humā'ī, 3:455; Khvāndamīr/Thackston, 257.
65. Shāmī/Tauer, 138.
66. Maqrīzī/ʻAshūr, 3:788; Ibn Taghrī Birdī/*Manhal*, 1:249.
67. Maqrīzī/ʻAshūr, 3:788; Ibn Taghrī Birdī/*Manhal*, 1:249; Ibn Ḥajar/*Inbā'*, 3:156.
68. Maqrīzī/ʻAshūr, 3:788; Ibn Taghrī Birdī/*Manhal*, 1:250.
69. Maqrīzī/ʻAshūr, 3:788; Ibn Taghrī Birdī/*Manhal*, 1:250.
70. Yazdī/*Ẓafar-nāma*, 1:456; Naṭanzī/Aubin, 169.
71. Maqrīzī/ʻAshūr, 3:788; Ibn Taghrī Birdī/*Manhal*, 1:250; Yazdī/*Ẓafar-nāma*, 1:455; Astarābādī/*Bazm*, 22–3.
72. Maqrīzī/ʻAshūr, 3:788.
73. Maqrīzī/ʻAshūr, 3:788; Ibn Taghrī Birdī/*Manhal*, 1:250.
74. Ibn Taghrī Birdī/*Manhal*, 1:250.
75. Maqrīzī/ʻAshūr, 3:788.
76. Maqrīzī/ʻAshūr, 3:799; Ibn Taghrī Birdī/*Manhal*, 1:251.
77. Maqrīzī/ʻAshūr, 3:799; Ibn Taghrī Birdī/*Manhal*, 1:252.
78. Maqrīzī/ʻAshūr, 3:799.
79. Maqrīzī/ʻAshūr, 3:799; Ibn Taghrī Birdī/*Manhal*, 1:252.
80. Ibn Taghrī Birdī/*Manhal*, 1:252–3.
81. Maqrīzī/ʻAshūr, 3:799.
82. Maqrīzī/ʻAshūr, 3:801.
83. Yazdī/*Ẓafar-nāma*, 1:458.
84. Yazdī/*Ẓafar-nāma*, 2:199.
85. Maqrīzī/ʻAshūr, 3:807; Ibn Taghrī Birdī/*Manhal*, 1:253.
86. Ann F. Broadbridge, *Kingship and Ideology in the Islamic and Mongol Worlds* (Cambridge: Cambridge University Press, 2008), 181.
87. Maqrīzī/ʻAshūr, 3:807; Ibn Taghrī Birdī/*Manhal*, 1:253–4.
88. Maqrīzī/ʻAshūr, 3:813.
89. Maqrīzī/ʻAshūr, 3:814; Ibn Taghrī Birdī/*Manhal*, 1:254.
90. A section from Shukr Allāh's *Bahjat al-Tavārīkh*, with a German translation, can be found in Theodor Seif, 'Der Abschnitt über die Osmanen in

Šükrüllāh's persischer Universalgeschichte', *Mitteilungen zur Osmanischen Geschichte* 2 (1923–25): 63–128. Here is cited p. 96: *az sharr-i tīmūr vaṭan tark karda va bi-ṭaraf-i shām rafta būdand.* For the history of Rūḥī, see the modern Turkish transcription published by Halil Erdoğan Cengiz and Yaşar Yücel, in *Belgeler. Türk Tarih Belgeleri Dergisi*, 14/18 (1989–92). Here is cited p. 397: *temūr şerrinden bū ikisī terk-i vaṭan īdūb şām diyārına vārūb* (transcription from Ottoman Turkish text). See also Meḥmed Neşrī, *Kitâb-i Cihan-nümâ: Neşrî Tarihi*, ed. Faik Reşit Unat and Mehmed A. Köymen (Ankara: Türk Tarih Kurumu Basımevi, 1995), 334–5.

91. Seif, 'Der Abschnitt über die Osmanen in Šükrüllāh's persischer Universalgeschichte', 96; Rūḥī, 'Rûhî Târîhi', ed. Cengiz and Yücel, 397; Ḳarāmānlı Nişāncı Meḥmed Pāşā, 'Tevārīḫ al-Salāṭin al-'O̱smāniyye', trans. Konyalı İbrahim Hakkı, in *Osmanlı tarihleri: Osmanlı tarihinin anakaynakları olan eserlerin, mütehassıslar tarafından hazırlanan metin, tercüme veya sadeleştirilmiş şekilleri külliyatı* (Istanbul: Türkiye Yayınevi, 1949), 348; 'Āşıḳpāşāzāde, *Tevārīḫ-i Āl-i 'O̱smān*, ed. H. Nihal Atsız, in *Osmanlı tarihleri: Osmanlı tarihinin anakaynakları olan eserlerin, mütehassıslar tarafından hazırlanan metin, tercüme veya sadeleştirilmiş şekilleri külliyatı* (Istanbul: Türkiye Yayınevi, 1949), 143; Necdet Öztürk (ed.), *Anonim Osmanlı Kroniği (1299–1512)* (Istanbul: Türk Dünyası Araştırmaları Vakfı, 2000), (Ottoman Turkish text), 28a; (modern Turkish transcription), 50; Neşrī, *Kitâb-i Cihan-nümâ*, 334–5.
92. Ibn Taghrī Birdī/*Manhal*, 1:254.
93. Maqrīzī/'Ashūr, 3:1,020; Ibn Taghrī Birdī/*Manhal*, 1:254; Ibn Taghrī Birdī/*Nujūm*, 6:44.
94. Maqrīzī/'Ashūr, 3:1,020; Ibn Taghrī Birdī/*Manhal*, 1:254.
95. Maqrīzī/'Ashūr, 3:1,020; Ibn Taghrī Birdī/*Manhal*, 1:254; Ibn Taghrī Birdī/*Nujūm*, 6:44.
96. According to Ḥāfiẓ Abrū, Shirvān b. Shaykh Barāq Manṣūrī was one of Sulṭān Aḥmad's most esteemed amirs, who turned against him after a failed siege of Shushtar, and instigated a conspiracy against Sulṭān Aḥmad in Baghdad. See Ḥāfiẓ Abrū/*Zubda*, 880. Sharaf al-Dīn 'Alī Yazdī writes that in fact Shirvān was Tīmūr's appointed governor of Khuzistan, but that he rebelled and went to Baghdad to offer his services to Sulṭān Aḥmad, after which he began to distribute money to the amirs in order to turn them against Sulṭān Aḥmad. See Yazdī/*Ẓafar-nāma*, 168. According to *al-Ta'rīkh al-Ghiyāthī*, which represents a combination of both Mamluk and Timurid historiography, Tīmūr himself had sent Shirvān to Sulṭān Aḥmad as an agent by which to gain influence at the Jalayirid court and turn the sultan's trusted amirs and intimates against him. See Ghiyāth/*Ta'rīkh*, 119.
97. Yazdī/*Ẓafar-nāma*, 2:169–70; Ghiyāth/*Ta'rīkh*, 122–3.
98. Maqrīzī/'Ashūr, 3:1,020; Ibn Taghrī Birdī/*Manhal*, 1:254–5; Ibn Taghrī Birdī/*Nujūm*, 6:44.
99. Ibn Taghrī Birdī has 22 Shawwāl in the *Manhal al-Ṣāfī*, and 24 Shawwāl in

the *Nujūm al-Zāhira*. See Ibn Taghrī Birdī/*Manhal*, 1:255; Ibn Taghrī Birdī/*Nujūm*, 6:44. Maqrīzī has 2 Shawwāl. See Maqrīzī/'Ashūr, 3:1,020.

100. Maqrīzī/'Ashūr, 3:1,020; Ibn Taghrī Birdī/*Manhal*, 1:255.
101. Maqrīzī/'Ashūr, 3:1,020; Ibn Taghrī Birdī/*Nujūm*, 6:44.
102. Maqrīzī/'Ashūr, 3:1,020; Ibn Taghrī Birdī/*Nujūm*, 6:44.
103. Ibn Taghrī Birdī/*Manhal*, 1:255.
104. Maqrīzī/'Ashūr, 3:1,023.
105. According to Ḥāfiẓ Abrū, Sulṭān Aḥmad and Qarā Yūsuf began to quarrel at Bahasna, after which Qarā Yūsuf stayed behind and Sulṭān Aḥmad proceeded to Anatolia. See Ḥāfiẓ Abrū/*Zubda*, 893.
106. Yazdī/*Ẓafar-nāma*, 2:196.
107. Ḥāfiẓ Abrū/*Zubda*, 894; 'Āşıḳpāşāzāde, *Tevārīḫ-i Āl-i 'O͟smān*, ed. 'Ālī Bey (Istanbul: Maṭba'a-yi 'Āmire, 1332 [1913–14]), 249.
108. Ḥāfiẓ Abrū/*Zubda*, 894.
109. Yazdī/*Ẓafar-nāma*, 2:268.
110. Although Yazdī writes that both Sulṭān Aḥmad and Qarā Yūsuf were with Bāyezīd at Erzincan, Shukr Allāh reports that Sulṭān Aḥmad had already returned to Baghdad by this time, and that Bāyezīd originally turned the city over to Qarā Yūsuf. However, Muṭahhartan was returned to power only sixteen days later, because 'Qarā Yūsuf could not get along with the people of Erzincan' (*bi-qawm-i arzinjān sāz-kārī natavānist kard*). See Seif, 'Der Abschnitt über die Osmanen in Šükrüllāh's persischer Universalgeschichte', 96. Neşrī provides an identical account (*erzincān ḥalḳīle mu'āmele īdemeyūb*). See Neşrī, *Kitâb-i Cihan-nümâ*, 334–5.
111. Yazdī/*Ẓafar-nāma*, 2:268. Little is known about Muṭahhartan before he became the amir of Erzincan in 781/1379. In the Timurid-era histories of Shāmī, Yazdī, Ibn 'Arabshāh and Ḥāfiẓ Abrū, as well as in the Ottoman sources written by Neşrī and 'Āşıḳpāşāzāde, his name is written as 'Ṭahartan' (or 'Ṭahirtan'). However, Yaşar Yücel has argued that the version used by Astarābādī in *Bazm u Razm* ('Muṭahhartan') is probably more proper, since Astarābādī, as the historian of Qāḍī Burhān al-Dīn in Sivas, would have been the source closest to the events in Erzincan in this period. In addition, in the contemporary *taḳvīm* written in Erzincan, the amir's name is also given as 'Muṭahhartan'. See Yaşar Yücel, *Anadolu Beylikleri hakkında Araştırmalar: Eretna Devleti, Kadı Burhaneddin Ahmed ve Devleti, Mutahharten ve Erzincan Emirliği, II* (Ankara: Türk Tarih Kurumu Basımevi, 1989), 253–4.
112. Yazdī/*Ẓafar-nāma* 2:268; Neşrī, *Kitâb-i Cihan-nümâ*, 334–5.
113. A series of four missives and responses between Tīmūr and Bāyezīd are preserved in Ferīdūn Aḥmed Bey, *Mecmū'a-yi Münşe'āt-i Selāṭīn* (Istanbul: Dār al-Ṭibā'a al-'Āmira, 1848), 118–19, 123–6, 126–30, 130–3. On the correspondence preserved by Ferīdūn Aḥmed Bey between Tīmūr and Bāyezīd, Sulṭān Aḥmad and Qarā Yūsuf, see Edward Granville Browne, *A*

Literary History of Persia, Volume 3: The Tartar Dominion (1265–1502) (Cambridge: Cambridge University Press, 1956), 2:204–6. Rūḥī wrote that Tīmūr sent an envoy to Bāyezīd, demanding that he turn over Sulṭān Aḥmad and Qarā Yūsuf. When Bāyezīd ignored the envoy, Tīmūr sent an army to attack Sivas. See Rūḥī, 'Rûhî Târîhi', ed. Cengiz and Yücel, 397. In addition, Ibn 'Arabshāh refers to a letter sent by Tīmūr, urging Bāyezīd not to give refuge to Sulṭān Aḥmad and Qarā Yūsuf. See Ibn 'Arabshāh/*'Ajā'ib*, 184–5.

114. Rūḥī, 'Rûhî Târîhi', ed. Cengiz and Yücel, 397; Seif, 'Der Abschnitt über die Osmanen in Šükrüllāh's persischer Universalgeschichte', 96. According to 'Ālī Bey's edition of 'Āşıḳpāşāzāde's history, Sulṭān Aḥmad received the city of Kütahya as a *tīmār* from Bāyezīd. See 'Āşıḳpāşāzāde, *Tevārīḫ-i Āl-i 'Os̱mān*, ed. 'Ālī Bey, 249.
115. Yazdī/*Ẓafar-nāma*, 2:257; Ibn 'Arabshāh/*'Ajā'ib*, 182.
116. Johannes Schiltberger, *The Bondage and Travels of Johann Schiltberger: A Native of Bavaria, in Europe, Asia, and Africa, 1396–1427*, ed. P. Bruun, trans. J. Buchan Telfer (New York: Burt Franklin, 1970; reprinted from London: Hakluyt Society, 1879), 24.
117. Yazdī/*Ẓafar-nāma*, 2:276.
118. Yazdī/*Ẓafar-nāma*, 2:277.
119. 'Āşıḳpāşāzāde, *Tevārīḫ-i Āl-i 'Os̱mān*, ed. Atsız, 142–3; Neşrī, *Kitâb-i Cihan-nümâ*, 342–3.
120. Halil İnalcık, 'Bāyazīd I', *Encyclopaedia of Islam*, 2nd edn (Leiden: Brill, 1960), 1:1,117–19.
121. In an account of Bāyezīd's captivity found in an anonymous *Tevārīḫ-i Āl-i 'Os̱mān*, and repeated by Luṭfī Pāşā, Tīmūr and Bāyezīd discuss the fortune-telling skills (*reml 'ilmi*) of Sulṭān Aḥmad Jalayir. See Öztürk (ed.), *Anonim Osmanlı Kroniği (1299–1512)*, 49; cf. Luṭfī Pāşā, *Tevārīḫ-i Āl-i 'Os̱mān* (Istanbul: Maṭba'a-yi 'Āmire, 1341 [1922–23]), 58.
122. Yazdī/*Ẓafar-nāma*, 2:324.
123. For the period following the defeat of Bāyezīd at Ankara, see Dimitris J. Katstritsis, *The Sons of Bayezid: Empire Building and Representation in the Ottoman Civil War of 1402–1413* (Leiden and Boston: Brill, 2007).
124. Yazdī/*Ẓafar-nāma*, 2:369.
125. Naṭanzī/Aubin, 169.
126. Maqrīzī reported that it was the Tigris river. See Maqrīzī/'Ashūr, 3:1,107.
127. Yazdī/*Ẓafar-nāma*, 2:370.
128. Yazdī/*Ẓafar-nāma*, 2:370.
129. Yazdī/*Ẓafar-nāma*, 2:370.
130. Ibn Taghrī Birdī/*Manhal*, 1:255.
131. Maqrīzī/'Ashūr, 3:1,118. The date of Sulṭān Aḥmad's arrival in Damascus is given by Maqrīzī as 6 Jumādá I 806/21 November 1403 (Maqrīzī/'Ashūr, 3:1,119), and by Ibn Ḥajar as 26 Jumādá I/11 December (Ibn Ḥajar/*Inbā'*, 5:145).

132. Maqrīzī/'Ashūr, 3:1,118; Ibn Ḥajar/*Inbā'*, 5:145–6.
133. Maqrīzī/'Ashūr, 3:1,120; Ibn Taghrī Birdī/*Nujūm*, 6:109.
134. Ibn Ḥajar/*Inbā'*, 5:145.
135. According to the *Rawżat al-Ṣafā'* of Mīrkhvānd, Sulṭān Aḥmad and Qarā Yūsuf were imprisoned together not in Damascus but in Cairo, where they swore to each other that, should they ever be free, they would not attack each other, but would be united. Qarā Yūsuf would take Tabriz and Sulṭān Aḥmad would take Baghdad, and they would not interfere in each other's affairs. See Mīrkhvānd/*Rawża*, 6:549. See also Khvāndamīr/Thackston, 2:314–15.
136. Īnāl Bāy was married to Barqūq's daughter Khawand Bayrām. See Maqrīzī/'Ashūr, 3:1,136; Ibn Taghrī Birdī/*Nujūm*, 6:111.
137. Maqrīzī/'Ashūr, 3:1,136; Ibn Taghrī Birdī/*Nujūm*, 6:110–11.
138. Maqrīzī/'Ashūr, 3:1,138–9; Ibn Taghrī Birdī/*Nujūm*, 6:112–13.
139. Ibn Taghrī Birdī/*Manhal*, 1:255.
140. Maqrīzī/'Ashūr, 3:1,154; Ibn Taghrī Birdī/*Nujūm*, 6:120.
141. Maqrīzī/'Ashūr, 3:1,147.
142. Maqrīzī/'Ashūr, 3:1,165; Ibn Taghrī Birdī/*Nujūm*, 6:126.
143. Yazdī/*Ẓafar-nāma*, 2:169.
144. Yazdī/*Ẓafar-nāma*, 2:169.
145. Mīrkhvānd/*Rawża*, 6:549.
146. Mīrkhvānd/*Rawża*, 6:550.
147. Khvāndamīr/Humā'ī, 3:571; Khvāndamīr/Thackston, 316–17.
148. Mīrkhvānd/*Rawża*, 6:557–8.
149. Mīrkhvānd/*Rawża*, 6:558.
150. Mīrkhvānd/*Rawża*, 6:560.
151. Mīrkhvānd/*Rawża*, 6:560.
152. Mīrkhvānd/*Rawża*, 6:560.
153. Mīrkhvānd/*Rawża*, 6:560.
154. Mīrkhvānd/*Rawża*, 6:560; Khvāndamīr/Humā'ī, 3:576; Khvāndamīr/Thackston, 319.
155. Mīrkhvānd/*Rawża*, 6:561.
156. Mīrkhvānd/*Rawża*, 6:578.
157. Tāj al-Salmānī, *Šams al-Ḥusn: Eine Chronik vom Tode Timurs bis zum Jahre 1409*, ed. Hans Robert Roemer (Wiesbaden: Franz Steiner Verlag, 1956), 96.
158. Naṭanzī/Aubin, 169.
159. Naṭanzī/Aubin, 169; Mīrkhvānd/*Rawża*, 6:578; Khvāndamīr/Humā'ī, 3:576; Khvāndamīr/Thackston, 319. Faṣīḥ Khvāfī writes that 'Alā' al-Dawla went to Baghdad, but does not report that he rebelled against his father. See Faṣīḥ Khvāfī/*Mujmal*, 170.
160. Vladimir Minorsky, 'Thomas of Metsop' on the Timurid-Turkman Wars', in *The Turks, Iran and the Caucasus in the Middle Ages* (London: Variorum Reprints, 1978), XI, 7; T'ovma Metsobets'i, *History of Tamerlane and His*

Successors, trans. Robert Bedrosian (New York: Sources of the Armenian Tradition, 1987), 59. Mīrkhvānd/*Rawża*, 6:579; Maqrīzī/'Ashūr, 4:133; Ibn Ḥajar/*Inbā'*, 6:226. Qarā Yūsuf was summoned by the Artuqid malik of Mardin. See John E. Woods, *The Aqquyunlu: Clan, Confederation, Empire* (Salt Lake City: University of Utah Press, 1999), 46.

161. Maqrīzī/'Ashūr, 4:137.
162. Maqrīzī and Ibn Ḥajar give his name as Ibn al-Shaykh Ibrāhīm, while Ibn Taghrī Birdī has al-Shaykh Ibrāhīm. See Maqrīzī/'Ashūr, 4:140; Ibn Ḥajar/*Inbā'*, 6:226; Ibn Taghrī Birdī/*Manhal*, 1:256.
163. Samarqandī/*Maṭla'*, 2:114; Mīrkhvānd/*Rawża*, 6:579; Khvāndamīr/Humā'ī, 3:577; Khvāndamīr/Thackston, 320.
164. Maqrīzī/'Ashūr, 4:140.
165. Mīrkhvānd/*Rawża*, 6:580.
166. Mīrkhvānd/*Rawża*, 6:580; Maqrīzī/'Ashūr, 4:140.
167. Samarqandī/*Maṭla'*, 2:115.
168. Mīrkhvānd/*Rawża*, 6:582.
169. Mīrkhvānd/*Rawża*, 6:582.
170. Mīrkhvānd/*Rawża*, 6:582.
171. According to Thomas of Metsop', Sulṭān Aḥmad was strangled. See Vladimir Minorsky, 'Thomas of Metsop' on the Timurid-Turkman Wars', 8; Metsobets'i, *History of Tamerlane and His Successors*, 60.
172. Mīrkhvānd/*Rawża*, 6:583.

9

Conclusions and the Legacy of the Jalayirids

The period of Jalayirid rule lasted only about seventy-five years in Baghdad, while Jalayirid rule in Tabriz was considerably less. The dynasty comprised only four rulers who held any considerable power, and perhaps can be understood as an irrelevant footnote to the fourteenth century, between the eras of the far more significant Ilkhanids and Timurids. Yet, an examination of the history of the Jalayirid dynasty requires an assessment of several of the most significant social and political changes in the central Islamic lands in the late medieval period. Tracing the origins of the Jalayirids and their emergence as the heirs to the Ilkhanate in the middle of the fourteenth century illuminates the complex process of politics in the context of the Mongol empire, and the relationship between the socio-political identities of tribe, *ulūs* and princely household.

Despite the significance of the Jalayirid period for the development of post-Mongol political identity, the legacy of the Jalayirids is perhaps most closely associated with cultural developments, particularly in the field of manuscript painting. Some of the most important changes in this distinctly Persian art form took place under the Jalayirids, bridging the masterpiece known as the Great Mongol *Shāh-nāma*, produced in the late Ilkhanid period, with fifteenth- and sixteenth-century Timurid and Safavid painting, commonly considered the pinnacle of the Persian miniature form. Although this study is primarily concerned with political history, considering the historical legacy of the Jalayirids without touching on their role as artistic patrons would be to ignore a central aspect of their contribution to the cultural history of Persianate society.

The fourteenth century has been characterised as the formative period of Persian painting, when the principal elements that formed later examples of painting were developed.[1] A fundamental feature of Persian manuscript illustrations in this period was the influence from Chinese painting.[2] In particular, Chinese-inspired landscape settings were adapted to Persian figure drawing in examples of paintings produced in Jalayirid workshops.[3] Certainly, the Jalayirid period was important for the development of manuscript painting and the art of the book. Yet, is it accurate to speak of 'Jalayirid painting', and, if so, what does it mean?

Jalayirid Tabriz and Baghdad were indeed important centres of book production,[4] although there is some scholarly debate about the extent to which we can refer to a definitive Jalayirid 'school' of painting. Several scholars have argued that the Jalayirid workshops at Tabriz and Baghdad produced works with a distinctive style, which were influential on Timurid painting in the fifteenth century.[5] In a 1939 article, Eric Schroeder surmised that when Muḥammad b. Muẓaffar occupied Tabriz for two months in 760/1359, he may have acquired some illustrated manuscripts, which he then would have taken back to Shiraz. The appearance of such manuscripts in Fars would help to explain the inspiration of a *Shāh-nāma*, produced in Shiraz in 772/1370–71, which resembled Jalayirid works but was quite different from earlier Inju and Muzaffarid paintings.[6] Schroeder described the Jalayirid style as characterised by an innovative representation of nature, stylised as a large system, in contrast to earlier paintings in which nature was not a subject for the artist.[7] Ernst Grube identified Jalayirid painting as the source of 'modern' Persian-Islamic painting, through the Jalayirid influence on Timurid painting.[8] For Grube, the difference between Muzaffarid and Jalayirid painting was quite distinct, with very few points of comparison between them.[9] Furthermore, works done under Inju or Muzaffarid patrons were of only local importance.[10] Stefano Carboni has written that the Jalayirid style of painting was characterised by 'lyrical scenes, with many graceful small figures set in lavish interiors or in gardens in full bloom'.[11] Jalayirid paintings feature pastel colours, integrate lines of text into the painting itself, and tend to take as their subjects romantic Persian poetry, rather than epic works. Deborah Klimburg-Salter has also identified the extension of the painting into the margins of the page, as well as the use of drawings in the margins, as among the major innovations of Jalayirid painting.[12]

Other scholars have been more cautious about identifying a particularly Jalayirid school of painting, suggesting that dynastic patronage had little to do with the choices artists were making in the fourteenth century. As Sheila Blair has pointed out, artists of the period moved from city to city in search of patronage and according to changing political circumstances, making it difficult to assign dynastic labels to artistic schools.[13] Christiane Gruber has followed this way of thinking, arguing that artistic 'schools' were still forming during the fourteenth century, and that when scholars have discussed schools, they are often referring to the work of one or two individuals who served a particular dynastic patron. In addition, artistic styles may have been more determined by a work's subject, rather than a particular 'school'.[14]

A closer examination of what we actually know about painting under the Jalayirids suggests that such caution against discussing fully developed artistic schools is warranted. The evidence we have about artists and works patronised by the Jalayirids is scanty, and can offer only a glimpse of artistic life in Tabriz and Baghdad under their rule. For the artists working under the Jalayirid patronage our most important source is the preface from an album of calligraphy and painting written by Dūst Muḥammad (fl. 1531–64), prepared for the Safavid prince Bahrām Mīrzā, brother of Shāh Tahmāsp (r. 1524–76). The album is today in the Topkapı Palace Museum in Istanbul, and its preface has been translated by Wheeler Thackston.[15] Dūst Muḥammad traces a chain of transmission of artistic knowledge from master to student from the end of the Ilkhanid period to the Timurids, beginning with the painter Ustād Aḥmad Mūsá. According to Dūst Muḥammad, Aḥmad Mūsá 'lifted the veil from the face of depiction, and the style of depiction that is now current was invented by him'.[16] In other words, the painting of the sixteenth century could be traced back to innovations made by a single artist in the service of Abū Sa'īd Bahādur Khan. Aḥmad Mūsá was responsible for illustrations in an *Abū-Sa'īd-nāma*, a copy of *Kalīla wa-Dimna*, a *Mi'rāj-nāma*, and a *Tārīkh-i Chīngīzī*.[17] Figure 9.1 is an example of a painting from the *Mi'rāj-nāma* attributed to Aḥmad Mūsá, which exists today in the Bahrām Mīrzā album. If we trust Dūst Muḥammad, it was painted during the reign of Abū Sa'īd (1317–35), although there is some scholarly debate about this.[18]

More important for the purposes of examining painting under the Jalayirids, Dūst Muḥammad identifies Aḥmad Mūsá's students and their legacy in connecting Ilkhanid painting to that of the Safavid period. However, Dūst Muḥammad's account is cursory, and does not provide any information about Aḥmad Mūsá after Abū Sa'īd's death in 736/1335,[19] nor any account of artists in the service of Shaykh Ḥasan Jalayir at Baghdad. It is generally assumed that Aḥmad Mūsá continued to work and train students during this period, since his students ended up in the service of the Jalayirids,[20] although there is no direct evidence of this. What we know is that one of his students, named Shams al-Dīn, worked in the service of Shaykh Uvays, presumably at Tabriz. It is likely that Shams al-Dīn was responsible for the paintings in a *Shāh-nāma* manuscript produced at Tabriz around 1370.[21] An example from this work is provided below in Figure 9.2.

However, it is not until the period of Sulṭān Aḥmad that we have any definitive dates or attribution of works to any particular artist.[22] Dūst Muḥammad tells us that Shams al-Dīn did not enter the service of any other patron after Shaykh Uvays's death in 776/1374, devoting himself to teaching.[23] One of his students, Khwāja 'Abd al-Ḥayy, provided Shams

Figure 9.1 *Mi'rāj-nāma* attributed to Aḥmad Mūsá, Tabriz, 1317–35. Topkapı Palace Museum ms. H.2154, fol. 107r.

Figure 9.2 Abduction of Zal by the Simurgh, from a *Shāh-nāma* manuscript, Tabriz, c. 1370. Topkapı Palace Museum ms. H.2153, fol. 23a.

Figure 9.3 *Dīvān* of Sulṭān Aḥmad, Baghdad, 1403. Freer and Sackler Galleries, Smithsonian Institution.

al-Dīn with a place to stay in his house and the necessities of life in return for the master's teaching.[24] 'Abd al-Ḥayy went on to become the most prominent painter during the reign of Sulṭān Aḥmad, and became the Jalayirid sultan's teacher.[25] When Tīmūr conquered Baghdad in 795/1393, 'Abd al-Ḥayy was captured and sent back to Tīmūr's capital at Samarqand, where he remained for the rest of his life.[26] We know little of 'Abd al-Ḥayy's work, beyond the fact that he specialised in ink drawings such as those illustrating the *dīvān* of Sulṭān Aḥmad.[27] Figure 9.3 shows a page from the *dīvān*, with the illustrations in the margins depicting human figures, animals and landscape features.

This *dīvān* manuscript is noteworthy for its marginal pen and ink illustrations (in a style known as *qalamsiyāhī*), consisting not of miniature illumination, but of decorative scenes not always connected with the poetic text.[28] Klimburg-Salter has argued that these illustrations fall within a period of experimental transition that saw the movement of the graphic image from the centre of the page to the margin.[29] Klimburg-Salter also contends that the prevalence of images of birds in the *dīvān* represents a conscious visual reference to the work of the Sufi poet Farīd al-Dīn 'Aṭṭār (d. 627/1230), the 'Conference of the Birds' (*Manṭiq al-Ṭayr*).[30]

Sulṭān Aḥmad was a connoisseur and active patron of painting. His workshops in Baghdad were active until Tīmūr's attack on the city in 803/1401, and produced several well-known works of art.[31] Following the death of Tīmūr in 807/1405, Sulṭān Aḥmad attempted to regain control of Tabriz, and in the process continued to patronise painters in the city. After the fall of Tabriz to the Qarāquyūnlū in 813/1410, artists who had worked in the Jalayirid ateliers there tended to migrate to Shiraz, where they sought the patronage of the Timurid prince Iskandar b. 'Umar Shaykh.[32]

Other works of visual art produced during the reign of Sulṭān Aḥmad have been the subject of art historians. Stefano Carboni has described a late eighth/fourteenth-century illustrated astrological treatise, also attributed to the workshop of Sulṭān Aḥmad. This treatise features illustrations of the mansions of the moon, lunar-planetary conjunctions, and a treatise on the zodiac, a so-called 'Book of Nativities' (*Kitāb al-Mawālid*).[33] A more recent study has focused on illustrations contained in a 'Book of Marvels' copied for Sulṭān Aḥmad in 790/1388.[34]

One of the finest examples of book illustration during the reign of Sulṭān Aḥmad can be found in a manuscript of Khwājū Kirmānī's *Khamsa*, produced in Baghdad in 1396.[35] The paintings are attributed to one of Shams al-Dīn's students named Junayd. The illustration of the wedding day of Humāy and Humāyūn (Figure 9.4) bears his signature, the earliest recorded signed Persian miniature painting.[36] We know nothing about

Figure 9.4 Wedding day of Humāy and Humāyūn, from the *Khamsa* of Khwājū Kirmānī, Baghdad, 1396, with the signature of the painter Junayd. British Library Add. 18113, fol. 45v.

Junayd beyond his works in the *Khamsa* manuscript; Dūst Muḥammad says only that he was a student of Shams al-Dīn.[37] In general, it is difficult to connect particular works to individual artists, given the rarity of signed paintings; Junayd's work is certainly exceptional in this regard.[38]

Although the Jalayirid influence on Timurid painting has been emphasised, the example of what we know about 'Abd al-Ḥayy and Junayd illustrates the difficulty in tracing definitively the influence of individual artists between royal courts. While we know that 'Abd al-Ḥayy was taken to Tīmūr's Samarqand, we do not have any confirmed examples of his work. On the other hand, while we do have an example of Junayd's work in the 1396 Baghdad *Khamsa* of Khwājū Kirmānī, we have no evidence that he was taken to or travelled himself to any Timurid court, making his influence on later artists uncertain. We do have an example of a Timurid manuscript, produced in Herat in the fifteenth century by a certain Khwāja 'Alī Tabrīzī. Zeren Tanındı has argued that Khwāja 'Alī probably did his apprenticeship in Jalayirid Tabriz or Baghdad,[39] thus offering an example of a more direct transmission of artistic training and production from the Jalayirid to the Timurid period.

In addition to painting, calligraphy and metalwork were also forms of artistic expression under the Jalayirids. According to the *Gulistān-i Hunar*, a treatise on calligraphers and painters written in 1005/1596–97 for the Safavid Shāh 'Abbās (r. 1587–1629) by Qāḍī Aḥmad Mīr Munshī al-Ḥusaynī, one of the outstanding calligraphers of Shaykh Uvays's time was a certain Mubārak Shāh, known as Zarīn-Qalam, or 'golden pen'.[40] Sheila Blair has dealt extensively with the career of Zarīn-Qalam, and has pointed out that Qāḍī Aḥmad confused him with another individual named Mubārak Shāh b. Quṭb, and that in fact the Zarīn-Qalam in the service of Shaykh Uvays was actually named Aḥmad Shāh.[41] According to Qāḍī Aḥmad's treatise, Shaykh Uvays had a dream in which 'Alī b. Abī Ṭālib commanded him to direct (Aḥmad) Shāh to make calligraphic inscriptions on the buildings of Najaf, the site of the tombs of both 'Alī and Shaykh Uvays's father Shaykh Ḥasan. It was for his work in Najaf that Aḥmad Shāh earned the nickname Zarīn-Qalam.[42] Aḥmad Shāh also left his mark in Jalayirid Baghdad, designing epigraphic decorations for the Mirjāniyya mosque-madrasa complex, founded by Khwāja Mirjān in 758/1357.[43] Another calligrapher, identified as a pupil of Zarīn-Qalam, was Pīr Yaḥyá Ṣūfī, who served Jalayirid, Chubanid and Ilkhanid patrons, and who also left inscriptions on many buildings in Najaf.[44] A third master of calligraphy, as well as of poetry, in Jalayirid Iraq was Mawlānā Ma'rūf-i Khaṭṭāt-i Baghdādī. Qāḍī Aḥmad writes that he turned away from Sulṭān Aḥmad in Baghdad and went to the court of the Timurid prince Iskandar b. 'Umar

Shaykh in Isfahan, and was later taken to Herat by Shāhrukh.[45] Like the painters 'Abd al-Ḥayy and Khwāja 'Alī, Khaṭṭāt-i Baghdādī began his career in the service of the Jalayirids and finished it under the Timurids.

We know little about individuals who produced metalwork for the Jalayirids, such as the copper basin from Ardabil bearing the name of Sultan Shaykh Uvays.[46] However, Linda Komaroff has identified similarities between this vessel and contemporary metalware produced in Mamluk Syria.[47] Alison Ohta has identified Jalayirid influence on Mamluk filigree bookbinding as well,[48] which seems to indicate a general pattern of artistic exchange and interaction between artists and craftsmen on either side of the Euphrates by the fifteenth century. Doris Behrens-Abouseif has suggested that contact between the Jalayirid and Mamluk courts, and the growing number of Iranians in Cairo in the fifteenth century, may account for artistic exchange between Iran and Syria in the period.[49]

How, then, can we sum up the artistic legacy of the Jalayirids? Given the available evidence, it seems that when we talk about Jalayirid painting in particular, we refer to a handful of artists working in Tabriz and Baghdad, continually developing and innovating a style of painting that emerged toward the late Ilkhanid period, inspired by Chinese influences, available due to the intensive cross-cultural interactions made possible and encouraged by the Mongols. Given the paucity of examples, and ongoing debates among historians, it seems best to consider painting done under Jalayirid patronage not as a distinct 'school' of painting, but as part of an ongoing process of experimentation and creativity among artists who moved between cities and dynastic courts, and whose work would continue to influence painters of the Timurid and Safavid periods. What must be kept in mind as we consider the artistic legacy of the Jalayirids is that even as we focus on a single dynasty and courtly patronage, the reality of the fourteenth and fifteenth centuries was that artists, as well as scholars and holy men, moved in circles not constrained by the political power of any one ruling family. The Jalayirid sultans, like their contemporary rulers in Cairo, Shiraz and Samarqand, offered material reward for artists' works, but in a cultural context in which the religious, literary and visual forms of their work were common to a community much larger than the frontiers of any single polity.

The complete history of artistic production, patronage and stylistic influences under the rule of the Jalayirids demands its own thorough study. The brief preceding summary can only highlight some of the most important points in a growing literature on manuscript painting and artistic culture in the fourteenth and fifteenth centuries. The purpose of the present study has been to trace the processes of dynastic state formation and ideological legitimation in the period in which such cultural developments were taking place. To summarise, this study has offered a chronological narrative of the relationship between the Chinggisid Ilkhans and the Jalayir tribe, particularly the Ilgayid Jalayirs whose descendants became sultans in the eighth/fourteenth century. However, the methodology has been one of working backwards, from the Jalayirid sultans themselves to their ancestors' roles in the enterprise of the Ilkhanate and the Mongol empire as a whole. By doing so, it is hoped that some new insight into the relationship between the tribal amirs and the institutions of the Mongol dynastic state has emerged.

As we have seen, the Jalayirid sultans were descended in part from the Mongolian Jalayir tribe, whose members participated in the great transformations of Mongolian society that accompanied the rise of Chinggis Qan's empire in the early seventh/thirteenth century. Pre-Chinggisid tribal identities, which were primarily (though not completely) political identities, changed as political allegiances were primarily directed to Chinggisid princes, to whose patrimonial inheritance (*ulūs*) the Jalayir, and other tribal groups, were sublimated. The social and political meaning that such tribal identities had before Chinggis Qan was diminished in the process of the redistribution of land and human resources among the family of the great qan. What mattered by the middle of the seventh/thirteenth century was not so much what tribe one belonged to, but which Chinggisid prince one served.

The Jalayirid sultans' ancestor Īlgā Noyan played a central role in the establishment of the Ilkhanate in the middle of the thirteenth century. The Ilkhanate became the *ulūs* of Hülegü and his descendants and was, at least originally, an extension of the authority of the Toluid branch of the Chinggisid family into the Oxus-to-Euphrates region. Īlgā Noyan was one of several Jalayir amirs among the elite of the early Ilkhanate. However, these amirs did not act as a group with a single purpose or leader. As the events of the internal struggles between 1282 and 1295 illustrate, tribal identity or allegiance did not define the conflicts between different amiral factions. Instead, the royal princes, the descendants of Hülegü, were the rallying points for these factional struggles. The Jalayirs did not fight the Sulduz or Oyrat in this period; rather, Jalayir fought Jalayir and Sulduz fought Sulduz, according to each individual's loyalty and obligations to a particular prince of the blood.

The reign of Ghazan Khan (1295–1304) was a major turning point in the course of Ilkhanid history. This period witnessed a decline in the power of the amirs and a centralisation of power in the hands of the khan. Amirs who had opposed Ghazan in 1295 – and did not have an alternative

Chinggisid prince around whom to organise – failed in attempts at rebellion. Jalayir amirs took part in uprisings in Anatolia around the turn of the seventh–eighth/thirteenth–fourteenth century. These rebellions were put down, and as a consequence the fortunes of the Ilgayid Jalayirs, who by this time had close ties to the royal households of Ghazan and his brother Öljeytü, greatly improved in the early fourteenth century. Īlgā Noyan's grandson, Amīr Ḥusayn (whose name indicates a new communal commitment to Islam in the generation of Ghazan), held the title of *güregen*, or royal son-in-law, by virtue of his marriage to Öljetey Sultan, the sister of Öljeytü. The status of *güregen* not only gave Amīr Ḥusayn and his son Shaykh Ḥasan access to the Ilkhanid court, but also ensured that they would survive and emerge stronger in the period of royal centralisation and attempts to limit the influence of the amirs during the reigns of Ghazan and Öljeytü. Although the Sulduz Amīr Chūpān took control of the Ilkhanate in the first part of Abū Sa'īd's reign, Shaykh Ḥasan became the prime beneficiary of his fall and the swing of the pendulum of power back to the khan-sultan after 1327. Shaykh Ḥasan was the highest-ranking Ilkhanid amir until Abū Sa'īd's death. His duties in this capacity were centred in Anatolia, a fact that gave him a distinct advantage when the Ilkhanid order collapsed in 1335. Shaykh Ḥasan's power in Rūm and the upper Tigris enabled him to win the support of the Oyrat tribesmen and take control of both eastern Anatolia and Baghdad in the chaotic years after Abū Sa'īd's death.

Thus, the emergence of Shaykh Ḥasan Jalayir as one of several contenders for power in post-Ilkhanid Iran was not the consequence of a 'retribalisation' of Mongol society in the Middle East after a century, and the falling away of the formidable, but temporary, Chinggisid imperial order. In fact, Shaykh Ḥasan owed his fortune and power to the Ilkhanid order itself. He was not a tribal leader, but someone intimately connected to the Ilkhanid court. If he commanded the allegiance of any tribal elements, it was not the Jalayirs but the Oyrats, after the defeat of their chief 'Alī Pādshāh. In the absence of a Chinggisid prince to succeed Abū Sa'īd, Shaykh Ḥasan attempted to take control of the Ilkhanid *ulūs* in the name of a powerless Chinggisid puppet. For the amirs who competed for control of the Ilkhanate, including the Jalayirids, Chubanids and Muzaffarids, the Ilkhanid *ulūs* remained the framework for political action.

Shaykh Ḥasan's son and successor, Shaykh Uvays, was able to build upon his father's military gains in Arab Iraq and take advantage of the upheaval in Azarbayjan in the late 1350s to capture Tabriz, the seat of Ilkhanid authority, as well as considerable commercial wealth. Shaykh Uvays's conquest of Tabriz not only brought the prestige and wealth of the former Ilkhanate under the control of the Jalayirid house, it also brought a number of administrators, littérateurs and others who had formerly served the Ilkhanate into the service of the Jalayirids. The men of the pen who became associated with the court of Shaykh Uvays, and who benefited from Jalayirid patronage, had an interest in the continuity of central sultanic authority in Tabriz on the pattern of the later Ilkhanate. It seems that for this reason, those in the service of Shaykh Uvays helped to construct an ideological foundation for the authority of the Jalayirids in the former Ilkhanid *ulūs*. The contemporary texts and material artifacts tend to present Shaykh Uvays as the inheritor of what we can call the Ilkhanid legacy. This ideology was based on the Jalayirid sultan's genealogical relationship to members of the Hülegüid house, and a rhetorical presentation of Shaykh Uvays as a dispenser of royal justice in the name of Islam, similar to how the later Ilkhans, such as Ghazan and Abū Sa'īd, had been. For the military and urban elites of Azarbayjan, the *ulūs* of Hülegü continued to provide the framework in which legitimate, Muslim royal authority was conceived. It was not important if the sultan was not a Chinggisid prince of the blood; the ideology was flexible enough to adapt to the political reality. Shaykh Uvays could be made a rightful Mongol khan and Muslim sultan, as long as the patterns of patronage and courtly life around Tabriz were maintained. However, once the notion of Jalayirid royalty was established during the reign of Shaykh Uvays, the doors were opened to challenges to dynastic authority by the amirs, who could organise opposition around one of several Jalayirid princes. Thus, the sultanate that Shaykh Uvays had established was, on the eve of Tīmūr's campaigns, divided between amiral power at Tabriz, Baghdad and Sultaniyya.

The campaigns of Tīmūr in Iran fundamentally altered the balance of power in the *ulūs* of Hülegü, and challenged the Ilkhanid legacy as promoted by the Jalayirids. The reign of Sulṭān Aḥmad b. Shaykh Uvays was defined by the threat from Tīmūr, not just to Jalayirid rule, but also to the political order from Oxus to Nile. The Mamluk sultanate, the Ottoman sultanate and the Qarāquyūnlū Turkman confederation all suffered to varying degrees from Tīmūr's campaigns. Sulṭān Aḥmad sought protection from the rulers of each of these polities. On the occasions when he found refuge (with Barqūq in 1394, with Bāyezīd in 1400–02 on two separate occasions, with Qarā Yūsuf on several occasions), Sulṭān Aḥmad was accommodated because of what he represented in symbolic terms, more so than any material advantage he could provide for his host: he was the rightful heir to the *ulūs* of Hülegü, and had not submitted to Tīmūr. In the period of the Timurid campaigns, Sulṭān Aḥmad was an alternative, a symbol of opposition and commitment to the Ilkhanid tradition, as opposed to the violent upheavals of the armies of Tīmūr. Furthermore, for Qarā Yūsuf, association with Sulṭān Aḥmad offered ideological capital upon which to make claims to authority in the Jalayirid lands in the early ninth/fifteenth century. The Ilkhanate still provided the framework for imagining the meaning of political power in Iran, Iraq and Anatolia by this time, and for the Qarāquyūnlū, the Jalayirid sultan was the link between themselves and the charisma of the Ilkhans.

Notes

1. Ernst J. Grube, *Persian Painting in the Fourteenth Century: A Research Report* (Naples: Istituto Orientale di Napoli, 1978), 1.
2. Basil Gray, 'A Timurid Copy of a Chinese Buddhist Picture', in Richard Ettinghausen (ed.), *Islamic Art in The Metropolitan Museum of Art* (New York: The Metropolitan Museum of Art, 1972), 35.
3. Gray, 'A Timurid Copy of a Chinese Buddhist Picture', 36. The ink drawings found in the *dīvān* of Sulṭān Aḥmad are often cited as clear examples of Chinese influence in the Jalayirid period. See David J. Roxburgh, 'Persian Drawing, ca. 1400–1450: Materials and Creative Procedures', *Muqarnas* 19 (2002): 55; Sheila R. Canby, *Persian Painting* (Northampton, MA: Interlink, 1993), 48.
4. Grube, *Persian Painting in the Fourteenth Century*, 22. We actually know very little about the activity that went on at the ateliers and libraries of Tabriz and Baghdad. In the case of Tabriz, it has been suggested that book production at Rashīd al-Dīn's library may have continued to function into the Jalayirid period, despite the fact that the Rab'-i Rashīdī was plundered twice in the first half of the fourteenth century. See Thomas W. Lentz and Glenn D. Lowry, *Timur and the Princely Vision: Persian Art and Culture in the Fifteenth Century* (Los Angeles and Washington, DC: Los Angeles County Museum of Art, Arthur M. Sackler Gallery, Smithsonian Institution and Smithsonian Institution Press, 1989), 51.
5. Eric Schroeder, 'Ahmed Musa and Shams al-Dīn: A Review of Fourteenth Century Painting', *Ars Islamica* 6:2 (1939): 115; Grube, *Persian Painting in the Fourteenth Century*, 23.
6. Schroeder, 'Ahmed Musa and Shams al-Dīn', 116–18.
7. Schroeder, 'Ahmed Musa and Shams al-Dīn', 116–18.
8. Grube, *Persian Painting in the Fourteenth Century*, 46. According to Grube, the elements of Timurid painting developed from a distinctively Jalayirid 'school' of painting. See Grube, *Persian Painting in the Fourteenth Century*, 23.
9. Grube, *Persian Painting in the Fourteenth Century*, 23.
10. Grube, *Persian Painting in the Fourteenth Century*, 46.
11. Stefano Carboni, 'Synthesis: Continuity and Innovation in Ilkhanid Art',

in *The Legacy of Genghis Khan: Courtly Art and Culture in Western Asia, 1256–1353* (New Haven and London: Yale University Press, 2002), 223.

12. Deborah E. Klimburg-Salter, 'A Sufi Theme in Persian Painting: The Diwan of Sultan Ahmad Gala'ir in the Freer Gallery of Art, Washington, D.C.', *Kunst des Orients* 11 (1976–77): 57–9.
13. Sheila Blair, 'Artists and Patronage in Late Fourteenth-Century Iran in the Light of Two Catalogues of Islamic Metalwork', *BSOAS* 48:1 (1985): 58–9.
14. Christiane Gruber, *The Ilkhanid Book of Ascension: A Persian-Sunni Devotional Tale* (London and New York: I. B. Tauris, 2010), 25.
15. Wheeler M. Thackston, *Album Prefaces and Other Documents on the History of Calligraphers and Painters* (Leiden: Brill, 2001), 4; Gruber, *The Ilkhanid Book of Ascension*, 24.
16. Thackston, *Album Prefaces*, 12.
17. Thackston, *Album Prefaces*, 12–13; Priscilla P. Soucek, 'Aḥmad Mūsā', *Encyclopaedia Iranica*, ed. Ehsan Yarshater (London and New York: Routledge and Kegan Paul, 1984), 1:652–3; Filiz Çağman and Zeren Tanındı, *The Topkapı Saray Museum: The Albums and Illustrated Manuscripts*, ed. and trans. J. M. Rogers (Boston: Little, Brown and Company, 1986), 70; Grube, *Persian Painting in the Fourteenth Century*, 33.
18. For the provenance of the Bahrām Mīrzā album *Mi'rāj-nāma* paintings, I follow Gruber in her *The Ilkhanid Book of Ascension*. On the scholarly debate surrounding the dating of these paintings, see Gruber, *The Ilkhanid Book of Ascension*, 25 and notes 147–8.
19. Canby, *Persian Painting*, 41; Grube, *Persian Painting in the Fourteenth Century*, 31–2, 34.
20. Schroeder, 'Ahmed Musa and Shams al-Dīn', 132. Schroeder wrote that it was 'highly probable' that Aḥmad Mūsá, along with the contents of the Tabriz library, were transferred to Baghdad when Shaykh Ḥasan Jalayir moved his court there in 1340.
21. Çağman and Tanındı, *The Topkapı Saray Museum*, 70.
22. Grube, *Persian Painting in the Fourteenth Century*, 41.
23. Grube, *Persian Painting in the Fourteenth Century*, 33; Schroeder, 'Ahmed Musa and Shams al-Dīn', 129; Priscilla P. Soucek, ''Abd-al-Ḥayy, K̲vājā', *Encyclopaedia Iranica*, ed. Ehsan Yarshater (London and New York: Routledge and Kegan Paul, 1982), 1:115.
24. Thackston, *Album Prefaces*, 13.
25. Schroeder, 'Ahmed Musa and Shams al-Dīn', 129.
26. Thackston, *Album Prefaces*, 13; Soucek, ''Abd-al-Ḥayy, K̲vājā', 115.
27. Soucek, ''Abd-al-Ḥayy, K̲vājā', 115; Lentz and Lowry, *Timur and the Princely Vision*, 52. Deborah Klimburg-Salter has argued that 'Abd al-Ḥayy was the likely artist for the illustrations from the *dīvān* found in the Freer Gallery. See Klimburg-Salter, 'A Sufi Theme in Persian Painting', 76–9.
28. Bernard O'Kane has pointed to the similarities between the pen and ink drawings in the *dīvān* of Sulṭān Aḥmad and the mysterious so-called *siyāh-qalam*

paintings, featuring distinctive depictions of demons, dervishes and scenes of everyday life. O'Kane suggests that these paintings have their origins in Jalayirid Tabriz during the reign of Shaykh Uvays. See Bernard O'Kane, 'Siyah Qalam: The Jalayirid Connections', *Oriental Art* 49:2 (2003): 2–18.

29. Klimburg-Salter, 'A Sufi Theme in Persian Painting', 57.
30. Klimburg-Salter, 'A Sufi Theme in Persian Painting', 65.
31. Works produced at Baghdad under Sulṭān Aḥmad Jalayir include *'Ajā'ib al-Makhlūqāt* (1388), *Kalīla wa Dimna* (1392), the *dīvān* of Khvājū Kirmānī (1396), and *Kitāb al-Buldan* (1399). See Klimburg-Salter, 'A Sufi Theme in Persian Painting', 70–3.
32. Klimburg-Salter, 'A Sufi Theme in Persian Painting', 59.
33. Stefano Carboni, 'Two Fragments of a Jalayirid Astrological Treatise in the Keir Collection and in the Oriental Institute in Sarajevo', *Islamic Art* 2 (1987): 149–50.
34. Anna Caiozzo, 'Une conception originale des cieux: planets et zodiaque d'une cosmographie jalayride', *Annales Islamologiques* 37 (2003): 59–78. Caiozzo examines a copy of the work *'Ajā'ib al-Makhlūqāt wa-Gharā'ib al-Mawjūdāt* by a certain Ṭūsī Salmānī, consisting of an illustrated cosmography, inspired by a seventh/thirteenth-century *'ajā'ib* work. Caiozzo argues that Salmānī's illustrations are unlike the illustrations in earlier versions.
35. Barbara Brend, 'Jonayd-e Naqqāš', *Encyclopaedia Iranica*, ed. Ehsan Yarshater (London and New York: Routledge and Kegan Paul, 2009), 15:5; Schroeder, 'Ahmed Musa and Shams al-Dīn', 129.
36. Bernard O'Kane, *Early Persian Painting:* Kalila *and* Dimna *Manuscripts of the Late Fourteenth Century* (London and New York: I. B. Tauris, 2003), 34; Soucek, ''Abd-al-Ḥayy, K̲vājā', 115; Canby, *Persian Painting*, 44.
37. Thackston, *Album Prefaces*, 13.
38. For example, an illustrated manuscript of the *Khamsa* of Niẓāmī was produced in Baghdad between 1386 and 1388, during the reign of Sulṭān Aḥmad. However, we do not know who the artist was. See Norah M. Titley, 'A 14th-Century Niẓāmī Manuscript in Tehran', *Kunst des Orients* 8 (1972): 120; Grube, *Persian Painting in the Fourteenth Century*, 22; Canby, *Persian Painting*, 42; O'Kane, *Early Persian Painting*, 34.
39. Zeren Tanındı, 'Additions to Illustrated Manuscripts in Ottoman Workshops', *Muqarnas* 17 (2000): 151.
40. Aḥmad b. Mīr Munshī al-Ḥusaynī, *Calligraphers and Painters: A Treatise by Qāḍī Aḥmad, Son of Mīr-Munshī (circa* A.H. *1015/*A.D. *1606)*, trans. V. Minorsky (Washington, DC: Smithsonian Institution, 1959), 61.
41. Blair, 'Artists and Patronage in Late Fourteenth-Century Iran', 55; Jonathan M. Bloom, 'Paper: The Transformative Medium in Ilkhanid Art', in Linda Komaroff (ed.), *Beyond the Legacy of Genghis Khan* (Leiden and Boston: Brill, 2006), 291–2.
42. Aḥmad b. Mīr Munshī al-Ḥusaynī, *Calligraphers and Painters*, 61.
43. Blair, 'Artists and Patronage in Late Fourteenth-Century Iran', 53–4.

44. Aḥmad b. Mīr Munshī al-Ḥusaynī, *Calligraphers and Painters*, 62.
45. Aḥmad b. Mīr Munshī al-Ḥusaynī, *Calligraphers and Painters*, 65; Priscilla P. Soucek, 'Eskandar b. 'Omar Šayx b. Timur: A Biography', *Oriente Moderno* 15:2 (1996): 84.
46. This example of Jalayirid metalwork was brought to light by Yedda Godard, and is discussed in Chapter 7. See Y. A. Godard, 'Bassin de cuivre au nom de Shaikh Uwais', *Athār-é Īrān: Annales du service archaeologique de Īrān* 1 (1936): 371–3.
47. Linda Komaroff, *The Golden Disk of Heaven: Metalwork of Timurid Iran* (Costa Mesa and New York: Mazda, 1992), 40, n. 112.
48. Alison Ohta, 'Filigree Bindings of the Mamluk Period', *Muqarnas* 21 (2004), 267–76.
49. Doris Behrens-Abouseif, 'The Jalayirid Connection in Mamluk Metalware', *Muqarnas* 26 (2009): 157–8.

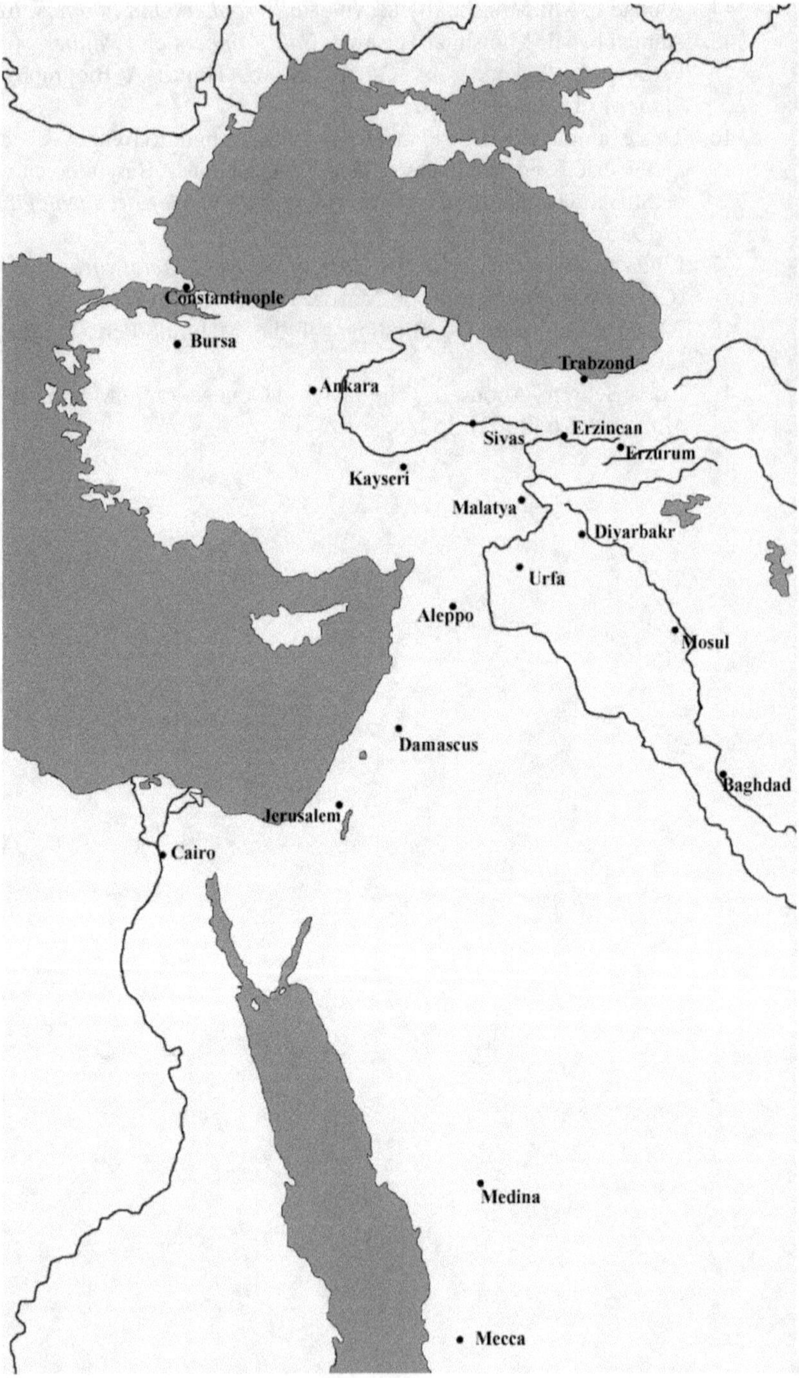

Map 1 Jalayirid dynasty.

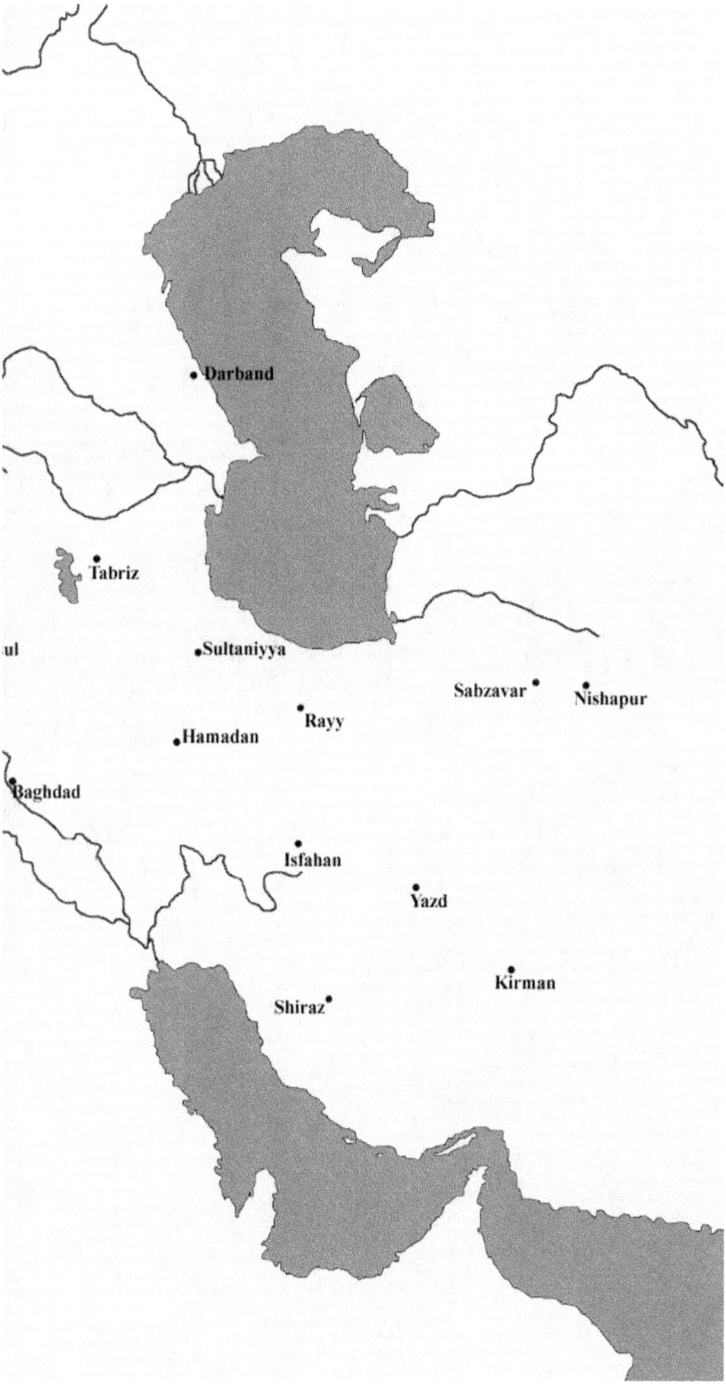
Darband
Tabriz
ul
Sultaniyya
Sabzavar
Nishapur
Rayy
Hamadan
Baghdad
Isfahan
Yazd
Kirman
Shiraz

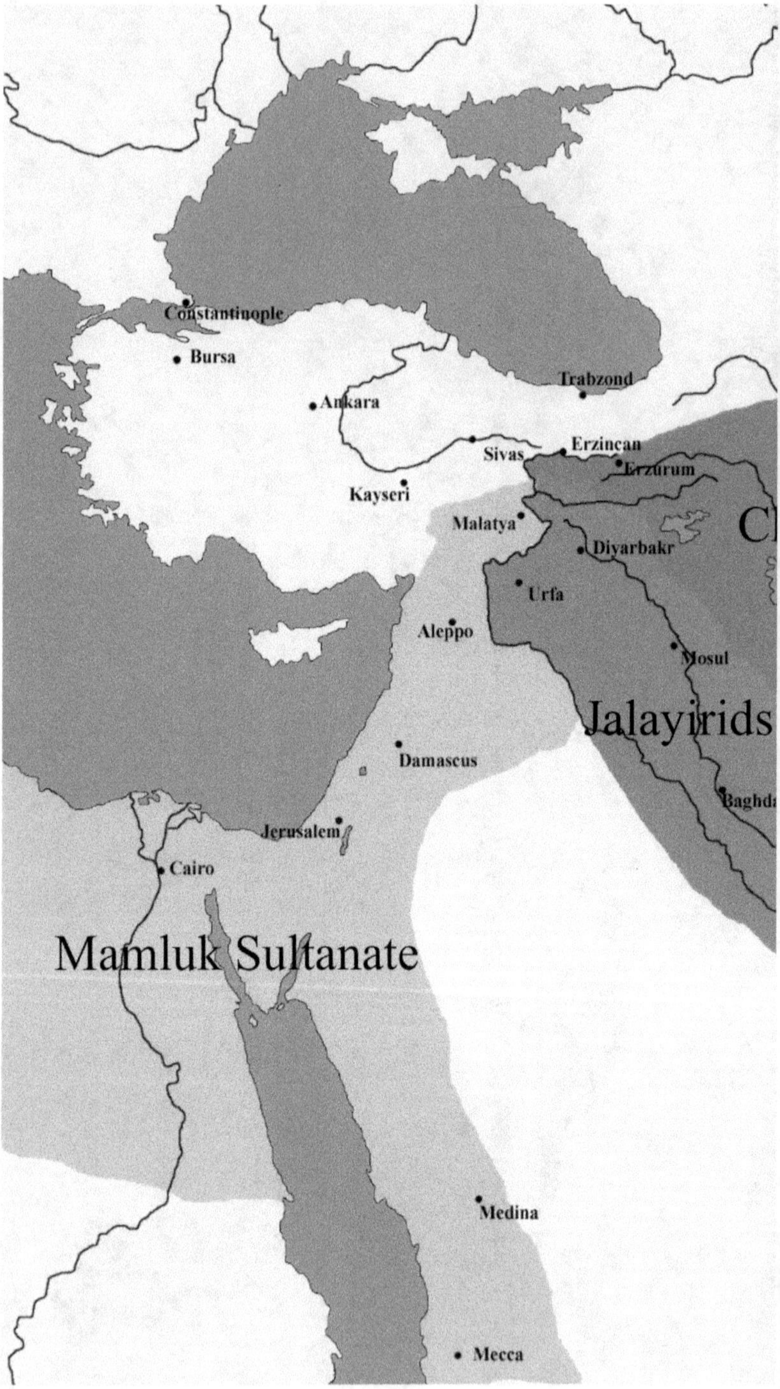

Map 2 Jalayirid dynasty, c. 1353.

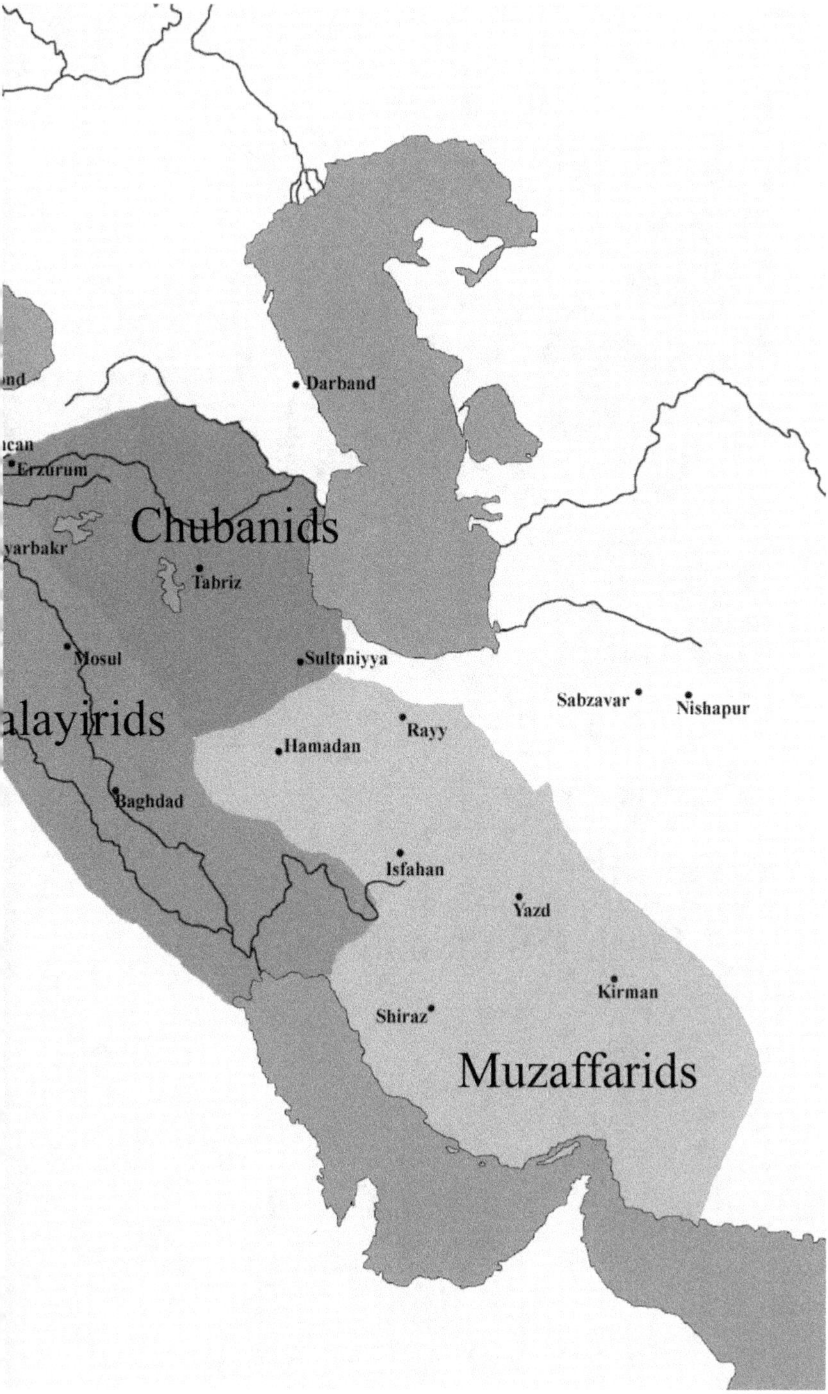
Darband
Erzurum
Chubanids
Tabriz
Mosul
Sultaniyya
Sabzavar
Nishapur
Rayy
Hamadan
Baghdad
Isfahan
Yazd
Kirman
Shiraz
Muzaffarids

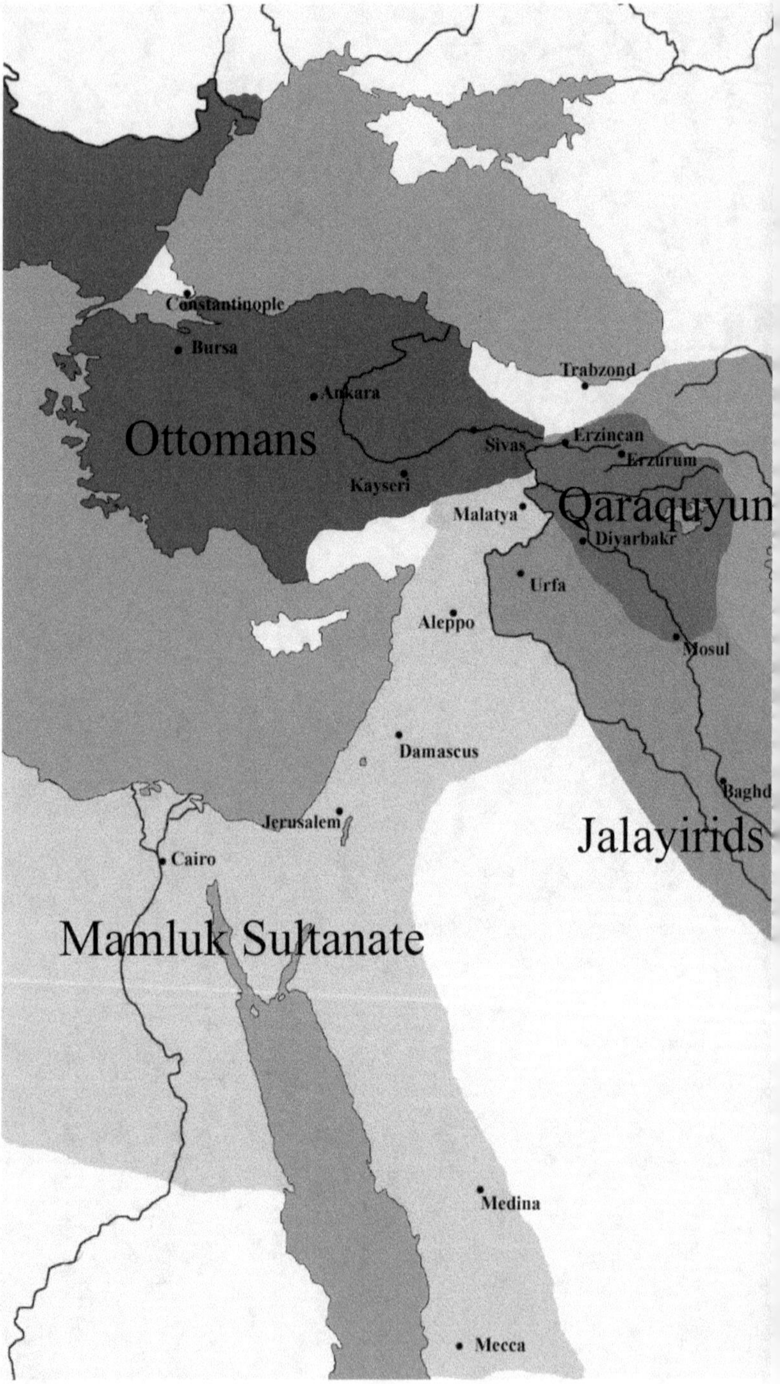

Map 3 Jalayirid dynasty, c. 1400.

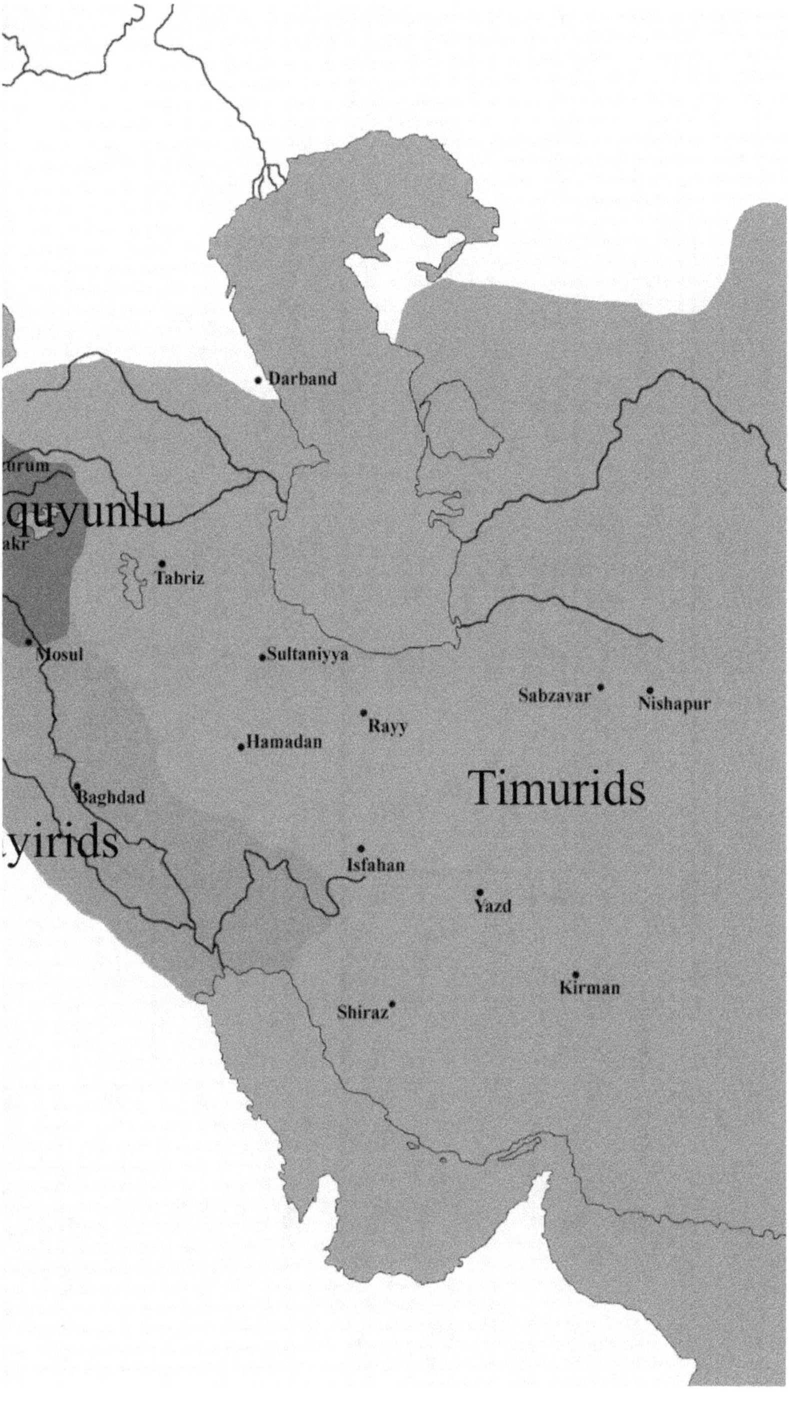
Darband
Tabriz
Mosul
Sultaniyya
Sabzavar
Nishapur
Rayy
Hamadan
Timurids
Baghdad
Isfahan
Yazd
Kirman
Shiraz

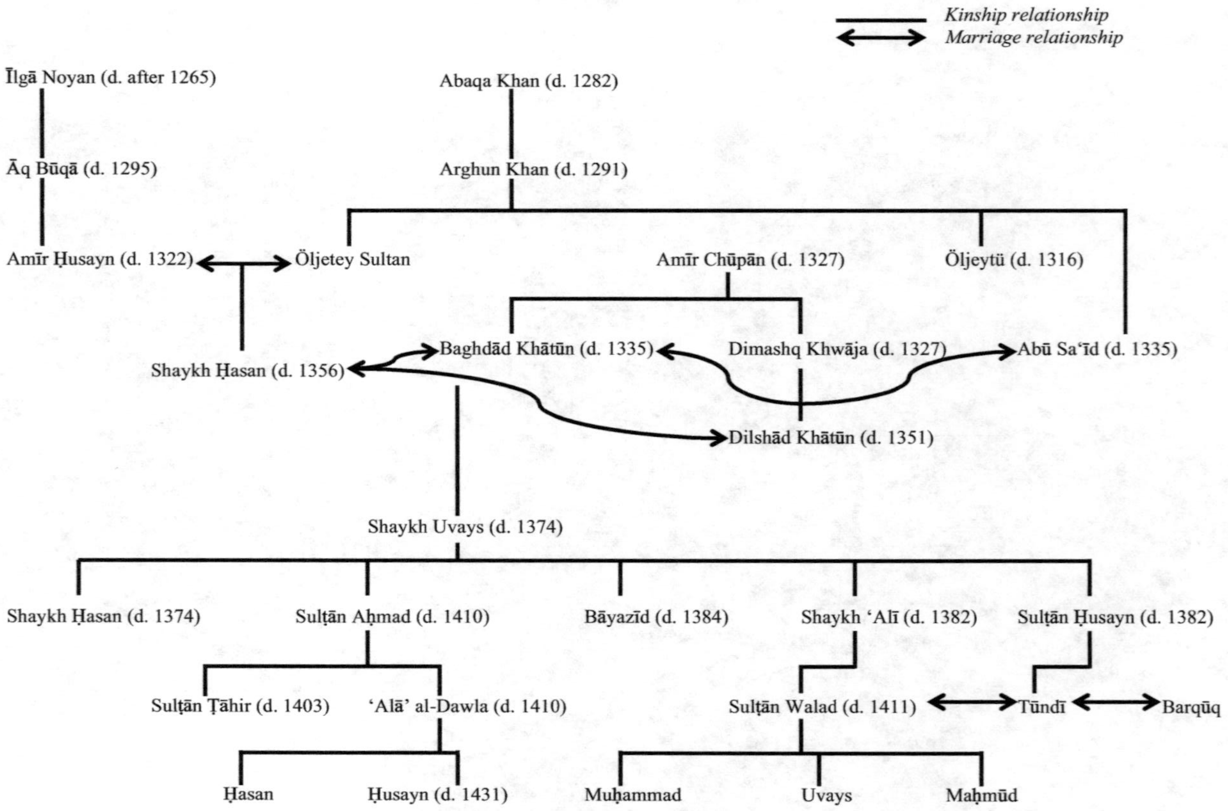

Genealogy of the Jalayirid dynasty.

Bibliography

Primary Sources

Abū al-Fidā', Ismā'īl b. 'Alī, *al-Mukhtasar fī Akhbār al-Bashar*, ed. Muḥammad Zaynahum Muḥammad 'Azab (Cairo: Dār al-Ma'ārif, 1998).

Aḥmad b. Mīr Munshī al-Ḥusaynī, *Calligraphers and Painters: A Treatise by Qāḍī Aḥmad, Son of Mīr-Munshī (circa* A.H. *1015/*A.D. *1606)*, trans. V. Minorsky (Washington, DC: Smithsonian Institution, 1959).

Ahrī, Abū Bakr al-Quṭbī, *Ta'rīkh-i Shaikh Uwais (A History of Shaikh Uwais): An Important Source for the History of Ādharbaijān in the Fourteenth Century*, trans. J. B. Van Loon (The Hague: Mouton & Co., 1954).

Āqsarāyī, Karīm al-Dīn Maḥmūd, *Musāmarat al-Akhbār va Musāyarat al-Akhyār*, ed. Osman Turan (Ankara: Türk Tarih Kurumu, 1993).

'Āşıkpāşāzāde, *Âşıkpaşaoğlu Tarihi*, ed. H. Nihal Atsız (Istanbul: Milli Eğitim Bakanlığı Yayınları, 1992).

—— *Tevārīḫ-i Āl-i 'Os̱mān*, ed. 'Ālī Bey (Istanbul: Maṭba'a-yi 'Āmire, 1332 [1913–14]).

—— *Tevārīḫ-i Āl-i 'Os̱mān*, ed. H. Nihal Atsız, in *Osmanlı tarihleri: Osmanlı tarihinin anakaynakları olan eserlerin, mütehassıslar tarafından hazırlanan metin, tercüme veya sadeleştirilmiş şekilleri külliyatı* (Istanbul: Türkiye Yayınevi, 1949), 77–318.

Astarābādī, 'Azīz b. Ārdashīr, *Bazm u Razm*, intro. Köprülüzāde Meḥmed Fu'ād Bey [Mehmed Fuad Köprülü] (Istanbul: Evḳāf Maṭba'ası, 1928).

Azhdarī, Nūr al-Dīn, *Ghāzān-nāma-yi Manẓūm*, ed. Maḥmūd Mudabbirī (Tehran: Bunyād-i Mawqūfāt-i Duktur Maḥmūd Afshār, 1380 [2001]).

Banākatī, Dāvūd ibn Muḥammad, *Tārīkh-i Banākatī: Rawżat Ūlā al-Albāb fī Ma'rifat al-Tavārīkh wa-al-Ansāb*, ed. Ja'far Shi'ār (Tehran, 1348 [1969]).

Bar Hebraeus, *The Chronography of Gregory Abû'l Faraj, the Son of Aaron, the Hebrew Physician Commonly Known as Bar Hebraeus Being the First Part of his Political History of the World*, trans. Ernest A. Wallis Budge (Oxford: Oxford University Press, 1932).

Clavijo, Ruy Gonzalez de, *Embassy to Tamerlane, 1403–1406*, trans. Guy Le Strange (London: George Routledge and Sons, 1928).

Cleaves, Francis Woodman (ed. and trans.), *The Secret History of the Mongols* (Cambridge, MA: Harvard University Press, 1982).

De Rachewiltz, Igor (trans.), *The Secret History of the Mongols: A Mongolian Epic Chronicle of the Thirteenth Century* (Leiden: Brill, 2004).
Faṣīḥ Khvāfī, Faṣīḥ al-Dīn Aḥmad, *Mujmal-i Faṣīḥī*, ed. Maḥmūd Farrukh (Mashhad: Kitābfurūshī-yi Bāstān, 1339 [1961]).
Ferīdūn Aḥmed Bey, *Mecmū'a-yi Münşe'āt-i Selāṭīn* (Istanbul: Dār al-Ṭibā'a al-'Āmira, 1848).
Ghiyāth, 'Abd Allāh b. Fatḥ Allāh, *al-Ta'rīkh al-Ghiyāthī*, ed. Ṭāriq Nāfi' al-Ḥamdānī (Baghdad: Maṭba'at As'ad, 1975).
Grigor of Akanc', 'History of the Nation of Archers', trans. Robert P. Blake and Richard N. Frye, *Harvard Journal of Asiatic Studies* 12:3/4 (1949): 269–399.
Ḥāfiẓ Abrū, *Cinq opuscules de Ḥāfiẓ-i Abrū concernant l'histoire de l'Iran au temps de Tamerlan*, ed. Felix Tauer (Prague: L'Académie Tchécoslovaque des sciences, 1959).
—— *Ẕayl-i Jāmi' al-Tavārīkh*, ed. Khānbābā Bayānī (Tehran: 'Ilmī, 1317 [1939]).
—— *Zubdat al-Tavārīkh*, ed. Sayyid Kamāl Ḥājj-i Sayyid Javādī (Tehran: Vizārat-i Farhang va Irshād-i Islāmī, 1380 [2001]).
Ibn 'Arabshāh, Muḥammad ibn Aḥmad, *'Ajā'ib al-Maqdūr fī Nawā'ib Tīmūr*, ed. 'Alī Muḥammad 'Umar (Cairo: Maktabat al-Anjilū al-Miṣriyya, 1399 [1979]).
Ibn Baṭṭūṭa, *Riḥlat Ibn Baṭṭūṭa: al-Musammā Tuḥfat al-Nuẓẓār fī Gharā'ib al-Amṣār wa-'Ajā'ib al-Asfār* (Miṣr: al-Maktaba al-Tijāriyya al-Kubrá, 1964).
—— *The Travels of Ibn Baṭṭūṭa, A.D. 1325–1354*, trans. H. A. R. Gibb (Cambridge: Hakluyt Society at the University Press, 1971).
Ibn Bībī, *El-Evāmirü'l-'Alā'iyye fī'l-Umūri'l-'Alā'iyye*, ed. Adnan Sadık Erzi (Ankara: Türk Tarih Kurumu Basımevi, 1956).
—— *Histoire des Seldjoucides d'Asie Mineure d'après l'Abrégé du Seldjouknāmeh d'Ibn-Bībī*, ed. M. Th. Houtsma (Leiden: Brill, 1902).
Ibn Ḥajar al-'Asqalānī, Aḥmad ibn 'Alī, *Durar al-Kāmina fī A'yān al-Mi'a al-Thāmina*, ed. 'Abd al-Wārith Muḥammad 'Alī (Beirut: Dār al-Kutub al-'Ilmiyya, 1977).
—— *Inbā' al-Ghumr bi-Abnā' al-'Umr* (Hyderabad: Maṭba'at Majlis Dā'irat al-Ma'ārif al-'Uthmāniyya, 1967).
—— *Inbā' al-Ghumr bi-Anbā' al-'Umr fī al-Ta'rīkh* (Beirut: Dār al-Kutub al-'Ilmiyya, 1986).
Ibn Taghrī Birdī, Abū al-Maḥāsin Yūsuf, *al-Manhal al-Ṣāfī wa al-Mustawfī ba'd al-Wāfī*, ed. Muḥammad Amīn (Cairo: al-Hay'a al-Miṣriyya al-'Āmma lil-Kitāb, 1984–).
—— *al-Nujūm al-Zāhira fī Mulūk Miṣr wa-al-Qāhira* (Cairo: Maṭba'at Dār al-Kutub al-Miṣriyya, 1929–72).
—— *al-Nujūm al-Zāhira fī Mulūk Miṣr wa-al-Qāhira*, ed. William Popper (Berkeley: University of California Press, 1960).
Juvaynī, 'Alā' al-Dīn 'Aṭā Malik, *Genghis Khan: The History of the World Conqueror*, trans. J. A. Boyle (Seattle: University of Washington Press, 1997).
—— *Tārīkh-i Jahān-gushāy*, ed. Muḥammad ibn 'Abd al-Wahhāb Qazvīnī, 4th

edn (Tehran: Intishārāt-i Arghavān, 1370 [1991]); originally published in E. J. W. Gibb Memorial Series 16 (Leiden: Brill, 1912).

Ḳarāmānlı Nişāncı Meḥmed Pāşā, 'Tevārīḫ al-Salāṭīn al-'Os̱māniyye (Osmanlı Sultanları Tarihi)', trans. Konyalı İbrahim Hakkı, in *Osmanlı tarihleri: Osmanlı tarihinin anakaynakları olan eserlerin, mütehassıslar tarafından hazırlanan metin, tercüme veya sadeleştirilmiş şekilleri külliyatı* (Istanbul: Türkiye Yayınevi, 1949), 321–69.

Khvāndamīr, Ghiyās̱ al-Dīn b. Humām al-Dīn, *Habibu's-siyar, Tome Three, The Reign of the Mongol and the Turk*, ed. and trans. Wheeler Thackston (Cambridge, MA: Department of Near Eastern Languages and Civilizations, Harvard University, 1994).

—— *Tārīkh-i Habīb al-Siyar fī Akhbār-i Afrād-i Bashar*, ed. Jalāl al-Dīn Humā'ī (Tehran: Kitāb-khāna-yi Khayyam, 1954).

Kirakos Gandzakets'i's, *History of the Armenians*, trans. Robert Bedrosian (New York: Sources of the Armenian Tradition, 1986).

Kutubī, Maḥmūd, *Tārīkh-i Āl-i Muẓaffar*, ed. 'Abd al-Ḥusayn Navā'ī (Tehran: Kitābfurūshī-yi Ibn Sīnā, 1956).

Luṭfī Pāşā, *Tevārīḫ-i Āl-i 'Os̱mān* (Istanbul: Maṭba'a-yi 'Āmire, 1341 [1922–23]).

Maqrīzī, Taqī al-Dīn Aḥmad b. 'Alī, *Kitāb al-Sulūk li-Ma'rifat Duwal al-Mulūk*, ed. Muḥammad Muṣṭafá Ziyāda (Cairo: Lajnat al-Ta'lif wa-al-Tarjama wa-al-Nashr, 1934).

—— *Kitāb al-Sulūk li-Ma'rifat Duwal al-Mulūk*, ed. 'Abd al-Fattāḥ 'Ashūr (Cairo, 1972).

Māzandarānī, 'Abd Allāh ibn Muḥammad ibn Kiyā, *Die Resālä-ye Falakiyyä des 'Abdollāh Ibn Moḥammad Ibn Kiyā al-Māzandarānī: Ein persischer Leitfaden des staatlichen Rechnungswesens (um 1363)*, ed. Walther Hinz (Wiesbaden: Franz Steiner Verlag, 1952).

Metsobets'i, T'ovma, *History of Tamerlane and His Successors*, trans. Robert Bedrosian (New York: Sources of the Armenian Tradition, 1987).

Mīrkhvānd, Muḥammad b. Khvāndshāh, *Tārīkh-i Rawżat al-Ṣafā'* (Tehran: Markazī-yi Khayyam Pīrūz, 1959–60).

Nakhjivānī, Muḥammad bin Hindūshāh, *Dastūr al-Kātib fī Ta'yīn al-Marātib*, ed. 'Abd al-Karīm 'Alīūghlī 'Alīzāda (Moscow: Izd-vo 'Nauka', Glav. red. vostochnoĭ lit-ry, 1964–76).

Naṭanzī, Mu'īn al-Dīn, *Extraits du Muntakhab al-tavārīkh-i Mu'īnī (Anonyme d'Iskandar)*, ed. Jean Aubin (Tehran: Librairie Khayyam, 1957).

—— *Muntakhab al-Tavārīkh-i Mu'īnī*, ed. Parvīn Istakhrī (Tehran: Intishārāt-i Asāṭīr, 2004).

Neşrī, Meḥmed, *Kitâb-i Cihan-nümâ: Neşrî Tarihi*, ed. Faik Reşit Unat and Mehmed A. Köymen (Ankara: Türk Tarih Kurumu Basımevi, 1995).

Onon, Urgunge (trans.), *The Secret History of the Mongols: The Life and Times of Chinggis Khan* (Richmond: Curzon, 2001).

Öztürk, Necdet (ed.), *Anonim Osmanlı Kroniği (1299–1512)* (Istanbul: Türk Dünyası Araştırmaları Vakfı, 2000).

Qāshānī, Abū al-Qāsim, *Tārīkh-i Ūljāytū*, ed. Mahin Hambly (Tehran, 1969).

Qazvīnī, Ḥamd Allāh Mustawfī, *The Geographical Part of the Nuzhat-al-Qulūb*, ed. Guy Le Strange (Leiden: Brill; London: Luzac & Co., 1915–19).

—— *Tārīkh-i Guzīda*, ed. ʻAbd al-Ḥusayn Navā'ī (Tehran: Amīr Kabīr, 1362 [1983]).

Qazvīnī, Zayn al-Dīn b. Ḥamd Allāh Mustawfī, *Ẕayl-i Tārīkh-i Guzīda*, ed. Īraj Afshār (Tehran: Naqsh-i Jahān, 1372 [1993]).

Rāmī, Sharaf al-Dīn Muḥammad b. Ḥasan, *Anīs al-ʻUshshāq*, ed. Muḥsin Kiyānī (Tehran: Intishārāt-i Rawzna, 1376 [1997–98]).

Rashīd al-Dīn Fażl Allāh Hamadānī, *Jāmiʻ al-Tavārīkh*, ed. Muḥammad Rawshan and Muṣṭafá Mūsavī (Tehran: Nashr-i Alburz, 1373 [1994]).

—— *Mukātabāt-i Rashīdī*, ed. Muḥammad Abarqūhī and Muḥammad Shafīʻ (Lahore: University of the Punjab Oriental Publications, 1945).

—— *Shuʻab-i Panjgāna* (Istanbul: Topkapı Sarayı Müzesi Kütüphanesi, Ahmet III ms. 2937).

Rūḥī, 'Rûhî Târîhi', ed. Halil Erdoğan Cengiz and Yaşar Yücel, in *Belgeler. Türk Tarih Belgeleri Dergisi*, 14/18 (1989–92).

Ṣafadī, Khalīl ibn Aybak, *Aʻyān al-ʻAṣr wa-Aʻwān al-Naṣr* (Beirut: Dār al-Fikr al-Muʻāṣir and Damascus: Dār al-Fikr, 1998).

Samarqandī, Dawlatshāh, *Taẕkirat al-Shuʻarā'-yi Dawlatshāh Samarqandī*, ed. Muḥammad ʻAbbāsī (Tehran: Kitāb-furūshī-yi Bārānī, 1337 [1958]).

Samarqandī, Kamāl al-Dīn ʻAbd al-Razzāq, *Maṭlaʻ-i Saʻdayn va Majmaʻ-i Baḥrayn*, ed. ʻAbd al-Ḥusayn Navā'ī (Tehran: Shāh Riżā Muqābil Dānishgāh, 1353 [1975]).

Sāvajī, Salmān, *Kullīyāt-i Salmān-i Sāvajī*, ed. ʻAbbās ʻAlī Vafā'ī (Tehran: Anjuman-i Ās̱ār va Mafākhir-i Farhangī, 1382 [2004]).

Schiltberger, Johannes, *The Bondage and Travels of Johann Schiltberger: A Native of Bavaria, in Europe, Asia, and Africa, 1396–1427*, ed. P. Bruun, trans. J. Buchan Telfer (New York: Burt Franklin, 1970; reprinted from London: Hakluyt Society, 1879).

Shabānkāra'ī, Muḥammad bin ʻAlī bin Muḥammad, *Majmaʻ al-Ansāb*, ed. Mīr Hāshim Muḥaddis̱ (Tehran: Mu'assasa-yi Intishārāt-i Amīr Kabīr, 1363 [1985]).

Shāmī, Niẓām al-Dīn, *Histoire des conquêtes de Tamerlan intitulée Ẓafar-nāma, par Niẓāmuddīn Šāmī, avec des additions empruntées au Zubdatu-t-Tawāriḫ-i Bāysunġurī de Ḥāfiẓ-i Abrū*, ed. Felix Tauer (Prague: Orientální ústav/Oriental Institute, 1937).

—— *Zafernâme*, ed. Necati Lugal (Ankara: Türk Tarih Kurumu Basımevi, 1949).

Shujāʻī, Shams al-Dīn, *Tārīkh al-Malik al-Nāṣir Muḥammad ibn Qalawūn al-Ṣāliḥī wa-Awlāduhu*, ed. Barbara Schäfer (Wiesbaden: Franz Steiner, 1978–85).

Tāj al-Salmānī, *Šams al-Ḥusn: Eine Chronik vom Tode Timurs bis zum Jahre 1409*, ed. Hans Robert Roemer (Wiesbaden: Franz Steiner Verlag, 1956).

ʻUmarī, Aḥmad b. Yaḥyá b. Faḍl Allāh, *Das Mongolische Weltreich: Al-ʻUmarī's*

Darstellung der mongolischen Reiche in seinem Werk Masālik al-Abṣār fī Mamālik al-Amṣār, ed. and trans. Klaus Lech (Wiesbaden: Otto Harrassowitz, 1968).
Vaṣṣāf, 'Abd Allāh b. Fażl Allāh, *Taḥrīr-i Tārīkh-i Vaṣṣāf*, ed. 'Abd al-Muḥammad Āyatī (Tehran: Mu'assasa-yi Muṭāla'at va Taḥqīqāt-i Farhangī [Pizhūhishgāh], 1372 [1993]).
—— *Tārīkh-i Vaṣṣāf* [Lithograph ed. Bombay, 1269 (1853); reprint] (Tehran: Ibn-i Sīnā, 1338 [1959]).
Yazdī, Sharaf al-Dīn 'Alī, *Ẓafar-nāma*, ed. Muḥammad 'Abbāsī (Tehran: Amīr Kabīr, 1336 [1957–58]).
Zāhidī, Ḥusayn ibn Abdāl, *Silsilat al-Nasab-i Ṣafaviyya, Nasabnāma-yi Pādishāhān bā 'Uẓmat-i Ṣafavī* (Berlin: Chāpkhāna-yi Īrānshahr, 1343 [1924]).

Secondary Literature

Abu-Lughod, Janet L., *Before European Hegemony: The World System* A.D. *1250–1350* (Oxford: Oxford University Press, 1989).
Aigle, Denise, *Le Fārs sous la domination mongole: Politique et fiscalité (XIIIe–XIVe s.), Studia Iranica, Cahier 31* (Paris: Association pour l'Avancement des Études Iraniennes, 2005).
—— 'Mythico-Legendary Figures and History Between East and West', in *The Mongol Empire Between Myth and Realities* (Leiden: Brill, 2014), 23–42.
Aka, İ., 'Aharī', *Encyclopaedia Iranica*, ed. Ehsan Yarshater (London and New York: Routledge and Kegan Paul, 1983), 1:634.
Album, Stephen, *Checklist of Islamic Coins*, 2nd edn (Santa Rosa: S. Album, 1998).
—— 'Studies in Ilkhanid History and Numismatics I: A Late Ilkhanid Hoard (743/1342)', *Iranian Studies* 13 (1984): 49–116.
Algar, H., 'Astarābādī, Fażlallāh', *Encyclopaedia Iranica*, ed. Ehsan Yarshater (London and New York: Routledge and Kegan Paul, 1987), 2:841–4.
Allsen, Thomas T., 'Changing Forms of Legitimation in Mongol Iran', in Gary Seaman and Daniel Marks (eds), *Rulers from the Steppe: State Formation on the Eurasian Periphery* (Los Angeles: Ethnographics Press, University of Southern California, 1991), 223–41.
—— *Culture and Conquest in Mongol Eurasia* (Cambridge: Cambridge University Press, 2001).
—— 'Guard and Government in the Reign of the Grand Qan Möngke, 1251–59', *Harvard Journal of Asiatic Studies* 46:2 (1986): 495–521.
—— *Mongol Imperialism: The Politics of the Great Qan Möngke in China, Russia, and the Islamic Lands, 1251–1259* (Berkeley: University of California Press, 1987).
—— 'Notes on Chinese Titles in Mongol Iran', *Mongolian Studies* 14 (1991): 27–39.
—— 'Sharing Out the Empire: Apportioning Lands under the Mongols', in

Anatoly M. Khazanov and André Wink (eds), *Nomads in the Sedentary World* (Richmond: Curzon, 2001), 172–90.

Amitai-Preiss, Reuven, 'Evidence for the Early Use of the Title *īlkhān* among the Mongols', *Journal of the Royal Asiatic Society* 3:1 (1991): 353–61.

—— 'New Material from the Mamluk Sources for the Biography of Rashid al-Din', in Julian Raby and Teresa Fitzherbert (eds), *The Court of the Il-khans, 1290–1340* (Oxford: Oxford University Press, 1994), 23–7.

'Ānī, Nūrī 'Abd al-Ḥamīd, *Al-'Irāq fī al-'Ahd al-Jalā'irī: 738–814 H/1337–1411 M: Dirāsa fī Awḍā'ihi al-Idāriyya wa-al-Iqtiṣādiyya* (Baghdad: Dār al-Shu'ūn al-Thaqāfiyya al-'Āmma, 1986).

Arioli, Angelo, 'Su una Fonte di Mustawfī Qazvīnī', in *La Bisaccia dello Sheikh: Omaggio ad Alessandro Bausani, Islamista nel Sessantesimo Compleanno* (Venice: Università degli Studi di Venezia, 1981), 29–41.

Arjomand, Said Amir, *The Shadow of God and the Hidden Imam: Religion, Political Order, and Societal Change in Shi'ite Iran from the Beginning to 1890* (Chicago and London: University of Chicago Press, 1984).

Atsız, H. Nihal, 'Hicri 858 Yılına Ait Takvim', *Selçuklu Araştırmaları Dergisi* 4 (1975): 223–83.

Aubin, Jean, 'Aux origins d'un movement populaire medieval le cheykhisme du Bayhaq et du Nichâpour', *Studia Iranica* 5 (1976): 213–24.

—— 'Un chroniqueur méconnu: Šabankara'i', *Studia Iranica* 10 (1981): 213–24.

—— *Émirs Mongols et vizirs Persans dans les remous de l'acculturation* (Paris: Association pour l'Avancement des Études Iraniennes, 1995).

—— 'L'Ethnogénèse de qaraunas', *Turcica* 1 (1969): 69–94.

—— 'La fin de l'état Sarbadār du Khorassan', *Journal Asiatique* (1974): 95–118.

Āzhand, Ya'qūb, *Ḥurūfiyya dar Tārīkh* (Tehran: Nashr-i Nay, 1369 [1990]).

Babinger, Franz, *Die Geschichtesschreiber der Osmanen und ihre Werke* (Leipzig: O. Harrassowitz, 1927).

—— 'Rūḥī', trans. Christine Woodhead, *Encyclopaedia of Islam*, 2nd edn (Leiden: Brill, 1994), 8:594.

Balard, Michel, 'Les Gênois en Asie centrale et en extrême-orient au XIVe siècle: un cas exceptionnel?', in *Économies et sociétés au moyen age: mélanges offerts à Eduoard Perroy* (Paris: Publications de la Sorbonne 5, 1973), 681–9.

Bardakçı, Murat, *Maragalı Abdülkadir: XV. yy. bestecisi ve müzik nazariyatçısının hayat hikâyesiyle eserleri üzerine bir çalışma* (Istanbul: Pan Yayıncılık, 1986).

Barfield, Thomas J., *The Perilous Frontier* (Cambridge: Blackwell, 1989).

Barthold, V. V., *Turkestan Down to the Mongol Invasion*, trans. H. A. R. Gibb (London: Luzac, 1928).

Bashir, Shahzad, 'Deciphering the Cosmos from Creation to Apocalypse: The Hurufiyya Movement and Medieval Muslim Esotericism', in Abbas Amanat and Magnus Bernhardsson (eds), *Imagining the End: Visions of Apocalypse from the Ancient Middle East to Modern America* (London: I. B. Tauris, 2002), 168–84.

—— *Fazlallah Astarabadi and the Hurufis* (Oxford: Oneworld, 2005).

Bauer, Thomas, 'Mamluk Literature as a Means of Communication', in Stephan Conermann (ed.), *Ubi sumus? Quo vademus? Mamluk Studies – State of the Art*, (Göttingen: V&R Unipress, Bonn University Press, 2013), 23–56.

—— 'Mamluk Literature: Misunderstandings and New Approaches', *Mamlūk Studies Review* 9:2 (2005): 105–32.

Bayānī, Shīrīn, *Tārīkh-i Āl-i Jalāyir* (Tehran: Intishārāt-i Dānishgāh-i Tihrān, 1962).

Behrens-Abouseif, Doris, 'The Jalayirid Connection in Mamluk Metalware', *Muqarnas* 26 (2009): 149–59.

Bernardini, Michele, 'Genoa', *Encyclopaedia Iranica*, ed. Ehsan Yarshater (London and New York: Routledge and Kegan Paul, 2001), 10:422–6.

Bese, Lajos, 'Some Turkic Personal Names in the *Secret History of the Mongols*', *Acta Orientalia Academiae Scientiarum Hungaricae* 32:3 (1978): 353–69.

Biran, Michal, *Qaidu and the Rise of the Independent Mongol State in Central Asia* (Richmond: Curzon, 1997).

Blair, Sheila, 'Artists and Patronage in Late Fourteenth-Century Iran in the Light of Two Catalogues of Islamic Metalwork', *Bulletin of the School of Oriental and African Studies* 48:1 (1985): 53–9.

—— 'The Coins of the Later Ilkhanids: A Typological Analysis', *Journal of the Economic and Social History of the Orient* 26 (1983): 295–317.

Bloom, Jonathan M., 'Paper: The Transformative Medium in Ilkhanid Art', in Linda Komaroff (ed.), *Beyond the Legacy of Genghis Khan* (Leiden and Boston: Brill, 2006), 289–302.

Boyle, J. A., 'Īndjū', *Encyclopaedia of Islam*, 2nd edn (Leiden: Brill, 1971), 3:1,208.

—— '*Iru* and *Maru* in the *Secret History of the Mongols*', *Harvard Journal of Asiatic Studies* 17 (1954): 403–10.

—— 'The Journey of Het'um I, King of Little Armenia, to the Court of the Great Khan Möngke', *Central Asiatic Journal* 9 (1964): 175–89.

—— 'Juvaynī and Rashīd al-Dīn as Sources on the History of the Mongols', in Bernard Lewis and P. M. Holt (eds), *Historians of the Middle East* (London: Oxford University Press, 1962), 133–7.

—— 'Kirakos of Ganjak on the Mongols', *Central Asiatic Journal* 7 (1962): 199–214.

—— 'Rashīd al-Dīn: The First World Historian', *Iran* 9 (1971): 19–26.

Brend, Barbara, 'Jonayd-e Naqqāš', *Encyclopaedia Iranica*, ed. Ehsan Yarshater (London and New York: Routledge and Kegan Paul, 2009), 15:5.

Broadbridge, Ann F., *Kingship and Ideology in the Islamic and Mongol Worlds* (Cambridge: Cambridge University Press, 2008).

Brockelmann, Carl, *Geschichte der Arabischen Literatur* (Leiden: Brill, 1949).

Browne, Edward Granville, *A Literary History of Persia, Volume 3: The Tartar Dominion (1265–1502)* (Cambridge: Cambridge University Press, 1956).

—— 'The *Mujmal* or "Compendium" of History and Biography of Faṣíḥí of Khwáf', *Le Muséon* ser. 3, 1:1 (1915): 48–78.

Buell, Paul D., 'Early Mongol Expansion in Western Siberia and Turkestan (1207–1219): A Reconstruction', *Central Asiatic Journal* 36 (1992): 1–32.

—— *Historical Dictionary of the Mongol World Empire* (Lanham, MD, and Oxford: The Scarecrow Press, 2003).

—— 'Tribe, Qan, and Ulus in Early Mongol China: Some Prolegomena to Yüan History', PhD dissertation, University of Washington, 1977.

Çağman, Filiz and Zeren Tanındı, 'Selections from Jalayirid Books in the Libraries of Istanbul', *Muqarnas* 28 (2011): 221–64.

—— *The Topkapı Saray Museum: The Albums and Illustrated Manuscripts*, ed. and trans. J. M. Rogers (Boston: Little, Brown and Company, 1986).

Cahen, Claude, 'Contribution à l'histoire du Diyār Bakr au quatorzième siècle', *Journal Asiatique* 243 (1955): 65–100.

—— *Pre-Ottoman Turkey: A General Survey of the Material and Spiritual Culture and History c. 1071–1330*, trans. J. Jones-Williams (New York: Taplinger, 1968).

Caiozzo, Anna, 'Une conception originale des cieux: planets et zodiaque d'une cosmographie jalayride', *Annales Islamologiques* 37 (2003): 59–78.

Canby, Sheila R., *Persian Painting* (Northampton, MA: Interlink, 1993).

Carboni, Stefano, 'Synthesis: Continuity and Innovation in Ilkhanid Art', in *The Legacy of Genghis Khan: Courtly Art and Culture in Western Asia, 1256–1353* (New Haven and London: Yale University Press, 2002), 197–225.

—— 'Two Fragments of a Jalayirid Astrological Treatise in the Keir Collection and in the Oriental Institute in Sarajevo', *Islamic Art* 2 (1987): 149–86.

Cleaves, Francis Woodman, '*DARUΓA* and *GEREGE*', *Harvard Journal of Asiatic Studies* 16 (1953): 237–59.

—— 'The Mongolian Names and Terms in the History of the Nation of Archers by Grigor of Akanc'', *Harvard Journal of Asiatic Studies* 12:3/4 (1949): 400–43.

Dawson, Christopher (ed.), *Mission to Asia* (Toronto: Toronto University Press, 1998).

De Rachewiltz, Igor, Hok-lam Chan, Hsiao Ch'i-ch'ing and Peter W. Geier (eds), *In the Service of the Khan: Eminent Personalities of the Early Mongol-Yüan Period (1200–1300)* (Wiesbaden: Harrassowitz Verlag, 1993).

DeWeese, Devin, *Islamization and Native Religion in the Golden Horde* (University Park: Penn State Press, 1994).

Di Cosmo, Nicola, 'State Formation and Periodization in Inner Asian History', *Journal of World History* 10 (1999): 1–40.

Doerfer, Gerhard, 'Āl Tamġā', *Encyclopaedia Iranica*, ed. Ehsan Yarshater (London and New York: Routledge and Kegan Paul, 1983), 1:766–8.

—— *Türkische und Mongolische Elemente im Neupersischen* (Wiesbaden: Franz Steiner Verlag, 1963).

Dols, Michael W., *The Black Death in the Middle East* (Princeton: Princeton University Press, 1977).

Dörfer, Sven (ed.), *Die Geschichte der Mongolen des Hethum von Korykos (1307) in der Rückübersetzung durch Jean le Long, Traitiez des estas des conditions de quatorze royaumes de Asie (1351)* (Frankfurt am Main: Peter Lang, 1998).

Fleischer, Cornell H., *Bureaucrat and Intellectual in the Ottoman Empire: The Historian Mustafa Ali (1541–1600)* (Princeton: Princeton University Press, 1986).

Fletcher, Joseph, 'The Mongols: Ecological and Social Perspectives', *Harvard Journal of Asiatic Studies* 46:1 (1986): 11–50.

Godard, Y. A., 'Bassin de cuivre au nom de Shaikh Uwais', *Athār-é Īrān: Annales du service archaeologique de Īrān* 1 (1936): 371–3.

Gölpınarlı, Abdülbâki, *Hurûfîlik Metinleri Kataloğu* (Ankara: Türk Tarih Kurumu Basımevi, 1973).

Gray, Basil, 'A Timurid Copy of a Chinese Buddhist Picture', in Richard Ettinghausen (ed.), *Islamic Art in The Metropolitan Museum of Art* (New York: The Metropolitan Museum of Art, 1972), 35–8.

Grousset, René, *The Empire of the Steppes: A History of Central Asia*, trans. Naomi Walford (New Brunswick, NJ, and London: Rutgers University Press, 1999).

Grube, Ernst J., *Persian Painting in the Fourteenth Century: A Research Report* (Naples: Istituto Orientale di Napoli, 1978).

Gruber, Christiane, *The Ilkhanid Book of Ascension: A Persian-Sunni Devotional Tale* (London and New York: I. B. Tauris, 2010).

Guo, Li, 'Mamluk Historiographic Studies: The State of the Art', *Mamlūk Studies Review* 1 (1997): 15–43.

Herrmann, Gottfried, 'Ein Erlaß des Ǧalāyeriden Solṭān Ḥoseyn aus dem Jahr 780/1378', in *Erkenntnisse und Meinungen I herausgegeben von Gernot Wießner* (Wiesbaden: Otto Harrassowitz, 1973), 135–63.

—— *Persische Urkunden der Mongolenzeit* (Wiesbaden: Harrassowitz Verlag, 2004).

Herrmann, Gottfried and Gerhard Doerfer, 'Ein persisch-mongolischer Erlaß des Ǧalāyeriden Šeyḫ Oveys', *Central Asiatic Journal* 19 (1975): 1–84.

Hodgson, Marshall G. S., *The Venture of Islam, Volume 2: The Expansion of Islam in the Middle Periods* (Chicago: University of Chicago Press, 1974).

İnalcık, Halil, 'Autonomous Enclaves in Islamic States: *Temlîk*s, *Soyurghal*s, *Yurdluḳ-Ocaḳlıḳ*s, *Mâlikâne-Muḳāṭa'a*s and *Awqāf*', in Judith Pfeiffer and Sholeh A. Quinn (eds), in collaboration with Ernest Tucker, *History and Historiography of Post-Mongol Central Asia and the Middle East: Studies in Honor of John E. Woods* (Wiesbaden: Harrassowitz, 2006), 112–34.

—— 'Bāyazīd I', *Encyclopaedia of Islam*, 2nd edn (Leiden: Brill, 1960), 1:1,117–19.

—— 'The Khan and the Tribal Aristocracy: The Crimean Khanate under Sahib Giray I', *Harvard Ukrainian Studies* 3/4 (1979–80): 445–66.

—— 'The Question of the Closing of the Black Sea under the Ottomans', in *Essays in Ottoman History* (Istanbul: Eren, 1998), 415–45.

Jackson, Peter, 'The Dissolution of the Mongol Empire', *Central Asiatic Journal* 22 (1978): 186–244.

—— 'Muẓaffarids', *Encyclopaedia of Islam*, 2nd edn (Leiden: Brill, 1992), 7:820–2.

Jackson, Peter and Charles Melville, 'Ğīāṯ al-Dīn Moḥammad', *Encyclopaedia Iranica*, ed. Ehsan Yarshater (London and New York: Routledge and Kegan Paul, 2001), 10:598–9.

Jagchid, Sechin and Paul Hyer, *Mongolia's Culture and Society* (Boulder: Westview, 1979).

Jahn, Karl, 'Čao', *Encyclopaedia of Islam*, 2nd edn (Leiden: Brill, 1961), 2:14.

—— 'Das iranische Papiergeld', *Archiv Orientalni* 10 (1938): 308–40.

—— 'Rashīd al-Dīn as World Historian', in *Yádnáma-ye Jan Rypka* (The Hague and Paris: Mouton & Co., 1967), 79–87.

—— 'The Still Missing Works of Rashīd al-Dīn', *Central Asiatic Journal* 9 (1964): 113–22.

al-Janabi, Tariq Jawad, *Studies in Medieval Iraqi Architecture* (Baghdad: Republic of Iraq, Ministry of Culture and Information, 1982).

Katstritsis, Dimitris J., *The Sons of Bayezid: Empire Building and Representation in the Ottoman Civil War of 1402–1413* (Leiden and Boston: Brill, 2007).

Kempiners, Jr, Russell G., 'Vaṣṣāf's *Tajziyat al-Amṣār wa Tazjiyat al-A'ṣār* as a Source for the History of the Chaghadayid Khanate', *Journal of Asian History* 22 (1988): 160–87.

Khazanov, Anatoly M., *Nomads and the Outside World* (Madison: University of Wisconsin Press, 1994).

Khoury, Philip S. and Joseph Kostiner, 'Introduction: Tribes and the Complexities of State Formation in the Middle East', in Philip S. Khoury and Joseph Kostiner (eds), *Tribes and State Formation in the Middle East* (Berkeley: University of California Press, 1990), 1–22.

Klimburg-Salter, Deborah E., 'A Sufi Theme in Persian Painting: The Diwan of Sultan Ahmad Gala'ir in the Freer Gallery of Art, Washington, D.C.', *Kunst des Orients* 11 (1976–77): 43–84.

Kolbas, Judith, *The Mongols in Iran: Chingiz Khan to Uljaytu 1220–1309* (London and New York: Routledge, 2006).

Komaroff, Linda, *The Golden Disk of Heaven: Metalwork of Timurid Iran* (Costa Mesa and New York: Mazda, 1992).

Köprülü, Mehmed Fuad, *Islam in Anatolia after the Turkish Invasion (Prolegomena)*, ed. and trans. Gary Leiser (Salt Lake City: University of Utah Press, 1993).

Krader, Lawrence, 'The Origin of the State among the Nomads of Asia', in *Pastoral Production and Society: Proceedings of the International Meeting on Nomadic Pastoralism* (Cambridge: Cambridge University Press, 1979), 221–34.

—— *Peoples of Central Asia* (Bloomington: Indiana University Press, 1963).

Kwanten, Luc, *Imperial Nomads: A History of Central Asia, 500–1500* (Philadelphia: University of Pennsylvania Press, 1979).
Lambton, A. K. S., 'Early Timurid Theories of State: Ḥāfiẓ Abrū and Niẓām al-Dīn Šāmī', *Bulletin d'Études Orientales* 30 (1978): 1–9.
Ledyard, Gari, 'The Mongol Campaigns in Korea and the Dating of the *Secret History of the Mongols*', *Central Asiatic Journal* 9 (1964): 1–22.
Lentz, Thomas W. and Glenn D. Lowry, *Timur and the Princely Vision: Persian Art and Culture in the Fifteenth Century* (Los Angeles and Washington, DC: Los Angeles County Museum of Art, Arthur M. Sackler Gallery, Smithsonian Institution and Smithsonian Institution Press, 1989).
Levy, Reuben, 'The Letters of Rashīd al-Dīn Faḍl Allāh', *Journal of the Royal Asiatic Society* (1946): 74–8.
Lindner, Rudi Paul, 'How Mongol Were the Early Ottomans?', in Reuven Amitai-Preiss and David O. Morgan (eds), *The Mongol Empire and its Legacy* (Leiden: Brill, 1999), 282–9.
—— 'What Was a Nomadic Tribe?', *Comparative Studies in Society and History* 24:4 (October 1982): 689–711.
Little, Donald P., 'Historiography of the Ayyūbid and Mamlūk Epochs', in Carl F. Petry (ed.), *The Cambridge History of Egypt, Volume I: Islamic Egypt, 640–1517* (Cambridge: Cambridge University Press, 1998), 412–44.
McChesney, R. D., 'A Note on the Life and Works of Ibn 'Arabshāh', in Judith Pfeiffer and Sholeh A. Quinn (eds), in collaboration with Ernest Tucker, *History and Historiography of Post-Mongol Central Asia and the Middle East: Studies in Honor of John E. Woods* (Wiesbaden: Harrassowitz, 2006), 205–49.
Manz, Beatrice Forbes, 'The Clans of the Crimean Khanate, 1466–1532', *Harvard Ukrainian Studies* 2 (1978): 282–309.
—— 'Mongol History Rewritten and Relived', *Revue des Mondes Musulmans et de la Méditerranée, Série Histoire* 89–90 (2000): 129–49.
—— *The Rise and Rule of Tamerlane* (Cambridge: Cambridge University Press, 1989).
—— 'The Ulus Chaghatay Before and After Temür's Rise to Power: The Transformation from Tribal Confederation to Army of Conquest', *Central Asiatic Journal* 27 (1983): 79–100.
Markov, G. E., 'Problems of Social Change among the Asiatic Nomads', in Wolfgang Weissleder (ed.), *The Nomadic Alternative: Modes and Models of Interaction in the African-Asian Deserts and Steppes* (The Hague: Mouton, 1978), 305–11.
Mashkūr, Muḥammad Javād, *Tārīkh-i Tabrīz tā Pāyān-i Qarn-i Nuhum-i Hijrī* (Tehran: Anjuman-i Āṡār-i Millī, 1352 [1973]).
May, Timothy, *The Mongol Art of War: Chinggis Khan and the Mongol Military System* (Yardley: Westholme, 2007).
Melville, Charles, 'Abū Sa'īd and the Revolt of the Amirs in 1319', in Denise Aigle (ed.), *L'Iran face à la domination mongole* (Tehran: Institut Français de Recherche en Iran, 1997), 89–120.

—— 'Delšād Ḵātūn', *Encyclopaedia Iranica*, ed. Ehsan Yarshater (London and New York: Routledge and Kegan Paul, 1996), 7:255.

—— 'The Early Persian Historiography of Anatolia', in Judith Pfeiffer and Sholeh A. Quinn (eds), in collaboration with Ernest Tucker, *History and Historiography of Post-Mongol Central Asia and the Middle East: Studies in Honor of John E. Woods* (Wiesbaden: Harrassowitz, 2006), 135–66.

—— *The Fall of Amir Chupan and the Decline of the Ilkhanate, 1327–1337: A Decade of Discord in Iran* (Bloomington: Indiana University, Research Institute for Inner Asian Studies, 1999).

—— 'Ḥamd Allāh Mustawfī's *Ẓafarnāmah* and the Historiography of the Late Ilkhanid Period', in Kambiz Eslami (ed.), *Iran and Iranian Studies: Essays in Honor of Iraj Afshar* (Princeton: Zagros, 1998), 1–12.

—— 'The Īlkhān Öljeitü's Conquest of Gīlān (1307): Rumour and Reality', in Reuven Amitai-Preiss and David O. Morgan (eds), *The Mongol Empire and its Legacy* (Leiden: Brill, 1999), 73–125.

—— '*Pādishāh-i Islām*: The Conversion of Sultan Maḥmūd Ghāzān Khān', *Pembroke Papers* 1 (1990): 159–77.

—— 'Wolf or Shepherd? Amir Chupan's Attitude to Government', in Julian Raby and Teresa Fitzherbert (eds), *The Court of the Ilkhans, 1290–1340* (Oxford: Oxford University Press, 1996), 79–93.

Minorsky, Vladimir, 'Thomas of Metsop' on the Timurid-Turkman Wars', in *The Turks, Iran and the Caucasus in the Middle Ages* (London: Variorum Reprints, 1978), XI, 1–26.

Morton, A. H., 'The Letters of Rashīd al-Dīn: Īlkhānid Fact or Timurid Fiction', in Reuven Amitai-Preiss and David O. Morgan (eds), *The Mongol Empire and its Legacy* (Leiden: Brill, 1999), 155–99.

al-Naqshbandī, Nāṣir, 'al-Madrasa al-Mirjāniyya', *Sumer* 2 (1946): 33–54.

Nicol, Norman D., Raafat el-Nabarawy and Jere L. Bacharach, *Catalog of the Islamic Coins, Glass Weights, Dies and Medals in the Egyptian National Library, Cairo* (Malibu, CA: Undena, 1982).

Ohta, Alison, 'Filigree Bindings of the Mamluk Period', *Muqarnas* 21 (2004): 267–76.

Okada, Hidehiro, '*The Secret History of the Mongols*, a Pseudo-Historical Novel', *Journal of Asian and African Studies* [Tokyo] 5 (1972): 61–8.

O'Kane, Bernard, *Early Persian Painting:* Kalila *and* Dimna *Manuscripts of the Late Fourteenth Century* (London and New York: I. B. Tauris, 2003).

—— 'Siyah Qalam: The Jalayirid Connections', *Oriental Art* 49:2 (2003): 2–18.

Peacock, A. C. S., 'The Saljūq Campaign against the Crimea and the Expansionist Policy of the Early Reign of 'Alā' al-Dīn Kayqubād', *Journal of the Royal Asiatic Society* 16:2 (2006): 133–49.

Petech, Luciano, 'Les Marchands Italiens dans l'Empire Mongol', *Journal Asiatique* 250 (1962): 549–74.

Petrushevsky, I. P., 'The Socio-Economic Condition of Iran under the Ilkhans', in J. A. Boyle (ed.), *The Cambridge History of Iran, Volume 5: The*

Saljuq and Mongol Periods (Cambridge: Cambridge University Press, 1968), 483–537.

Pfeiffer, Judith, 'Conversion Versions: Sultan Öljeytü's Conversion to Shi'ism (709/1309) in Muslim Narrative Sources', *Mongolian Studies* 22 (1999): 35–67.

—— 'Reflections on a "Double Rapprochement": Conversion to Islam among the Mongol Elite during the Early Ilkhanate', in Linda Komaroff (ed.), *Beyond the Legacy of Genghis Khan* (Leiden: Brill, 2006), 369–89.

Poppe, Nicholas, 'On Some Proper Names in the *Secret History*', in G. Décsy (ed.), *Eurasia Nostratica: Festschrift für Karl Heinrich Menges, Band I–II* (Wiesbaden: Otto Harrassowitz, 1977), 161–7.

Rabino, H. L., 'Coins of the Jalā'ir, Ḳara Ḳoyūnlū, Mu<u>sh</u>a'<u>sh</u>a', and Aḳ Ḳoyūnlū Dynasties', *Numismatic Chronicle* 6:10 (1950): 94–139.

Ratchnevsky, Paul, *Genghis Khan: His Life and Legacy*, ed. and trans. Thomas Nivison Haining (Oxford and Cambridge, MA: Blackwell, 1991).

Riasanovsky, Valentin A., *Fundamental Principles of Mongol Law* (Bloomington: Indiana University Press, 1965).

Richard, Jean, 'Buscarello de Ghizolfi', *Encyclopaedia Iranica*, ed. Ehsan Yarshater (London and New York: Routledge and Kegan Paul, 1990), 4:569.

Riḍwān, Yumná, *Al-Dawla al-Jalā'iriyya: wa-Ahamm Maẓāhir al-Ḥaḍāra fī al-'Irāq wa-Adhirbayjān khilāla al-Qarnayn al-Thāmin wa-al-Tāsi' ba'da al-Hijra* (Cairo: Maṭābi' al-Ahrām, 1993).

Roemer, H. R., 'The Jalayirids, Muzaffarids and Sarbadārs', in Peter Jackson and Laurence Lockhart (eds), *The Cambridge History of Iran, Volume 6: The Timurid and Safavid Periods* (Cambridge: Cambridge University Press, 1986), 1–41.

Roxburgh, David J., 'Persian Drawing, ca. 1400–1450: Materials and Creative Procedures', *Muqarnas* 19 (2002): 44–77.

Rypka, Jan, *History of Iranian Literature* (Dordrecht: D. Reidl, 1968).

Sanjian, Avedis K. (ed. and trans.), *Colophons of Armenian Manuscripts, 1301–1480: A Source for Middle Eastern History* (Cambridge, MA: Harvard University Press, 1969).

Schamiloğlu, Uli, 'Tribal Politics and Social Organization in the Golden Horde', PhD dissertation, Columbia University, 1986.

Schroeder, Eric, 'Ahmed Musa and Shams al-Dīn: A Review of Fourteenth Century Painting', *Ars Islamica* 6:2 (1939): 113–42.

Seif, Theodor, 'Der Abschnitt über die Osmanen in Šükrüllāh's persischer Universalgeschichte', *Mitteilungen zur Osmanischen Geschichte* 2 (1923–25): 63–128.

Shastina, N. P., 'Mongol and Turkic Ethnonyms in the *Secret History of the Mongols*', in Louis Ligeti (ed.), *Researches in Altaic Languages* (Budapest: Akadémia Kiadó, 1975), 231–44.

Smith, Jr, John Masson, ''Alī b. Oways', *Encyclopaedia Iranica*, ed. Ehsan Yarshater (London and New York: Routledge and Kegan Paul, 1983), 1:853–4.

—— 'Djalayir, Djalayirid', *Encyclopaedia of Islam*, 2nd edn (Leiden: Brill, 1962), 2:401–2.
—— *The History of the Sarbadār Dynasty, 1336–1381 A.D. and its Sources* (The Hague: Mouton, 1970).
Sneath, David, *The Headless State: Aristocratic Orders, Kinship Society and Misrepresentations of Nomadic Inner Asia* (New York: Columbia University Press, 2007).
Soucek, Priscilla P., ''Abd-al-Ḥayy, K̲vājā', *Encyclopaedia Iranica*, ed. Ehsan Yarshater (London and New York: Routledge and Kegan Paul, 1982), 1:115.
—— 'Aḥmad Mūsā', *Encyclopaedia Iranica*, ed. Ehsan Yarshater (London and New York: Routledge and Kegan Paul, 1984), 1:652–3.
—— 'Art in Iran: vii. Islamic, Pre-Safavid', *Encyclopaedia Iranica*, ed. Ehsan Yarshater (London and New York: Routledge and Kegan Paul, 1987), 2:603–18.
—— 'Eskandar b. 'Omar Šayx b. Timur: A Biography', *Oriente Moderno* 15:2 (1996): 73–87.
Soudavar, Abolala, 'In Defense of Rašīd-od-dīn and his Letters', *Studia Iranica* 32 (2003): 77–120.
Spuler, Bertold, *Die Mongolen in Iran: Politik, Verwaltung, und Kultur der Ilchanzeit, 1220–1350* (Berlin: Akademie-Verlag, 1955).
Storey, Charles Ambrose, *Persian Literature: A Bio-Bibliographical Survey* (London: Luzac & Co., 1927–).
Strika, Vincenzo and Jābir Khalīl, *The Islamic Architecture of Baghdad: The Results of a Joint Italian-Iraqi Survey* (Naples: Istituto Universitario Orientale, 1987).
Sümer, Faruk, *Kara Koyunlular (Başlangıçtan Cihan-Şah'a kadar)*, I. Cilt (Ankara: Türk Tarih Kurumu Basımevi, 1962).
Tanındı, Zeren, 'Additions to Illustrated Manuscripts in Ottoman Workshops', *Muqarnas* 17 (2000): 147–61.
Tapper, Richard, 'Anthropologists, Historians, and Tribespeople on Tribe and State Formation in the Midde East, in Philip S. Khoury and Joseph Kostiner (eds), *Tribes and State Formation in the Middle East* (Berkeley: University of California Press, 1990), 48–73.
Thackston, Wheeler M., *Album Prefaces and Other Documents on the History of Calligraphers and Painters* (Leiden: Brill, 2001).
—— *A Century of Princes: Sources on Timurid History and Art* (Cambridge, MA: The Aga Khan Program for Islamic Architecture, 1989).
Titley, Norah M., 'A 14th-Century Niẓāmī Manuscript in Tehran', *Kunst des Orients* 8 (1972): 120–5.
Togan, İsenbike, *Flexibility and Limitation in Steppe Formations* (Leiden: Brill, 1998).
Togan, Zeki Velidi, 'The Composition of the History of the Mongols by Rashīd al-Dīn', *Central Asiatic Journal* 8 (1963): 60–72.
—— 'References to Economic and Cultural Life in Anatolia in the Letters of Rashīd al-Dīn', trans. Gary Leiser, in Judith Pfeiffer and Sholeh A. Quinn

(eds), in collaboration with Ernest Tucker, *History and Historiography of Post-Mongol Central Asia and the Middle East: Studies in Honor of John E. Woods* (Wiesbaden: Harrassowitz, 2006), 84–111.

Turan, Osman, *İstanbul'un Fethinden önce Yazılmış Tarihî Takvimler* (Ankara: Türk Tarih Kurumu Basımevi, 1954).

Ṭurṭūr, Sha'bān Rabī', *Al-Dawla al-Jalā'iriyya* (Cairo: Dār al-Hidāya, 1987).

Ürekli, Muzaffer, 'Celâyirliler', *Türkiye Diyanet Vakfı İslâm Ansiklopedisi* (Istanbul: Türkiye Diyanet Vakfı Vakıf Yayınları İşletmesi, 1993), 7:264–5.

Uzunçarşılı, İsmail Hakkı, *Anadolu Beylikleri ve Akkoyunlu, Karakoyunlu Devletleri* (Ankara: Türk Tarih Kurumu Basımevi, 1988).

Vásáry, István, 'The Origin of the Institution of *Basqaq*s', *Acta Orientalia Academiae Scientiarum Hung. Tomus* 32:2 (1978): 201–6.

Vladimirtsov, B. I., *The Life of Chingis-Khan*, trans. Prince D. S. Mirsky (London: George Routledge and Sons, 1930).

Werner, Christoph, Daniel Zakrzewski and Hans-Thomas Tillschneider, *Die Kuğuğī-Stiftungen in Tabrīz: Ein Beitrag zur Geschichte der Ǧelāyiriden* (Wiesbaden: Dr. Ludwig Reichert Verlag, 2013).

Wittek, Paul, 'Niğde', *Encyclopaedia of Islam*, 2nd edn (Leiden: Brill, 1993), 8:15–16.

Woods, John E., *The Aqquyunlu: Clan, Confederation, Empire* (Salt Lake City: University of Utah Press, 1999).

—— 'Ebn 'Arabšāh', *Encyclopaedia Iranica*, ed. Ehsan Yarshater (London and New York: Routledge and Kegan Paul, 1996), 7:670.

—— 'The Rise of Timurid Historiography', *Journal of Near Eastern Studies* 46:2 (1987): 81–108.

Yınanç, Mükrimin Halil, 'Celâyir', *İslam Ansiklopedisi* (Istanbul: Millî Eğitim Basımevi, 1945), 3:64–5.

Yücel, Yaşar, *Anadolu Beylikleri hakkında Araştırmalar: Eretna Devleti, Kadı Burhaneddin Ahmed ve Devleti, Mutahharten ve Erzincan Emirliği, II* (Ankara: Türk Tarih Kurumu Basımevi, 1989).

Index

Abā Bakr b. Mīrānshāh (Timurid), 158, 166, 171–2
Abaqa Khan, 38, 41, 49, 50–1, 54, 57, 64, 74, 102, 104, 208
'Abbās Āqā, 151
Abbasid, 38, 48–9, 64, 80, 135–6, 138
'Abd al-Ḥayy *see* Khwāja 'Abd al-Ḥayy (painter)
Abū Sa'īd Bahādur Khan, 1, 2, 7–8, 10, 12, 14–16, 57, 67–70, 74–6, 78, 80–1, 83, 86, 91, 93, 104, 107, 113, 115, 119, 130–3, 137, 140–2, 162, 187, 196–7
Abū Sa'īd b. Muḥammad, 10
Abūghān, 42
'Ādil Āqā *see* Amīr 'Ādil Āqā
Āghā Fīrūz, 166
Aghachkī, 157
Aḥmad Mūsá (painter), 187–8
Aḥmad Tegüder Khan, 38, 50–3, 55–7, 101, 130, 140
Ahrī, Abū Bakr al-Quṭbī, 8, 16, 67, 90, 103–7, 130–3
Akhī Jūq, 104–6, 108, 116
Akrunj, 77, 85
'Alā' al-Dawla b. Sulṭān Aḥmad Jalayir, 160, 173, 175
Ālādāgh, 83, 85
Aleppo, 13–14, 89, 160, 164, 167
'Alī Pādshāh, 76–8, 81–4, 88, 111, 137, 196
'Alī Pīltan, 106, 108
'Alī Shāh, Khwāja Tāj al-Dīn, 67
altan urugh, 36, 37, 77
Amīr 'Ādil Āqā, 113, 115, 147–57, 159
Amīr Chūpān, 7, 57, 66–70, 75, 78–9, 86–7, 91–2, 94, 103, 105–6, 120, 140, 196
Amīr Ḥusayn Gūrgān, 4, 6, 17, 65, 66, 67, 71n, 72n, 94, 140, 196
Amīr Muḥammad Pīltan, 108
Amīr Qāsim, 118
Amīr Valī, 10, 113–15, 118, 149, 151, 175n, 176n
Amīr Zāhid, 118, 126n
amīr-i ulūs, 82–4, 86, 94
Anatolia, 5–7, 9, 11–12, 17, 50, 53–7, 63, 67, 69–70, 76–81, 83, 86–9, 94, 102, 111, 113, 132, 155–6, 158, 164, 166, 169, 196, 198
Ankara (battle), 166
Anūshirvān Khan, 92, 102, 122n
Āq Būqā Jalayir, 6, 17, 51, 53, 55–8, 62n, 65–6
Āq Khvāja (battle), 51, 56
Āqquyūnlū, 81, 174
Arab Iraq, 2, 8, 63, 77–8, 80, 83, 87–8, 90–4, 102, 109–11, 113, 139, 143, 153, 158–9, 162, 165, 167–9, 171, 173, 175, 196
Ardabil, 15, 16, 66, 103, 139, 151, 176n, 177n, 194
Arghun Khan, 7, 38, 50–3, 55–7, 59n, 60n, 66, 68, 79, 102, 130, 208
Arghūniyya, 79
Arigh Böke, 37, 42, 75
Arpā Khan, 75–8, 82, 85, 87, 94n, 95n
Arran, 35, 66–7, 72n, 79, 87, 151
Arūq, 51–2
al-Ashraf Sha'bān (Mamluk sultan), 109
Assassins *see* Nizārī Ismā'īlīs
atabeg, 41, 124n
Āyna Beg, 56–7
Azarbayjan, 2–3, 8–9, 11, 14–16, 35, 39, 48, 51, 53, 57, 66, 74–5, 79–81, 83, 85–94, 101–8, 110–16, 118, 121, 129, 132, 137, 141–3, 147, 151–4, 157–9, 168–74, 196–7
Azhdarī, Khwāja Nūr al-Dīn, 8, 131–3

Baghdad, 3, 10–11, 13, 16, 18–20, 39, 48–9, 52–3, 56, 70, 72n, 76–8, 80–94, 95n, 105–13, 117, 121, 122n, 124n, 125n, 126n, 133–7, 140–1, 147–51, 153–60, 163–70, 172–5, 177n, 178n, 179n, 180n, 181n, 183n, 185–7, 190–4, 196–7, 198n, 199n, 200n
Baghdād Khātūn, 67, 69–70, 80, 83
Bahā' al-Dīn Jūlāh, 174
Bahrām Mīrzā, 187
Bala, 40
Bāltū, 56–7
Barāq Khan, 42, 50
Bardā'ī, Qāḍī Muḥyī al-Dīn, 103
Barhashīn b. Ḥājī Ṭaghāy, 89

Barqūq (Mamluk sultan), 159–64, 167–8, 183n, 197
Batu Khan, 37
Bāyazīd b. Shaykh Uvays Jalayir, 148, 153–4
Baybars (Mamluk sultan), 6, 54, 61n
Baydu Khan, 38, 55–7, 61n, 62n, 65, 76, 95n
Bāyezīd I (Ottoman sultan), 11–12, 15–16, 159, 165, 182n, 197
Bāyezīd II (Ottoman sultan), 11–12
Bāyjū Noyan, 53
Bayrām Beg, 112, 118, 125n
Bayrām Khwāja, 110–12, 114, 148, 154–5, 178n
Bāysunqur Mīrzā, 10
Birdī Beg Khan, 104
Birdī Khwāja, 111
Bisṭām Jāgīr, 175
bītikchī, 54
Börte, 36
Būqā Jalayir, 50–3, 55–7, 60n, 63–4
Burhān al-Dīn, Qāḍī, 11, 13, 151, 179n, 181n
Bursa, 120, 164, 166

Caffa, 119
Cairo, 13, 53, 68, 92–3, 161–4, 167–8, 170, 183n, 194
Chaghatay Khan, 37–8, 42, 47n, 156
Chaghatayids, 3, 37, 41–3, 49–50, 67, 107, 139, 156–7, 168
chao, 55
China, 2–3, 35–6, 38–40, 42–3, 45n, 52, 67, 119, 139, 156
Chinggis Qan, 3–5, 10, 29, 32–43, 45n, 51, 64, 76, 82, 84–5, 113, 121, 133–4, 142, 156, 158, 162, 195
chīngsāng, 42, 52, 60n
Chubanids, 12–14, 18, 23n, 55, 61n, 67–70, 80, 85–93, 99n, 101–2, 104–8, 114, 116–19, 122n, 127n, 129, 140, 143n, 153, 193, 196
Clavijo, Ruy Gonzalez de, 16, 81, 119–20

Damascus, 13, 58n, 68, 126n, 163–4, 167–9, 173, 182n, 183n
Dānishmand, 41
Davātī, Muḥammad, 151
Dilshād Khātūn, 15, 19, 75–7, 83, 92–3, 101, 105, 130, 139–41, 146n
Dimashq Khwāja, 67–9, 72n, 75, 80, 92, 101–2, 105, 140, 208
Dimashqiyya, 80, 175
Diyarbakr, 2, 17, 49, 53, 74, 76, 78, 88–93, 95n, 102, 109–11, 113–14, 143, 158, 171, 173
Dū'a Khan, 42
Dūst Muḥammad, 187, 193

Eretna, 11, 78
Erzincan, 54, 164, 171, 174, 181n
Erzurum, 54, 56, 155

Euphrates, 1, 3, 7, 35, 38–9, 48, 53, 90, 164, 167, 171, 194–5

Faraj, al-Nāṣir (Mamluk sultan), 164, 167–8
Faraj Jalayir, 165
Fars, 8, 73n, 103, 116, 143n, 169, 176n, 187
Fażl Allāh Astarābādī, 116, 117, 139

Genoa, 118–20, 127n
Geykhatu Khan, 38, 52, 55–7, 65, 71n, 88
Ghazan Khan, 5, 7–8, 38, 52, 55–8, 62n, 63–6, 71n, 74, 78–81, 99n, 104, 131–2, 134, 137, 142, 143n, 174, 195–7
Ghāzāniyya, 79, 81
Ghiyāth al-Dīn Muḥammad 'Alīshāhī, 87
Ghiyāth al-Dīn Muḥammad Rashīdī, 8, 14, 72n, 74–7, 80, 94n, 95n, 97n, 131, 137, 143n
Golden Horde, 22n, 49, 64, 85, 103, 139
Great Mongol *Shāh-nāma*, 185
gūrgān (*güregen*), 63, 66–7, 71n, 105, 196
Güyük Qan, 37, 42, 99n

Ḥāfiẓ Shīrāzī, 1, 15, 19
Ḥāfiẓ Abrū, 6, 9–10, 16, 23n, 74–5, 77, 82–3, 86, 90, 96n, 101, 107–10, 112–14, 149–50, 157
Ḥājī Khātūn, 73n, 75, 95n
Ḥājī Māmā Khātūn, 119
Ḥājī Ṭaghāy, 78, 89–91, 96n
Hama, 12, 165
Harqay, 40
hazāra, 40–2
Herat, 9–10, 20, 68, 81, 171
Hilla, 99n, 166–7
Hindūqūr Noyan, 42
Ḥukumdār 'Alī Beg, 11
Hülegü Khan, 4–7, 17–18, 37–9, 43, 48–51, 53, 55, 58n, 65, 74–75, 79, 82, 84, 88, 93, 99n, 102–3, 105, 108, 110, 133, 157–8, 195, 197
Hülegüids, 48, 50, 63, 65, 76–8, 92–3, 140, 197
Ḥurūfiyya, 117, 126n, 139
Hūshang (Shīrvānshāh), 112, 125n

Ibn 'Arabshāh, 13, 159
Ibn Baṭṭūṭa, 16, 72n, 79, 81
Ibrāhīm al-Darbandī (Shīrvānshāh), 174
Ibrāhīm Shāh, 89–91
Ikeres, 32
Īlchīdāy, 41–2
Īlgā Noyan, 2, 17, 48–51, 54–8, 60n, 63, 65, 195–6
Ilgayids, 7, 48, 53, 56, 63, 65, 67–8, 94, 195–6
Īlūgā, 41, 42
īnāq, 50–1
Īnāl Bāy b. Qajmās, 168, 183n
īnchū, 49, 52, 54
Injuids, 73n, 75, 79, 103
Iqbāl, 57

Īsan Qutlugh, 85, 98n
Ishāk Tughlī, 56
Iskandar Sulṭān Mīrzā, 19, 174, 191, 193

Jahān Tīmūr Khan, 88, 91
Jahānshāh Qarāquyūnlū, 81
Jahānshāh (Timurid amir), 166
Jakam, 168
Jalayirid style of painting, 19, 186
Jamāl Ḥājī b. Tāj al-Dīn 'Alī Shīrvānī, 77
Jāngqī Kūrgān, 42
Jānī Beg Khan, 103–4, 106, 116, 122n
Jochi Khan, 37
Jochids, 37, 39, 49, 66, 103–4, 106–7, 112, 116, 119–20, 139, 160
Julbān Qarāsaqal, 160

Karbala, 139, 140, 160
Karts, 18, 68, 81
Kā'ūs (Shīrvānshāh), 104, 108, 111–12, 114, 118
Kayseri, 11, 54
Kemah fortress, 70
Kereyit, 32–4, 40
keshig, 33–4, 66
Khalīl Sulṭān, 174
Khiżr Shāh, 107
Khurasan, 3, 6, 9, 11, 21n, 35, 42, 48, 50–1, 55–6, 76, 80–1, 85–8, 91, 98n, 99n, 107, 113, 115, 169
Khvājū Kirmānī, 15, 18, 28n
Khwāja 'Abd al-Ḥayy (painter), 187, 191, 193–4
Khwāja Bāyazīd Dāmghānī, 117
Khwāja Mirjān, 108–12, 114, 116, 118, 124n, 126n, 134, 153, 193
Khwarazm, 35, 40, 106, 126n, 160
Khwārazmshāh, 35, 40, 162
Kirman, 8, 40, 79, 116
Kuhūrgāy, 55
Kujujī, Khwāja Shaykh, 150
Kujujī shaykhs, 150
Kūnjak Khātūn, 101

mahdī, 69, 89, 117
Maḥmūd b. Walad b. Shaykh 'Alī Jalayir, 175
Maḥmūd Shāh, Sharaf al-Dīn (Injuid), 73n, 75, 95n
Maḥmūd Sulṭān, 166
al-Mālik al-Ṣāliḥ (Artuqid), 90–1, 103, 121n
Malik Ashraf, 69, 87, 91–3, 102–7, 118–19, 121n, 122n, 123n, 127n, 129
Malik Tīmūr, 42
Mamluks, 6–7, 12–13, 24n, 49, 53–4, 66, 68–9, 78, 86, 89–93, 98n, 105, 108–9, 120, 147, 159–64, 167–9, 180n, 194, 197
Mangqut, 32
Marāghī, 'Abd al-Qādir, 136, 178n
Mas'ūd Beg, 49
Mazandaran, 9–10, 113, 115, 118
Mehmed II (Ottoman sultan), 11
Merkit, 30, 34
Mingāsār Noyan, 42, 47n
Mirjān *see* Khwāja Mirjān
Mirjāniyya madrasa, 133, 135, 136, 193
Misāfir Īradājī, 151, 152, 177n
Möngke Qa'an, 5, 37–9, 41–2, 48, 50, 99n
Morosini, Marco, 119
Mosul, 78, 89, 93, 111, 154, 163, 171
Mubāriz al-Dīn Muḥammad (Muzaffarid), 103, 106, 115–16
Mughan, 35, 79, 98n, 151
Muḥammad Khan, 8, 83–7, 98n
Muḥammad Sulṭānshāh, 157
Mu'īn al-Dīn Sulaymān (*parvāna*), 54, 61n
Mūngka Noyan, 42
Muqālī, 40
Muż, 111, 154
Mūsá Khan, 76–8, 82, 85, 87–8, 95n, 98n
Muṣṭafá b. Bāyezīd, 166
Musta'ṣim bi-llāh (caliph), 49
Muṭahhartan, 11, 164, 174, 181n
Muzaffarids, 1, 8–9, 18, 20n, 79, 103, 106–7, 115–16, 141, 149–50, 152–3, 155, 160, 176n, 186, 196

Nakhjivan, 106, 143n, 155
Nakhjivānī, Muḥammad b. Hindūshāh, 14–16, 131, 133–6, 143n
al-Nāṣir Ḥasan (Mamluk sultan), 92–3
al-Nāṣir Muḥammad (Mamluk sultan), 12, 78, 86, 89–91, 162
Navā'ī, 'Alī Shīr, 10
Nayman, 32–4, 40, 58n
Niẓāmī, 19, 200n
Nizārī Ismā'īlīs (Assassins), 48
nöker, 33–4, 64–5, 152, 166, 167
noyan, 33
Nu'ayr (Āl Faḍl), 160, 161

Oghul Ghaymish, 42, 47n, 99n
Ögödey Qa'an, 4–5, 22n, 35, 37, 41–3, 99n
Öljetey Sultan (Khatun), 6, 65–8, 70, 94, 102, 130, 134, 196, 208
Öljeytü Khan, 5–6, 52, 54, 66–8, 72n, 75, 78, 85, 87, 99n, 134, 137, 196, 208
Onon river, 17
Otchigin (Ūtikīn), 85
Oxus, 3, 7, 38–9, 42, 48, 54, 95n, 107, 159, 195, 197
Oyrat, 2, 42, 63, 74, 76–8, 81, 83–9, 93–4, 96n, 108, 110–11, 123n, 137, 147, 149, 158, 167, 171, 195–6

pādishāh, 52, 82, 87, 104, 136
pādishāh-i islām, 58, 71n, 132, 134

Pādishāh Luqmān, 114–15
parvāna see Mu'īn al-Dīn Sulaymān
Persian Iraq, 8, 79, 89, 102, 106, 114, 116, 136, 143n, 160
Pīr 'Alī Bādīk, 153–6
Pīr Budāq, 170, 172–3, 175
Pīr Sulṭān, 77
plague, 92–3, 117, 127n
Pūlād Chīngsāng, 66, 71n

Qadā'an, 41
Qādāgāch Khātūn, 42
Qarā Būqā, 49
Qarā Ḥasan, 167
Qarā Jurī, 86–9
Qarā Muḥammad Qarāquyūnlū, 11, 155–6
Qarā 'Usmān, 174
Qarā Yūsuf Qarāquyūnlū, 14, 147–8, 156, 159, 163–75, 181n, 182n, 183n, 184n, 197–8
Qaraqorum, 38, 48, 133
Qarāquyūnlū, 3, 11, 14, 19, 81, 110–11, 113, 147–8, 154–6, 159, 164, 167, 169–75, 191, 197–8
Qaydu, 41
Qipchaqs, 42
Qipchaq (father of Āyna Beg), 56
Qipchaq steppe, 103, 112, 156, 160
Qiyat, 34
Qongqirat, 32, 34
qorchi, 33
Qubilay Qan, 37–9, 42, 52, 55, 60n, 99n
Qūnqūrtāy, 51
quriltay, 37, 40, 51, 82, 87, 155, 178n
Qūshūq Noyan, 42, 47n
Qutlughshāh, 66, 78
Qūtū, 54

Rab'-i Rashīdī, 77, 80, 198n
Rayy, 114–15, 148–9, 151, 175n, 176n
Rukn al-Dīn Shaykhī Rashīdī, 87

Sa'd al-Dawla (vizier), 55
Ṣadr al-Dīn Ardabīlī (Ṣafavī), 103, 126n, 139, 151, 176n, 177n
Ṣadr al-Dīn Zanjānī, 52, 55
Ṣafaviyya, 16, 103, 139, 151, 177n
ṣāḥib-qirān, 129, 136, 171, 178n
Saljūqs, 6, 53, 54, 57, 61n, 79, 146n
Salmān Sāvajī, 15, 18–19, 121n, 125n, 136–42
Samāghar, 55
Samarqand, 13, 157–8, 160, 173, 191, 193–4
Saray, 103–4, 106, 119
Sarbadārs, 1, 81, 97n, 114
Sāṭī Beg, 72n, 75, 85, 87–8, 99n
Sāvajī, Sa'd al-Dīn, 5, 137
Sāvajī, Salmān *see* Salmān Sāvajī
Schiltberger, Johannes, 16, 81, 120, 165
Seche Domoq, 40
Shāh Maḥmūd b. Mubāriz al-Dīn, 116, 126n
Shāh Manṣūr, 160
Shāh Muḥammad b. Qarā Yūsuf, 174–5
Shāh Shujā', 116, 141, 149–50, 152, 155, 176n
Shāh-nāma, 6, 22n, 92, 131, 140–1, 185–7, 189
Shāhrukh, 9–10, 174, 194
Shams al-Dīn (painter), 187, 191, 193
Sharaf al-Dīn Mas'ūd b. Khaṭīr, 54, 61n
Shaykh 'Alī b. 'Alī Qūshchī, 85
Shaykh 'Alī b. Shaykh Uvays Jalayir, 148, 153–6, 169, 175, 178n
Shaykh 'Alī, Qāḍī, 116, 124n, 126n
Shaykh al-Maḥmūdī, 167, 169
Shaykh Ḥasan Chūbānī, 83, 86–91, 98n, 99n, 119
Shaykh Ḥasan Jalayir, 4, 8, 10, 12–19, 22n, 63, 67–70, 73n, 74, 76–8, 80–94, 97n, 98n, 99n, 100n, 101, 108, 110, 114, 116, 118, 121, 129–30, 132, 134, 137, 139–41, 145n, 153, 171, 187, 193, 196, 199n
Shaykh Sāvahī, 161
Shaykh Uvays Jalayir, 2–4, 8, 13–15, 18–19, 67, 74, 80–1, 84, 92–4, 101–2, 105–21, 122n, 123n, 124n, 125n, 126n, 129–42, 143n, 145n, 147–54, 159, 162, 173, 175, 177n, 178n, 187, 193–4, 196–7, 200n, 208
Shīktūr Noyan, 50–1, 55–6, 59n, 71n
Shīrāmun, 42
Shīrvān (amir), 164, 180n
Sivas, 11, 13, 151, 164, 179n, 181n, 182n
siyah-qalam (*qalamsiyāhī*), 19, 191, 199n
Sorqaqtani Beki, 37–8, 42, 99n
Sulaymān Khan, 88, 91, 143n
Sulaymān Shāh Khāzin, 109, 124n
Sulaymish, 57, 62n
Sulduz, 30, 34, 54–5, 57, 67–8, 86, 91, 102, 140, 195–6
Sulṭān Aḥmad Jalayir, 3–4, 10–16, 19–20, 108, 147–8, 150–7, 159–75, 177n, 178n, 179n, 180n, 181n, 182n, 183n, 184n, 187, 190–1, 193, 197–8, 199n, 200n
Sulṭān Dilshād, 164
Sulṭān Ḥusayn Bāyqarā, 20, 171
Sulṭān Ḥusayn Jalayir, 4, 116, 119–20, 124n, 126n, 141, 148–55, 162, 175, 176n, 177n, 178n
Sulṭān Maḥmūd Khan, 158
Sulṭān Ṭāhir, 13, 166–7, 169, 173
Sulṭānbakht, 104, 106
Sultaniyya, 16, 54, 60n, 79, 85, 87–9, 93, 106, 110, 114, 119–20, 147–50, 152, 154, 173, 176n, 197
Sūtāy Akhtājī, 78, 89
Sutayids, 12–13, 89–90, 93
suyūrghāl, 149, 152, 155, 174, 176n
Suyurghatmish, 67

Tabriz, 2–3, 16, 19–20, 39, 52, 54–7, 66, 74, 77–81, 83, 87–91, 93–4, 103–7, 109–10, 112–20, 121n, 122n, 124n, 126n, 127n, 129, 133, 141–2, 143n, 147–57, 159, 165, 170, 172–5, 176n, 177n, 183n, 185–9, 191, 193–4, 196–7, 198n, 199n, 200n
Ṭaghāchār, 55–7
Ṭaghāy Tīmūr Khan, 18, 81, 85, 87–9, 98n, 99n, 113–15
Tahmāsp (Safavid shah), 187
tamghāchī, 50–1
Tana, 119
Ṭaraqāy, 38, 55
Tatar, 40
Tāyjī, 56
Temüjin *see* Chinggis Qan
Tīmūr, 1, 3, 8–11, 13–17, 19, 22n, 81, 101, 107–8, 113, 115, 142, 147–8, 152, 154, 156–69, 171–3, 180n, 181n, 182n, 191, 193, 197–8
Tīmūr Tāsh b. Amīr Chūpān, 7, 68–9, 86–9, 91, 98n, 99n, 105–6
Timurids, 1, 3, 6, 9–11, 13–14, 18–20, 101–2, 107–8, 112–13, 117, 120, 123n, 136, 147, 152, 156–60, 162–3, 165, 167–72, 180n, 181n, 185–7, 191, 193–4, 197
Tolui Khan, 36, 37, 42, 75, 76, 82, 99n
Toluids, 37–9, 41–3, 195
Töregene, 37, 99n
Trabzond, 120
Transoxiana, 3, 9, 11, 35–6, 38, 40, 45n
Tūdā'ūn Sulduz, 54, 55, 61n
Ṭughā Khātūn, 68
Ṭughān, 53, 55–6, 60n, 61n
tümen (tūmān), 40, 77–8, 95n
Tūndī Khātūn (Sulṭān), 162–3, 175
Tuqtāmīsh Khan, 160
Tūqū (Ṭūghū), 54–6
Tūrsun Khātūn, 101, 140

Ughan, 40
Ūgulāy Qūrchī, 50, 56
Ugulayids, 53, 56
Ujan, 118, 127n, 149, 155
ulūs, 4, 36–43, 45n, 48–9, 55, 70, 79, 82–4, 86, 99n, 103–8, 120, 125n, 139, 157–8, 185, 195–7
Ulus Chaghatay, 139, 154, 156
'Umar b. Mīrānshāh, 158, 171
Ūrūghtū Jalayir, 54, 56
Uvays (rebel in Baghdad), 173
Uyghur, 31, 59n, 77, 132, 143n, 144n

Vafā Qutlugh, 156
Vajīh al-Dīn Ismā'īl b. Shams al-Dīn, 153, 177n, 178n
Venice, 118–20

Xiongnu, 31, 34–5

yārghūchī, 42, 46n
yārlīgh, 52, 103
Yashbak al-Sha'bānī, 168
Yazd, 8, 79, 103, 116
Yīsūr Noyan, 42
Yüan dynasty, 3, 37, 64, 67, 72n

al-Ẓāhir Barqūq *see* Barqūq (Mamluk sultan)
Zakarīyā, Khwāja Shams al-Dīn, 83, 97n, 134, 153

EU representative:
Easy Access System Europe
Mustamäe tee 50, 10621 Tallinn, Estonia
Gpsr.requests@easproject.com

www.ingramcontent.com/pod-product-compliance
Lightning Source LLC
Chambersburg PA
CBHW051115230426
43667CB00014B/2594
* 9 7 8 1 4 7 4 4 2 6 3 7 4 *